THE BEHOLDEN STATE

THE BEHOLDEN STATE

California's Lost Promise and How to Recapture It

Edited by Brian C. Anderson

Foreword by William E. Simon, Jr.

ROWMAN & LITTLEFIELD PUBLISHERS, INC.

Lanham • Boulder • New York • Toronto • Plymouth, UK

All illustrations in this book courtesy of their illustrators: Sean Delonas, Alberto Mena, Robert Pizzo, Arnold Roth.

Published by Rowman & Littlefield Publishers, Inc.
A wholly owned subsidiary of The Rowman & Littlefield Publishing Group, Inc.
4501 Forbes Boulevard, Suite 200, Lanham, Maryland 20706
www.rowman.com

10 Thornbury Road, Plymouth PL6 7PP, United Kingdom

British Library Cataloguing in Publication Information Available

Library of Congress Cataloging-in-Publication Data

The beholden state : California's lost promise and how to recapture it / edited by Brian C. Anderson ; foreword by William E. Simon, Jr.
    pages cm
  ISBN 978-1-4422-2343-1 (cloth : alk. paper) — ISBN 978-1-4422-2344-8 (ebook) 1. California—Economic conditions—21st century. 2. California—Social conditions—21st century. 3. California—Politics and government—21st century. I. Anderson, Brian C., 1961-
  HC107.C2B44 2013
  330.9794—dc23

                                                                2013007398

∞™ The paper used in this publication meets the minimum requirements of American National Standard for Information Sciences—Permanence of Paper for Printed Library Materials, ANSI/NISO Z39.48-1992.

Printed in the United States of America

Contents

Part II: The Urban Fiscal Crisis

Part III: Of Energy and Environment

Part IV: Public Order

Part V: Immigration Dilemmas

Part VI: Education

Foreword

William E. Simon, Jr.

THROUGHOUT MUCH OF THE twentieth century, California was *the* destination for the striving, industrious middle class. Opportunities for entrepreneurial risk-taking abounded, and millions of Californians took full advantage of America's grand promise of upward mobility. Critical cutting-edge infrastructure projects, including a vast system of freeways and the California Aqueduct, opened up the state for farms and homes. The University of California offered a world-class education to youngsters of modest means and infused the state's labor pool with tremendous human capital. For decades, all anyone really needed in California was a willingness to work hard.

But recently, that has fundamentally changed. Poor policy decisions in recent decades have made California less welcoming for enterprising business owners, middle-class families with college-aged kids, and young families starting out in life. Thanks to its exceptional climate and beautiful Pacific vistas, California will always maintain pockets of affluence, particularly in places like Sausalito, Malibu, and Newport Beach. But for people who live outside those premier ZIP codes, middle-class life has become far harder to attain. You have to wonder: Has the Golden State lost its glitter?

Consider California's employment situation, which was in trouble well before the Great Recession began. Between 1992 and 2000, as demographer Wendell Cox notes in chapter 5, California added 776,000 more jobs from business start-ups than it lost to business closures. But then, between 2000 and 2008, job loss from closures outpaced job growth from start-ups, resulting in a net *loss* of more than 262,000 jobs. During the same eight-year span, nearly 80,000 jobs migrated to other states. I've lost count of the business-people I know personally who have either decided to expand their operations out of state or simply pulled up stakes and left entirely.

One reason for their departure is that starting a business in California has never been more onerous, because of the endless accretion of regulations and rising taxes. For example, the state's "Global Warming Solutions Act," passed in 2006, is making the cost of doing business even worse by forcing utilities to obtain one-third of their electricity from expensive renewable sources, such as wind and solar. Manufacturing is steadily bleeding away. For the past decade, California consistently ranks last on national surveys of the best states in which to do business.

Yet another deeply troubling fact is that California's public schools, once among the nation's best, now compete with Mississippi's for the dubious distinction of the lowest student achievement in reading and math on the National Assessment of Educational Progress. It should be possible to fix these schools—but the California Teachers Association and its lesser partner, the California Federation of Teachers, have steadfastly opposed every attempt at reform, especially those emphasizing accountability.

In 2009, the Manhattan Institute informed me of its plans to drive a serious discussion about the problems and possibilities of California. The new research initiative couldn't have been more timely. While most parts of the country were struggling during the depths of the Great Recession, the California economy was performing especially poorly. Massive deficits had forced Sacramento to issue IOUs to creditors, and the state's unemployment rate significantly outpaced the national average. California's history of poor policy decisions and frustrated reform efforts could no longer be ignored. So over the past four years, the Manhattan Institute's flagship magazine, *City Journal*, has published scores of articles and essays elucidating the origins of the state's challenges and introducing solutions. This book brings together some of the most penetrating and insightful pieces.

As many chapters in the book point out, California's troubles don't have to be permanent. For example, chapter 22 describes the so-called parent trigger, which lets parents at a failing public school petition their local district for reforms. The law was the first of its kind in the nation, and lawmakers in other states are looking to California as a model.

California can be a model to the nation in other ways, including public safety. Take the astounding feat accomplished by Bill Bratton, the police chief of Los Angeles until 2009: driving down crime there for six consecutive years. Bratton's success was perhaps less surprising to those of us who had followed his career. Back in the 1980s, when I had the honor of working for Rudy Giuliani—a no-nonsense U.S. attorney at the time—I could see that he understood that <mark>law and order were the sine qua non of prosperity.</mark> When Giuliani became mayor of New York, perhaps his most important hire was Bratton, who as police commissioner presided over Gotham's famous 1990s crime drop. Two of Bratton's most powerful tools were Broken Windows policing—enforcing seemingly minor laws to deter major crimes—and the now-renowned Compstat system, which tracked crime and held precinct commanders accountable for crime surges in their areas. Some years later, Bratton brought both innovations to Los Angeles and introduced other reforms as well, as chapter 15 shows.

In fact, there are many ways to restore the Golden State's lost luster. For example, California is sitting on top of an ocean of oil that could be extracted in an environmentally responsible way. Millions of entrepreneurs would love to open businesses in California, if only the state would give them a reason, instead of more barriers. Fiscal disasters at the state and local level, immigration conundrums, the inefficient tax code, persistent crime and disorder in many cities—all these problems could be solved. Just as policy mistakes helped turn the world's fifth-largest economy into the world's ninth-largest, with Greek-sized financial statements, wise policies could get the state back on track. My hope is that policymakers and the public will begin by taking the lessons of this important book to heart.

Acknowledgments

THE BEHOLDEN STATE WOULDN'T HAVE been possible without the great thinking and writing of its many contributors. Nor would it have been put together without the tireless work and good judgment of my *City Journal* editorial colleagues Ben Plotinsky, Paul Beston, Ben Boychuk (who oversees City Journal California, our website's ongoing source of weekly commentary on the Golden State), Nicole Gelinas, and Steven Malanga (whose insightful writings make up a substantial part of this book). This was truly a collaborative effort. Four talented people—Sean Delonas, Alberto Mena, Robert Pizzo, and Arnold Roth—provided the graphs and illustrations that accompany several chapters; I'm happy we could reproduce their artistry here. Janice Meyerson provided expert copy editing. Bernadette Serton lined up *The Beholden State*'s publisher and kept reminding everyone when everything was due. Jon Sisk of Rowman & Littlefield welcomed this project and expedited its publication with assistance from Benjamin Verdi.

The Manhattan Institute continues to be a remarkable home for intellectual inquiry. My thanks to the institute's president, Lawrence Mone, for his enthusiasm for *City Journal*, his vision, and his recognition of California's need for the kind of research and analysis that MI and *CJ* provide. MI's executive vice president, Vanessa Mendoza, and Daniel Geary in the MI development office find *City Journal* the support that allows us to operate. We are grateful to the Arthur N. Rupe Foundation, the Hertog/Simon Fund for Policy Analysis, and especially the William E. Simon Foundation for their support of the magazine's California focus and the publication of this volume.

—Brian C. Anderson

Introduction

Brian C. Anderson

A GENERATION AGO, California was widely expected to be the dynamo of the twenty-first-century American economy—"California, Inc.," as Joel Kotkin and Paul Grabowicz called it in a book published in the early 1980s. The Golden State had everything going for it: a famously sunny, temperate climate; a culture of innovation and entrepreneurialism; a growing population that easily found work in a diverse economy; good public schools that prepared students for success, and an even better state university system; sturdy infrastructure; and geographical proximity to increasingly prosperous Asian nations. The future was Californian.

Today, few would describe California as dynamic. Signs of decline are everywhere. In 2012, the state's economy seemed to be recovering, at last, from the Great Recession—but that was long after the national recovery had gotten under way. In fact, California's unemployment rate has remained above the nation's for years now, climbing to a frightening 13 percent in 2010 and still hovering around 10 percent. In parts of the state, the numbers are worse still. New business investment, both from within California and from without, has vaporized. The public schools, once near the top in national rankings, have sunk to the bottom. Roads and bridges creak and crumble as infrastructure spending dwindles. State and municipal budgets have reeled from crisis to crisis, with several cities falling into bankruptcy. People and firms are leaving the state in record numbers.

What caused this reversal? In the broadest terms, the answer is misguided policy, rooted in a political culture too often disconnected from reality. To finance its profligate spending, California governments have taxed too much and borrowed too much. Those mistakes, combined with excessive regulations, have poisoned the state's business climate, which business leaders rank as the nation's worst. Public schools have been protected from needed reforms. Trendy environmentalism has damaged agriculture. Politically correct "diversity" initiatives have ravaged public universities. The private-sector coalitions that once turned cities like Los Angeles into powerhouses have been replaced by public-sector machines. Governing institutions have produced unintended consequences and corruption.

A few years ago, *City Journal* set out to provide ongoing analysis and reporting about California's problems and to offer workable proposals on how the state could regain its mojo. This book collects and updates the best of that work, carried out by some of the leading social thinkers of our time—many of them, including Kotkin and Victor Davis Hanson, long-time Californians worried about their state's darkening future. At once pathology and prescription, these essays tell a story important not only for Californians but for all Americans, since many of the developments that have harmed the Golden State are present elsewhere in the country. For example, California's "big-spending, high-taxing, lousy-services paradigm," as William Voegeli describes it in chapter 2, will sound familiar to many readers.

The book's title, *The Beholden State*, refers to a major reason for the bad policy plaguing California. As Steven Malanga argues in the eponymous opening chapter, California's public-sector unions have grown so mighty that they can make the state's politicians do their bidding. The pols, as a consequence, have lavished money on government employees, who often get paid more than their counterparts in other states and enjoy job protections unheard of in the private sector. They also get crazily generous pensions and frequently retire at 55 making nearly as much as they did while working, and sometimes more. The giant government-worker pension fund CalPERS, Malanga shows in another chapter, operates more like an advocacy group—fighting in the political arena for expansive benefits for employees—than like a program with a fiduciary responsibility to taxpayers.

The first two parts of *The Beholden State*, "The Politics and Economics of Decline" and "The Urban Fiscal Crisis," explore in detail the destructive effects of this union hijacking of California's political economy, as well as other forms of economic harm that the state has inflicted on itself, including environmental regulations hard to justify on any cost-benefit analysis. The reader will find a series of pointed proposals for change, ranging from economist Arthur B. Laffer's call for a simple, low-rate flat tax to replace the state's byzantine tax system to Troy Senik's recipe of political reforms to check the excessive influence of special interests, rein in the more dysfunctional aspects of California's initiative and referendum process, and make regulations more sensible. If enacted, these policies would help restore California's proud tradition of growth and opportunity.

So would a more practical attitude toward the state's abundant natural resources, as part III, "Of Energy and Environment," underscores. In "A Crude Awakening," Tom Gray describes how California's aversion to fossil fuels has resulted in underuse of its massive onshore oil reserves and a near-refusal to develop its offshore oil wealth—sources of employment and revenue that could go a long way toward solving the state's fiscal and economic difficulties. Hanson's "The Water Wars" decries the utopian environmentalist demand that California's inland waters flow as purely as they did in preindustrial times so as to protect salmon runs and a certain tiny fish. The environmental effort threatens to dry up some of the most fertile irrigated farmland on the planet, costing the state many jobs and billions in revenue.

Luckily, California's cities have shown better sense, at least when it comes to policing. In part IV, "Public Order," Heather Mac Donald and John Buntin look at William Bratton's tenure as chief of the Los Angeles Police Department, which brought safety to anarchic and dangerous Skid Row and drove crime down across the city while improving relations with minority neighborhoods that had viewed the police as a hostile force. Bratton's crime-fighting achievement rivaled his success in New York as Mayor Rudolph Giuliani's first police commissioner. Mac Donald also reports on the ongoing battle against street vagrancy in San Francisco, where a "homelessness-industrial complex" fights every attempt to make sidewalks passable and neighborhoods safe.

Part V of *The Beholden State* covers California's "Immigration Dilemmas." These include growing tensions between blacks and Hispanics in Los Angeles, which have erupted in gang violence. They include, too, the struggle of the state's Hispanics to overcome family breakdown, educational failure, and the temptations of the street and to lift themselves into the middle class.

Nowhere has public-sector unionism done more damage to California than in the public schools, as part VI reveals. Senik deems the powerful California Teachers Association "the worst union in America" for good reason. It has successfully lobbied to make California's teachers the highest-compensated in the country, while student outcomes have plummeted. It has ruthlessly fought every push to establish greater teacher accountability, even to the extent of protecting incompetent and sometimes criminal teachers from getting fired. And it has showered the dues that it collects from its members on a host of left-wing causes and politicians, adding to the state's troubles. The University of California system, long a springboard to middle-class success, has also lost its way, as Mac Donald shows. Acting as though its über-tolerant campuses seethed with racism, UC has wasted millions on diversity initiatives and hiring, threatening its own tradition of scientific and engineering excellence. The reader will find in the education chapters, too, an array of reform proposals.

One of *City Journal*'s abiding concerns is the condition of the culture, and this volume doesn't neglect that theme. Part VII features screenwriter and novelist Andrew Klavan on Hollywood's contempt for American values; Mac Donald on the Los Angeles art world's trendy celebration of graffiti, which effectively encourages vandals to prey on the hard-working owners of small businesses; and Michael Anton on Tom Wolfe's depiction of the state in his early journalistic classics.

The book's final section, "Keep Hope Alive," reflects our ultimate optimism. With our central office situated in New York City, at the Manhattan Institute, we've seen vividly how good policy can quickly transform things for the better. When *City Journal*'s first issue appeared in 1990, New York City was caught in a downward vortex. Crime and disorder raged out of control. Violence claimed six lives a day, and rape, theft, and other felonies were endemic. Parks were colonized by the homeless and the drugged. Graffiti covered subway cars and buses, sending the message that authority had lost its meaning. Welfare rolls exceeded one million people, with multigenerational dependency becoming the norm. Businesses, subject to higher and higher taxes, fled in droves, and many New Yorkers said in polls that they'd join them as soon as they could. The city, in short, was gravely ill—sicker than California is today. And this urban decline was predestined, the experts claimed, the inevitable product of an unjust and uncaring society.

The writers and editors of *City Journal* didn't buy it. New York could flourish again—if the right policies were put in place. Mayor Giuliani did just that. Implementing many ideas on crime-fighting, welfare reform, and growth economics that *City Journal* had advocated, Giuliani brought New York back from the brink and unleashed an urban renaissance. It was one of the great public-policy successes in history.

There's no question that returning California to the path of greatness requires a similarly dramatic new vision. This book presents key components of it. California can regain its lost promise—if it takes the right steps, as outlined not only in part VIII but in almost every chapter of the book.

I

THE POLITICS AND ECONOMICS OF DECLINE

1

The Beholden State

How Public-Sector Unions Broke California

Steven Malanga

THE CAMERA FOCUSES ON AN OFFICIAL of the Service Employees International Union (SEIU), California's largest public-employee union, sitting in a legislative chamber and speaking into a microphone. "We helped to get you into office, and we got a good memory," she says matter-of-factly to the elected officials outside the shot. "Come November, if you don't back our program, we'll get you out of office."

The video has become a sensation among California taxpayer groups for its vivid depiction of the audacious power that public-sector unions wield in their state. The unions' political triumphs have molded a California in which government workers thrive at the expense of a struggling private sector. The state's public school teachers are the highest paid in the nation. Its prison guards can easily earn six-figure salaries. State workers routinely retire at 55 with pensions higher than their base pay for most of their working life. Meanwhile, what was once the most prosperous state now suffers from an unemployment rate far steeper than the nation's and a flood of firms and jobs escaping high taxes and stifling regulations. This toxic combination—high public-sector employee costs and sagging economic fortunes—has produced recurring budget crises in Sacramento and in virtually every municipality in the state.

How public employees became members of the elite class in a declining California offers a cautionary tale to the rest of the country, where the same process is happening in slower motion. The story starts half a century ago, when California public workers won bargaining rights and quickly learned how to elect their own bosses—that is, sympathetic politicians who would

Illustration by Sean Delonas.

grant them outsize pay and benefits in exchange for their support. Over time, the unions have turned the state's politics completely in their favor. The result: unaffordable benefits for civil servants, fiscal chaos in Sacramento and in cities and towns across the state, and angry taxpayers finally confronting the unionized masters of California's unsustainable government.

* * *

California's government workers took longer than many of their counterparts to win the right to bargain collectively. New York City mayor Robert Wagner started a national movement back in the late 1950s when he granted negotiating rights to government unions, hoping to enlist them as allies against the city's Tammany Hall machine. The movement intensified in the early 1960s, after President John F. Kennedy conferred the right to bargain on federal workers. In California, a more politically conservative environment at the time, public employees remained without negotiating power through most of the 1960s, though they could join labor associations. In 1968, however, the state legislature passed the Meyers-Milias-Brown Act, extending bargaining rights to local government workers. Teachers and other state employees won the same rights in the 1970s.

These legislative victories happened at a time of surging prosperity. California's aerospace industry, fueled by the Cold War, was booming; investments in water supply and infrastructure nourished the state's agribusiness; cheaper air travel and a famously temperate climate burnished tourism. The twin lures of an expanding job market and rising incomes pushed the state's population higher, from about 16 million in 1960 to 23 million in 1980 and nearly 30 million by 1990. This expanding population in turn led to rapid growth in government jobs—from a mere 874,000 in 1960 to 1.76 million by 1980 and nearly 2.1 million in 1990—and to exploding public-union membership. In the late 1970s, the California teachers' union boasted about 170,000 members; that number jumped to about 225,000 in the early 1990s and stands at well over 320,000 today.

The swelling government payroll made many California taxpayers uneasy, eventually encouraging the 1978 passage of Proposition 13, the famous initiative that capped property tax hikes and sought to slow the growth of local governments, which feed on property taxes. Government workers rightly saw Proposition 13 as a threat. "We're not going to just lie back and take it," a California labor leader told the *Washington Post* after the vote, adding that Proposition 13 had made the union "more militant." The next several years proved him right. In 1980 alone, unionized employees of California local governments went on strike 40 times, even though doing so was illegal. And once the Supreme Court of California sanctioned state and local workers' right to strike in 1985—something that their counterparts in most other states still lack—the unions quickly mastered confrontational techniques like the "rolling strike," in which groups of workers walk off jobs at unannounced times, and the "blue flu," in which public-safety workers call in sick en masse.

But in post–Proposition 13 California, strikes were far from the unions' most fearsome weapons. Aware that Proposition 13 had shifted political action to the state capital, three major blocs—teachers' unions, public-safety

unions, and the Service Employees International Union, which now represents 350,000 assorted government workers—began amassing colossal power
in Sacramento. Over the past 30 years, they have become elite political givers
and the state's most powerful lobbying factions, replacing traditional interest
groups and changing the balance of power. Today, they vie for the title of
mightiest political force in California.

* * *

Consider the California Teachers Association (see also chapter 19). Much
of the CTA's clout derives from the fact that, like all government unions,
it can help elect the very politicians who negotiate and approve its members' salaries and benefits. Soon after Proposition 13 became law, the union
launched a coordinated statewide effort to support friendly candidates in
school board races, in which turnout is frequently low and special interests
can have a disproportionate influence. In often bitter campaigns, union-
backed candidates began sweeping out independent board members. By 1987,
even conservative-leaning Orange County saw 83 percent of board seats up
for grabs going to union-backed candidates. The resulting change in school
board composition made the boards close allies of the CTA.

But with union dues somewhere north of $1,000 per member and hun-
dreds of thousands of members, the CTA can afford to be a player not just
in local elections but in Sacramento, too (and in Washington, for that matter, where it's the National Education Association's most powerful affiliate).
The CTA entered the big time in 1988, when it almost single-handedly led
a statewide push to pass Proposition 98, an initiative—opposed by taxpayer
groups and Governor George Deukmejian—that required 40 percent of the
state's budget to fund local education. To drum up sympathy, the CTA ran
controversial ads featuring students; in one, a first-grader stares somberly
into the camera and says, "Pay attention—today's lesson is about the school
funding initiative." Victory brought local schools some $450 million a year
in new funding, much of it discretionary. Unsurprisingly, the union-backed
school boards often used the extra cash to fatten teachers' salaries—one reason that California's teachers are the country's highest paid, even though the
state's total spending per student is only slightly higher than the national average. "The problem is that there is no organized constituency for parents and
students in California," says Lanny Ebenstein, a former member of the Santa
Barbara Board of Education and an economics professor at the University of
California at Santa Barbara. "No one says to a board of education, 'We want
more of that money to go for classrooms, for equipment.'"

With its growing financial strength, the CTA gained the ability to shape
public opinion. In 1996, for instance, the union—casting covetous eyes on

surplus tax revenues from the state's economic boom—spent $1 million on an ad campaign advocating smaller classes. Californians began seeing the state's classrooms as overcrowded, according to polls. So Governor Pete Wilson earmarked some three-quarters of a billion dollars annually to cut class sizes in kindergarten through third grade. The move produced no discernible improvements in student performance, but it did require a hiring spree that inflated CTA rolls and produced a teacher shortage. (The union drew the line, however, when it faced the threat of increased accountability. Two years later, when Wilson offered funds to reduce class sizes even more but attached the money to new oversight mechanisms, the CTA spent $6 million to defeat the measure, living up to Wilson's assessment of it as a "relentless political machine.")

During this contentious period, the CTA and its local affiliates learned to play hardball, frequently shutting down classes with strikes. The state estimated that in 1989 alone, these strikes cost California students collectively some 7.2 million classroom days. Los Angeles teachers provoked outrage that year by reportedly urging their students to support them by skipping school. After journalist Debra Saunders noted in L.A.'s *Daily News* that the striking teachers were already well paid, the union published her home phone number in its newsletter and urged members to call her.

Four years later, the CTA reached new heights of thuggishness after a business-backed group began a petition to place a school-choice initiative on the state ballot. In a union-backed effort, teachers shadowed signature gatherers in shopping malls and aggressively dissuaded people from signing up. The tactic led to more than 40 confrontations and protests of harassment by signature gatherers. "They get in between the signer and the petition," the head of the initiative said. "They scream at people. They threaten people." The CTA's top official later justified the bullying: some ideas "are so evil that they should never even be presented to the voters," he said.

The rise of the white-collar CTA provides a good example of a fundamental political shift that took place everywhere in the labor movement. In the aftermath of World War II, at the height of its influence, organized labor was dominated by private workers; as a result, union members were often culturally conservative and economically progrowth. But as government workers have come to dominate the movement, it has moved left. By the mid-1990s, the CTA was supporting causes well beyond its purview as a collective bargaining agent for teachers. In 1994, for instance, it opposed an initiative that prohibited illegal immigrants from using state government programs and another that banned the state from recognizing gay marriages performed elsewhere. Some union members began to complain that their dues were helping

Illustration by Sean Delonas.

to advance a political agenda that they disagreed with. "They take our money and spend it as they see fit," says Larry Sand, founder of the California Teachers Empowerment Network, an organization of teachers and former teachers opposed to the CTA's noneducational politicking.

* * *

Public-safety workers—from cops and sheriffs to prison guards and highway-patrol officers—are the second part of the public-union triumvirate ruling California. In a state that has embraced some of the toughest criminal laws in the country, police and prison guards' unions own a precious currency: their political endorsements, which are highly sought after by candidates wanting to look tough on crime. But the qualification that the unions usually seek in candidates isn't, in fact, toughness on crime; it's willingness to back better pay and benefits for public-safety workers.

The pattern was set in 1972, when State Assemblyman E. Richard Barnes—an archconservative former navy chaplain who had fought pension and fringe benefit enhancements sought by government workers, including police officers and firefighters—ran for reelection. Barnes had one of the toughest records on crime of any state legislator. Yet cops and firefighters walked his district, telling voters that he was soft on criminals. He narrowly lost. As the *Orange County Register* observed years later, the election sent a message to all legislators that resonates even today: "Your career is at risk if you dare fiddle with police and fire" pay and benefits.

The state's prison guards' union has exploited a similar message. Back in 1980, when the California Correctional Peace Officers Association (CCPOA) won the right to represent prison guards in contract negotiations, it was a small fraternal organization of about 1,600 members. But as California's inmate population surged and the state went on a prison-building spree—constructing 22 new institutions over 25 years—union membership expanded to 17,000 in 1988, 25,000 by 1997, and 31,000 today. Union resources rose correspondingly, with a budget soaring to $25 million or so, supporting a staff 70 deep, including 20 lawyers.

Deploying those resources, the union started to go after politicians who didn't support higher salaries and benefits for its members and an ever-expanding prison system. In 2004, for example, the CCPOA spent $200,000—a whopping amount for a state assembly race—to unseat Republican Phil Wyman of Tehachapi. His sin: advocating the privatization of some state prisons in order to save money. "The amount of money that unions are pouring into local races is staggering," says Joe Armendariz, executive director of the Santa Barbara County Taxpayers Association. A recent mayoral and city council election in Santa Barbara, with a population of just 90,000, cost more than $1 million, he observes.

The symbiotic relationship between the CCPOA and former governor Gray Davis provides a remarkable example of the union's power. In 1998, when Davis first ran for governor, the union threw him its endorsement. Along with those much-needed law-and-order credentials, it also gave Davis $1.5 million in campaign contributions and another $1 million in independent ads supporting him. Four years later, as Davis geared up for reelection, he awarded the CCPOA a stunning 34 percent pay hike over five years, increasing the average base salary of a California prison guard from about $50,000 a year to $65,000—and this at a time when the unemployment rate in the state had been rising for nearly a year and a half and government revenues had been falling. The deal cost the state budget an additional $2 billion over the life of the contract. A union official described it admiringly as "the best labor contract in the history of California." Eight weeks after the offer, the union donated $1 million to Davis's reelection campaign.

Even cops who run for office have felt the wrath of public-safety unions. Allan Mansoor served 16 years as a deputy sheriff in Orange County but angered police unions by publicly backing an initiative that would have required them to gain their members' permission to spend dues on political activities. When the conservative Mansoor ran successfully for city council in Costa Mesa several years ago, local cops and firefighters poured resources into helping his more liberal opponents. "I didn't like seeing my dues go to candidates like Davis, so I supported efforts to curb that," Mansoor says. "Union leaders didn't like it, so they endorsed my opponents by claiming they were tougher on crime than I was."

Even more troubling are the activities of the California Organization of Police and Sheriffs (COPS), a lobbying and advocacy group that has raised tens of millions of dollars from controversial soliciting campaigns. In one, COPS fund raisers reportedly called residents of heavily immigrant neighborhoods and threatened to cut off their 911 services unless they donated. In another, a COPS fund raiser reportedly offered to shave points off Californians' driving records in exchange for donations. The group has dunned politicians, too. In 1998, it began publishing a voter guide in which candidates paid to be included. Pols considered the money well spent because of the importance of a COPS endorsement—or at least the appearance of one. "We all use them [COPS] for cover, especially in years when law enforcement is a big issue in elections," one state senator, Santa Clara's John Vasconcellos, admitted to the *Orange County Register*. "It stopped the right wing from calling me soft on crime."

The results of union pressure are clear. In most states, cops and other safety officers can typically retire at 50 with a pension of about half their final working salary; in California, they often receive 90 percent of their pay if they retire at the same age. The state's munificent disability system lets public-safety workers retire with rich pay for a range of ailments that have nothing to do with their jobs, costing taxpayers hundreds of millions of dollars. California's prison guards are the nation's highest paid, a big reason that spending on the state's prison system has blasted from less than 4.3 percent of the budget in 1986 to more than 11 percent today.

* * *

California's third big public-union player is the state wing of the SEIU, the nation's fastest-growing union, whose chief, Andy Stern, earned notoriety by visiting the White House 22 times during the first six months of the Obama administration. Founded in 1921 as a janitors' union, the SEIU slowly transformed itself into a labor group representing government and health care workers—especially health care workers paid by government medical programs like Medicaid. In 1984, the California State Employees Association, which represented many state workers, decided to affiliate with the SEIU. Today, the SEIU represents 700,000 California workers—more than a third of its nationwide membership. Of those, 350,000 are government employees: noninstructional workers in schools across the state; all non-public-safety workers in California's burgeoning prisons; 2,000 doctors, mostly residents and interns, at state-run hospitals; and many others at the local, county, and state levels.

The SEIU's rise in California illustrates again how modern labor's biggest victories take place in back rooms, not on picket lines. In the late 1980s, the SEIU began eyeing a big jackpot: tens of thousands of home health care workers being paid by California's county-run Medicaid programs. The SEIU initiated a long legal effort to have those workers, who were independent contractors, declared government employees. When the courts finally agreed, the union went about organizing them—an easy task because governments rarely contest organizing campaigns, not wanting to seem antiworker. The SEIU's biggest victory was winning representation for 74,000 home health care workers in Los Angeles County, the largest single organizing drive since the United Auto Workers unionized General Motors in 1937. Taxpayers paid a steep price: home health care costs became the fastest-growing part of the Los Angeles County budget after the SEIU bargained for higher wages and benefits for these new recruits. The SEIU also organized home health care workers in several other counties, reaching a whopping statewide total of 130,000 new members.

The SEIU's California numbers have given it extraordinary resources to pour into political campaigns. The union's major locals contributed a hefty $20 million in 2005 to defeat a series of initiatives to cap government growth and rein in union power. The SEIU has also spent millions over the years on initiatives to increase taxes, sometimes failing but on other occasions succeeding, as with a 2004 measure to impose a millionaires' tax to finance more mental health spending. With an overflowing war chest and hundreds of thousands of foot soldiers, the SEIU has been instrumental in getting local governments to pass living-wage laws in several California cities, including Los Angeles and San Francisco. And the union has also used its muscle in campaigns largely out of the public eye, as in 2003, when it pressured the board of CalPERS, the giant California public-employee pen-

Illustration by Sean Delonas.

sion fund, to stop investing in companies that outsourced government jobs to private contractors.

* * *

Armed with knowledge about California's three public-union heavy-weights, one can start to understand how the state found itself in its nightmarish fiscal situation. The beginning of the end was the 1998 gubernatorial election, in which the unions bet their future—and millions of dollars in members' dues—on Gray Davis. The candidate traveled to the SEIU's headquarters to remind it of his support during earlier battles against GOP governors ("Nobody in this race has done anywhere near as much as I have for SEIU"); the union responded by pumping $600,000 into his campaign. Declaring himself the "education candidate" who would expand funding of public education, Davis received $1.2 million from the CTA. Added to this was Davis's success in winning away from Republicans key public-safety endorsements—and millions in contributions—from the likes of the CCPOA.

Davis's subsequent victory over Republican Dan Lungren afforded public-worker unions a unique opportunity to cash in the IOUs that they had accumulated, because Davis's Democratic Party also controlled the state legislature. What followed was a series of breathtaking deals that left California state and municipal governments careening from one budget crisis to another for the next decade.

Perhaps the most costly was far-reaching 1999 legislation that wildly increased pension benefits for state employees. It included an unprecedented retroactive cost-of-living adjustment for the already retired and a phaseout of a cheaper pension plan that Governor Wilson had instituted in 1991. The deal also granted public-safety workers the right to retire at 50 with 90 percent of their salaries. To justify the incredible enhancements, Davis and the legislature turned to CalPERS, whose board was stocked with members who were either union reps or appointed by state officials who themselves were elected with union help. The CalPERS board, which had lobbied for the pension bill, issued a preposterous opinion that the state could provide the new benefits mostly out of the pension systems' existing surplus and future stock market gains. Most California municipalities soon followed the state enhancements for their own pension deals (see chapter 6).

When the stock market slid in 2000, state and local governments got slammed with enormous bills for pension benefits. The state's annual share, estimated by CalPERS back in 1999 to be only a few hundred million dollars, reached $3 billion by 2010. Counties and municipalities were no better off. Orange County's retirement system saw its payouts to retirees jump to $410 million a year by 2009, from $140 million in 2000. Many legislators who had voted for the pension legislation (including all but seven Republicans) later claimed that they'd had no idea that its fiscal impact would be so devastating. They had swallowed the rosy CalPERS projections even though they knew very well that the board was, as one county budget chief put it, "the fox in the henhouse."

The second budget-busting deal of the Davis era was the work of the teachers' union. In 2000, the CTA began lobbying to have a chunk of the state's budget surplus devoted to education. In a massive rally in Sacramento, thousands of teachers gathered on the steps of the capitol, some chanting for TV cameras, "We want money! We want money!" Behind the scenes, Davis kept up running negotiations with the union over just how big the pot should be. "While you were on your way to Sacramento, I was driving there the evening of May 7, and the governor and I talked three times on my cell phone," CTA president Wayne Johnson later boasted to members. "The first call was just general conversation. The second call, he had an offer of $1.2 billion. . . . On the third call, he upped the ante to $1.5 billion." Finally, in meetings, both sides agreed on $1.84 billion. As *Sacramento Bee* columnist Dan Walters later observed, that deal didn't merely help blow the state's surplus; it also locked in higher baseline spending for education. The result: "When revenues returned to normal, the state faced a deficit that eventually not only cost Davis his governorship in 2003 but has plagued his successor, Arnold Schwarzenegger."

* * *

Having wielded so much power effortlessly, the unions miscalculated the antitax, anti-Davis sentiment that erupted when, shortly after his autumn 2002 reelection, Davis announced that the state faced a massive deficit. The budget surprise spurred an enormous effort to recall the governor, which the unions worked to defeat, with the SEIU spending $2 million. At the same time, union leaders used their influence in the Democratic Party to try to save Davis, telling other Democrats that they would receive no union support if they abandoned the governor. "If you betray us, we won't forget it," the head of the 800,000-member Los Angeles County Federation of Labor proclaimed to Democrats. Only when it became apparent from polls that the recall would succeed did the unions shift their support to Lieutenant Governor Cruz Bustamante, who finished a distant second to Schwarzenegger. Taxpayer groups were euphoric.

But as they and Schwarzenegger soon discovered, most of California's government machinery remained union controlled—especially the Democratic state legislature, which blocked long-term reform. Frustrated, Schwarzenegger backed a series of 2005 initiatives sponsored by taxpayer groups to curb the unions and restrain government growth, including one that made it harder for public-employee unions to use members' dues for political purposes. The controversial proposals sparked the most expensive statewide election in American history. Advocacy groups and businesses spent a staggering $300 million (some of it, however, coming from drug companies trying to head off an unrelated initiative). The spending spree included $58 million from the CTA, which mortgaged its Sacramento headquarters for the cause. All of the initiatives went down to defeat.

California taxpayers nevertheless received a brief respite, thanks to the mid-decade housing boom that drove the economy and tax collections higher and momentarily eased the state's budget crisis. Predictably, state politicians forgot California's Davis-era deficit woes and gobbled up the surpluses, increasing spending by 32 percent, or $34 billion, in four years. Then the housing market crashed in 2007, prompting a cascade of budget crises in Sacramento and around the state. Only too late have Californians recognized the true magnitude of their fiscal problems, including a $21 billion deficit by mid-2009 that forced the state to issue IOUs when it temporarily ran out of cash. In the municipal bond market, fears began rising that the Golden State could actually default on its debt.

Municipalities around the state are also buckling under massive labor costs. One city, Vallejo, has already filed for bankruptcy to get out from under onerous employee salaries and pension obligations. (To stop other cities from going this route, unions are promoting a new law to make it harder for municipalities to declare bankruptcy.) Other local California governments, big and small, are nearing disaster. The city of Orange, with a budget of just $88 million in 2009, spent $13 million of it on pensions and expects that figure to rise to $23 million in just three years. Contra Costa's pension costs rose from $70 million in 2000 to $200 million by the end of the decade, producing a budget crisis. Los Angeles, where payroll constitutes nearly half the city's $7 billion budget, faces budget shortfalls of hundreds of millions of dollars in 2011, projected to grow to $1 billion annually in several years. In October 2007, even as it was clear that the area's housing economy was crashing, city officials had handed out 23 percent raises over a five-year period to workers.

In the past, California could always rely on a rebounding economy to save it from its budgetary excesses. But these days, few view the state as the land of opportunity. Throughout the national recession that began in December 2008 and carried through 2009, California's unemployment rate consistently ran several points higher than the national rate. Major California companies like Google and Intel have chosen to expand elsewhere, not in their home state. Put off by the high taxes and cumbersome regulatory regime that the public-sector cartel has led the way in foisting on the state, executives now view California as a noxious business environment. In a 2008 survey by a consulting group, Development Counsellors International, business executives rated California the state where they were least likely to locate new operations.

* * *

More and more California taxpayers are realizing how stacked the system is against them, and the first stirrings of revolt are breaking out. Voters defeated a series of ballot initiatives in May 2009 that would have allowed politicians to

solve the state budget crisis temporarily through a series of questionable gimmicks, including one to let the state borrow against future lottery receipts and
another to let it plug budget holes with money diverted from a mental health
services fund. In a clear message from voters, the only proposition to gain
approval banned pay raises for legislators during periods of budget deficit.

With anger rising, taxpayer advocates now plan to revive older initiatives
to cut the power of public-sector unions. Mark Bucher, head of the Citizens
Power Campaign, is pushing for an initiative that's similar to propositions
that failed in 1998 and in 2005—but their prospects may be brighter today,
he argues, because the woes of municipalities like Vallejo have made citizens
more aware of union power and more supportive of reform. "The mood has
clearly shifted in California," Bucher says. "You can see that in the rise of local
Tea Party antitax groups around the state. People are fed up."

Another initiative that could mend California's broken politics is a 2008
vote that took the power to delineate electoral districts away from the state
legislature—which had used it to make it difficult to defeat incumbents—and
gave it to a nonpartisan commission. If this commission succeeds in making
legislative races more competitive and incumbents more responsive to voter
sentiment, the legislature would almost certainly become less beholden to
narrow union interests, and a whole series of reforms would be possible: a
new, cheaper pension plan for state employees; fewer restrictions on charter
schools, which often educate kids more effectively and less expensively than
public schools do; and regulatory reforms that would reduce the estimated
$493 billion cost that regulations impose on California businesses each year.

It will take an enormous effort to roll back decades of political and economic gains by government unions. But the status quo is unsustainable. And
at long last, Californians are beginning to understand the connection between
that status quo and the corruption at the heart of their politics.

[2010]

2

The Big-Spending, High-Taxing, Lousy-Services Paradigm

California Taxpayers Don't Get Much Bang for Their Bucks

William Voegeli

IN 1956, THE ECONOMIST CHARLES TIEBOUT provided the framework that best explains why people vote with their feet. The "consumer-voter," as Tiebout called him, challenges government officials to "ascertain his wants for public goods and tax him accordingly." Each jurisdiction offers its own package of public goods, along with a particular tax burden needed to pay for those goods. As a result, "the consumer-voter moves to that community whose local government best satisfies his set of preferences." In selecting a jurisdiction, the mobile consumer-voter is, in effect, choosing a club to join based on the benefits that it offers and the dues that it charges.

America's federal system allows, at the state level, for 50 different clubs to join. At first glance, the states seem to differ between those that bundle numerous high-quality public benefits with high taxes and those that offer packages of low benefits and low taxes. These alternatives, of course, define the basic argument between liberals and conservatives over the ideal size and scope of government. Except for Oregon, John McCain carried every one of the 17 states with the lowest tax levels in the 2008 presidential election, while Barack Obama won every one of the 17 at the top of the list except for Wyoming and Alaska.

It's not surprising, then, that an intense debate rages over which model is more satisfactory and sustainable. What is surprising is the growing evidence that the low-benefit, low-tax alternative succeeds not only on its own terms but also according to the criteria used by defenders of high benefits and high taxes. Whatever theoretical claims are made for imposing high taxes to provide generous government benefits, the practical reality is that these public

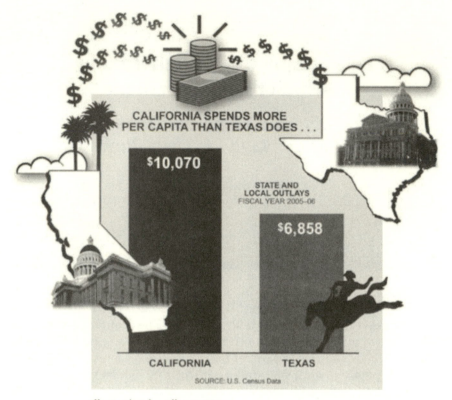

Illustration by Alberto Mena.

goods are, increasingly, neither public nor good: their beneficiaries are mostly the service providers themselves, and their quality is poor. For evidence, look to the two largest states in the nation, which are fine representatives of the liberal and conservative alternatives.

* * *

One out of every five Americans is either a Californian or a Texan. California became the nation's most populous state in 1962; Texas climbed into second place in 1994. They are broadly similar: populous Sun Belt states with large metropolitan areas, diverse economies, and borders with Mexico producing comparable demographic mixes. Both are "majority-minority" states, where non-Hispanic whites make up just under half of the population and Latinos just over a third.

According to the most recent data available from the Census Bureau, for the fiscal year ending in 2006, Americans paid an average of $4,001 per person in state and local taxes. But Californians paid $4,517 per person, well above that national average, while Texans paid $3,235. It's worth noting, by the way, that while state and local governments in both California and Texas get most of their revenue from taxes, the revenue is augmented by subsidies from the federal government and by fees charged for governmental services and facilities, such as trash collection, airports, public university tuition, and mass transit. California had total revenues of $11,160 per capita, more than every state but Alaska, Wyoming, and New York, while Texas placed a distant 44th on this scale, with revenues of all governmental entities totaling $7,558 per person.

What might interest Tiebout is that while California and Texas are comparable in terms of sheer numbers, their demographic paths are diverging. Before 1990, both states grew much faster than the rest of the country. Since then, only Texas has continued to do so. While its share of the nation's population has steadily increased, from 6.8 percent in 1990 to 7.9 percent in 2007, California's has barely budged, from 12 percent to 12.1 percent.

Unpacking the numbers is even more revealing—and, for California, disturbing. The biggest contrast between the two states shows up in "net internal migration," the demographer's term for the difference between the number of Americans who move into a state from another and the number who move out of it to another. Between April 1, 2000, and June 30, 2007, an average of 3,247 more Americans moved out of California than into it every week, according to the Census Bureau. Over the same period, Texas saw a net gain, in an average week, of 1,544 people. Aside from Louisiana and Mississippi, which lost population to other states because of Hurricane Katrina, California is the only Sun Belt state that had negative net internal migration after 2000. All the other states that lost population to internal migration were Rust Belt basket cases, including New York, Illinois, New Jersey, Michigan, and Ohio.

As Tiebout might have guessed, this outmigration has to do with taxes. Besides Mississippi, every one of the 17 states with the lowest state and local tax levels had positive net internal migration from 2000 to 2007. Except for Wyoming, Maine, and Delaware, every one of the 17 highest-tax states had negative net internal migration over the same period. Conservative researchers' technical explanation for this phenomenon is: "Well, duh." Or, as Arthur Laffer and Stephen Moore wrote in the *Wall Street Journal* in 2009: "People, investment capital and businesses are mobile: They can leave tax-unfriendly states and move to tax-friendly states."

Summarizing the findings of a report they wrote for the American Legislative Exchange Council, Laffer and Moore pointed out that between 1998 and 2007, the states without an individual income tax "created 89 percent more jobs and had 32 percent faster personal income growth" than the states with the highest individual income tax rates. California's tax and regulatory policies, the report predicts, "will continue to sap its economic vitality," while Texas's "pro-growth" policies will help it "maintain its superior economic performance well into the future." The clear implication is that California should become more like Texas.

* * *

At this point, defenders of the high-benefit, high-tax paradigm push back. Remember the other half of Tiebout's equation, they say. There's no need for a state to be like Texas if its high taxes and extensive regulations are part of a package deal that yields more and better public goods and an attractive quality of life.

But that, it turns out, is a big "if." It's true that many people are less sensitive to taxes and more concerned about public goods, and these consumer-voters will congregate in places with extensive services. But it's also true, all things being equal, that everyone would rather pay lower than higher taxes. The high-benefit, high-tax model can work, but only if the high taxes actually purchase high benefits—that is, public goods that far surpass the quality of those available to people who pay low taxes.

And here, California is decidedly lacking. The biggest factor accounting for California's loss of population to the other 49 states, bond ratings that would embarrass Chrysler or GM, and state politics contentious and feckless enough to shame a banana republic, has to be its public sector's diminishing willingness and capacity to fulfill its promises to taxpayers. "Twenty years ago, you could go to Texas, where they had very low taxes, and you would see the difference between there and California," social thinker and *City Journal* contributing editor Joel Kotkin told the *Los Angeles Times* in March 2009. "Today, you go to Texas, the roads are no worse, the public schools are not great but are better than or equal to ours, and their universities are good. The bargain between California's government and the middle class is constantly being renegotiated to the disadvantage of the middle class."

Similarly, the CEO of a manufacturing company in suburban Los Angeles told a *Times* reporter that his business suffered less from California's high taxes than from its ineffectual services. As a result, the company pays "a fortune" to educate its employees, many of whom graduated from California public schools, "on basic things like writing and math skills." According to a 2009 report issued by McKinsey & Company, Texas students "are, on average, one to two years of learning ahead of California students of the same age," though expenditures per public school student are 12 percent higher in California.

State and local government expenditures as a whole were 46.8 percent higher in California than in Texas in 2005–2006—$10,070 per person compared with $6,858. And Texas not only spends its citizens' dollars more effectively; it emphasizes priorities that are more broadly beneficial. In 2005–2006, per capita spending on transportation was 5.9 percent lower in California than in Texas, and highway expenditures in particular were 9.5 percent lower, a discovery both plausible and infuriating to any Los Angeles commuter losing the will to live while sitting in yet another freeway traffic jam. With tax revenues scarce and voters strongly opposed to surrendering more of their income, Texas officials devote a large share of their expenditures to basic services that benefit the most people. In California, by contrast, more and more spending consists of either transfer payments to government dependents (as in welfare, health, housing, and community development programs) or generous payments to government employees and contractors (reflected in administrative costs, pensions, and general expenditures). Both kinds of spending weaken California's appeal to consumer-voters, the first because redistributive transfer payments are the least publicly beneficial type of public good, and the second because the dues paid to Club California purchase benefits that, increasingly, are enjoyed by the staff instead of the members.

Californians have the best possible reason to believe that the state's public sector is not holding up its end of the bargain: clear evidence that it used to do a better job. Bill Watkins, executive director of the Economic Forecast Project at the University of California at Santa Barbara, has calculated that once you adjust for population growth and inflation, the state government spent 26 percent more in 2007–2008 than in 1997–1998. Back then, "California had teachers. Prisoners were in jail. Health care was provided for those with the least resources." Today, Watkins asks, "Are the roads 26 percent better? Are schools 26 percent better? What is 26 percent better?"

* * *

The steady deterioration of California's public services hasn't gone unnoticed. Shortly after his stunning ascension to the governor's office in 2003, Arnold Schwarzenegger established an advisory commission, the California Performance Review (CPR), to recommend ways to make governance in California smarter, cheaper, and better. The commission labored through 2004 before delivering a doorstop report with more than 1,200 recommendations for streamlining this and consolidating that, along with an assessment that implementing the full list of changes could save California $32 billion over the first five years.

And then . . . nothing, really. The 2,500-page report was "dead on arrival," according to Bill Whalen of the Hoover Institution, "because it was too complicated for voters to rally behind and legislators didn't want to see it enacted." Citizen Schwarzenegger may have assumed that his personal star

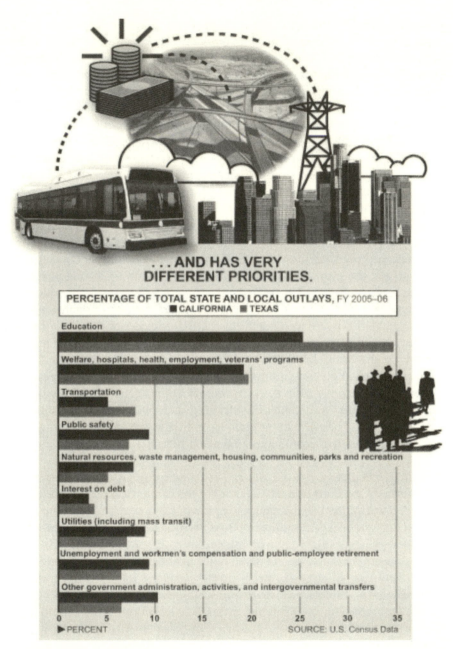

...AND HAS VERY DIFFERENT PRIORITIES.

PERCENTAGE OF TOTAL STATE AND LOCAL OUTLAYS, FY 2005–06
■ CALIFORNIA ■ TEXAS

Education

Welfare, hospitals, health, employment, veterans' programs

Transportation

Public safety

Natural resources, waste management, housing, communities, parks and recreation

Interest on debt

Utilities (including mass transit)

Unemployment and workmen's compensation and public-employee retirement

Other government administration, activities, and intergovernmental transfers

0   5   10   15   20   25   30   35
► PERCENT   SOURCE: U.S. Census Data

Illustration by Alberto Mena.

power and the CPR recommendations' plodding good sense would make a politically irresistible combination. Such reckoning failed to account for the formidable ability of even the most obscure and otiose governmental body to hunker down, defend its turf, and outlast mere politicians.

The CPR, for example, recommended abolishing dozens of California's commissions and advisory boards, either outright or by folding their activities into a simpler and more rational organizational structure. Five years later, few of these vestigial organs had been removed. The many that remained included the Commission on Aging, whose lead accomplishment for 2009 was getting the legislature to declare a Fall Prevention Week (which began on the first day of autumn, naturally); the Apprenticeship Council, "which has been in place since the 1930s," according to the CPR, and "is no longer needed to perform regulatory and advisory responsibilities"; the Board of Barbering and Cosmetology; the Court Reporters Board; and the Hearing Aid Dispensers Bureau.

The point is not that turning a flamethrower on every item in the Museum of Governmental Anachronisms would have saved California a great deal of money. It is, rather, that abolishing these boards and commissions, whose names are talk-radio punch lines, would have been the easy calls, the obvious first steps toward giving California's taxpayers a decent return on their surrendered dollars. Yet even the low-hanging fruit proved out of reach. The path of least resistance was to do the same old thing, not the sensible thing.

The resistance comes from the blob of interest groups, inside and outside government, that like California's public sector just fine the way it is and see reform as a threat to their comfortable, lucrative arrangements. It turns out, for example, that all the pointless boards and commissions are bulletproof because they provide golden parachutes to politicians turned out of the state legislature by California's strict term limits. In the middle of the state's most recent budget crisis, State Senator Tony Strickland proposed a bill to eliminate salaries paid to members of boards and commissions who, despite holding fewer than two formal hearings or official meetings per month, had received annual compensation in excess of $100,000. The bill died in committee.

* * *

James Madison would have to revise—or possibly burn—Federalist No. 10 if he were forced to account for the new phenomenon of the government itself becoming the faction decisively shaping its own policy and conduct. This faction dominates because it's playing a much longer game than the politicians who come and go, not to mention the citizens who rarely read the enormous owner's manual for the Rube Goldberg machine they feed with their dollars. They rarely stay outraged long enough to make a difference.

Take entitlements and public-employee pensions, which are, Watkins says, "the real source of the state's fiscal distress." A 2005 study by the Legislative Analyst's Office (California's version of the Congressional Budget Office) found that pensions for California's government employees "surpassed the other states—often significantly—at all retirement ages." California government workers retiring at age 55 received larger pensions than their counterparts in any other state (leaving aside the many states where retirement as early as 55 isn't even possible). The California Foundation for Fiscal Responsibility periodically posts a list of retired city managers, state administrators, public university deans, and police chiefs who receive pensions of at least $100,000 per year. The latest report shows 5,115 lucky members in this six-figure club. The state's annual bill for polishing their gold watches is $610 million.

Again, the most vivid part of the problem is not the most important. California would move only slightly closer to regaining fiscal health if it scraped the gilding off the pensions and health benefits of its most lucratively retired employees. But when even a flagrant example of a government's serving its workforce better than its citizens is politically unassailable, it's hard to be hopeful about the mundane reforms needed to change the rest of the economically debilitating public-employee retirement system. The California Performance Review suggested the sensible thing: gradually substituting defined-contribution for defined-benefit pension plans. (According to a report by the Pew Center on the States, just 20 percent of the nation's private-sector employees are enrolled in a defined-benefit pension plan, compared with 90 percent of public-sector employees.) To no one's shock, the state legislature has rejected all proposals to curb the state's financial obligations to its retired and retiring employees.

* * *

If California doesn't want to be Texas, it must find a way to be a better California. The easy thing about being Texas is that the government has a great deal of control over the part of its package deal that attracts consumer-voters—it must merely keep taxes low. California, on the other hand, must deliver on the high benefits promised in its sales pitch. It won't be enough for its state and local governments to spend a lot of money; they have to spend it efficiently and effectively.

The optimistic assessment is that things are going to get worse in California before they get better. The pessimistic assessment is that they're going to get worse before they get much worse. As is often the case, hanging around with the pessimists is less fun but more instructive. The current recession has driven California's state government into what amounts to a five-month budget cycle, according to Dan Walters of the *Sacramento Bee*. He estimated that the budget deal tortuously wrought in July would start falling apart in October, because it was predicated on pie-in-the-sky revenue estimates and because so many of its spending cuts are being challenged, often successfully, in the courts.

The recession will eventually end and California's finances will improve, say the optimists. Given the state's pervasive political bias against efficient and effective public services, however, the question is whether its finances will ever get truly well. States that have grown accustomed to thinking of the engine that drives their economies as an inexhaustible resource—whether it's Michigan and the auto industry, New York and Wall Street, or California and the vision of the sunlit good life that used to attract new residents—find it tough to compete again for what they thought would be theirs forever and to plan budgets for lean years that turn into lean decades. Instead, they invest their hopes in a deus ex machina that will rescue them from the hard choices they dread.

For California's governmental-industrial complex, a new liberal administration and Congress in Washington offer plausible hope for a happy Hollywood ending. Federal aid will replace the dollars that California's taxpayers, fed up with the state's lousy benefits and high taxes, refuse to provide. Americans will continue to vote with their feet, either by leaving California or disdaining relocation there, but their votes won't matter, at least in the short term. Under the coming bailout, the new 49ers—Americans in the other 49 states, that is—will be extended the privilege of paying California's taxes. At least they won't have to put up with its public services.

[2009]

3

The Golden State's War on Itself

How Politicians Turned the California Dream into a Nightmare

Joel Kotkin

C ALIFORNIA HAS LONG BEEN a destination for those seeking a better place to live. For most of its history, the state enacted sensible policies that created one of the wealthiest and most innovative economies in human history. California realized the American dream but better, fostering a huge middle class that, for the most part, owned their homes, sent their kids to public schools, and found meaningful work connected to the state's amazingly diverse, innovative economy.

Recently, though, the dream has been evaporating. Between 2003 and 2007, California state and local government spending grew 31 percent, even as the state's population grew just 5 percent. The overall tax burden as a percentage of state income, once middling among the states, has risen to the sixth-highest in the nation, says the Tax Foundation. Since 1990, according to an analysis by California Lutheran University, the state's share of overall U.S. employment has dropped a remarkable 10 percent. When the state economy has done well, it has usually been the result of asset inflation—first during the dot-com bubble of the late 1990s, and then during the housing boom, which was responsible for nearly half of all jobs created earlier in this decade.

After the financial crisis began in 2008, the state fared even worse. In 2009, California personal income fell 2.5 percent, the first such fall since the Great Depression and well below the 1.7 percent drop for the rest of the country. Unemployment had started to ebb nationwide by 2010, but not in California, where it approached 13 percent, among the highest rates in the nation. Between 2008 and 2009, not one of California's biggest cities outperformed such traditional laggards as New York, Pittsburgh, and Philadelphia in employment growth, and four cities—Los Angeles, Oakland, Santa Ana, and San Bernardino–Riverside—sit very close to the bottom among the nation's largest metro areas, just slightly ahead of basket cases like Detroit. Long a global exemplar, California is in danger of becoming, as historian Kevin Starr has warned, a "failed state."

What went so wrong? The answer lies in a change in the nature of progressive politics in California. During the second half of the twentieth century, the state shifted from an older progressivism, which emphasized infrastructure investment and business growth, to a newer version, which views the private sector much the way the Huns viewed a city—as something to be sacked and plundered. The result is two separate California realities: a lucrative one for the wealthy and for government workers, who are largely insulated from

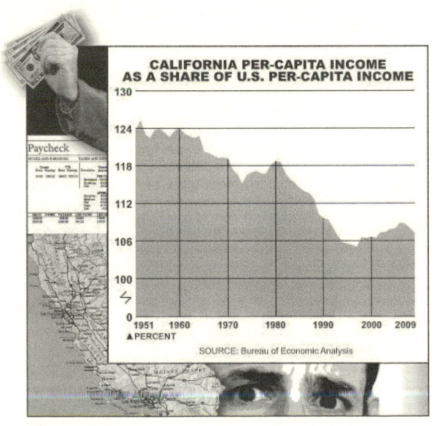

CALIFORNIA PER-CAPITA INCOME AS A SHARE OF U.S. PER-CAPITA INCOME

SOURCE: Bureau of Economic Analysis

Illustration by Alberto Mena.

economic decline; and a grim one for the private-sector middle and working classes, who are fleeing the state.

* * *

The old progressivism began in the early 1900s and lasted for half a century. It was a nonpartisan and largely middle-class movement that emphasized fostering economic growth—the progressives themselves tended to have business backgrounds—and building infrastructure, such as the Los Angeles Aqueduct and the Hetch Hetchy Reservoir. One powerful progressive was Republican Earl Warren, who governed the state between 1943 and 1953 and spent much of the prospering state's surplus tax revenue on roads, mental health facilities, and schools. Another was Edmund G. "Pat" Brown, elected in 1958, who oversaw an aggressive program of public works, a rapid expansion of higher education, and the massive California Water Project.

But by the mid-1960s, Brown's traditional progressivism was being destabilized by forces that would eventually transform liberal politics around the nation: public-sector workers, liberal lobbying organizations, and minorities, all demanding more and more social spending. This spending irritated the business interests that had formerly seen government as their friend, contributing to Brown's defeat in 1966 by Ronald Reagan. Reagan was far more budget-conscious than Brown had been, and large declines in infrastructure spending occurred on his watch, mostly to meet a major budget deficit.

The decline of progressivism continued under the next governor: Pat Brown's son, Edmund G. "Jerry" Brown, Jr., who took office in 1975. Brown scuttled infrastructure spending, in large part because of his opposition to growth and concern for the environment. Encouraged by "reforms" backed by Brown—such as the 1978 Dill Act, which legalized collective bargaining for them—the public-employee unions became the best-organized political force in California and currently dominate Democrats in the legislature (see chapter 1, "The Beholden State"). According to the unions, public funds should be spent on inflating workers' salaries and pensions—or else on expanding social services, often provided by public employees—and not on infrastructure or higher education, which is why Brown famously opposed new freeway construction and water projects and even tried to rein in the state's university system.

The power of the public-employee lobby would come to haunt the recall-shortened gubernatorial reign of Gray Davis, Brown's former chief of staff. The government workers' growing demands on the budget, green groups' opposition to expanding physical infrastructure, and Republican opposition to tax increases made it impossible for either Davis or his successor, Arnold

Schwarzenegger, to expand the state's infrastructure at a scale necessary to accommodate its growing population.

* * *

The new progressives were as unenthusiastic about welcoming business as about building infrastructure. Fundamentally indifferent or even hostile to the existing private sector, they embraced two peculiar notions about what could sustain California's economy in its place. The first of these was California's inherent creativity—a view held not only by liberal Democrats. David Crane, Governor Schwarzenegger's top economic advisor, once told me that California could easily afford to give up blue-collar jobs in warehousing, manufacturing, or even business services because the state's vaunted "creative economy" would find ways to replace the lost employment and income. California would always come out ahead, he said, because it represented "ground zero for creative destruction."

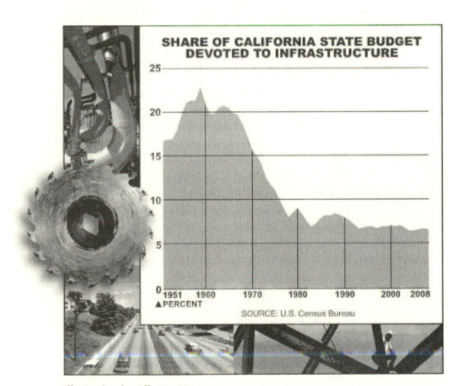

Illustration by Alberto Mena.

The second engine that could supposedly keep California humming was the so-called green economy. In a 2009 *Time* cover story, for example, Michael Grunwald argued that venture capital, high tech, and, above all, "green" technology were already laying the foundation of a miraculous economic turnaround in California. Though there are certainly opportunities in new energy-saving technologies, this is an enthusiasm that requires some serious curbing. One study hailing the new industry found that California was creating some 10,000 green jobs annually before the recession. But that won't heal a state that has lost 700,000 jobs since then.

At the same time, green promoters underestimate the impact of California's draconian environmental rules on the economy as a whole. Take the state's Global Warming Solutions Act, which will force any new development to meet standards for being "carbon-neutral." It requires the state to reduce its carbon-emissions levels by 30 percent between 1990 and 2020, virtually assuring that California's energy costs, already among the nation's highest, will climb still higher. The legislation seems certain to slow any future recovery in the suffering housing, industrial, and warehousing sectors and to make California less competitive with other states. Costs of the act to small businesses alone, according to a report by two California State University professors, will likely cut gross state product by $182 billion over the next decade and cost some 1.1 million jobs.

It's sad to consider the greens such an impediment to social and economic health. Historically, California did an enviable job in traditional approaches to conservation—protecting its coastline, preserving water and air resources, and turning large tracts of land into state parks. But much like the public-sector unions, California's environmental movement has become so powerful that it feels free to push its agenda without regard for collateral damage done to the state's economy and people. With productive industry in decline and the business community in disarray, even the harshest regulatory policies often meet little resistance in Sacramento.

In the Central Valley, for instance, regulations designed to save certain fish species have required 450,000 acres to go fallow. Unemployment is at 17 percent across the valley; in some towns, like Mendota, it's higher than 40 percent. Rick Wartzman, director of the Peter Drucker Institute, has described the vast agricultural region around Fresno as "California's Detroit," an area where workers and businesspeople "are fast becoming a more endangered species than Chinook salmon or delta smelt." The fact that governments dominated by "progressives" are impoverishing whole regions isn't merely an irony; it's an abomination.

* * *

So much for the creative green economy. As for the old progressives' belief that government shouldn't scare away productive, competitive, long-term enterprise, that, too, has been abandoned by their successors. "Our economy is not inducing the right kind of business," says Larry Kosmont, a prominent business consultant in Los Angeles. "It's too expensive to operate here, and managers feel squeezed. They feel they can't control the circumstances any more and have to look somewhere else." The problem isn't just corporate costs, either. The regulatory restraints, high taxes, and onerous rules enacted by the new progressives lead to high housing prices, making much of California too expensive for middle- and working-class employees and encouraging their employers to move elsewhere.

Silicon Valley, for instance—despite the celebrated success of Google and Apple—has 130,000 fewer jobs now than it had a decade ago, with office vacancy above 20 percent. In Los Angeles, garment factories and aerospace companies alike are shutting down. Toyota has abandoned its Fremont plant. California lost nearly 400,000 manufacturing jobs between 2000 and 2007, according to a report by the Milken Institute—even as industrial employment grew in Texas and Arizona. A sign of the times: transferring factory equipment from the Bay Area to other locales has become a thriving business, notes Tom Abate of the *San Francisco Chronicle*.

Optimists sometimes point out that "new economy" companies like Disney, Google, Hewlett-Packard, and Apple, as well as scores of smaller innovative firms, continue to keep their headquarters in the state. But this is to ignore the fact that many of these companies are sending their middle- and working-class employees to other locales. Evidence of middle-class flight: since 1999, according to California Lutheran University, the state has seen a far steeper decline in households earning between $35,000 and $75,000 than the national average. And blue-collar areas—Oakland, the eastern expanses of greater Los Angeles, and much of central California—have been hit even harder. California's overall poverty rate has been consistently higher than the national average. In Los Angeles County alone, some 20 percent of the population—2.2 million people—receives some form of public aid.

* * *

In short, the economy created by the new progressives can pay off only those at the peak of the employment pyramid—top researchers, CEOs, entertainment honchos, highly skilled engineers and programmers. As a result, California suffers from an increasingly bifurcated social structure. Between 1993 and 2007, the share of the state's income that went to the top 1 percent of earners more than doubled, to one-quarter—the eighth-largest share in the country.

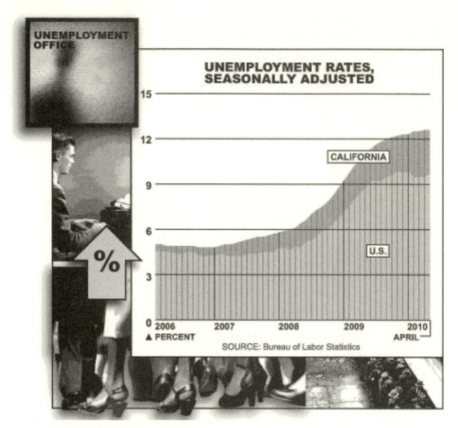

UNEMPLOYMENT OFFICE

UNEMPLOYMENT RATES, SEASONALLY ADJUSTED

CALIFORNIA

U.S.

15

12

9

6

3

0

2006   2007   2008   2009   2010

▲ PERCENT   APRIL

SOURCE: Bureau of Labor Statistics

%

Illustration by Alberto Mena.

For these lucky earners, a low-growth or negative-growth economy works just fine, so long as stock prices rise. For their public-employee allies, the same is true, so long as pensions remain inviolate. Global-warming legislation may drive down employment in warehouses and factories, but if it's couched in rhetoric about saving the planet, these elites can even feel good about it.

Under the new progressives, it's always hoi polloi who need to lower their expectations. More than four out of five Californians favor single-family homes, for example, but progressive thinkers like Robert Cruickshank, writing in *California Progress Report*, want to replace "the late 20th century suburban model of the California Dream" with "an urban, sustainable model that is backed by a strong public sector." Of course, this new urban model will apply not to the wealthy progressives who own spacious homes in the suburbs but to the next generation, largely Latino and Asian. Robert Eyler, chair of the economics department at Sonoma State University, points out that wealthy aging yuppies in Sonoma County have little interest in reviving growth in the local economy, where office vacancy rates are close to those in

Detroit. Instead, they favor policies, such as "smart growth" and an insistence on "renewable" energy sources, that would make the area look like a gated community—a green one, naturally.

* * *

California's supposedly progressive economics have had profound demographic consequences. After serving as a beacon for millions of Americans, California now ranks second to New York—and just ahead of New Jersey—in the number of moving vans leaving the state. Between 2004 and 2007, 500,000 more Americans left California than arrived; in 2008, the net outflow reached 135,000, much of it to the very "dust bowl" states, like Oklahoma and Texas, from which many Californians trace their origins. California now has a lower percentage of people who moved there within the last year than any state except Michigan. Even immigration from abroad seems to be waning: a recent University of Southern California study shows the percentage of Californians who are foreign-born declining for the first time in half a century. After the 2010 census, as political analyst Michael Barone predicted, California did not gain a new congressional district for the first time in its history as a state.

This demographic pattern only reinforces the hegemony of environmentalists and public employees. In the past, both political parties had to answer to middle- and lower-middle-class voters sensitive to taxes and dependent on economic growth. But these days, with much of the middle class leaving, power is won largely by mobilizing activists and public employees. There is little countervailing pressure from local entrepreneurs and businesses, which tend to be poorly organized and with an employee base consisting heavily of noncitizens. And the legislature's growing Latino caucus doesn't resist regulations that stifle jobs—perhaps because of the proliferation of the California equivalent of "rotten boroughs": Latino districts with few voters where politicians can rely on public employees and activists to dominate elections.

* * *

Blessed with resources of topography, climate, and human skill, California does not need to continue its trajectory from global paragon to planetary laughingstock. A coalition of inland Latinos and Anglos, along with independent suburban middle-class voters in the coastal areas, could begin a shift in policy, reining in both public-sector costs and harsh climate-change legislation. Above all, Californians need to recognize the importance of the economic base—particularly such linchpins as agriculture, manufacturing, and trade—in reenergizing the state's economy.

The changes needed are clear. For one thing, California must shift its public priorities away from lavish pensions for bureaucrats and toward the infrastructure critical to reinvigorating the private sector. The state's once-vaunted power system routinely experiences summer brownouts; water supplies remain uncertain, thanks to environmental legislation and a reluctance to make new investments; the ports are highly congested and under constant threat of increased competition from the southeastern United States, the Pacific Northwest, and eventually Mexico's Baja California. Fixing these problems would benefit the state's middle and working classes. Lower electrical costs would help preserve industrial facilities—from semiconductor and aerospace plants to textile mills. Reinvestment in trade infrastructure, such as ports, bridges, and freeways, would be a huge boon to working-class aspirations, since ports in Southern California account for as much as 20 percent of the area's total employment, much of it in highly paid, blue-collar sectors.

Another potential opportunity lies in energy, particularly oil. California has enormous reserves not just along its coast but also in its interior. The Democrats in the legislature, which seems determined to block expanded production, want to increase taxes on oil producers. A better solution would be a reasonable program of more drilling, particularly inland, which would create jobs and also bring a consistent, long-term stream of much-needed tax revenue.

These shifts would likely appeal to voters in the areas—such as the Central Valley and the "Inland Empire" around Riverside—that have been hurt most by the recession and the depredations of the hyperregulatory state. Indeed, the disquiet in the state's interior could make the coming gubernatorial election the most competitive in a decade. Jerry Brown, the Democratic candidate, certainly appears vulnerable: his campaign is largely financed by the same public-sector unions whose expansion he fostered as governor; more recently, serving as state attorney general, he was the fiercest enforcer of the Global Warming Solutions Act, which opens him to charges that he opposes economic growth. One hopeful sign that pragmatism may be back in fashion: a new proposed ballot measure to reverse the act until unemployment drops below 5.5 percent, where it stood before the recession.[1]

Still, it isn't certain that California's inept and often clueless Republicans will mount a strong challenge. For them to do so, business leaders need to get back in the game and remind voters and politicians alike of the truth that they have forgotten: only sustained, broadly based economic growth can restore the state's promise.

[2010]

Note

1. California's seasonally adjusted unemployment rate in December 2012 was 9.8 percent, compared with 7.8 percent nationally.

4

Cali to Business: Get Out!

Firms Are Fleeing the State's Senseless Regulations and Confiscatory Taxes

Steven Malanga

IN 2010, A MEDICAL-TECHNOLOGY FIRM called Numira Biosciences, founded in 2005 in Irvine, California, packed its bags and moved to Salt Lake City. The relocation, CEO Michael Beeuwsaert told the *Orange County Register*, was partly about the Utah destination's pleasant quality of life and talented workforce. But there was a big "push factor," too: California's steepening taxes and ever-thickening snarl of government regulations. "The tipping point was when someone from the Orange County tax [assessor] wanted to see our facility to tax every piece of equipment I had," Beeuwsaert said. "In Salt Lake City at my first networking event I met the mayor and the president of the Utah Senate, and they asked what they could do to help me. No [elected official] ever asked me that in California."

California has long been among America's most extensive taxers and regulators of business. But at the same time, the state had assets that seemed to offset its economic disincentives: a famously sunny climate, a world-class public university system that produced a talented local workforce, sturdy infrastructure that often made doing business easier, and a history of innovative companies.

No more. As California has transformed into a relentlessly antibusiness state, those redeeming characteristics haven't been enough to keep firms from leaving. Relocation experts say that the number of companies exiting the state for greener pastures has exploded. In surveys, executives regularly call California one of the country's most toxic business environments and one of the least likely places to open or expand a new company. Many firms still headquartered in California have forsaken expansion there. Reeling from

Illustration by Sean Delonas.

the burst housing bubble and suffering an unemployment rate well above the national level, California can't afford to remain on this path.

* * *

California first began to tarnish its business-friendly reputation in 1974, when Democrat Jerry Brown became governor. Government's job, in

Brown's view, was to restrain growth, not to unleash it (see chapter 3, "The Golden State's War on Itself"). His administration proceeded to scuttle some infrastructure spending, limit development, and expand environmental regulations. In 1977, *Time* declared that "the California of the 60s, a mystical land of abundance and affluence, vanished some time in the 70s." And by 1978, the Fantus Company, a corporate-relocation firm, was ranking California the fourth-worst state for business.

Brown's two Republican successors determined to restore California's economic luster. George Deukmejian, who served two terms as governor starting in 1983, and Pete Wilson, governor from 1991 through 1998, worked to cut back existing regulations and reject new ones, and they trimmed some taxes and other costs of doing business, including onerous workers' compensation assessments. Sacramento also created economic "quick-response" teams, whose mission was to persuade companies considering relocation to stay. California's tax burden, ranked fourth-highest in the nation in 1978 by the Tax Foundation, had dropped to 16th place by 1994. "Companies are once again looking at California as a good place to do business," a Fantus executive declared a few years later.

All that changed for the worse again when Gray Davis, Brown's chief of staff during the late 1970s, became governor in 1999. Elected with heavy support from labor unions and trial lawyers, the Democrat signed 33 bills that the state's chamber of commerce called "job killers." One of the bills, for example, contributed to an increase in the payments that companies made into workers' compensation funds from $2.30 per $100 of payroll to $6.44; the annual cost to businesses nearly tripled, from $9 billion to $25 billion. After voters booted Davis out of office in a 2003 recall election and replaced him with Arnold Schwarzenegger, the new governor promised to address the business community's complaints. Schwarzenegger did pass one significant pro-business reform—reducing those workers' compensation fees—but otherwise made little headway. Worse, in 2006, he signed the Global Warming Solutions Act, a measure to reduce greenhouse-gas emissions that, some critics say, could boost electricity costs in the state by 20 percent or more.

As the 2000s proceeded, firms got more and more disgruntled. In a 2004 survey of California executives by the consulting firm Bain & Company, half of those interviewed said that they planned to halt job growth within the state, while 40 percent said that they planned to send jobs elsewhere, with Texas the most frequently mentioned domestic destination. Flash-forward to the present, and you'll find bosses' views grimmer still. In a 2011 poll by various California business groups, 82 percent of executives and owners said that if they weren't already in the state, they wouldn't consider starting up there, and 64 percent said that the main reason they stayed in California was that it was tough to relocate their particular kind of business. Nor do executives think that things will get better. For several years in a row, California has ranked dead last in *Chief Executive*'s poll about states' business environments.

*　*　*

Labor groups, environmentalists, and some politicians say that such polls merely reflect businesses' craving to get fair taxes lowered and reasonable regulations repealed. Responding to the most recent *Chief Executive* poll, for example, Steve Smith of the Labor Federation of California charged that it represented "little more than corporate honchos throwing around their weight to try to further strip working people of important protections that improve lives." Similarly, though an older Jerry Brown—returned to the governor's office in 2010—has acknowledged that California's approach to retaining businesses may need some work, his administration considers worry about the business environment overblown. "Rhetoric aside, there are many indications that California is outperforming most of the country from an economic and productivity standpoint," Joel Ayala, director of the governor's Office of Economic Development, said in early 2011.

But numbers from the National Establishment Time Series database tell a more disturbing story. During the period from 1994 through 2008, the latest year for which data are available, California ranked 47th among the states in net jobs created through business relocation, losing 124,000 more jobs *to* other places than it gained *from* other places. Some argue that this exodus is inconsequential; a 2010 study by the California Public Policy Institute found that jobs leaving the state through relocations amounted to only a small percentage of California's total job loss. But the numbers show that California isn't creating jobs in other ways, either. It generated just 285,000 more jobs from new businesses than it lost to business failures, placing 29th in the country (first-place Florida gained 2.4 million net jobs). What's particularly disturbing, as demographer Wendell Cox has demonstrated (see chapter 5), is that nearly none of those net jobs were created between 2000 and 2008, meaning that start-ups haven't contributed to California employment for more than a decade.

The evidence also shows that California is losing the battle for new investment. From 2007 through 2010, according to a study by the California Manufacturers and Technology Association, 10,763 industrial facilities were built or expanded across the country—but only 176 of those were in California. That amounted to 4.8 facilities per 1 million people, the lowest rate of any state; the national average was more than 40. The same study found that of the nation's $350 billion in investments in manufacturing facilities, just $8.7 billion was spent in California, a per-capita rate of investment less than one-fifth the national average.

California's defenders argue that the state continues to incubate cutting-edge companies in places like Silicon Valley, where investment remains vigorous, thanks in part to the area's muscular venture-capital industry. And it's true that California entrepreneurs and early-stage firms still get one-third of all venture funding nationwide. Unfortunately, if those firms actually succeed and start creating jobs, California has difficulty cashing in. In 2007, California-based Google built a new generation of server farms not in its home state but in Oregon, employing 200 people. The following year, one of California's most successful tech companies, Intel, opened a $3 billion production facility in Phoenix, Arizona. In 2011, eBay, based in San Jose, said that it would add some 1,000 back-office jobs in Austin, Texas, over the next decade.

Smaller firms have exhibited the same pattern of expanding outside the state. In fact, Silicon Valley lost one-quarter of its computer, microchip, and communications-equipment manufacturing jobs from 2001 to 2008, say valley entrepreneurs (see chapter 28, "The Silicon Lining"). "Every state in America is focusing on California," Dave White, an economic-development official who tries to lure companies to Colorado Springs, told the *Orange County Register* in 2010. "It's low hanging fruit."

* * *

California's suffocating regulations have a lot to do with these lousy indicators, says Andrew Puzder, the chief executive of CKE Restaurants, which operates more than 3,000 Hardee's, Carl's Jr., and other eateries. In February 2011, Puzder called his company's home state "the most business-unfriendly state we operate in. While we kept our corporate headquarters here, our company's real job-creating engine has already moved." Indeed, CKE has stopped opening restaurants in California, where the process can take up to two years because of regulations, and plans to open 300 in Texas, where a new place can debut in just six weeks. Because those two years are spent on expensive administrative work—everything from negotiating permits to filing planning documents—it can cost $200,000 more to open a restaurant in California than in Texas. And once open, a California restaurant costs more to operate, too, thanks in part to the state's complex labor laws, including the requirement that employers pay overtime after eight hours of work in a day. California treats even service employers like CKE as if the harsh industrial conditions of the 1930s were still prevalent, Puzder complained: "It's not like we have kids working in coal mines or women working in sweatshops."

Many firms share this frustration with California's regulations, and for good reason. A 2009 study by California State University finance professors Sanjay Varshney and Dennis Tootelian estimated that regulations cost the state's businesses $493 billion annually, or nearly $135,000 per company.

That weight, the study found, fell disproportionately on small firms and pushed California's overall employment down by some 3.8 million jobs.

California's regulations often utterly defeat entrepreneurs. John Bowen, the owner of an 82-year-old family-run business, King Kelly Marmalade, sold his firm to an out-of-state operator in 2007 after tiring of the ceaseless regulatory battle. At one point, Bowen started counting the government agencies that he had to deal with to run his business; he gave up when he reached 44. Bowen's biggest woe was complying with the state's aggressive air-pollution laws, wastewater regulations, and workplace rules. "I loved the work," he says. "This decision [to sell] was largely as a result of excessive and oppressive government rules."

As Bowen's example suggests, California's environmental regulations are particularly intrusive. Cemex, a manufacturing firm, announced in 2010 that it would shutter its Davenport, California, plant, which employed 120 people, citing environmental regulations as one reason that the facility was the most expensive to operate of its 14 American plants. Solar Millennium, an energy company, canceled plans to build a facility in Ridgecrest, California—an undertaking that would have created 700 temporary jobs and 75 permanent ones— after lengthy delays caused by state environmental reviews, including one on the project's impact on the Mojave ground squirrel. CalPortland, a cement company, recently shut down its 109-year-old Colton facility, laying off about 125 workers and blaming the closure on California's environmental rules.

California prides itself on being a leader in the environmental movement, but now even some green manufacturers say that they can't afford to stay there. In 2011, Bing Energy, a fuel-cell maker, announced that it would relocate from Chino in San Bernardino County to Tallahassee, Florida, where it expected to hire nearly 250 workers. "I just can't imagine any corporation in their right mind would decide to set up in California today," Bing CFO Dean Minardi said. Other California green firms staffing up elsewhere include Be Green Packaging, a Santa Barbara recycling company, which decided to build its first U.S. manufacturing facility in South Carolina; AQT Solar, an energy-cell maker based in Sunnyvale, which will employ 1,000 people at a new 184,000-square-foot manufacturing plant, also in South Carolina; Biocentric Energy Holdings, a Santa Ana energy company that moved to Salt Lake City; and Calisolar, a Santa Clara–based green-energy company building a factory in Ontario, Canada, that will employ 350 workers.

California seems to find innovative ways to expand environmental regulations every few years. Construction firms, recyclers, and other users of big off-road machinery, for instance, now face significant additional costs because new emissions standards will require them to replace much of that equipment. Executives at SA Recycling in Anaheim testified at a 2010 forum on business costs that their company had to spend $5 million for new parts and equipment to meet the standards. Of even broader concern are aggressive environmental mandates, signed into law by Governor Brown, that require the state to produce one-third of its energy from renewable sources by 2020. In a state where average energy costs are 50 percent higher than the national

Illustration by Sean Delonas.

average, businesses are understandably nervous about how such a shift will influence their bottom lines.

Yet the business community's appeals fall on deaf ears. These days, it simply doesn't have as much clout in Sacramento as the environmental lobby does. "The state's environmentalists think capitalism is harmful to the environment," says Assemblyman Dan Logue, chair of a GOP task force on jobs and the economy. "They think jobs and people leaving the state are good."

With liberal politicians and the environmental lobby setting the tone, the state's regulatory bureaucracy has become uncompromising, with officials frequently interpreting regulations in the most punitive manner. The owners of one small San Clemente business, Racing Optics, departed for Las Vegas after enduring harassment and threats of fines from state and local authorities over trivial issues concerning their homes, including failure to recycle water properly and to obtain the proper hazardous-waste permit for disposing of oil. Expenses for the small company, which produces laminated stickers for helmets, goggles, and vehicles, are now 20 to 30 percent lower than they were in California, the owners told the *Orange County Register*. Similarly, a small hair-salon chain out of Sacramento, Hoppin' Shears, fed up with the antibusiness attitude of the state, aborted plans to open 20 new California locations and is now looking across state lines. "We eventually want 20 units, but California is too unpredictable," firm co-owner Alice Wagner says. "Mostly it is the adversarial environment in California—like business and their owners are the nasty unwanted necessity—that we face every day when running our business."

* * *

Taxes are another big reason for companies to leave California. According to the Tax Foundation, California imposes the nation's second-heaviest tax burden on businesses. True, property taxes are relatively light, thanks to the 1978 initiative Proposition 13, which capped increases. But spendthrift California politicians responded to Prop. 13 by increasing revenues from other sources—including business owners, who get socked with a crushing array of levies.

Start with the state's high individual income-tax rates, which disproportionately affect business owners, since their incomes are generally greater than the average worker's. Though the highest bracket, 10.3 percent, applies only to millionaires, the second-highest, 9.3 percent, starts at incomes above just $47,000 annually.[1] By contrast, in New Jersey, another high-tax state, the top bracket of 8.97 percent doesn't kick in until filers hit $500,000 in income. California also extracts one of the nation's highest marriage penalties for couples filing jointly, the Tax Foundation reports. Since married couples are more likely to be business owners than single filers, the marriage penalty creates yet another disincentive for entrepreneurs to locate or remain in California.

Add to that California's corporate income tax, one of the few that has its own alternative minimum tax feature, which excludes companies from taking deductions beyond a certain point. And California's sales tax, the country's most onerous, reduces demand for in-state retail sales, with residents turning instead to "out-of-state, catalog, or internet purchases, leaving less business activity in state," the Tax Foundation notes. All this piles up. "The tax burden for a company to operate a business in California is 13 to 14 percent higher than the rest of the country," says Gino DiCaro of the California Manufacturers and Technology Association.

Sacramento is on the prowl for yet more tax revenues, one reason why financial executives surveyed by *CFO* recently ranked California's tax bureaucracy among the country's most aggressive. In 2011, even as business groups pointed to the growing number of firms leaving the state, California instituted a so-called Amazon tax, a sales levy that online retailers must collect from customers. To avoid having to collect taxes, Amazon, the giant Internet marketplace where many online retailers sell their wares, immediately severed ties with California-based merchants, leaving many without any business. In July 2011, the *Contra Costa Times* reported that states like Texas and Arizona were wooing these affiliates and that up to 70 had already left California to set up shop elsewhere and resume their Amazon ties, with perhaps hundreds of others contemplating doing the same.

Defenders of high taxes often claim that such levies rarely drive a firm from a location, at least on their own. But many academic studies have shown that states with lower taxes are winning the jobs war. Plenty of low-tax spots, moreover, boast congenial lifestyles and great weather, just as California does. Take Colorado Springs, which has made poaching Golden State firms a specialty. The area's economic-development agency estimates that 30 percent of its relocated firms come from Southern California. Dave White, the Colorado Springs economic-development official, told the *Orange County Register* that his area offered significant savings, including income- and corporate-tax rates less than half California's and workers' compensation charges 25 percent lower. The only thing that cost less in California, White boasted, was "citrus." Owners who have fled California for Colorado Springs concur. When Howell Precision Machine and Engineering, a Los Angeles County–based maker of military and aerospace parts, announced that it was moving to Colorado Springs in 2011, its owner said bluntly, "Our survival depends on our relocating to another state."

* * *

As if California's regulations and taxes weren't sufficiently deadly to businesses, the state can also claim what may be America's most expensive litigation environment for firms. The American Tort Reform Foundation recently named California one of the country's five worst "judicial hellholes," in part for its long history of "wacky consumer class actions." Blame the state's infamous consumer-rights law, which allows trial lawyers to sue firms for minor violations of California's complex labor and environmental regulations. Abuses of the law earned California the reputation of being a "shakedown state," with lawyers regularly sending out threatening letters in mass mailings to thousands of small businesses, demanding payments in return for not suing over purported minor paperwork violations. Outrage over the lawsuits led voters to pass a reform initiative, Proposition 64, in 2004. The new law, though, limited only the most egregious of the lawsuits by forcing attorneys, before they could sue, to show that they were representing plaintiffs who claimed to have been harmed.

One particularly troublesome source of nuisance suits is the Americans with Disabilities Act (ADA). California law allows plaintiffs to sue for damages over even minor violations of the act's architectural guidelines for accommodating the disabled. One plaintiff has sued 1,000 businesses, mostly restaurants, and won an average settlement of $4,000. At the same time, brick-and-mortar retailers find themselves under siege from lawsuits based on an obscure provision of California labor law that requires stores to have enough seats for all employees. Wielding that law, trial attorneys have filed about 100 lawsuits, claiming damages of up to $100 per employee, against chain retailers.

* * *

California business leaders and advocacy groups have proposed various reforms to improve California's awful business environment. At the top of the list is creating an independent commission to evaluate the impact on employment of all proposed regulations before legislators vote on them. Another idea is a requirement for new regulations to sunset within four or five years unless the legislature renews them. This would force lawmakers to revisit regulations and consider their cost after several years. Assemblyman Logue has also proposed diverting regulatory fines imposed on California businesses into the state's general fund, instead of letting them fill the coffers of the agencies that impose the fines. Bureaucrats would then no longer have an incentive to step up fines during periods of budget stress.

California should also pursue tax reforms, including lowering the state's top corporate and personal income rates and sharing the tax burden among more taxpayers. The sharing could be achieved by eliminating features in the tax code that target certain firms or filers, such as the alternative minimum tax on corporations and the marriage penalty on individuals. And California urgently needs to find a way to lower its sales taxes, or it will keep driving retail sales out of state.

Finally, California must reform its civil-litigation laws so that they no longer encourage frivolous lawsuits. One practical reform proposed in Sacramento would require plaintiffs to inform a business of an alleged ADA violation and then give it 90 days to fix the problem before they could file a lawsuit. Similar legislation applied to a broader range of lawsuits against businesses, such as the wave of suits against retailers for not providing chairs, would greatly improve the legal environment in the state. As Tom Scott of California Citizens Against Lawsuit Abuse recently asked: "Why can't we just give the employee a chair rather than filing a lawsuit?"

* * *

Back in April 2011, when California sent a delegation to study Texas's job-development strategies, Governor Rick Perry agreed to meet with the group because he said that California's economic fortunes were important to the future of the United States. That's true—but then, New York State's economic performance was once crucial to the country's economy, too, back when the Empire State boasted a more robust private sector. America eventually passed New York by, and California assumed New York's place as the driver of the national economy.

Now, California is in danger of giving up that role to other states. Officials in California who doubt that that can happen aren't listening to what the state's businesses are telling them.

[2011]

Note

1. Proposition 30, which California voters passed in November 2012, raised income and sales tax rates and created new brackets. The measure, which is supposed to sunset after seven years, imposes a 10.3 percent rate on income between $250,000 and $300,000; an 11.3 percent rate on income between $300,000 and $500,000; a 12.3 percent rate on income between $500,000 and $1 million; and a 13.3 percent rate on income over $1 million. The measure also raised the state sales tax for four years from 7.25 percent to 7.5 percent.

5

The Long Stall

California's Jobs Engine Broke Down Well before the Financial Crisis

Wendell Cox

EVERYBODY KNOWS THAT CALIFORNIA's economy has struggled mightily since the 2008 financial crisis and subsequent recession. Liberal pundits and politicians tend to blame the dismal performance entirely on the Great Recession; as Jerry Brown put it while campaigning (successfully) for governor in 2010, "I've seen recessions. They come, they go. California always comes back."

But a study commissioned by *City Journal* using the National Establishment Time Series database, which has tracked job creation and migration from 1992 through 2008 (so far) in a way that government statistics can't, reveals the disturbing truth. California's economy during the second half of that period—2000 through 2008—was far less vibrant and diverse than it had been during the first. Well before the crisis struck, then, the Golden State was setting itself up for a big fall.

* * *

One of the starkest signs of California's malaise during the first decade of the twenty-first century was its changing job dynamics. Even before the downturn, California had stopped attracting new business investment, whether from within the state or from without.

Economists usually see business start-ups as the most important long-term source of job growth, and California has long had a reputation for nurturing new companies—most famously, in Silicon Valley. As chart 1 shows, however, this dynamism utterly vanished in the 2000s. From 1992 to 2000, California saw a net gain of 776,500 jobs from start-ups and closures; that is,

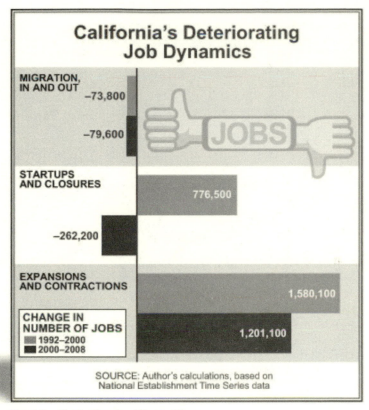

Chart 1   Illustration by Alberto Mena.

the state added that many more jobs from start-ups than it lost to closures. But during the first eight years of the new millennium, California had a net *loss* of 262,200 jobs from start-ups and closures. The difference between the two periods is an astounding 1 million net jobs.

Between 2000 and 2008, California also suffered net job losses of 79,600 to the migration of businesses among states—worse than the net 73,800 jobs that it lost from 1992 through 2000. The leading destination was Texas, with Oregon and North Carolina running second and third (see chart 2). California managed to add jobs only through the expansion of existing businesses, and even that was at a considerably lower rate than before.

Another dark sign, largely unnoticed at the time: California's major cities became invalids in the 2000s. Los Angeles and the San Francisco Bay Area

Chart 2   Illustration by Alberto Mena.

had been the engines of California's economic growth for at least a century. Since World War II, the L.A. metropolitan area, which includes Orange County, has added more people than all but two *states* (apart from California): Florida and Texas. The Bay Area, which includes the San Francisco and the San Jose metro areas, has been the core of American job growth in information technology and financial services, with San Jose's Silicon Valley serving as the world's incubator of information-age technology. During the 1992–2000 period, the L.A. and San Francisco Bay areas added more than 1.1 million new jobs—about half the entire state total. But between 2000 and 2008, as chart 3 indicates, California's two big metro areas produced fewer than 70,000 new jobs—a nearly 95 percent drop and a mere 6 percent of job creation in the state. This was a collapse of historic proportions.

* * *

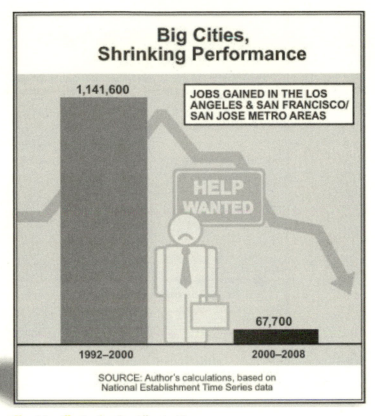

Chart 3   Illustration by Alberto Mena.

Not only did California in the 2000s suffer anemic job growth; the new jobs paid substantially less than before. Chart 4 reveals the sad reversal. From 2000 to 2008, California had a net job loss of more than 270,000 in industries with an average wage higher than the private-sector state average. That marked a turnaround of nearly 1.2 million net jobs from the 1992–2000 period, when 908,900 net jobs were created in above-average-wage industries. Further, during the earlier period, more than 707,000 net jobs were created in the very highest-wage industries—those paying over 150 percent of the private-sector average.

Chart 5, which indicates job growth or decline in selected industries, again suggests that a lopsided amount of California's economic growth in the 2000s was in below-average-wage fields. It included nearly 590,000 net jobs in "administration and support"—clerical and janitorial jobs, for example, as well

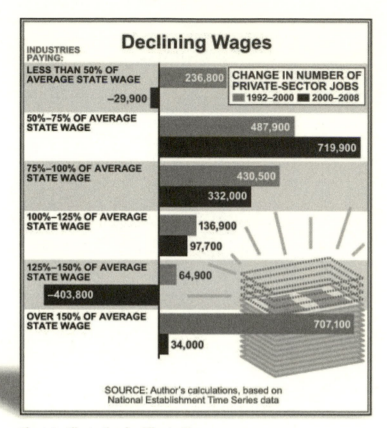

Chart 4 Illustration by Alberto Mena.

as positions in temporary-help services, travel agencies, telemarketing and telephone call centers, and so on. The largest losses in the state during the 2000s were in manufacturing, which traditionally provided above-average wages. After adding a net 64,900 manufacturing jobs from 1992 to 2000, California hemorrhaged a net 403,800 from 2000 to 2008. But information jobs also went into negative territory, while professional, scientific, and technical-services employment experienced far lower growth than in the previous decade.

The chart also shows that California's growth in the 2000s, such as it was, took place disproportionately in sectors that rode the housing bubble. In fact, 35 percent of the net new jobs in the state were created in construction and real estate. All those jobs have vaporized since 2008, according to Bureau of Labor Statistics data. They are unlikely to come back any time soon.

These are troubling numbers. Fewer jobs and lower wages do not a robust economy make. A continuation of this trend would result in a far more un-

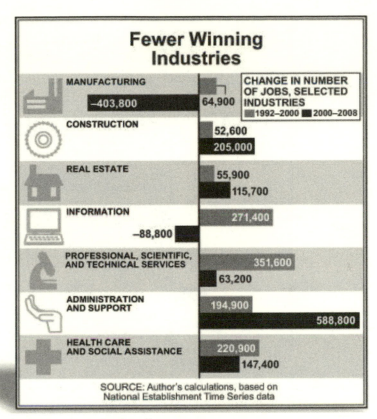

Fewer Winning Industries

MANUFACTURING −403,800 | 64,900

CHANGE IN NUMBER OF JOBS, SELECTED INDUSTRIES
■1992–2000 ■2000–2008

CONSTRUCTION 52,600 | 205,000

REAL ESTATE 55,900 | 115,700

INFORMATION 271,400 | −88,800

PROFESSIONAL, SCIENTIFIC, AND TECHNICAL SERVICES 351,600 | 63,200

ADMINISTRATION AND SUPPORT 194,900 | 588,800

HEALTH CARE AND SOCIAL ASSISTANCE 220,900 | 147,400

SOURCE: Author's calculations, based on National Establishment Time Series data

Chart 5   Illustration by Alberto Mena.

equal economy, shrunken tax revenues, and a likely increase in state public assistance—all at a time when officials are struggling with massive deficits.

* * *

A final indicator of California's growing economic weakness during the 2000–2008 period is that the average size of firms headquartered in the state shrank dramatically. As chart 6 shows, California had a huge increase over the 1992–2000 period in the number of jobs added by companies employing just a single person or between two and nine people, even as larger firms cut hundreds of thousands of jobs. Many of the single-employee companies may simply be struggling consultancies: if they were doing better, they'd likely have to start hiring at least a few people. While start-ups are indeed crucial to economic growth, small companies are especially vulnerable to economic

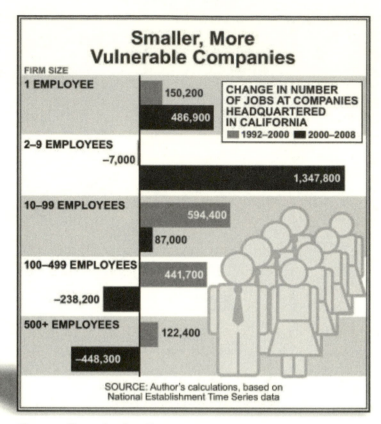

Smaller, More Vulnerable Companies

FIRM SIZE

1 EMPLOYEE — 150,200; 486,900

CHANGE IN NUMBER OF JOBS AT COMPANIES HEADQUARTERED IN CALIFORNIA
■ 1992–2000 ■ 2000–2008

2–9 EMPLOYEES — −7,000; 1,347,800

10–99 EMPLOYEES — 594,400; 87,000

100–499 EMPLOYEES — 441,700; −238,200

500+ EMPLOYEES — 122,400; −448,300

SOURCE: Author's calculations, based on National Establishment Time Series data

Chart 6   Illustration by Alberto Mena.

downturns and often feel the brunt of taxes and regulations more acutely than larger firms do. The awful job numbers for the bigger companies—including a net loss of nearly 450,000 positions for firms with 500 or more employees—suggest the toxicity of California's business climate. After all, bigger firms have the resources to settle and expand in other locales; in the 2000s, they clearly wanted nothing to do with the Golden State.

What is behind California's shocking decline—its snuffed-out start-ups, unproductive big cities, poorer jobs, and tinier, weaker, or fleeing companies—during the 2000–2008 period? Steven Malanga (see chapter 4, "Cali to Business: Get Out!") identifies the major villains: suffocating regulations, inflated business taxes and fees, a lawsuit-friendly legal environment, and a political class uninterested in business concerns, if not downright hostile to them. One could add to this list the state's extraordinarily high cost of living, with housing prices particularly onerous, having skyrocketed in the major metropolitan areas before the downturn—thanks, the research suggests, to overzealous land-use regulation.

One thing is for sure: California will never regain its previous prosperity if it leaves these problems unaddressed. Its profound economic woes aren't just the result of the Great Recession.

[2011]

6

The Pension Fund That Ate California

CalPERS's Corruption, Insider Dealing, and Politicized Investments Have Overwhelmed Taxpayers with Debt

Steven Malanga

AFTER SPENDING YEARS DOGGED BY unpaid debts, California labor leader Charles Valdes filed for bankruptcy in the 1990s—twice. At the same time, he held one of the most influential positions in the American financial system: chair of the investment committee for the California Public Employees' Retirement System, or CalPERS, the nation's largest pension fund for government workers. Valdes left the board in 2010 and now faces scrutiny for accepting gifts from another former board member, Alfred Villalobos—who, the state alleges, spent tens of thousands of dollars trying to influence how the fund invested its assets. Questioned by investigators about his dealings with Villalobos, Valdes invoked the Fifth Amendment 126 times.

California taxpayers help fund CalPERS's pensions and ultimately guarantee them, so they might wonder: How could a financially troubled former union leader occupy such a powerful position at the giant retirement system, which manages roughly $230 billion in assets? The answer lies in CalPERS's three-decade-long transformation from a prudently managed steward of workers' pensions into a highly politicized advocate for special interests. Unlike most government pension funds, CalPERS has become an outright lobbyist for higher member benefits, including a huge pension increase that is now consuming California state and local budgets. CalPERS's members, who elect representatives to the fund's board of directors, ignored concerns over Valdes's suitability because they liked how he fought for those plusher benefits.

CalPERS has also steered billions of dollars into politically connected firms. And it has ventured into "socially responsible" investment strategies, making bad bets that have lost hundreds of millions of dollars. Such dubious

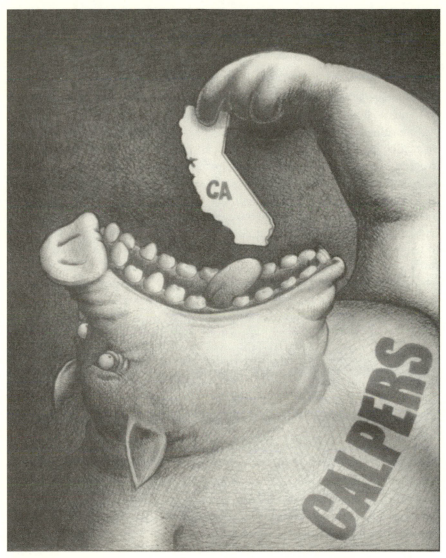

Illustration by Sean Delonas.

practices have piled up a crushing amount of pension debt, which California residents—and their children—will somehow have to repay.

* * *

When California's government-employee pension system was established in 1932, it was a model of restraint. Private-sector pensions were still rare back then, but California lawmakers had a particular reason for wanting a public-sector pension system: without one, unproductive older workers had an incentive to stay on the job and just "go through the motions" to get a paycheck, as a 1929 state commission put it. Pensions would encourage those workers to retire. The commission cautioned, however, against setting a retirement age so low that it would "encourage or permit the granting of any retirement allowance to an able-bodied person in middle life."

Accordingly, California set its initial retirement age for state workers (and, beginning in 1939, for local-government employees) at 65, at a time when the average 20-year-old entering the workforce could expect to live for another 46 years, until 66. The system's first pensions were modest, though far from miserly. An employee's pension equaled 1.43 percent of his average salary over his last five years on the job, multiplied by the total number of years he had worked. That formula typically provided workers with pensions equal to half or more of their final salaries, noted California's Little Hoover Commission, a government agency, in a 2010 study. For example, a state worker who retired at 65 after 40 years on the job would qualify for a pension equal to 57.2 percent of his average final salary (that's 40 times 1.43). If that salary was $50,000, his pension would be nearly $29,000.

The pensions were funded by three sources: contributions from employers (that is, state and local governments); contributions from employees (though some governments opted to cover that expense); and money that the pension fund would gain by investing those contributions. With the 1929 stock-market crash in mind, California opted for a cautious investment approach, allowing the fund to buy only safe federal Treasury bonds and state municipal bonds. "An unsound system," the 1929 commission warned, would be "worse than none." The employees' contributions were fixed, so if investment returns weren't sufficient to fund the promised pensions, the employers' contributions would have to increase to make up the difference.

In 1961, California enhanced non-public-safety state workers' retirement packages by enrolling them in federal Social Security, a program that's optional for state and local government employees. But the state made few other changes to the pension system over its first 30 years.

* * *

Then came the late 1960s, a time of rapidly growing public-sector union power. In 1968, the California state legislature added one of the most expensive of all retirement perks, annual cost-of-living adjustments, to CalPERS pensions. Other enhancements followed quickly, including, in 1970, a far more generous pension formula: a worker's pension was calculated from 2 percent, not 1.43 percent, of his average final salary, and he could start getting his pension at 60, rather than 65. Thus, an employee who worked for 40 years and retired at 60 with an average final salary of $50,000 could collect an annual pension equal to 80 percent of that sum, or $40,000; if he kept working for another five years, his pension fattened to 90 percent of his final average. In 1983, public-safety workers got an even better pension formula: 2.5 percent of average final salary for every year worked, which could be taken starting at 55. A police officer or firefighter who began work at 20 and retired 35 years later with a final average salary of $50,000 now qualified for a yearly pension of almost $44,000.

As benefits increased, so did pressure to pay for them by boosting CalPERS's investment returns. The shift started in 1966 when voters approved Proposition 1, a measure, promoted by CalPERS, that let it invest up to 25 percent of its portfolio in stocks. The timing wasn't ideal, since the long economic stagnation of the late 1960s and 1970s had left equity markets struggling for gains. But by the early 1980s, markets were roaring again, and CalPERS asked for permission to invest up to 60 percent of its portfolio in stocks. Voters rejected that ballot initiative but approved another, Proposition 21, in 1984, which likewise let CalPERS expand its investments—and didn't specify a percentage limit. Instead, Prop. 21 supposedly protected taxpayers with a clause that held CalPERS board members personally responsible if they didn't act prudently. The proposition received the enthusiastic backing of government unions and CalPERS board president Robert Carlson, former head of the powerful California State Employees Association. CalPERS's conservative investment approach, Carlson and other supporters argued, was shortchanging the state's taxpayers. After all, the better the investment returns were, the less state and local governments would need to pay into the pension fund.

Despite the new investment strategy, the costs of the enlarged pensions weighed heavily on California's budget. In 1991, with the nation mired in a recession and the state in a fiscal crisis, the California legislature closed the existing pension system to new workers, for whom it created a second "tier." This less expensive plan no longer required the worker to make a pension contribution, and it lowered the value of his pension to 1.25 percent of his final average salary for every year he had worked; further, he could begin to receive the pension only at 65. A 40-year veteran with a final average salary of $50,000 would thus qualify for a $25,000 pension, plus Social Security benefits.

The state's public-sector unions hated the new tier, of course, and their growing influence over CalPERS's board of directors meant that it, too, was soon lobbying against the 1991 reform. Six of the board's 13 members are chosen by government workers, and as union power grew in California, those six increasingly tended to be labor honchos. Two more members are statewide elected officials (California's treasurer and controller), and another two are appointed by the governor—so by 1999, when union-backed Gray Davis became governor and union-backed Phil Angelides became state treasurer, the CalPERS board was wearing a "union label," noted the *New York Times*. As the newspaper added, critics worried that the board had become so partisan that its "ability to provide for the 1.3 million public employees whose pensions it guarantees" was in doubt.

* * *

The critics were right to worry about CalPERS's bias. In 1999, the fund's board concocted an astonishing proposal that would take all the post-1991 state employees and retroactively put them in the older, more expensive pension system. The initiative went still further, lowering the retirement age for all state workers and sweetening the pension formula for police and firefighters even more. Public-safety workers could potentially retire at 50 with 90 percent of their salaries, and other government workers at 55 with 60 percent of their salaries.

CalPERS wrote the legislation for these changes and then persuaded lawmakers to pass it. In pushing for the change, though, the pension fund downplayed the risks involved. A 17-page brochure about the proposal that CalPERS handed to legislators reads like a pitch letter, not a serious fiscal analysis. The state could offer these fantastic benefits to workers at no cost, proclaimed the brochure: "No increase over current employer contributions is needed for these benefit improvements." The state's annual contribution to the pension fund—$776 million in 1998—would remain relatively unchanged in the years ahead, the brochure predicted.

CalPERS board members also minimized the plan's risks. Board president William Crist contended in the press that the bigger benefits would be covered by the pension fund's market returns. Labor leader Valdes blasted critics who warned about potential stock-market declines, saying that they were trying to deny workers a piece of the good times. What the board members didn't mention was that California law protected government pensions, so that taxpayers would be on the hook for any shortfall in pension funding. In essence, the CalPERS position was that government workers should carry zero risk, sharing the bounty when the fund's investments did well but losing nothing when the investments went south.

But the board members knew that there was a downside. CalPERS staff had provided them with scenarios based on different ways the market might perform. In the worst case, a long 1970s-style downturn, government contributions to the fund would have to rise by billions of dollars (which is basically what wound up happening). CalPERS neglected to include that worst-case scenario in its legislative brochure. And though the board later claimed that it had offered a full analysis to anyone who asked, key players at the time deny it. Even the state senator who sponsored the law, Deborah Ortiz, says that lawmakers received little of substance from the fund's representatives. "We probed and probed and asked questions 100 times," she told the *San Jose Mercury News* in 2003. "The CalPERS staff assured us that even in the worst-case scenario the state's general fund would take a $300 million hit," a manageable sum in a $99 billion state budget. (The actual cost to the state budget, it turned out, was more than ten times that estimate—and it's still climbing.)

CalPERS also misled legislators and the press about the 1991 pension tier that it was pushing to repeal. In its brochure, the fund implied that the retirement pay that rank-and-file service workers got under the 1991 plan was tantamount to poverty. It didn't mention that many state workers also received Social Security payments, which add substantially to retirement income.

California lawmakers easily passed the new pension deal in 1999. The bill, signed by Governor Davis with little fanfare, immediately generated pressure on local governments to match the new benefits for their own employees. In 2001, legislators passed a measure allowing municipal workers covered by the CalPERS system to bargain for the same benefits that the state workers had just won. Like state legislators, many local officials believed that CalPERS surpluses would pay for the benefits. Expensive new benefits spread across the state "like a grass fire," Tony Oliveira, president of the California State Association of Counties, remembered in 2010.

* * *

That frenzy to expand benefits took place even though the air was already coming out of the economy. The tech-stock bubble deflated in the spring of 2000, shattering the NASDAQ market and driving down the Dow Jones Industrial Average. The American economy plunged into recession the following year, a slowdown made far worse by the terrorist attacks of September 11. By the close of trading on September 17, 2001, the Dow stood at 8,920.70, down nearly a quarter from its early-2000 all-time high of 11,722.

CalPERS has the exclusive power to determine the size of state and local governments' contributions into the fund. As its investments tanked, it quickly boosted those contributions to compensate. By mid-decade, local officials were frantically telling the California press that the contributions were squeezing out other forms of spending. Glendale, a Los Angeles suburb, watched its annual pension bill rocket from $1.3 million in 2003 to $13.7 million in 2007—nearly a tenfold increase. San Jose's tab almost doubled, from $73 million in 2001 to $122 million in 2007, and then rose even faster over the next three years, hitting a jaw-dropping $245 million in 2010. San Bernardino's annual pension obligations rose from $5 million in 2000 to about

$26 million in 2012. The state budget took a massive hit, too, its pension costs lurching from $611 million in 2001 to $3.5 billion in 2010.

Even those sums understated the problem. As a backlash grew to the larger bills that it was sending to municipalities and the state, CalPERS used a series of fiscal gimmicks to limit the immediate impact on balance sheets. Typically, to protect governments from violent swings in contributions every year, pension funds like CalPERS average their investment returns over three years, hoping that good years offset bad years. In 2005, CalPERS extended the performance average to 15 years, an extraordinarily long period that blended the fund's losses in the 2000s with its gains way back in the 1990s—thus reducing state and local governments' immediate costs, which remained overwhelming nevertheless. Then, in 2009, CalPERS told governments that they could pay off the higher bills from the previous year's scary market drop over the next three decades, pushing the bill for the financial meltdown to the next generation. The pension fund made a similar move in 2011: after revising downward its absurdly optimistic predictions of future investment gains, it gave governments 20 years to finance the higher resulting costs.

Both Governor Arnold Schwarzenegger and his successor, Jerry Brown, scorched CalPERS for the tricks. "The state should decline to participate in any effort to shift more costs to our children," said Schwarzenegger, who offered to give CalPERS $1.2 billion more out of his budget for pensions. Still trying to minimize the impact on current budgets, the fund declined and took a $200 million hike instead.

CalPERS contended that the state's escalating pension costs shouldn't be blamed on the expensive 1999 legislation. The real culprit, it claimed, was the stock market's slump, which hurt investment returns. But back when it was promoting the legislation in 1999, CalPERS had hyped Pollyannaish projections of 8 percent average annual returns, which proved crucial to getting the change through the legislature.

* * *

Another reason not to buy CalPERS's stock-market excuse is that its losses have been far worse than they should have been, thanks to a number of overly risky investment practices. Wilshire Consulting reported in 2012 that CalPERS's returns over the past five years had trailed those of 99 percent of large public pension funds.

Why? Recall that back in 1984, Proposition 21 gave CalPERS's board greater latitude in allocating investments. Initially, the shift seemed to bolster the fund's assets: CalPERS's investment income rose from $1.5 billion in 1982 to $3.3 billion in 1985 to $6.1 billion in 1990. Even more spectacularly, CalPERS earned $68 billion during the tech boom of 1994 through 1998. But those rich gains had an unforeseen consequence: they prompted the call for

Illustration by Sean Delonas.

higher benefits that resulted in the lavish new pension deal of 1999, which, in turn, led to a search for even greater investment returns in progressively riskier investment strategies.

CalPERS's investments in real estate, which had begun cautiously in the 1960s, exemplify the wrong turn. The fund started expanding its real-estate portfolio during the 1990s tech boom. Then, as its stock investments slid at the turn of the millennium, it chased even higher returns in real estate. Between 2004 and 2006, as the country's real-estate bubble was inflating, CalPERS pumped $7 billion into the sector, most of it in a few places that later became ground zero for the housing bust. By 2008, the fund owned 288,000 homes and lots, 80 percent of them in property-bubble states California, Florida, and Arizona. The fund's real-estate portfolio grew from 5 percent of its assets in mid-2005 to 10 percent by June 2008, even as real estate was already collapsing in CalPERS's biggest markets.

The portfolio included a $500 million bet on two large apartment complexes in New York City—Peter Cooper Village and Stuyvesant Town—that went bust in a high-profile default. There was also an investment of nearly $1 billion in Landsource Communities, which planned to develop some 15,000 acres in California's Santa Clarita Valley but eventually filed for bankruptcy. By 2011, the value of the fund's real-estate holdings had declined by 49 percent, resulting in $11 billion in losses.

Desperate for higher returns, CalPERS also bought the riskiest portions of collateralized-debt obligations, accumulating $140 million of them by 2007. These were the packages of debt, largely subprime mortgages, whose defaults helped trigger the 2008 financial meltdown. According to a 2007 story by Bloomberg News, CalPERS bought these investments, known as "toxic waste" on Wall Street, from Citigroup, one of the sinking firms that the government later bailed out. "I have trouble understanding public pension funds' delving into equity tranches, unless they know something the market doesn't know," Edward Altman of New York University told Bloomberg about the CalPERS buys. "If there's a meltdown, which I expect, it will hit those tranches first."

The decline in property values also squeezed CalPERS's cash flow, forcing the fund to sell off weakened stocks "at exactly the wrong time," concludes a study by Andrew Ang, a professor at Columbia University's business school, and Knut Kjaer, an investment manager. Their paper on CalPERS's panic selling in 2008 notes that the cash-hungry fund sold 2.3 million shares of Apple Inc. for $370 million; those shares would be worth nearly $1.5 billion today.

* * *

Prop. 21 had another effect that proved disastrous for CalPERS's performance: turning the fund into a mammoth would-be activist. The initiative passed at a time when many companies were closing down their own corporate-directed pension funds and switching to defined-contribution plans, in which the assets are directed by the wishes of individual employees, not concentrated in a single fund. As a consequence, the newly empowered CalPERS was left one of the biggest shareholders in America. And over time, the CalPERS board started using its newfound power to enforce its own political agenda, often without meeting its fiduciary responsibility to invest the fund's money wisely.

Leading the charge after becoming state treasurer in 1999 was Phil Angelides, who announced that he wanted to "mobilize the power of the capital markets for public purpose." During Angelides' tenure, according to a *Sacramento Bee* analysis, a third of his office's press releases concerned his actions on the boards of CalPERS and of CalPERS's sister fund, the California State Teachers' Retirement System (CalSTRS). For example, soon after Angelides took his board seats, he persuaded CalPERS and CalSTRS to divest shares in tobacco companies. Depressed at the time, those shares soon began to rise; a 2008 CalSTRS report estimated that the funds missed $1 billion in profits because of the divestiture. CalPERS also banned investments in developing countries like India, Thailand, and China because they didn't meet Angelides' labor or ethical standards. A 2007 CalPERS report calculated that its investments in developing markets underperformed an international emerging-markets index by 2.6 percent. Cost to the fund: $400 million.

Angelides wasn't alone. Union officials and other CalPERS board members pursued their own political agendas, demanding, for instance, that the fund not invest in firms and countries that lacked worker-friendly labor policies. By 2011, according to a Mercer Consulting report, CalPERS had adopted 111 different policy statements on the environment, social conditions, and corporate governance, all dictating or restricting how its funds could be invested.

CalPERS leaped into "social investing" at exactly the wrong time. That trend had gained currency in the 1990s with an emphasis on buying into environmentally "clean" companies. Tech firms were high on the list, so the 1990s Internet start-up boom made social investing seem like a sound financial strategy. But when CalPERS debuted its Double Bottom Line initiative in 2000—so called because it would supposedly produce both good returns and good social policy—the tech bubble had already popped.

Many socially conscious investors then turned their attention to another industry that didn't pollute: finance. One social-investing research firm named Fannie Mae the leading corporate citizen in America from 2000 through 2004. Other finance firms that attracted big cash from social investors included AIG, Citigroup, and Bank of America, according to an analysis by American Enterprise Institute adjunct fellow Jon Entine. When the market for shares of these firms imploded in 2008, so did the performance of social investors.

* * *

Yet another feature of CalPERS that has cost taxpayers is double-dealing by the board, ranging from awarding contracts to political donors to alleged outright corruption. In 2010, Jerry Brown, California's attorney general at the time, launched a lawsuit accusing Alfred Villalobos of trying to bribe current board members (including Charles Valdes) to win investment business for his clients, mostly large financial firms that wanted a piece of the huge CalPERS portfolio. Villalobos pulled in $47 million as a go-between, the suit charged. A month after the lawsuit was announced, Villalobos filed for personal bankruptcy, temporarily blocking the suit. In 2011, the Internal Revenue Service accused him of intentionally depleting his assets while in bankruptcy, including gambling some away in Nevada casinos. News reports revealed that Villalobos had previously filed for bankruptcy, a decade before serving on the CalPERS board.

The lawsuit also accused former CalPERS chief executive Fred Buenrostro of accepting gifts from Villalobos. Separately, a Securities and Exchange Commission lawsuit filed in 2012 accused Buenrostro of forging a document to help Villalobos win a big payment from a client. An internal CalPERS investigation quoted Buenrostro's wife as calling her husband a "puppet" of Villalobos. The report also pointed out that Buenrostro often intervened with the CalPERS staff on behalf of his acquaintances in the investment world—"friends of Fred," as the staffers called them.

Buenrostro and Villalobos have denied any wrongdoing, and investigations continue. In December 2011, after more than a year's delay, a judge finally ruled that the state's case against Villalobos could proceed, his bankruptcy filing notwithstanding.

These blockbuster allegations of influence-peddling came after nearly a decade of warnings of apparent conflicts of interest within CalPERS, prompting *Businessweek* to observe "an unpleasant whiff of pork-barrel politics rising from the board." One example involved Ron Burkle, a major political donor in California. Burkle was a significant giver to Angelides's campaign for treasurer, and he employed another board member, former San Francisco mayor Willie Brown, to do legal work for him. But Burkle's closest ties were with Governor Gray Davis: he gave $600,000 to Davis's gubernatorial campaign and appointed Davis's wife to the board of directors of one of his companies. CalPERS invested some $760 million in Burkle's private equity funds from 2000 through 2002.

Another disturbing case involved board member Sean Harrigan, also an officer of the United Food and Commercial Workers International Union. Between 2000 and 2004, the *Sacramento Bee* reported, Harrigan openly solicited donations for a union campaign fund from various investment companies that won multimillion-dollar deals from CalPERS. The companies ponied up $300,000. A CalPERS spokesperson said that the fund was unaware that

Harrigan was soliciting donations from firms that did business with it, adding that there was no prohibition within CalPERS against the practice.

* * *

Criticized for scandals and for its staggering long-term pension debt, CalPERS has endorsed a series of minor reforms. They include an assessment of the board's performance every two years by an independent auditor and the online posting of board members' and staffers' travel expenses. CalPERS also now limits to $50 the gifts that board members can receive from anyone doing business with the fund. However, Governor Brown's proposal to reform the CalPERS board by adding two new members with financial expertise failed to make it past the union-friendly state assembly, which argued that any changes to the board's composition should be negotiated between government unions and the state. For now, it seems, CalPERS will remain under union control.

CalPERS and its legislative allies keep resisting the one reform that would truly free California taxpayers from this ruinous pension system: moving it toward a 401(k)-style defined-contribution plan, as other states and municipalities, including Utah and Rhode Island, have done. In a defined-contribution plan, the government's commitment ends after it makes its annual required contribution into a worker's retirement account; the taxpayer's liability also ends there. Under the CalPERS regime, by contrast, employees are guaranteed benefits even if the government hasn't put aside money to pay for them, placing all the future liability on the taxpayer. Defined-contribution systems like Utah's also aren't as easy to manipulate politically as CalPERS-style pension plans because the money goes into workers' individual accounts, not into a massive portfolio controlled by a politically appointed or an elected board of directors.

Right now, the pension bill that Californians owe because of CalPERS is enormous. In a December 2011 study, former Democratic assemblyman Joe Nation, a public finance expert at Stanford University, estimated that CalPERS's long-term pension debt is a sizable $170 billion if CalPERS achieves an average annual investment return of 6.2 percent in years to come. If the return is just 4.5 percent annually—a rate close to what more conservative private pensions often shoot for—the fund's long-term liability rises to a forbidding $290 billion. By contrast, CalPERS itself estimated its long-term unfunded liability at merely $80 billion, using a lofty projected annual investment return of 7.75 percent. (The fund has recently cut that estimate to 7.5 percent.)

In August 2012, California did pass modest pension reforms, which apply mostly to new workers hired starting in 2013. Nation estimates that the reforms cut the state's long-term pension debt by 10 percent at most. Clearly,

Illustration by Sean Delonas.

the state needs to do much more. In the last five years, three California municipalities—Vallejo, Stockton, and San Bernardino—have filed for bankruptcy, each citing retirement costs as a significant factor. But bankruptcy may not afford cities any relief from pension costs; CalPERS argues that cities have no right in federal bankruptcy court to reduce pensions, since the fund is not a creditor of these municipalities but an arm of state government. Vallejo, which has already emerged from bankruptcy, did nothing to reduce its pension costs in Chapter 9, and its employee costs remain sky-high. To employ a cop in Vallejo still requires $230,000 a year, including $47,000 in annual CalPERS costs.

* * *

Meanwhile, CalPERS's rejoinders to its growing chorus of critics continue to mislead. Responding to a September 2012 opinion piece by Gary Jason, a California State University professor, about the impact of pension costs on municipal bankruptcies, CalPERS claimed that pensions were only a small part of the problem, accounting for just 10 percent of Stockton's budget, for instance. But in 2011, when Stockton declared a fiscal emergency, it listed $29 million in payments to CalPERS and $7 million to repay previous pension borrowings, which together equaled 21 percent of its total general-fund spending of $168 million. In a March 2011 analysis of its fiscal plight, city officials blamed "uncontrolled pension, health, and other benefit cost increases" (see chapter 11, "Broken Windows, Broken City").

CalPERS also understates the growing financial stress caused by pension obligations. In August 2012, for instance, board member Rob Feckner published a disingenuous op-ed in the *Sacramento Bee* responding to critics of CalPERS's most recent poor investment performance. Feckner said that the media misunderstand the fund's investment strategy, which focuses not on a single year but on long-term results. He noted that over the last 20 years, the fund had hit its investment targets more frequently than it had missed them. Yet he ignored the sharp increases in taxpayer contributions that CalPERS demanded when it missed its targets, as well as the fiscal smoothing gimmicks that it wielded to keep contributions from rising even more.

CalPERS's advocacy for higher benefits and its poor investment performance in recent years have locked in long-term debt in California and driven up costs, problems for which there are no easy solutions. As former Schwarzenegger economic advisor David Crane, a California Democrat, has said of the fund's managers and board: "They are desperate to keep truths hidden."

[2013]

7

Flatten Taxes!

A Proposal to Fix the
State's Business-Killing Tax Regime

Arthur B. Laffer

OVER HALF A DECADE AGO, I decided to leave Rancho Santa Fe, California, for Nashville, Tennessee. That's a major undertaking for anyone, but particularly for a 25-year resident of Southern California, dragging his whole family and company along with him. I still remember decision day: January 5, 2006. I'd been disappointed in November by the defeat of Governor Arnold Schwarzenegger's ballot initiatives, which aimed at reining in state spending, but I was utterly aghast as I read the transcript of the governor's State of the State speech just days into the new year. Clearly, he had resolved to move in a big-government direction, making proposals that included issuing billions of dollars' worth of new bonds to pay for statewide infrastructure projects. The last thing California needed was more government spending. It was time for me to go.

I've had a lot of company of late. Firms, people, investments, and tax revenues are fleeing California, repelled by the most onerous antigrowth business environment in the United States. California's after-tax rate of return for doing business lags so far behind other states' (especially zero-income-tax competitors such as Texas, Tennessee, and Florida) that the exodus shouldn't surprise anyone. Yet the state's Democratic leadership continues to look to tax increases to make up for lost revenue.

Tax hikes, especially during trying economic times, make no sense. Economies don't tax themselves into prosperity. What California needs is a radical tax overhaul—to be precise, a single, low-rate flat tax. Such a reform would spur a renewal of economic activity and investment while continuing to raise the revenues that the state needs.

* * *

The 2012 edition of *Rich States, Poor States*, a publication that I coauthor annually with Stephen Moore and Jonathan Williams, shows just how anti-growth California's business environment is. Our study uses 15 progrowth attributes to rank the states' economic competitiveness. In the first four years of the index, California never ranked outside the bottom ten states; in 2012, it will probably manage that feat—just barely—thanks to the expiration of numerous temporary tax increases.

Taxes are indeed a big part of California's economic problem. At 10.3 percent, the state's top marginal personal income-tax rate is the fourth-highest in the country, and its top marginal corporate income-tax rate of 8.84 percent is 25 percent above the national average. Excessive taxation is an equal-opportunity tormentor, afflicting labor and capital, poor and rich, men and women, old and young. In the short run, higher taxes on labor or capital will reduce after-tax earnings. Some people will violate the law and fail to report taxable income; others will use legal options, including tax deductions and credits, to reduce their payments. In the long run, residents—those who can afford to, anyway—will vote with their feet and leave the state, shifting the tax burden to lower-wage workers, as well as to immobile land and property.

California's income-tax system is also the nation's most progressive—and that's not a good thing. Progressive tax systems magnify tax-revenue volatility, with lots of money pouring in during periods of growth and the till running dry during downturns. This volatility occurs because wealthy people, who pay more taxes in a progressive system, experience sharp income swings from boom to bust. Depending disproportionately on the wealthy for its own revenues, the state experiences the same swings. This dynamic has a bad effect on politicians, who go on spending sprees during booms and then raise taxes during busts, harming competitiveness.

Worse, a highly progressive tax structure means that the most productive California residents and businesses—the primary employers of others—wind up taxed the most on the margin. State government figures show that in 2008, 61.3 percent of all personal income taxes—by far the state's most important source of revenue—were paid by filers with adjusted gross incomes of over $200,000, who constituted just 4.1 percent of the population and earned 34.5 percent of all income. It's a wonder that California has any entrepreneurs or venture capitalists left.

* * *

In the late 1800s, economist Henry George, a Californian, neatly summarized the main points of a good tax system. It should "bear as lightly as possible upon production—so as least to check the increase of the general fund from which taxes must be paid and the community maintained," he wrote. It should be "easily and cheaply collected, and fall as directly as may be upon the ultimate payers—so as to take from the people as little as possible in addition to what it yields the government." It should be "certain—so as to give the least opportunity for tyranny or corruption on the part of officials, and the least temptation to law-breaking and evasion on the part of the taxpayers." Finally, George argued, a good tax system should "bear equally—so as to give no citizen an advantage or put any at a disadvantage, as compared with others."

California should follow George's instructions by scrapping all its state and local taxes and fees (except for sin taxes, which exist to modify behavior rather than to raise revenue) and replacing them with a flat tax of about 6 percent on two distinct bases. One tax base would be personal unadjusted gross income from all sources, with only a few deductions: charitable contributions; interest payments, including on home mortgages; and rent on one's primary residence, to remove the current system's preference for homeowners. A single tax rate would apply across the board, from the first dollar earned to the last. The other tax base would be businesses' net sales, or "value added"—that is, the difference between sales and production costs, which equals the state's gross domestic product when aggregated across California. The low 6 percent rate would reduce the incentive to avoid earning taxable income in California, and the very broad base would reduce the number of places where people could hide their income to avoid taxation.

That's it. This tax system would yield as much revenue as all of California's current state and local taxes. At the state level, the taxes on business profits, payroll, gas, capital gains, and stock options would disappear. Locally, property taxes would follow suit. All sales taxes—state, county, city, and special-district—would likewise be abolished.

Such a tax reform would spark a surge in economic activity in California, since the after-tax rate of return for doing business would rise, both from the decline in tax rates and from the elimination of myriad fees that harm productivity. The result would be more businesses moving into California, fewer moving out, and more economic activity emerging from the underground economy. The California economy would soar, generating higher tax revenues, which would reduce the state budget deficit. The revenue stream would also be far more stable from year to year.

Californians may recognize this proposal as similar to one offered two decades ago by, of all people, Jerry Brown. When Brown was running for president in 1992, he campaigned on a flat tax—a 13 percent national rate for everyone, regardless of income. In fact, Brown and I developed that proposal together.

* * *

As of May 2012, California had a projected general-fund deficit of $16 billion—and that didn't include local government deficits or the state's growing unfunded entitlement and pension liabilities. Governor Brown is intent on raising taxes to avert further spending cuts. But with California's unemployment rate among the highest in the nation, raising taxes on those still holding jobs will only make things worse. The governor should recall his old enthusiasm for the flat tax, which the state needs more than ever.

Without question, other major reforms are also needed in California. One could get lost for weeks in the state budget, with its vast unfunded liabilities, and come up with innumerable ways to save money that most Californians would find reasonable. But the tax reform that I've outlined would be a big step toward California's becoming the Golden State again.

[2012]

8

The Radical Reform That California Needs

Can Once and Future Governor Jerry Brown Deliver Political Change to Save the State's Economy?

Troy Senik

IN THE AFTERMATH OF THE 2010 midterm elections, a piece of conventional political wisdom—"Where California goes today, the rest of the nation goes tomorrow"—sounds a lot like a threat. A state that has long been a standard-bearer for liberal ideas and policies is finally coming apart at the seams. On Election Day, California suffered from the country's third-highest unemployment rate, the worst business climate, and a public-pension shortfall of more than $500 billion.

Yet as the rest of the nation voted for smaller government and economic restraint, California moved decisively in the opposite direction. On a night when Republicans picked up six seats in the U.S. Senate, California gave ultraliberal senator Barbara Boxer a 10-point margin over an articulate conservative, Carly Fiorina. While Republicans acquired more than 60 seats in the House of Representatives—the biggest one-party swing in 72 years—not one of those seats came from California. And though other double-digit-unemployment states like Michigan, Nevada, South Carolina, and Florida used the midterms to bring reformist Republicans to their governors' mansions, the Golden State elected Jerry Brown, the Democrat whose previous tenure as governor was the high-water mark for liberalism in the executive branch.

California needs to develop an economic-policy agenda that can save it from irredeemable second-class status. But the state's economic problems are inseparable from its considerable institutional and political problems. And fixing those will likely prove highly difficult under Governor Brown.

* * *

To get a sense of the institutional problems, first understand that California is as polarized as the nation is as a whole. San Francisco is so left-leaning that the city's name has become an adjective for liberalism. Orange County, by contrast, regularly boasts of being the most Republican municipality in the nation. Farmers in the state's vast Central Valley tend to one-sixth of the irrigated land in the United States. Environmentalists in Los Angeles, meanwhile, mount regular bids to reduce water supplies to the valley in order to protect a local fish species. One-third of the U.S. Navy's Pacific Fleet makes home port in San Diego. Up the coast in San Francisco, residents voted in 2005 to shut military recruiters out of high schools.

California's byzantine political structure is woefully unsuited to resolve all these tensions. This is a state with the world's third-longest constitution. It has a legislature that, until November 2010, required a two-thirds majority to pass annual budgets and that still needs a two-thirds majority to pass tax increases (though California remains one of the highest-taxed states in the country). The state has more than 300 unelected boards and commissions, which range from the picayune (the Speech-Language Pathology and Audiology and Hearing Aid Dispensers Board) to the oppressive (the California Coastal Commission, whose land-use policies were once denounced by Supreme Court Justice Antonin Scalia as "out-and-out extortion").

It's also a state in love with the plebiscite, with a dozen popular initiatives or referenda on the ballot during most general elections. While initiatives dealing with hot-button social issues—illegal immigration, gay marriage, abortion, marijuana—grab the most headlines, proposals doing long-term economic damage go largely unnoticed. Particularly harmful are popularly approved mandatory spending requirements, such as the requirement that the state spend approximately 40 percent of its revenues each year on education. These measures leave as little as 15 percent of the budget to the discretion of the legislators in Sacramento. (And, like all popularly enacted policies, they can be altered or undone only by another round of citizen approval.) Thanks partly to these spending requirements, California's budget deficit will widen to more than $25 billion by mid-2012, the Legislative Analyst's Office reports—a dizzying shortfall that must be closed, in accordance with the state's balanced-budget requirement.

The budget crisis is only the beginning of California's economic difficulties. Regulation is a silent killer of California's prosperity, and much of it is imposed by unknown, unelected bureaucrats operating within the bowels of state departments and agencies. The regulatory environment is so uninviting that a recent survey of more than 650 corporate executives ranked it the worst state in the nation in which to do business. Each year, "the total cost of regulation to the State of California is $492.994 billion," which is "almost five times the

State's general fund budget, and almost a third of the State's gross product," wrote Sanjay Varshney and Dennis Tootelian of California State University at Sacramento in a 2009 study. "The cost of regulation results in an [annual] employment loss of 3.8 million jobs, which is a tenth of the State's population."

California's biggest long-term economic threat—implanted by an earlier generation of legislators in ways difficult to remove today—is its public-pension time bomb. For years, Governor Arnold Schwarzenegger's doomsday projection for pension liabilities was a figure around $300 billion. It turns out that for once in his life, the governor was being too conservative. A study released by the Stanford Institute for Economic Policy Research in April 2009 put the total figure for California's three largest public-pension funds—responsible for financing the retirement of 2.6 million government workers—at $535 billion, all of which, of course, will have to be paid somehow.

* * *

To address the institutional problems at the core of California's economic crisis, a cottage industry of policy entrepreneurs has sprung up, such as Repair California, a group formed by Bay Area business leaders in 2008 for the sole purpose of calling a statewide constitutional convention. The appeal was undeniable: If the state is ungovernable, why not alter its governing charter? But Repair California's agenda embraced California's unfortunate tendency to believe that ever-greater citizen participation can make its problems disappear. Under a mind-numbingly complex series of representation formulas intended to factor in assembly districts, counties, and Indian tribes, Repair California would have 465 citizens chosen for the convention through a process too incoherent to be explained in paragraph form (the organization itself relies on an illustrated chart). In a rare moment of political sobriety, voters withheld the support that would have been necessary for Repair California's plan to qualify for the 2010 ballot.

A far more useful reform would be reining in the excesses of direct democracy. On contentious social issues, referenda and initiatives may be beneficial, but on more technical aspects of government, oversimplified ballot language tends to obscure more than it clarifies. The most telling examples are those spending initiatives—often totaling billions of dollars at a time—that promise improvements in emotionally appealing areas like education, health care, and social welfare. Under current rules, these initiatives aren't required to establish funding sources, so voters are essentially being asked if they'd like to feel socially virtuous free of charge. Mandating pay-as-you-go initiatives—that is, requiring initiatives that would spend money to propose offsetting spending cuts or tax increases—would at least require Californians to take responsibility for the sprawling debt increases that inevitably accompany such profligacy.

But what can California do about its current fiscal situation? To balance its budget, the state needs either to cut spending or to increase taxes (or both). The first option will be exceedingly difficult because of the ballot initiatives and locked-in spending requirements that have left legislators so little discretion over the budget. Ideally, California would eliminate all these complex spending formulas and start every year's budgeting process from zero. But that would require a ballot initiative itself, and such an initiative would be strenuously opposed by the broad coalition of special interests that benefit from the current system.

The second option, hiking taxes, looks no more promising. In the past few decades, California's requirement of a two-thirds majority to increase taxes hasn't always been prohibitive, especially when Republican governors make common cause with Democratic legislators (a trend that continued into the Schwarzenegger era). But in today's economic environment, increases are politically poisonous, as shown by a 2009 ballot proposal for widespread tax hikes that was defeated with just under two-thirds of the vote. Californians already labor under sales-tax rates usually reserved for states without income taxes (at 8.25 percent, the nation's highest) and sharply progressive income-tax rates usually reserved for states without sales taxes (the state's top rate is 10.3 percent, and it doesn't allow you to deduct your federal taxes, as some states with income taxes do). These taxes, in turn, are a big reason that residents are fleeing the state; in 2008, 135,000 more people left California than moved there. If California keeps raising taxes, it can expect the migration of its tax base to continue unabated.

California would therefore do well to take the advice of economist Arthur Laffer, not just because of his status as one of the authors of Reaganomics but because he is an example of the state's woes, having packed up his California-based fund-management business in 2006 and relocated to Tennessee (see chapter 7, "Flatten Taxes!"). By Laffer's estimates, if California abandoned its current, highly progressive income-tax system in favor of a statewide flat tax of no more than 6 percent on personal income and net business sales, it could completely abolish all property taxes, state gas taxes, and state payroll taxes, as well as all current state and local sales taxes, without losing revenue. And that's without factoring in the increased economic activity that such a dramatic change to the tax code would almost certainly generate. This change would once again require the support of a two-thirds majority in the legislature, but its appeal just might be broad enough to attract such a coalition.

No matter how California taxes or spends, its heavy regulatory burden will hamper the state in rediscovering its former economic dynamism. The state should create a commission to subject its regulations to rigorous cost-benefit analyses. Any regulation that fails to generate more in social benefits than it does in social costs should be prevented from becoming law unless it is passed by a two-thirds majority of the legislature, rather than by the executive branch through the rule-making process. This approach would recognize that excessive regulation is just as economically poisonous as excessive taxation (which already enjoys the protection of the two-thirds requirement) and force legislators to take responsibility for job-killing policies.

And unless it defuses its pension bomb, California will become Greece on the Pacific. In the short term, avoiding that fate means renegotiating pension deals with current employees, increasing their retirement age, and requiring higher contribution levels from them. In the long term, it means shifting to a system of defined contributions instead of defined benefits. California's organized-labor establishment is the state's single most powerful political interest group, which will make achieving these reforms awfully tough sledding through the legislature. Real change on pensions is more likely to come through an initiative campaign that manages to hit the electorate's panic button.

* * *

Jerry Brown's gubernatorial victory, combined with a total Democratic sweep of statewide offices and pronounced Democratic majorities in both houses of the state legislature, leaves California subject to virtually unimpeded one-party rule. The big question is thus whether the impetus for reform can come from within the Democratic Party.

Among his defenders, Brown is often lauded for being ideologically heterodox. This is, after all, a man who supported the flat tax in his 1992 bid for the Democratic presidential nomination and who threatened to "starve the schools financially until I get some educational reforms" during his time as governor. Optimistic pundits have convinced themselves that this policy eccentricity will give Brown the reformist spirit necessary to keep California from being the nation's best argument against federalism. That claim, however, is dubious. It was the state's public-employee unions—the single biggest force behind California's spendthrift ways—whose money allowed Brown to stay afloat in his campaign against former eBay CEO Meg Whitman. Will a Democratic governor with solid Democratic majorities in the state legislature be willing to spend most of his political capital to weaken the influence of his own financial base?

California's future may depend on it. The state is on an unsustainable course. As the economist Herbert Stein famously noted, "If something cannot go on forever, it will stop." As a new administration takes the helm in the Golden State, that's another piece of conventional wisdom that sounds like a threat.

[2011]

II

THE URBAN FISCAL CRISIS

9

Lost Angeles

The City of Angels Goes to Hell

Joel Kotkin

IT SEEMS APPROPRIATE THAT THE CITY where America's movies are made has enjoyed such a dramatic trajectory. Los Angeles began the twentieth century with barely 100,000 residents. By century's end, 4 million people were living there, making it the nation's second-largest city, while another 6 million were occupying the rest of Los Angeles County.

But in the new century, Los Angeles has begun to fade, and it can't blame its sorry condition on the recent recession. The unemployment rate is one of the highest among the nation's largest urban areas. Streets are potholed. Businesses and residents are fleeing. In virtually every category of urban success, from migration of educated workers to growth of airport travel, Los Angeles lags behind not only such fast-growth regions as Dallas, Houston, and Raleigh-Durham, but also historical rivals like New York.

Perhaps worst of all is the perception, both in the city and elsewhere, that Los Angeles no longer matters as much as it once did. "I've traveled the world, and there was once a great mystique about L.A., but it's gone," says Robert Hertzberg, a former mayoral candidate and onetime speaker of the California State Assembly. "And I look at the leadership, and it's gone. No one much cares."

* * *

Such pessimism, commonly heard these days, is an unwelcome development in a city that once epitomized the promise of twentieth-century America. L.A.'s greatness stemmed from its willingness to be different. Other New York rivals—Chicago, Denver, Kansas City—tried to turn themselves into

Los Angeles's lousy economy . . .

EMPLOYMENT CHANGE, 20 LARGEST METROPOLITAN AREAS, 2001–2011

HOUSTON	12.1%
WASHINGTON, D.C.	9.9%
RIVERSIDE	8.8%
PHOENIX	5.8%
DALLAS–FT. WORTH	3.8%
SAN DIEGO	1.6%
BALTIMORE	0.7%
SEATTLE	0.2%
MIAMI	−0.3%
NEW YORK	−1.9%
PHILADELPHIA	−2.3%
DENVER	−2.5%
ATLANTA	−2.6%
TAMPA	−2.7%
ST. LOUIS	−3.2%
MINNEAPOLIS	−3.9%
CHICAGO	−6.9%
LOS ANGELES	−7.1%
SAN FRANCISCO	−12.8%
DETROIT	−19.6%

SOURCE: Bureau of Labor Statistics

Illustration by Alberto Mena.

mini-Manhattans. The Los Angeles metro area, by contrast, was boldly designed not around a central core but on a series of centers, connected first by railcars and later by the freeways: Pasadena, the San Fernando Valley, West Los Angeles, Culver City, Burbank, West Hollywood, and others. Los Angeles was also one of the first cities in the nation to impose comprehensive zoning.

The result was what the early-twentieth-century clergyman Dana Bartlett called "a better city," a dispersed metropolis where most people occupied single-family houses in middle-class neighborhoods. Here, said geographer J. Russell Smith, the differences among "city life, suburban life and country life" blurred. Blessed with a mild climate, clear vistas, ample land, and a lightly industrialized economy, the city, Bartlett predicted, would become "a place of inspiration for nobler living." Los Angeles, said journalist Carey McWilliams, was "the first modernized decentralized industrial city in America"—and it would not be the last, as anyone familiar with Dallas, Denver, or Houston will recognize.

But Los Angeles wasn't satisfied with just being a better place; its turn-of-the-century business leaders saw the potential for greatness. Business leaders have always been key to cities' economic growth, whether in New York's overcoming Boston and Philadelphia as the country's most important city in the early nineteenth century or, some years later, in Chicago's conquest of St. Louis for midwestern dominance. In Los Angeles, forward-looking and often ruthless men, such as Harrison Gray Otis of the *Los Angeles Times*, pushed a city with no natural port or secure water supply ahead of its two more naturally favored rivals, San Francisco and San Diego. In a move enthusiastically endorsed by its business leadership, L.A. secretively purchased land in the southern Sierras to lock up mountain glaciers and the water that flowed from them. The region also created artificial ports, one at Long Beach and another, inside the city limits, at San Pedro. Needing electricity, it turned to its large oil supply and to federal hydroelectric plants (and, much later, to coal-fired electricity imported from distant Utah).

The strategy, a combination of vaulting ambition and careful planning, worked brilliantly. Lured by the pleasant climate and a business-dominated political economy, industries and entrepreneurs flocked to the Los Angeles area. Initially, the growth came largely from oil and agriculture, but by the 1920s, the nascent movie industry had settled in Hollywood, putting Los Angeles on the world map. By 1940, the county's population, barely 300,000 in 1900, had grown fivefold, bumping San Francisco off the top of the list of California's biggest urban areas. The L.A. region as a whole had grown even more rapidly, to 3.5 million people.

World War II fattened Los Angeles still further. The city was a staging ground for the war against Japan, with a defense industry built up from nothing. Between 1940 and 1944, over $800 million was invested in 5,000 new industrial plants in the region, and the county's industrial output grew from $5 billion to $12 billion during the war. Afterward, L.A.'s manufacturing firms seized opportunities in the emerging market for commercial planes and then the new military requirements of the Cold War, such as electronics-based aircraft and missiles. This fostered the growth of a vast industrial base for the city—oil and gas companies like Getty Oil, Atlantic Richfield, and Occidental Petroleum, utility giants like Southern California Edison, and eventually a garment industry. These firms attracted both high-end engineers and a large cadre of skilled and semiskilled blue-collar workers. From 1940 to the mid-1970s, the number of technical and professional workers statewide jumped at five times the rate along the East Coast.

As these opportunity-seeking newcomers rushed to L.A., the city experienced a remarkable real-estate boom. That, in turn, ignited the growth of scores of ancillary industries to serve the needs of the new residents, such as the manufacturing of auto parts, plumbing fixtures, and furniture. These industries were widely dispersed, and so were their employees, who could commute great distances at high speeds along the newly built freeway network. East Coast urbanists hated the form; Jane Jacobs, for instance, denounced Los Angeles as a "vast, blind-eyed reservation." But people continued to move to a place that offered the promise of urban opportunity along with a single-family house, a swimming pool, and access to beaches and mountains.

By the 1980s, Los Angeles had surpassed New York as the nation's largest port and Chicago as the nation's leading industrial center. And by the 1990s, its garment district—fed by immigrant entrepreneurs and workers—employed more people than New York's did and increasingly dominated even the fashion side, particularly in the growing sportswear market. Add to this the glitter of Hollywood, and you saw a city of superlatives.

True, the region hit a rough spot in the late 1980s, as the end of the Cold War led to massive federal cutbacks in aerospace, hammering the city's economy. Los Angeles County lost nearly 500,000 jobs between 1990 and 1993. The high unemployment was accompanied by a climate of rising political dysfunction under Mayor Tom Bradley. In 1992 came the infamous Rodney King riots, which damaged the city's reputation as a place of multicultural tolerance.

But Los Angeles, unlike postriot Detroit and postindustrial Cleveland, recovered from its tough times. Between 1993 and 1999, the county regained nearly 400,000 of its lost jobs. Though aerospace never fully recovered, other parts of the industrial belt, including the port and the apparel and entertainment industries, gained jobs. Perhaps even more important was that an entrepreneurial class of immigrants—Middle Eastern, Korean, Chinese, Latino—began nurturing new businesses in everything from textiles and ethnic food to computers. The probusiness mayoralty of Richard Riordan and the governorship of Pete Wilson restored confidence among the city's beleaguered businesses.

* * *

Yet around the beginning of the millennium, this progress stalled. Employment stayed relatively flat from 2001 until 2005, when Mayor Antonio Villaraigosa was elected, and then started to drop, falling back to the levels of the troubled early 1990s. As of March 2011, the unemployment rate was over 12 percent in the county, while in the entire L.A. metropolitan area, which includes adjacent Orange County, it was 11.4 percent—the third-highest unemployment rate of the nation's 20 largest metro areas.

Job losses, too, were more severe in Los Angeles than in all but two of the nation's top ten urban areas. Between 2001 and 2011, the number of jobs in the county contracted by 7.1 percent. According to research from the California Lutheran Economic Forecast, the decline was particularly marked in manufacturing, with the hemorrhaging of more than 150,000 jobs since 1990; only New York has lost more industrial jobs over the past 20 years. So it isn't surprising that Los Angeles County's share of the nation's employment has dropped by a fifth since 1990 and is now just 4 percent, the lowest level in decades. That decline in share of national employment has taken place in virtually every high-wage industry except entertainment.

Perhaps even more troubling than the economic data is the city's demographic profile. The recent census showed that over the last decade, the population of Los Angeles County grew from 9.5 million people to 9.8 million—a growth rate of just 3.1 percent, far lower than the national average of 10 percent, and also the smallest number of new city residents in any decade since the turn of the *last* century. The reason is a steady out-migration of residents. Over the last decade, Los Angeles County, once a magnet for newcomers, has lost more migrants to other domestic locales than any of the nation's other top 20 metropolitan areas. It also doesn't do well with the most educated of its residents. If you look at the nation's largest 52 metropolitan areas and the percentages by which their populations of college graduates grew between 2007 and 2009, you'll find that L.A. ranks just 37th.

* * *

Why has Los Angeles lost its mojo? A big reason is a decline in the power and mettle of the city's once-vibrant business community. Between the late 1980s and the end of the millennium, many of L.A.'s largest and most influential firms—ARCO, Security Pacific, First Interstate, Union Oil, Sun America—disappeared in a host of mergers that saw their management shift

... has given it one of the highest unemployment rates in the country ...

RIVERSIDE	13.9%
DETROIT	11.8%
LOS ANGELES	11.4%
TAMPA	11.0%
MIAMI	10.9%
SAN DIEGO	10.2%
SAN FRANCISCO	10.0%
ATLANTA	9.8%
ST. LOUIS	9.3%
DENVER	9.3%
SEATTLE	9.2%
CHICAGO	8.9%
PHOENIX	8.7%
PHILADELPHIA	8.5%
NEW YORK	8.4%
HOUSTON	8.3%
DALLAS–FT. WORTH	8.1%
BALTIMORE	7.4%
MINNEAPOLIS	6.8%
WASHINGTON, D.C.	5.8%

UNEMPLOYMENT RATE, 20 LARGEST METROPOLITAN AREAS, MARCH 2011

SOURCE: Bureau of Labor Statistics

NO POSITIONS AVAILABLE

APPLICATION FOR EMPLOYMENT

Illustration by Alberto Mena.

to places like London, New York, and San Francisco. Others, such as the *Los Angeles Times* and the Dodgers, were sold to outsiders. The most influential business leader downtown today, according to a recent *Los Angeles Downtown News* ranking, is Timothy Leiweke, president and CEO of AEG Entertainment—a subsidiary of the Anschutz Company, which is controlled by Philip Anschutz, a Denver billionaire. The fact that essentially a regional manager is so influential would make the city's past leaders spin in their graves.

Meanwhile, says David Abel, a Democratic Party activist and publisher of the influential *Planning Report*, once-powerful groups like the Los Angeles Chamber of Commerce and the Los Angeles County Economic Development Corporation (LAEDC) have atrophied. Today, there is virtually no business leader who speaks for the city's broader economic interest. Yes, a few individual Medicis, such as David Geffen and Eli Broad, support their pet causes, notably the arts. But Abel says that these people don't make up for the lack of a cohesive, independent, and committed business leadership. The most influential businesspeople, he adds, are professionals, or corporate vice presidents charged with sending earnings from L.A. back to their headquarters. As a result, they have little independence and few resources to challenge what he calls "the public emperors."

Those "emperors" are the leaders of L.A.'s public sector. As business retreated, power in Los Angeles, largely by default, shifted toward the government and its workers. Through the long decline that started in the 1990s and accelerated after 2005, government employment has climbed. Back in 1990, 13 percent of employed Angelenos worked for the government; by 2008, that figure had jumped to 16 percent. Even after a deep recession, the public sector—both county and city—continues to pull in big payouts. Today, almost 18,000 county workers earn more than $100,000 annually. The city has followed a similar path, with its city council the highest-paid in the nation. In L.A., as in much of California, public employees' pensions have risen at unsustainable rates.

The machine that controls Los Angeles these days consists of an alliance between labor and the political leadership of the Latino community, the area's largest ethnic population. Once virtually powerless in the region, Latinos elected to office now control many of the smaller municipalities along the industrial belt that stretches from downtown to the county line. But since they serve at the whim of labor interests, they seldom speak up for the area's many small businesses and homeowners. It's a familiar story: because Democrats are almost assured of victory in L.A.'s general elections, candidates must win only the low-turnout, union-dominated party primaries. John Pérez, a long-time union political operative and now speaker of the California State Assembly, won the Democratic nomination in 2008 with fewer than 5,000 votes and

then easily crushed the GOP candidate. Pérez's predecessor as speaker was
Fabian Núñez—another L.A. labor official. No wonder the *Sacramento Bee*'s
Dan Walters calls the labor movement "the closest thing to an omnipotent
political machine anywhere in the state."

* * *

The Latino-labor machine has two major priorities: expanding the power
of labor unions, particularly in the public sphere, and self-perpetuation.
Unsurprisingly, it cares little, and seems to understand less, about L.A.'s
economic environment. An excellent example is Mayor Villaraigosa himself,
another former labor organizer, whom the machine elevated first to the city
council and then to the mayoralty.

A common complaint about Villaraigosa is his governing style, which
many see as detached from long-term issues and focused on cultivating powerful friends, perhaps in preparation for a future Senate run. But a far greater
problem has been the mayor's single-minded emphasis on downtown development, especially high-density residential development. He has supported
heavy subsidies and tax advantages for L.A. Live, a downtown entertainment
complex, as well as for other projects in the area, and he has backed public investment in the surrounding infrastructure. He's currently supporting a push
to build a massive new downtown football stadium, even though L.A. has
no professional football team, and to displace much of the taxpayer-backed
Convention Center, which would presumably need to be rebuilt with public
funds.[1] And his biggest priority is to build the so-called subway to the sea,
a $40 billion train that would connect downtown with the Pacific. All these
government contracts feed the machine and its supporters.

This downtown push has done little to resuscitate the city's economy,
however, probably because it misses the entire point of Los Angeles, says Ali
Modarres, chairman of the geography department at California State University in Los Angeles. Remember that L.A.'s economy is built on multiple cores,
which operate largely independently of downtown. Downtown Los Angeles
employs a mere 2.5 percent of the region's workforce; New York's central
business districts, by contrast, employ roughly 20 percent. "To put the entire
focus of development on downtown L.A.," Modarres says, "is to ignore the
historical, cultural, economic, [and] social forces that have shaped the larger
geography of this metropolitan area."

It's true that between 1995 and 2005, the downtown area lost nearly
200,000 jobs, many of them in the industrial sector, which has historically
been concentrated in and around the central core. But Villaraigosa's accent is
on housing, not manufacturing—and as Cecilia Estolano, former head of the
Community Redevelopment Agency, points out, "downtown housing simply

doesn't create the jobs that small manufacturers do." So why hasn't Villaraigosa worked to revive downtown's industrial base? Because, though much of the industrial workforce is Latino, it has little influence with the mayor and his allies. "Manufacturing doesn't contribute to campaigns," says Estolano. "The only business interests that have any power are the real-estate interests, their lawyers and consultants." But the price of Villaraigosa's approach has become evident as the housing boom has petered out, leaving large numbers of condos empty or dumped on the rental market.

Meantime, business-strangling regulations proliferate. Many of these originate with the environmental movement, which Villaraigosa and other Democrats count on for political support and media validation. The city has tried repeatedly to control emissions at the port from ships and trucks, for example. Also harmful are various labor-friendly regulations, such as the city's effort to expand unions' presence from the docks to the entire network of trucks serving the port—essentially forcing out independent carriers, many of them Latino entrepreneurs, in favor of larger firms using Teamster drivers.

Such policies could backfire, says economist John Husing, who has done extensive research on the port sector and who calls L.A.'s port by far the largest generator of blue-collar employment in the region. They could lead shippers to transfer their business to cheaper and less heavily regulated ports elsewhere, precipitating a shift of blue-collar employment to Charleston, Houston, Savannah, and other growth-oriented southern cities. This is particularly dangerous given the planned 2014 widening of the Panama Canal, which will make southeastern ports far more competitive for Asia-based trade. "Our ferocious concentration on the environment and other issues has created a huge potential issue of social justice bigger than we might want to deal with," Husing says. "We are telling blue-collar workers here that we don't want you to have a job."

When criticized for the poor economy, the mayor cites some minor changes in policies favoring business. But Los Angeles remains one of the least hospitable places for business in the country, says consultant Larry Kosmont. Companies need to hire consultants, lawyers, and other fixers to complete even small-scale projects, he says; the system is particularly tough on smaller businesses, and firms without subsidies are unlikely to locate or expand in the region. "It usually takes two to three times more to process anything in L.A., compared even to surrounding cities," Kosmont says, "It makes a big difference if you are a major Korean airline or AEG or if you are an independent entrepreneur." If the system doesn't change, he predicts, "we're going to end up like a better-looking Detroit."

* * *

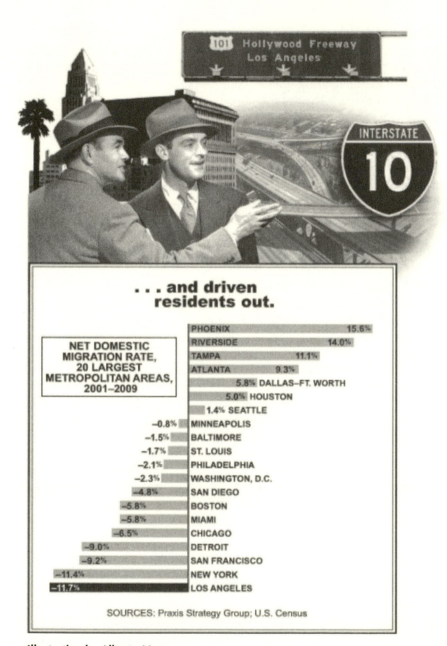

. . . and driven residents out.

NET DOMESTIC MIGRATION RATE, 20 LARGEST METROPOLITAN AREAS, 2001–2009

PHOENIX	15.6%
RIVERSIDE	14.0%
TAMPA	11.1%
ATLANTA	9.3%
DALLAS–FT. WORTH	5.8%
HOUSTON	5.0%
SEATTLE	1.4%
MINNEAPOLIS	−0.8%
BALTIMORE	−1.5%
ST. LOUIS	−1.7%
PHILADELPHIA	−2.1%
WASHINGTON, D.C.	−2.3%
SAN DIEGO	−4.8%
BOSTON	−5.8%
MIAMI	−5.8%
CHICAGO	−6.5%
DETROIT	−9.0%
SAN FRANCISCO	−9.2%
NEW YORK	−11.4%
LOS ANGELES	−11.7%

SOURCES: Praxis Strategy Group; U.S. Census

Illustration by Alberto Mena.

That prediction is probably too dire. Los Angeles still enjoys enormous natural advantages, including what may be the kindest climate of all the world's megacities. The inertia of such key institutions as Hollywood and the port has preserved them as great assets for the city. "Information" jobs, which include not only entertainment but also software and data processing, are an abiding strength: in 2010, information employment in Los Angeles surged by 5.1 percent, ten times New York's growth rate and well ahead of such high-tech locales as Austin, Boston, San Francisco, and Seattle. L.A. has the largest concentration of information-sector workers in the country—200,000 work-ers—with New York, at 164,000, coming in second. At the same time, ocean container traffic has recovered from the dreary days of the global recession, with total container volume growing by over 10 percent since early 2010. Em-ployment in technology, professional business services, and finance appears to have bottomed out and begun to make modest gains.

But perhaps the region's most hopeful harbinger is its vibrant ethnic economy. Many of the city's largest banks are either run by local ethnics— Korean, Chinese, Armenian, Israeli—or controlled from Asia. (These play a far larger role in Los Angeles than in established financial centers like New York and Chicago.) Scores of vital shopping and business districts, particu-larly the huge Asian economy in the San Gabriel Valley, have withstood the recession. L.A.'s self-made, immigrant-run businesses include garment firms like Guess, Jonathan Martin, American Apparel, Koos Manufacturing, and Bebe; supermarket chains like the Iranian-run K.V. Mart and Mexican Val-larta; low-budget fashion retailer Forever 21; yogurt chain Pinkberry; and a host of Chinese-American firms involved in everything from computers to noodles to wastepaper.

Los Angeles greatly outperforms its big-city competitors in ethnic en-trepreneurship. The percentage of minorities who are self-employed is the third-highest among the 52 largest America metro areas, behind only Atlanta and Miami. In contrast, New York ranks 27th and Chicago 43rd. Part of the reason for this, Modarres says, is the city's multipolar geography. Dispersion allows entrepreneurs to access large specialized markets in modestly priced strip malls and commercial centers.

* * *

But the Los Angeles region will never fully recover unless there is a huge shift in its political culture. Even liberal Democrats are beginning to realize that the current system isn't sustainable. Writing recently in the *Los Angeles Business Journal*, Roderick Wright, a Democratic state senator from south Los Angeles, compared the state and local governments with the Mafia. The "vig" that government took from local businesses, Wright argued—both in taxes and in the cost of regulation—was undermining job creation, particularly in working-class districts like his. He also warned that renewable-energy mandates recently imposed by the state would boost the cost of energy in the region, already 53 percent above the national average, by an additional 20 to 25 percent.

So L.A. needs a challenge to the machine and its ruinous economic policies. That challenge isn't likely to come from the city's enervated business sector, but there are other potential sources of reform. One may be the state and federal governments themselves, whose budget crises may finally start depleting the machine's pocketbook. For instance, Governor Jerry Brown wants to save money by eliminating the state's redevelopment agencies,[2] and L.A.'s agency has been a major source of funds for downtown developers, who in turn have heavily backed the machine. In Washington, the GOP Congress may put an end to Villaraigosa's subway to the sea, which relies heavily on federal funding.

Another possible challenger to the machine is the city's network of 93 "neighborhood councils," local groups that receive some city funding. "The city establishment has no use for the NCs or any other meaningful source of public input," says Greg Nelson, former chief of staff for Councilman Joel Wachs. "If just one leader comes along, NCs could emerge into a major force."

Challenges to the machine might also come from the city's working and middle classes, says Ron Kaye, former editor of the San Fernando Valley–based *Daily News*. He points to the city's remaining middle-class homeowners, who are concentrated in the Valley but who also occupy scores of other neighborhoods, from black Leimert Park to white sections of the west side to the Latino east side. "These are the places that reflect the whole idea of L.A., as opposed to the Villaraigosa vision of a city of apartment dwellers," Kaye says. However, homeowners are becoming rarer in Los Angeles; since the 1970s, he estimates, they have dropped from 60 percent of the population to roughly 40 percent. Further, it will surely be difficult to persuade voters on the city's Latino east side to oppose the machine: "The ethnic communities are all walled off and have trouble challenging the elite center that wants to siphon off their wealth and move it downtown."

Still, for evidence that homeowners might mount real opposition to the machine, Kaye indicates recent local elections. Despite the machine's nearly total power over the city council, voters in 2010 rejected Measure B, a well-financed insider deal that would have given control of the city's solar installations to unionized workers from the Department of Water and Power. Similarly, the machine-favored candidate for city attorney, Jack Weiss, was defeated in 2009 by an outsider candidate, Carmen Trutanich. There are even signs of rebellion from the usually complacent city council, some of whose members are questioning the idea of having the city provide help for the proposed downtown football stadium.

Will Los Angeles get the Sunshine Revolution that it so desperately needs? Only time will tell. What's certain for now is that only when the machine and its masters no longer dictate L.A.'s fate can this diverse and dynamic region resume its ascent toward greatness.

[2011]

Notes

1. The Los Angeles City Council on September 28, 2012 unanimously approved the plan by AEG to build the 76,000-seat, $314 million stadium. The plan calls for demolishing the convention center's West Hall and repaying municipal bonds to fund a new convention hall—also estimated to cost $314 million. The stadium was expedited by a bill, signed in 2011 by Governor Jerry Brown, to waive most of the state's environmental-permitting rules. The project will proceed as soon as the NFL approves a team for L.A., which hasn't had a franchise since 1994.

2. Governor Brown eliminated the state's redevelopment agencies as part of the 2011 state budget deal.

10

How the Road to Bell Was Paved

Not with Good Intentions but with the Avarice of Professional Government Bureaucrats

William Voegeli

B EFORE THE SUMMER OF 2010, even many Southern Californians had never heard of Bell, a modest Los Angeles suburb of 37,000 located near enough to the big city for views of the downtown skyscrapers. Then the *Los Angeles Times* ran a front-page story revealing that Bell's city manager, Robert Rizzo, was receiving a salary of $787,637, while the police chief got $457,000 a year and the assistant city manager made $376,288.

Overnight, Bell became America's most famous kleptocracy, featured in national publications and on network news programs. The quick resignations of the three hypercompensated civil servants failed to kill the story. Further efforts by *Times* reporters uncovered extravagant pay packages for other city employees, outlandish fringe benefits, and loans of public funds to city workers and favored businesses. The state attorney general filed a lawsuit against Rizzo and other Bell officials, while the Los Angeles County district attorney indicted him, the assistant city manager, and six current or former city council members on corruption charges. If none of those legal actions succeeds, taxpayers throughout California can expect to fund a pension for Rizzo worth $600,000 per year, according to the *Times*'s calculations, while the retired police chief makes ends meet on a pension of $411,000.[1]

Bell's all-you-can-eat personnel policies are outrageous but not surprising. The abuse of power, after all, is an endemic political problem, one so old that it's often rendered in Juvenal's Latin: *Quis custodiet ipsos custodes?* Who will guard the guardians themselves?

America's answer to that question made its republic distinctively successful. If ambition could be made to counteract ambition, in James Madison's formulation, then the guardians would guard one another, which was why Madison's Constitution incorporated checks and balances. Madison saw these, however, as especially vital to the success of a distant national government, expecting that Americans would pay careful attention to the conduct of their own state and local governments. That's exactly what Alexis de Tocqueville found during his trip through America 40 years later: "Municipal institutions constitute the strength of free nations. Town meetings are to liberty what primary schools are to science; they bring it within the people's reach, they teach men how to use and how to enjoy it."

Though fundamentally tawdry, the Bell scandal raises two important questions about the prospect of American self-government. First, can a post-Madisonian development in America—the professionalization of government that began a century ago—be reconciled to the Madisonian framework of counteracting ambitions? Second, can we still rely on conscientious civic engagement at the *local* level to be the elevating political force that Tocqueville applauded—and, if not, can our republic endure without it?

* * *

These are dilemmas much older than the plundering of one Los Angeles suburb. Even before the Constitution was 100 years old, America was undergoing profound changes that tested whether the political structures familiar to Madison and Tocqueville could continue to prevent the abuse of power. One of these changes was urbanization. The entire American population stood at just over 5 million people in 1800. By 1900, the three largest cities alone—Philadelphia, Chicago, and New York—had 6.4 million inhabitants.

The drivers of this population growth included waves of immigration, which transformed the homogeneous nation that Tocqueville analyzed into one of the world's most diverse. The proportion of the American population born in other countries peaked at 14.8 percent in 1890, half again as high as it had been in 1850. (The figure in the 2000 census was 11.1 percent.) Some 14 million people immigrated between 1860 and 1900, many from countries in eastern and southern Europe, where government was something done *to* people, not by them. The presence of millions of novice democrats leading economically precarious lives in crowded cities quickly gave rise to the shock-and-awe corruption of political machines, exemplified by New York's Tammany Hall.

These transformations convinced many Americans that it was no longer sufficient for the guardians to guard one other or realistic to believe that politically engaged citizens could scrutinize their behavior. In the late nineteenth and early twentieth centuries, the progressive movement sought to solve the problem by making government, especially local government, less political.

Regarding the superintendence of government as an essentially technical, rather than political, task, they decided to professionalize it.

Consider, in this light, Louis Brownlow, best known as the principal figure in the commission that President Roosevelt named in 1936—the Brownlow Committee—to reorganize the federal bureaucracy. Two years earlier, Brownlow had already weighed in on professionalization at the city level, welcoming changes that rendered municipal government "less legalistic, less partisan, and more technical." Thus, he said, "let whoever will be mayor, but the bacteriologist in the health department, the chemist in the water department, the superintendent of schools and his teachers, the nurses in the city hospital—these must be technicians." In large cities, professionals trained in the new discipline of public administration would run large departments and coordinate the provision of municipal services. In smaller ones, administration could be carried out by city managers, who "represent in their professional capacity" the "determination to keep the technical services of local government 'out of politics,'" according to Brownlow.

The first of these city managers had been hired in 1906 by Staunton, Virginia. Soon the "council-manager plan" became the dominant template for governing small and medium-size cities. In that structure, the elected city council answers to a town's citizens in the way that a corporation's board of directors answers to its shareholders. The city manager, in turn, resembles a chief executive officer: a professional administrator who manages the delivery of public services, hired by and reporting to the city council.

* * *

Like the members of any profession, city managers are jealous about their reputation, and they rallied to defend themselves after the Bell story broke. An organization of public administrators in Los Angeles County published a letter less than a week after the initial *Times* story, contending that Bell's government salaries were "outrageous and a huge aberration." Girard Miller, a *Governing* columnist, wrote: "The vast majority of America's public officials and public employees are more likely to be underpaid, not overpaid. In thousands of communities across America, most public officials, public managers and millions of public servants earn every penny of salary they receive. We need to curb the extreme abuses and go no further."

The problem, however, is more fundamental than a few bad apples among legions of diligent officials. What Louis Brownlow welcomed, James Madison feared: a "will in the community independent of the majority" could, wrote Madison, embrace and act on "unjust views." The very word "professional" points us to the great problem with the professionalization of government: though it can refer to a person with extensive training and expertise, it also distinguishes, from "amateur," a person who performs activities for a living—for money. In the geography of public administration, a slippery slope separates the idealistic and rigorous from the self-serving. The calling begets a guild, which turns into a mutual protection society and winds up a racket.

For evidence of the racket, look to the documented cases of battered-taxpayer syndrome on the rise in places far from Bell. The Milwaukee Teachers' Education Association, whose website declares that it has "one, constant focus—putting children at the center of education," sued the city's school district in 2010, demanding that it make erectile-dysfunction drugs like Viagra available through the teachers' health insurance. The school board estimates that complying with the demand would cost as much as hiring a dozen entry-level teachers.

In Illinois, local officials are virtuosos in the art of "pension spiking." The *Chicago Tribune* reports that the 55-year-old administrator of Bellwood, a predominantly black, working-class suburb just outside Chicago, retired in 2010 with a pension of $252,689—based on a salary of $472,255 in 2009, boosted from $168,593 in 2005. In his final year of employment, this frantic go-getter was paid under *ten* different job titles. At the same time, one of the state's most affluent cities, Highland Park, paid three park officials bonuses worth almost $700,000 as they got ready to retire. One 58-year-old official will receive a pension of $166,000—more than he ever made as an executive with the parks district until his final months on the job.

Back in California, the struggles of two public-administration students interning with a city council candidate in Orange County suggest the existence of related abuses in the state, less extreme but more common than Bell's. According to Fred Smoller, the Brandman University professor directing the students' program, it took them "nearly four months and hundreds of hours of work" to complete what should have been a simple project: gathering data on how much local city managers were paid. "While several cities cooperated, many others gave the students the runaround," says Smoller. "Two cities charged for access to this information. Two others said that the public was not entitled to know the details of city-official compensation packages." Several local officials, according to Smoller and the city council candidate, threatened the professor and his students, saying that publicizing the salary information would be a bad career move.

* * *

Some argue that the Bell story has less to do with the dangers of professionalizing government than with the town's demographics. More than half of Bell's residents are foreign-born (mostly from South and Central America), and nearly two-thirds over the age of 25 lack a high school diploma. Perhaps its residents were as vulnerable to Rizzo's exploitation as Manhattan tenement dwellers once were to Boss Tweed's. *Los Angeles Times* columnist

George Skelton accused the Rizzo gang of "ripping off vulnerable, uninformed taxpayers in one of the county's poorest cities, exploiting their public trust and, sadly, apathy." A crucial point on the road to the scandal was a 2005 special election in which residents voted to make Bell's local government exempt from state laws on municipal compensation. The turnout in that election was fewer than 400 people—less than 5 percent of Bell's registered voters.

But the incidents in Milwaukee, Bellwood, Highland Park, and Orange County suggest that the reassuring explanation—that Bell's problems are due to unique circumstances and that those of us who live in more educated communities could never be fleeced by a manipulator like Rizzo—isn't correct. They remind us that guarding the guardians has become harder everywhere.

For one thing, if "town meetings are to liberty what primary schools are to science," as Tocqueville had it, then America has a long-term, worsening drop-out problem. Apathy isn't confined to poor or immigrant communities. Indeed, the word "community" is increasingly used, contrary to the term's long history, to denote people who attend to things they have in common other than the affairs of the particular geographic location where they reside. Our time, attention, and affinities are not limitless, so as we increasingly concern ourselves with the environmentalist community, the bluegrass-music community, or the office-supplies wholesalers' community, we have less left over for the patch-on-the-map communities where we live. Our waking hours are enveloped by communications technologies that Madison and Tocqueville couldn't have imagined; we are a polity turned inside-out, familiar with the distant and estranged from the nearby. Americans are likelier to know the names of the president's pets than to know those of their own city council members.

We rely on the media to conduct the due diligence that they distract us from doing ourselves. The Bell story was featured in the *Los Angeles Times* every day for weeks, and the journalists who broke it can start working on their Pulitzer acceptance speeches.[2] But the *Times*, like all daily newspapers and television and radio stations, has only a fraction of the reporters, revenues, and resources that it once did. Had the Rizzo gang postponed its assault on Bell's treasury until after a few more rounds of *Times* layoffs—or had it picked a more distant city to plunder, one policed by a mom-and-pop weekly instead of a metropolitan daily—its members might have retired happily and lavishly without ever having to answer for it.

* * *

The final lesson from the Bell story is that professionalism can do only so much good and can do a considerable degree of harm in obliging a government to control itself. Many educators, public-safety and health officials, and administrators are professionals in the best sense, motivated by a sense of duty and a desire to serve the public honorably. In the absence of an avalanche of stories about other Bells, we can hope that only a small minority are professionals in the worst, most rapacious, sense of the term.

There's a group in the middle, however. They may employ their professional training and specialized technical knowledge to solve problems, but they're not above using such know-how to stifle criticism or impede scrutiny. Having chosen careers devoted to the public welfare, they lose the ability to distinguish what's good for the public from what's good for their own careers. They're not necessarily cynical when they insist that it's for the sake of schoolchildren that teachers must receive virtually automatic tenure after three years on the job. They may mean it when they say that the public sector cannot attract and retain the personnel it needs without offering health, retirement, and job-security benefits found nowhere else in the American economy. But being sincere isn't the same as being right.

Yielding so much of the political space once occupied by elected officials to "disinterested experts"—who sometimes turn out to be neither—has harmed governance and civic engagement. This contention requires no illusions about the virtues of elected politicians. Having grown up in Chicago during the final years of America's last graft- and patronage-based big-city machine, I understand the point of having a trained chemist monitoring the safety of the city's drinking water, instead of handing the lab coat and test tubes to some alderman's idiot nephew. Even as we cannot count on the guardians to guard themselves, however, we cannot rest assured that the professionals will professionalize themselves. Neither advanced degrees nor mid-career training programs that include ethics refresher courses will banish the danger that power will be abused.

The problem of power is inherently a political rather than a technical one. To survive, self-government requires citizens who understand that their rights are never finally secure and that their civic duties can never be safely delegated.

[2010]

Notes

1. In 2012, the California Public Employees' Retirement System (CalPERS) board voted to cut Rizzo's pension to $50,000 a year. As of January 2013, Rizzo was still awaiting trial, but the trial of the six former Bell city council members began late that month.

2. *Times* reporters Ruben Vives and Jeff Gottlieb, in fact, won the 2011 Pulitzer Prize for public service reporting.

11

Broken Windows, Broken City

Stockton Faces Pending Insolvency and an Unraveling Social Fabric

Steven Greenhut

WHERE'S A GOOD OCCUPY PROTEST when you need one? Those scraggly protesters are making mischief on behalf of "the 99 percent" in Oakland, and they're raging against university tuition increases in San Diego, Los Angeles, and Santa Cruz. Yet as a municipal crisis unfolds in one of California's former boomtowns, "Occupy Stockton" is nowhere to be found. If the movement cared about ordinary people as much as it claims, it would have plenty to keep it busy in Stockton, where the greed and shortsightedness of the public sector have sent a relatively poor city careening toward insolvency and unraveled its social fabric.

Because California's municipalities have squandered so much of their budgets on government workers and retired employees, they haven't been able to provide the essential services that justify government's existence. Stockton is a case in point. City manager Bob Deis told reporters in 2012 that the city's finances resembled a Ponzi scheme. He had never seen the kind of unaffordable health plan that Stockton employees receive: complete medical care for the employee and spouse *for life*, available, in some rare circumstances, after only a month on the job. "Employee costs are weighing down the city in the wake of a recessionary slump in revenues," *City Journal*'s Steven Malanga observes. "Stockton has spent the last two years trying to reduce its budget to avoid insolvency. The city has cut about a quarter of its police, but rich pension and health benefit deals still make it difficult for the city to pay its bills. . . . Employee costs make up 81 percent of the city's general fund spending."

Stockton has taken out pension-obligation bonds and followed other California cities in squandering tens of millions of tax dollars on redevelopment projects—in its case, a new minor-league baseball stadium and a waterfront entertainment project—that it hopes will bring an urban renewal. Yet downtown Stockton, despite its beautiful old buildings dating to the Gold Rush era, is largely a ghost town. An ineffective government, which can't control crime or even keep the streets clean, is the main source of the problem.

Stockton is the first city to operate under a new California law designed to put the brakes on bankruptcy. Under the law, the city will stop paying some of its debts and is heading toward a 90-day mediation process, now a requirement before seeking Chapter 9 bankruptcy protection.[1] The state legislature passed the new law at the urging of public-employee unions after Vallejo declared bankruptcy in 2008. Unions feared that California municipalities would use bankruptcy protection to abrogate their labor contracts. Both Vallejo and Stockton are suffering under crime waves as police staffing is reduced, but public-safety officials share the blame for the city's budget disaster. Their salaries and defined-benefit retirements still allow them to retire with 90 percent or more of their final year's pay. Stockton lost more than 41 police officers between 2009 and 2012. But the city participates in the generous "3 percent at 50" retirement benefit, a formula that allows public-safety workers to retire at age 50 with 3 percent of their final year's salary multiplied by the number of years on the job. Vallejo made headlines for providing a $300,000 compensation package to a police captain. Stockton has double the number of $100,000-plus retirees found in similar-size cities.

Only a few years ago, Stockton was thriving. Long-distance commuters who couldn't afford the Bay Area's sky-high housing prices crossed the Altamont Pass into the Central Valley. Housing prices soared throughout the region. Like most inland California cities, Stockton lacks coastal glamour. But it's a decent working-class city with historic homes, leafy neighborhoods, a fine private university with an ivy-covered campus (University of the Pacific), and modern suburbs, though it does have its run-down neighborhoods.

Today, though, the city is starting to epitomize the "broken windows" problem that *City Journal* readers understand so well. Residents share a widespread sense that the city doesn't respond to problems or do a good job handling basic services. I own two rental houses in Stockton, which I purchased as foreclosures after they lost about 75 percent of their value from the market peak. Overgrown trees entangled with utility wires stand in front of one of my houses. It's the city's legal responsibility to provide maintenance for such things, but officials told me they have no plans—let alone a budget—to do so. I see shopping carts abandoned in neighborhoods and trash-strewn parks. When my houses were vacant, preventing break-ins by homeless squatters and copper-pipe thieves was a constant struggle. I like Stockton—its neighborhoods, its climate, its terrain (on the edge of the magnificent California

Delta), and its proximity to the big cities across the coastal ranges—but the civic disorder takes a heavy toll.

When private firms don't provide good services, consumers have choices. When city governments fail to perform adequately because they have squandered their budgets, residents are left waiting, hoping, and eventually moving. As an elected supervisor in another beleaguered California county once opined: "County government is becoming a pension provider that provides government services on the side." That's true practically everywhere in the once Golden State. In Stockton, the results are plain to see.

[2012]

Note

1. Stockton officially declared bankruptcy on June 26, 2012. As of January 2013, several creditors, including the city's bond underwriters, were challenging Stockton's workout plan in federal bankruptcy court, claiming the city hadn't adequately addressed its pension liabilities.

III

OF ENERGY AND ENVIRONMENT

12

A Crude Awakening

Black Gold Could Revive the Golden State—If Politicians Got Out of the Way

Tom Gray

A FTER THE *DEEPWATER HORIZON* OIL RIG exploded in the Gulf of Mexico in April 2010, the Obama administration slapped a moratorium on deepwater drilling in the Gulf and backed away from plans to expand drilling along the eastern United States. Louisiana's governor, Bobby Jindal, saw thousands of jobs at stake and demanded that the moratorium be lifted. But the governor of California, Arnold Schwarzenegger, responded differently: he withdrew his support for Tranquillon Ridge, an offshore drilling project that would have delivered up to $100 million in yearly revenue to the financially struggling state government.

Schwarzenegger's reaction was a prime example of California's animus toward oil drilling. Tranquillon Ridge wouldn't have required a new drilling platform; it would have used an existing one. That platform stands in a safe 242 feet of water—*Deepwater Horizon* was drilling in about 5,000 feet—and is far from any coastal towns. Environmental activists had even cut a deal with the driller to retire the platform after 14 years. It was a deal with low risks and no losers. But news coverage from the Gulf blinded Schwarzenegger. "I see on TV the birds drenched in oil, the fishermen out of work, the massive oil spill, and the oil slick destroying our precious ecosystem," he declared at a May 2010 news conference. "That will not happen here in California."

California pays a high price for its aversion to oil. By refusing to tap much of the oil wealth off its shoreline, the state is forgoing a resource that could go far to revive its economy and bring state and local governments back to fiscal health. On dry land, too, California is missing an opportunity: its vast onshore oil reserves are underused, thanks to a green-energy agenda that raises the cost of oil production and refining. Policymakers have to realize that their quixotic quest to outgrow fossil fuels isn't helping the state.

* * *

You wouldn't know it from recent history, but the Golden State's gold has been as much black as yellow. A century ago, California's cities and future suburbs bristled with oil towers, especially in and around Los Angeles. At one point, in the mid-1920s, the state produced about a quarter of the world's oil; today, this would be a bigger share than that of the largest two producers— Saudi Arabia and Russia—combined. With all this oil came plenty of money. In the words of author Eric Schlosser: "In many ways Southern California was the Kuwait of the Jazz Age." Oil was part of the California dream.

But California's attitude toward oil began to shift in January 1969, when a well six miles off the Santa Barbara coast blew out just after workers had finished drilling it. The spill—the largest in American waters at the time, now ranked third, behind the *Deepwater Horizon* and *Exxon Valdez* spills—received saturation press coverage, united Santa Barbara residents in outrage, and caught the oil industry flat-footed. "I am amazed at the publicity for the loss of a few birds," said Fred Hartley, president of the Union Oil Company. His words simply raised the outrage level higher.

The impact of the Santa Barbara spill extended far beyond California; more than any other single event, it brought the various strands of environmentalism and conservation together into a national movement. Among other things, it inspired Gaylord Nelson, then a U.S. senator from Wisconsin, to promote the first Earth Day, and it spurred the creation of the Environmental Protection Agency. But the spill's most immediate result was that California stopped leasing tidelands—the zone within three nautical miles of shore, whose resources the state owns—to oil companies. Not a single acre of this oil-rich seabed has been auctioned since, though drilling continues in areas leased before 1969.

Natural resources more than three miles offshore belong to the federal government, which continued to lease tracts off California through 1984. But then Congress cut off funding for further leases. Consequently, California's onshore and offshore production hit its all-time peak in 1985—424 million barrels, 13 percent of the U.S. total—and then began declining. Falling oil prices in the 1980s also took their toll on production, both onshore and off. In 1990, President George H. W. Bush issued a moratorium on new leasing in most of the waters under federal jurisdiction, including all zones off California. Plans to open up the California areas briefly revived under George W. Bush in 2008, but the Obama administration has put them back on hold.

Onshore, the situation is less dire: new wells are continually being drilled, mostly on private or federal land. But the state no longer goes out of its way to attract oil investment, and environmental and land-use laws give local opponents tools to stymie drilling plans. Outside of regions like the southern San Joaquin Valley—where drilling has been an important part of the economy and landscape for a century or so—Californians don't like drilling rigs and can block projects at the local government level. In March 2012, to take one example, the planning commission in San Luis Obispo County rejected a plan to drill a dozen new wells, with one commissioner arguing that "the isolated and pastoral Huasna Valley" was "not a suitable place for oil production," as the local *Tribune* put it.

Another problem for onshore oil producers is California's ambitious climate-change law, Assembly Bill 32, passed in 2006 but only now starting to take hold in the form of specific regulations. When fully in effect, it will slam drillers with a double whammy. First, as users of fossil-fuel energy for such extraction techniques as steam injection, they will be placed under a cap-and-trade system that amounts to a carbon tax. If they can't reduce their greenhouse-gas output to the required levels, they and other affected businesses will have to pay $500 million a year or more to buy carbon credits.

Second, AB 32's Low Carbon Fuel Standard (LCFS) requires that the "carbon intensity" of all transportation fuels sold in California—a measure of how much greenhouse gas they emit in their entire life cycle, from production and transportation to combustion—fall by 10 percent by 2020. The problem is that at least half of California's crude oil must be extracted from the ground by means of energy-intensive steam injection, according to a 2011 analysis from the state's energy commission. That crude, therefore, will have a high carbon intensity, and under the LCFS, it will be at a competitive disadvantage with imported crude oil, which tends to have a lower carbon intensity. So despite having ample in-state refining capacity, California producers may have to send much of their oil overseas to find a market for it. (Worsening America's dependence on oil imports is another probable effect of the LCFS.)

* * *

Despite its evident distaste for oil, California is still the country's fourth-largest producer—behind Texas, Alaska, and North Dakota—and yields more than 15 million barrels per month, about 9 percent of the U.S. total. That doesn't count the output from offshore federal tracts, which is much smaller than that of the Gulf of Mexico but still a respectable 22 million barrels per year.

And the state's roughly 50,000 wells, both onshore and offshore, still have plenty of oil available for pumping. According to 2011 estimates from the U.S. Department of the Interior, federal tracts off the shore of Southern California alone probably hold 5.32 billion barrels of recoverable oil. Onshore, rising prices have breathed new life into old fields, and drillers are using methods such as steam injection to coax oil out of wells that would be dry by now with conventional pumping. "What has been produced in California is only 25 percent of what is in the ground," says Iraj Ershaghi, a professor of petroleum engineering at the University of Southern California. "Lots of small producers are going after small fields that have been abandoned."

The biggest onshore story is the potential of the Monterey Formation (also known as the Monterey Shale), a zone of petroleum-rich rock that extends much of the state's length. The Monterey holds an enormous amount of oil, estimated at up to 500 billion barrels. Though it has long been difficult to extract oil directly from it, advancing technology, along with rising oil prices, has put much more of its oil within reach. If even a small fraction of its reserves proves accessible, the Monterey would be the biggest shale oil play in the nation. In July 2011, the federal Energy Information Administration (EIA) estimated that the Monterey had 15.4 billion barrels of recoverable crude—four times what's estimated to lie within the Bakken Shale formation, which is fueling North Dakota's current oil boom. Those 15.4 billion barrels would be worth about $1.5 trillion at today's crude prices.

The potential impact of 15.4 billion barrels of oil is enormous. Even if California managed to tap just half of that quantity over the next 35 years, the state would be adding an average of 220 million barrels a year—doubling its current output and matching its peak year of 1985. It would also be pumping $22 billion each year into its economy if crude prices stayed near their current levels (in light of global demand, it's more likely that prices will rise). If the EIA estimate is reasonably close to the mark, the Monterey Formation would be in a class with oil fields in Saudi Arabia. "Having a field like this on American soil would be a game changer for American dependence on foreign imports," says Chris Faulkner, CEO of the Dallas-based exploration company Breitling Oil and Gas.

* * *

The state could certainly use an oil boom right now. Its jobless rate is stubbornly running nearly 3 percentage points above the national average, and most new drilling in the Monterey Formation would be taking place in the San Joaquin Valley, where unemployment is chronically high. (In the four counties most likely to be sites for drilling—Kern, Fresno, Tulare, and Kings—the March 2012 jobless rate averaged 17.5 percent.)

Simply looking for oil provides an economic boost. Operating one drilling rig creates 100 jobs, says Rock Zierman, head of the California Independent Petroleum Association. The oil-field service firm Baker Hughes reports that 46 rigs are currently active in California. If drilling were to return to early-

1980s levels, tripling that count to more than 130 rigs, the 100-to-one ratio means that more than 8,400 new jobs would be the result. And oil-field jobs are well paid. According to the Bureau of Labor Statistics, the average pay in the Kern County oil fields in 2010 was $66,700 a year for a rotary-drill operator, $46,580 for a derrick operator, and nearly $36,000 for a roustabout (an oil-field maintenance worker)—not counting overtime, which can be generous in oil and gas work. None of these jobs requires more than a high school education.

Oil drilling also produces plenty of revenue for the government. For starters, there are the sales, income, and property taxes that oil producers pay—and it's worth noting that the state's property assessments take the value of proved reserves and extracted oil into account, meaning that the more oil is discovered, the higher the assessment and the higher the tax revenue. Then there's the 16.67 percent royalty that California takes from oil pumped from state-owned land and waters. In just the first decade of the 2000s, state leases inside the three-nautical-mile limit pumped $2.4 billion in royalties into the state treasury. The state also gets half of the royalties on oil pumped from federal land in California, as well as 27 percent of royalties from oil produced in federal waters up to six nautical miles offshore. In a 2011 study, University of Wyoming energy economists Timothy Considine and Edward Manderson estimated that fully developing the oil and gas reserves in the state and federal waters in the Santa Barbara Channel would generate nearly $33 billion (in 2010 dollars) in tax and royalty revenues for state and local governments over 20 years.

It's too early to tell how much of a boost the state would gain from tapping the Monterey, but the impact could be huge—"potentially at a much larger scale" than the development of the offshore resources, Considine and Manderson say. The state government would reap these rewards without having to spend much initially, since the oil industry provides its own infrastructure of pipelines, tanks, pumps, drilling rigs, and refineries. All the drillers need is a green light.

Well before the state flashes that light, revenue-starved *local* governments may create an oil boom of their own. The city of Whittier, just east of Los Angeles, has agreed to let the Santa Barbara–based Matrix Oil Corporation drill on 22 acres of city-owned land, now part of a 1,290-acre open-space preserve. The project is tied up in lawsuits (three, at last count), but if it can run that gauntlet, it could net the city as much as $115 million a year, according to an economic study done as part of its environmental-impact report.

Oil is appealing not only because it brings in a substantial sum of money through royalties but also because it can be extracted from small surface footprints. Slant-drilling equipment taking up just a few acres can reach oil five miles away or farther. In the same way, onshore rigs can easily reach oil under state-leased seabed up to three miles offshore. The risks of such land-to-sea drilling are almost nil, since any spills at the drilling site would be on land and easily manageable. In fact, the risks of drilling in water are low as well, to judge from the record. Estimates of the 1969 Santa Barbara spill run from 80,000 to 100,000 barrels. But in the more than four decades since, according to federal data, all oil spills off California's coast totaled less than 900 barrels. The Coal Oil Point seep, a natural feature just off the Santa Barbara coast, releases that much oil in a typical week.

* * *

Despite California's history of discouraging drilling with environmental laws and land-use regulations, the state's track record with the oil industry has not been completely bleak. Governor Jerry Brown sent a positive signal in the fall of 2011 when he fired two officials who had sharply slowed down the process for issuing new drilling permits. He followed that with the year-end appointment of Tim Kustic—"a geologist who knows the industry," says Zierman—as the chief drilling regulator. Occidental Petroleum CEO Steve Chazen gave Brown a nod at the company's fourth-quarter conference call in January 2012: "We are pretty encouraged by the way things are going now.... The governor is very pro-jobs."

But the larger balance of political forces hasn't changed. The state shows no signs of abandoning its quest for freedom from fossil fuels. Until California surrenders to realism, its oil drillers will be fighting political and regulatory headwinds. If they can look anywhere for hope, it's not to the political elites but to the broader public. Ordinary Californians are not anti-oil ideologues, and a fair number favor drilling off the state's coast. In a July 2011 poll by the Public Policy Institute of California (PPIC), the drilling question produced a nearly even split, with 46 percent in favor and 49 percent opposed. As might be expected, support was lower in coastal regions but still significant, at 40 percent. Nearly half of Californians, then, understand the connection between their automobile-based lifestyle and those platforms dotting the channel off Santa Barbara.

And prodrillers aren't always a minority in these polls. In the summer of 2009, a low point for the U.S. and California economies, 51 percent of the PPIC respondents said yes to offshore drilling. The following year, just after the *Deepwater Horizon* blowout, opinion lurched to the negative, with only 36 percent in favor of offshore drilling and 59 percent opposed. The lesson is that Californians' views on oil aren't set in stone. They can change dramatically, depending on what they see on the news or feel in their pocketbooks.

The pocketbook issue that matters most, says political scientist Eric R. A. N. Smith, is the price of gasoline. Smith, a professor at the University of California at Santa Barbara, has been studying public opinion on oil drilling since the mid-1990s. He says that the main objection to offshore drilling is its risk, followed by aesthetics; people prefer not to see oil platforms when they look out at the blue Pacific. Green ideology—such as the argument that drilling will make California more dependent on fossil fuels—is less important. That may explain why Californians consistently back the goals of AB 32, at least in PPIC polls, while blowing hot and cold on offshore drilling. That is, despite their wish to cut down on greenhouse gases, they'll take the oil if they think that the state needs it to keep the price of gasoline down. "If gasoline prices are stable, then probably opinions would stay the same as they are," says Smith. But he thinks that global supply and demand will drive prices up—and then, he says, new drilling will finally commence off the coast.

If he's correct, the prospects for the local economy would be bright. California was once a genuine petro-state, one of global importance. If it so chooses, it stands a good chance of becoming one again.

[2012]

13

The Water Wars

Environmentalist Efforts to Save the Delta Smelt Threaten to Create a New Dust Bowl

Victor Davis Hanson

CALIFORNIA'S WATER WARS AREN'T ABOUT SCARCITY. Even with 37 million people and the nation's most irrigation-intensive agriculture, the state usually has enough water for both people and crops, thanks to the brilliant hydrological engineering of past generations of Californians. But now there is a new element in the century-old water calculus: a demand that the state's inland waters flow as pristinely as they supposedly did before the age of dams, reservoirs, and canals. Only that way can California's rivers, descending from their mountain origins, reach the Sacramento–San Joaquin River Delta year-round. Only that way, environmentalists say, can a three-inch delta fish be saved and salmon runs from the Pacific to the interior restored.

Such green dreams are not new to California politics. But their consequences, in this case, have been particularly dire: rich farmland idled, workers laid off, and massive tax revenues forfeited. Worse still, they coincide with a $25 billion annual state deficit, an overtaxed and fleeing elite populace, unsustainable pension obligations for public employees, a growing population of illegal aliens—and a world food shortage. This insolvent state is in far too much trouble to predicate its agricultural future on fish.

* * *

You can learn an important fact about the water wars simply by driving the width of California's vast Central Valley, where most of the battles erupt. True, there is a rich agricultural economy of dairy, wine, row crops, and rice elsewhere in the state, both to the north and to the south. But the farming engine that drives California's $14 billion export industry is centered in the hot flatlands of the 450-mile-long Central Valley, bounded by the mountains of the Sierra Nevada to the east and those of the Coast Range to the west.

I make that drive sometimes, starting from a cabin high in the snowy Sierra Nevada, near Huntington Lake. After descending the pass into the Central Valley, I reach my small raisin farm, homesteaded by my great-great-grandmother in 1875: 40 acres of Thompson seedless vines, part of what was once my family's 135-acre property within the small-farming patchwork of Fresno County, full of lush orchards and vineyards. As I continue across the state toward the Pacific, I pass through the valley's very different, sparsely settled western region, with its vast corporate latifundia. Finally, I reach the Coast Range and descend into the Bay Area sprawl, where much of contemporary California's environmental policy gets made.

What the drive teaches you is that there is no single Central Valley agriculture. Rather, the state is divided longitudinally, right down its middle, into two farming landscapes. These regions—the East Side and the West Side of the Central Valley—differ not only in the nature of the crops grown there but also in the relative availability of water and, more specifically, in the origins of the water that their farms so desperately need. Start with the East Side, which looks like a verdant, well-tended park from the air, thanks to the Sierra Nevada watershed—a freakish development of nature. On their steeper western slopes, the mountains rise precipitously to jagged peaks ranging from 9,000 feet high to more than 14,000. The towering wall collects massive snowfalls from Pacific winter storms that often pass over the valley without producing much rain. In the spring, the snow melts and flows into such rivers as the Kings, Kaweah, and San Joaquin, which then descend into the Central Valley.

Proximity to this guaranteed runoff from the Sierra prompted early homesteaders to prefer the Central Valley's East Side to its West. It explains why the area's small towns thrived on permanent orchards and vineyards, which represented more than a single year's investment, rather than on annual row crops, beef, and dairy. Originally, the East Side's grape and tree-fruit growers dug their own ditches to tap river water. I grew up on water stories from my grandfather, who would tell me how the combination of hot, sunny weather, rich soil, and plentiful Sierra water created prosperous vineyards and orchards from the scrub and desert of his youth.

In the early twentieth century, power companies and the state improved on what nature had bestowed, tapping the massive snow runoff with an ingenious system of dams. Engineers built vast lakes that stored millions of acre-feet (a unit of volume measuring one acre wide by one foot deep) of snowmelt. In the most ambitious systems of exploitation—for example, Henry Huntington's brilliant Big Creek Hydroelectric Project, begun in earnest in 1912—huge penstocks connected several reservoirs to produce abundant electricity, the water spinning turbines as it rushed down, step-fashion, from lake to lake. For farmers, though, the chief benefit was irrigation. The engineers linked the reservoirs and rivers with an intricate system of gravity-fed canals that channeled the stored water into millions of acres of farmland below. In July, the water that pours out of the ditch and into my vineyard remains ice-cold, despite the scorching outdoor temperatures. Mere hours earlier, it was roaring down from mountain canyons.

To this day, gravity-fed irrigation usually supplies the East Side with enough summer runoff for its crops. But in rare drought seasons, farmers have a second resource: an enormous, centuries-old aquifer, originally perhaps as large as a billion acre-feet, with a water table just 100 feet below the ground or even less. The water is good and the cost of pumping cheap. In some years, the Sierra runoff is so massive that when it reaches the valley floor, it is channeled into a system of on-farm storage ponds that recharges this aquifer. The result is a bountiful underground reserve water bank from which farmers can make withdrawals during drier years.

* * *

There isn't much controversy over water on the East Side. That's partly because of proximity to the generous Sierra, of course. Snowfalls and rainfalls during the recent period from 2009 to 2011 were among the heaviest on record. In May 2011, there were still eight feet of snow outside the front door of my mountain cabin, the irrigation ponds and ditches around my farm far below were still brimming, and the local ditch-tenders were begging farmers to draw on the surplus water so that the ditches wouldn't overflow and back up the system. These wet years are about as unusual as drought years, the norm being something in between.

And the Sierra watershed isn't going anywhere. Yes, Secretary of Energy Steven Chu, shortly before his appointment, pontificated that he could envision global warming's reducing the Sierra snowpack to just 10 percent of its current size. But Chu was drawing on politically correct supposition, not the evidence. Recent studies of the central Sierra by climatologist John Christy show that levels of snowfall have been almost unchanged over some 100 years of record-keeping.

There is another reason why water wars won't break out on the East Side: suburbanization. Suburbanites enjoy living not on the arid West Side, even though it's closer to the booming coastal economy, but on the picturesque, well-watered East. Over the last four decades, the region's farming towns have metamorphosed into a 400-mile, multimillion-person sprawl, clustering along the lines of the 99 freeway and the Southern Pacific railroad, from south of Bakersfield to north of Sacramento. In just the last 20 years, more

Illustration by Robert Pizzo.

than 100,000 acres of the nation's best farmland have been torn out to create housing developments with names like Vineyard Estates and Orchard Knolls. But the destruction of an acre of irrigated agriculture, along with its replacement by four to six suburban homes, means not less but more available water for the remaining—and often next-to-be-targeted—farms. A family of four or five often consumes less water per year than the irrigated peaches or grapes that once grew on their property.

Perpetually postmodern California is ambivalent about its legacy of development. But the East Side depends on the wealth created by the engineering marvels of the past—and not just agriculturally. Hydroelectricity supplies millions of homes between Bakersfield and Sacramento. Man-made alpine lakes are popular recreation spots. We may chide our ancestors for their audacity in altering nature and may dream of returning the Sierra to its pristine state, but we do not dare—not when millions below can live well where they otherwise would struggle to survive. So for now, the East Side has plenty of water and few political fights over irrigation.

* * *

The far larger, far more fragile West Side is a different story. It is too distant from the Sierra to tap easily much of the snow runoff through gravity-fed canals. In most years, moreover, the Sierra-sprung rivers run dry long before they near the Coast Range. And the water table can be more than 1,000 feet underground. On my East Side farm, the water table is reached at only 55 feet—and is rising; I can run a 15-horsepower electric pump for less than $3 per hour and get well over 1,000 gallons of pure water per minute. On the West Side, a mere 40 miles away, a 200-horsepower pump, struggling to bring up brackish water from deep below, might consume $30 per hour of electricity to deliver a fifth of the water per minute. In other words, pumping from the aquifer is as cheap and easy on the East Side as it is difficult—indeed, nearly prohibitive—on the arid West.

No wonder, then, that this vast interior land was once a desert outback— sparsely populated, mostly unfarmed, and owned by large ranching concerns. I remember driving out to the West Side with my father in the early 1960s to shoot squirrels and jackrabbits. There were desolate, seemingly limitless, tracts of range land, dotted by a few ramshackle hamlets, such as San Joaquin and Five Points, a world away from the East Side's settled agrarian towns.

The government changed all that in the 1960s. California, though hot and dry in its interior, is wet and cool in its northern and eastern mountain ranges. So the federal and state governments, in a series of complex partnerships, built the Central Valley Project and the California State Water Project—sprawling networks of dams, pumping stations, and canals that tapped water from the water-rich north and sent it more than 400 miles south, including to the water-short West Side of the Central Valley. Once West Side farmland was brought into irrigated production, it proved to be some of the world's most fertile and productive acreage, and a multibillion-dollar farming industry was born from desert.

That industry, however, was dominated by often expansive corporate and family-held operations, the largest between 20,000 and 40,000 acres in extent. The farms' owners, with imagination and audacity, found ways to produce an ever-greater variety of crops. But in the process, they seemed to alienate almost everyone. The Left harped that taxpayers were subsidizing corporate farming—that the $130 and more that the federal government and irrigation districts charged farmers per acre-foot of water represented far less than it cost to build and maintain the irrigation system. Farmers on the East Side originally resented the fact that lateral components of the system diverted some of their precious Sierra water to the west and south; they worried, too, about the competition posed by millions of new acres of subsidized farmland. Millions of thirsty northern California suburbanites eyed the long supply lines and began dreaming about stopping the water as it flowed past them or sending it over the mountains for sale to Los Angeles. Most recently, environmentalists argued that the diversion of the northern rivers degraded the ecology of the Sacramento–San Joaquin River Delta—a picturesque area near affluent, environmentally sensitive San Francisco.

It didn't help the West Side's cause that its lightly populated society was pyramidal. Unlike their counterparts on the more prosperous East Side, West Side towns were composed mostly of farm laborers and lacked an agrarian middle class. In the 1960s, a series of university studies and critical books noted that the per-capita income of some of these communities was lower than the average in Mexico. It was hard to contemplate the poor workers and the vast corporate holdings where they labored without thinking of medieval peasants and barons. The consequence was that most Californians didn't like what they heard about the West Side's economy, despite the collective wealth and inexpensive food that the region produced. So it became easier for the Bay Area environmental lobby—which, by the start of the new century, had begun to dominate California politics—to fight an easily caricatured corporate agribusiness in the west than to meddle with the romantic notion of small family farmers in the east.

✦ ✦ ✦

In late summer 2007, a federal judge in Fresno, Oliver Wanger, finally ruled in favor of an environmentalist lawsuit demanding that the federal government curtail its water deliveries to the West Side by 80 percent and more.

The suit involved salmon and especially the three-inch delta smelt, a fragile, short-lived fish. The number of smelt in the Sacramento–San Joaquin River Delta had plummeted over the years, the environmentalists claimed, because the California water projects had diverted far too much northern freshwater away from the delta, leading to lower oxygen levels there and ruining the eco-system; in addition, the huge pumps that sent the water around the delta sup-posedly destroyed young smelt populations. The solution was to shut down the irrigation pumps, allowing California rivers to flow year-round—not just in the wet season—to the delta and the sea.

So in 2008 and 2009, water deliveries to farmers were reduced to a fraction of their previous levels. Chaos followed. Thousands of acres of irrigated crops were idled. Farmworkers were laid off. Adding to the scarcity was that 2007 and 2008 proved drier than usual. In some cases, newly developed orchards and vineyards on the West Side died without summer irrigation—often near the frequently traveled north-south I-5 freeway, where thousands of passing motorists daily saw dead trees and signs erected by angry landowners pro-claiming MAN-MADE DUST BOWL. Yet despite the cutoffs, the delta smelt did not rebound much.

Exact figures for the economic damage were difficult to obtain, but the two most reliable studies were performed by the University of California at Davis and the University of the Pacific in Stockton. While differing in details, both analyses suggested figures of about 250,000 acres idled, 5,000 to 7,000 farmworkers laid off, and $350 million in annual agricultural revenue lost. Of course, those were only the more direct results of the cutoffs. One reason that Central Valley cities like Fresno and Bakersfield are currently suffering 18 percent unemployment rates is that West Side farms have been forced to cut back on the many purchases that help support those commercial centers, from equipment, material, and fuel to insurance, real estate, trucking, ship-ping, and consulting contracts.

Farmers are resourceful people. Some were able to switch to drought-resistant crops; others had cash reserves to pay the exorbitant costs of pump-ing some scarce groundwater. Still others purchased irrigation supplements from East Side canals. Also, the cutoffs came at a time of spiraling agricultural prices, meaning greater profits per acre and sometimes, counterintuitively, greater profitability on less land farmed. Another lucky break for the farmers came from China and India, where a newly affluent consumer class started importing California nuts, cotton, raisins, beef, and vegetables. But luckiest of all was that, by the winter of 2009, California had entered a wet cycle. The result is that, though the state certainly lost hundreds of millions of dollars in agricultural revenue, California will probably still export a record $14 billion in farm commodities in 2011.

The politics of the water cutoffs became bizarre. East Side farmers, worried about the shape of the state's green politics to come—and also fearful that the well-connected corporate farming interests at the south of the valley might, at some date, make up some of their water losses with larger draws on the Sierra supply—mostly rallied to the side of their West Side rivals.

Conservative northern California farmers, by contrast, were happy that less of their water was being diverted south; many fishermen, too, backed court decisions and legislative compromises that seemed to increase the number of salmon in the rivers. Both joined their usual enemies, the environmentalists, in praising the shutting down of the pumps.

Weirder still, corporate farms charged liberal environmentalists with destroying the jobs of downtrodden Mexican workers—citizens, green-card holders, and illegal aliens alike. The Latino Water Coalition demanded that the government restore water to their employers—their old foes during nearly constant labor litigation. And liberal activists, portrayed as opposed to both "family farmers" and "illegal aliens," sometimes confirmed that illiberal portrayal. After a contentious debate over water, a Fresno environmental icon, Lloyd Carter, blurted out to a local news reporter that Mexican farm laborers

> bring a lot of social problems with them, the next generation. On any given day in Fresno, there's 3,500 people in jail; 1,500 of those people are gang members, and a lot of those people are second-generation farm workers. . . . What parent raises their child to become a farm worker? These kids, they are the least educated people in America or in the southwest corner of this valley. They turn to lives of crime. They go on welfare. They get into drug trafficking, and they join gangs.

Some West Side farmers were also East Side farmers and had sizable operations not solely dependent on federal water from the far north. What is clear in this confused mess is that concerns for salmon and smelt now endanger a vast California agribusiness sector that provides thousands of jobs, earns the state billions in revenue, and ships produce worldwide at a time of global food crisis.

* * *

At the end of my frequent drives across the state, I descend into the environmentalists' stronghold, the San Francisco Bay Area. Here—particularly at Stanford University and the University of California at Berkeley—is where much of the environmental research and ideological advocacy took place that privileged the salmon and the smelt over the giants of agribusiness.

Ironies abound in the Bay Area. Few, for example, appreciate the fact that the region owes much of its enormous wealth to sophisticated waterworks.

San Francisco gets 30 to 50 percent of its drinking water from the Hetch Hetchy Reservoir, whose water is transported from the distant Sierra. The city houses a wide variety of firms dependent on Central Valley irrigation—everything from Pacific Gas and Electric, which runs sizable hydroelectric projects, to legal offices for the largest corporate farms, to tour companies offering Sierra lake excursions. And San Francisco, of course, consumes much of the produce grown cheaply on the West Side.

Another irony: while biologists are mostly sure that there are fewer smelt in the estuaries and argue that at least one cause is the diversion of freshwater inflows, they don't know whether that's the only reason that the smelt are disappearing. According to many analyses sponsored by advocacy groups and confirmed by disinterested scientific studies, the hundreds of Bay Area municipalities that dump their treated wastewater into the delta and bay contaminate the estuaries, raise nitrogen levels, and also endanger the smelt. It may be that the reason a few thousand conservative southern farmers are being asked to surrender their precious freshwater is to neutralize the wastewater that millions of affluent and environmentally correct residents are dumping into their own bay.

Environmentalists are unsurprisingly reluctant to concede that the riches of California, which have allowed their own movement to flourish, are derived from the entrepreneurialism and vision that created the West Side out of desert. They likewise dispute the claim that their own communities contribute to rising nitrogen levels in the bay and estuaries. They do not appreciate that West Side corporate barons export produce to feed an increasingly hungry planet. They tend, too, to ignore a final fact: that back in the unspoiled nineteenth century, many of the tributary rivers that they now want to flow year-round to the sea sometimes didn't, because in the absence of today's vast system of mountain reservoirs, yesteryear's snowmelt was largely gone by midsummer.

California lakes and canals are a testament to our fathers' using nature to bring water, power, and prosperity to the Central Valley—often under the tutelage of a past generation of scientists, engineers, and researchers from the coastal universities. These visionaries saw the massive federal West Side irrigation projects as the logical twentieth-century successors to the smaller state and local enterprises that had irrigated the East Side in the nineteenth century. But today, coastal scientists have tired of such visions. They consider them destroyers of nature, not catalysts of wealth, and so they use their academic expertise to thwart them.

* * *

The smelt and the salmon are now back in court, thanks to the hypothesis that Bay Area wastewater, not just river diversions and massive delta pumps, is to blame for their still-diminished numbers. Judge Wanger approved a temporary compromise that tries—in wet years like 2011, when there is more than enough water for everyone—to grant farmers 80 to 85 percent of their contracted water deliveries. The deal has made environmentalists happy, since the rivers are still flowing into the delta and out to sea; indeed, if not for the diversions to farmers, the rivers would overflow their banks. The farmers are less happy, reasoning that if they're getting little more than three-quarters of their deliveries during one of the wettest seasons on record, they'll surely receive even less in drier years—and someday, they may not be able to count on supplementing their lost water through near-prohibitive pumping, purchases of East Side Sierra water, crop diversions, or more efficient irrigation technology.

In the wake of the 2010 midterm elections, some local Democratic congressmen, such as Jim Costa and Dennis Cardoza, are bucking their party leadership and the environmental lobby and joining with conservative representatives to try to exempt the Central Valley Project and elements of the California State Water Project from federal environmental law. If they succeed, the issue could, in the future, be decided by state and federal legislators rather than trial lawyers and federal judges.

But in today's California—with vast Democratic majorities in the state legislature, statewide officeholders mostly Democratic, and a delegation to Congress that's also mostly Democratic—there is almost no chance of restoration of the original 100 percent delivery contracts, no matter what weather the future brings. When the wet cycle passes, thousands of acres on the West Side of the Central Valley will once again become idle—until Californians accept that unused farmland is a luxury that a still-growing but now-bankrupt state can no longer afford.

[2011]

IV
PUBLIC ORDER

14

The Reclamation of Skid Row

The LAPD's Efforts Are Reviving America's Most Squalid Neighborhood— and the Homeless Industry Is Hopping Mad

Heather Mac Donald

DRIVE AROUND LOS ANGELES'S SKID Row with Commander Andrew Smith and you can barely go a block without someone's congratulating him on his recent promotion. Such enthusiasm is certainly in order. Over the last year, this tall, high-spirited policeman has achieved what for a long while seemed impossible: a radical reduction of Skid Row's anarchy. What is surprising about Smith's popularity, however, is that his fans are street-wizened drug addicts, alcoholics, and mentally ill vagrants. And in that fact lies a resounding refutation of the untruths that the American Civil Liberties Union and the rest of the homeless industry have used to keep Skid Row in chaos—until now.

For 25 years, the advocates used lawsuits and antipolice propaganda to beat back every effort to restore sanity to Skid Row. They concealed the real causes of homelessness under a false narrative about a callous, profit-mad society that abused the less fortunate. The result: a level of squalor that had no counterpart in the United States. Smith's policing initiatives—grounded in the Broken Windows theory of order maintenance—ended that experiment in engineered anarchy, saving more lives in ten months than most homeless advocates have helped over their careers. The forces of lawlessness are re-grouping, however, and Smith's successes may wind up reversed in a renewed attack on the police.

* * *

Before Smith's Safer City Initiative began in September 2006, Skid Row's 50 blocks had reached a level of depravity that stunned even longtime observers. Encampments composed of tents and cardboard boxes covered practically every inch of sidewalk. Their 1,500 or so occupants, stretched out in lawn chairs or sprawled on the pavement, injected heroin and smoked crack and marijuana in plain view, day and night. Feces, urine, and drug-resistant bacteria coated the ground. Even drug addicts were amazed at the scene. Fifty-year-old Vicki Williams arrived from Las Vegas in December 2005 with a heavy habit. "I couldn't believe what I was seeing: people getting high on the streets like it was legal," she says. "Down here was like a world of its own. Anything you can imagine I've seen: women walking down the street buck naked, people stabbed in front of me."

The human chaos hid entrenched criminal networks. The biggest heroin gang in downtown Los Angeles operated from the area's west end, using illegal aliens to peddle dope supplied by the Mexican Mafia. Able-bodied dealers sold drugs from wheelchairs and from tents color-coded to signal the wares within. Young Bloods and Crips from Watts's housing projects battled over drug turf and amused themselves by robbing the elderly.

A pitiless law of the jungle ruled social relations. "Everyone is out for himself out there," says Ken Williams (no relation to Vicki), a 50-year-old recovering drug user and ten-year veteran of the streets. "If people see a weakness, they will go for it." Officer Deon Joseph, who has dedicated himself to bringing safety to Skid Row, calls up on his computer recent photos recording the area's still-not-fully suppressed violence: facial welts on a homeless woman assaulted by a homeless man while she was drunk and sleeping on Gladys Street; red gashes across a man's back from a rake wielded by gangsters. In May 2006, a mentally ill woman who had repeatedly resisted offers of housing and services was stomped to death by a homeless parolee. That night, 82 shelter beds were available on Skid Row; a business improvement district's homeless outreach team could persuade only two people to accept them.

Nonviolent crime also metastasized on Skid Row, fed by government welfare. General relief payments—California's little-copied welfare program for able-bodied childless adults—arrive early in the month, followed a few days later by federal Supplemental Security Income for drug addicts and the mentally ill. Skid Row's population and partying spiked around check days. When the money was gone, smoked away in crack pipes or injected into veins, the hustling began. A doctors' clinic in the Hispanic MacArthur Park neighborhood sent a van out to collect volunteers for Medicaid fraud; it offered $20 to anyone willing to take a fake health exam, and then billed the exams to the government at exorbitant rates. Two food-stamp rings, paying homeless recipients 50 cents for every dollar's worth of stamps, stole $6 million from federal taxpayers. The spending money handed out in these scams went right back into the drug trade, keeping the homeless addicted and the drug sellers in diamond tooth caps.

This lawlessness hurt Skid Row's law-abiding residents the most. The area's century-old residential hotels and missions house thousands of senior citizens, non-drug-abusing mentally ill persons, and addicts trying to turn their lives around. "The people we serve are very vulnerable," says Anita Nelson, director of a government-funded nonprofit that rehabilitates and manages single-room-occupancy hotels (SROs). "The elderly and the mentally ill were victimized by the crime and the dealers. When you're afraid to go into the park, you're a prisoner in your 120-square-foot unit." Temptation confronted recovering addicts every time they stepped outside.

With formal controls on behavior almost completely absent, the last vestiges of civility broke down. In 2005, young volunteers for the Union Rescue Mission set out to deliver 4,000 boxes of Christmas food to every SRO in the area. As they tried to navigate the streets, encampment residents cursed them, hurled racial taunts, and mockingly defecated in front of them. The area's intrepid businesses faced constant assault. "We had to fortify the buildings with razor wire and barricade ourselves in," a shrimp processor recalls. "The homeless would take or steal anything." His roll-up door, constantly exposed to bodily fluids, rotted away. In September 2006, the owner of one of the district's landmark businesses, ABC Toys, caught a typical moment on film: a mail carrier reaches through the store's gate to drop off letters, when she notices that the man at her feet is shooting heroin into a prominent vein. She flees in dismay without leaving the mail.

* * *

This ugly scene was not the by-product of economic dislocations or of social upheaval; it was the consequence of a destructive ideology that turned a seedy neighborhood for the down-and-out into a hell.

Skid Row began as a vital accessory to what was once Los Angeles's thriving heart, decades before the automobile spread the city across hundreds of square miles to the mountains and ocean. Farmland surrounded what is now downtown, requiring workers for the fields, for the adjacent factories that processed the produce, and for the railroad that shipped it out. Skid Row's cheap hotels, saloons, and theaters catered to these transient single males.

Though this low-rent district was located just a few blocks from the elegantly sculpted banks and office buildings of Spring Street and Broadway, the two worlds coexisted in relative peace because public order was maintained. Over the course of the twentieth century, Skid Row's population became older and more disabled by alcoholism, as industrial and agricultural jobs moved elsewhere. The local missions tried to reclaim lives lost to drink, offering a free meal in exchange for attendance at a sermon, but their success rate was never particularly high. Alcoholics congregated on the street in bottle gangs—a group of drinkers who pooled their nickels for booze. Still, if one collapsed at a business's front door, he stood a good chance of getting picked up by the police for public inebriation.

But in the 1960s, laws against public intoxication, vagrancy, and loitering came under attack in court and in the press, and by the 1980s, the enforcement of such public-order statutes had all but ceased. In 1975, approximately 50,000 arrests took place in Los Angeles for public intoxication, more than half of those on Skid Row; in 1985, the entire city generated only 4,000 such arrests. This enforcement halt was not the humanitarian advance that its architects claimed, says Clancy Imislund, the former director of Skid Row's Midnight Mission and an ex–Skid Row alcoholic himself. "The police picked up street drunks for their own protection," he notes. "Sometimes they sent them to a farm north of L.A. for six months. By the 1970s, however, the police started leaving them lying there, where gangs took their money and beat the hell out of them." A 1971 federal law tried to substitute rehabilitation for the policing cycle, but the success rate of federally funded alcoholism services wasn't noticeably better than that of the jails, according to sociologist Ronald Miller.

One further change in the legal landscape paved the way for the chaos that would engulf Skid Row by the century's end. Inspired partly by the then-fashionable belief that mental illness was an artificial construct for oppressing nonconformists, California passed landmark legislation in 1967 that virtually ended the involuntary commitment of the mentally ill. A decade later, hospital professionals were noticing with alarm that patients whom they had no power to hold for long-term treatment were cycling between the streets, jails, and short-term mental wards.

By the early 1980s, a new Skid Row population had emerged: drug addicts, overwhelmingly black, often mentally ill, who camped out on the streets. The era of the "homeless" had begun. This population was younger, more hostile, and more predatory than the old Skid Row rummies were; it brought in its train a criminal element that hadn't previously existed downtown. "In the seventies, I'd rather have my daughter walk through Skid Row than on Hollywood Boulevard," recalls Imislund. "Some of the alcoholics slept outside because they didn't want to clean up. They may have looked dangerous, but they weren't." The "homeless" were a different matter. Local crime jumped 28 percent in 1986 alone. "I started with my mommy and daddy 50 years ago; it was not this bad, uh-uh," says Rosy Rios, who runs a ministry in the area. "All [the older Skid Row alcoholics] did was drink they wine and talk about what they did in France. Now they all into they heroin. This place is running all the time. . . . Most of these guys are sex offenders. This is the place you can hide away."

An Urban Land Institute study warned in 1987 that the "invasion of the homeless" was threatening the older SRO population and local businesses; stronger police protection was essential, argued the institute. The recommendation failed to take into account a second new population invading Skid Row: homeless advocates. Some of the same groups that had challenged public-order laws and pushed for the deinstitutionalization of the mentally ill now seized on the resulting homeless for a host of ends, including a right to housing and further restrictions on the police. A made-for-the-media "tent city" erected by sundry homeless advocates outside City Hall in December 1984, for example, sought to end workfare and job-search requirements for welfare recipients—measures that had nothing to do with why people were on the streets.

* * *

A third new population sprang up around Skid Row, however, that would repeatedly clash with the homeless advocates over public safety: immigrant entrepreneurs. The eastern section of downtown adjacent to Skid Row, known as Central City East, had retained some food-processing and cold-storage businesses from the days of the ranchos, but most of its warehouses and factories were abandoned. In the late 1970s, a lone Chinese family spotted potential in the area, with its dense network of freeways leading to the Southland's ports and airports. Charlie Woo and his three brothers started a toy import-export business, and encouraged customers to become competitors by leasing space in the Woos' newly acquired warehouses. "People thought we were crazy to enter this blighted area and then to promote competition," says Shu Woo, one of the brothers, "but we wanted to create a gravitational center that would draw customers in." Today, the Woos' several multimillion-dollar toy companies are surrounded by about 500 other toy, electronics, and novelty enterprises, which generate nearly $1 billion in annual sales.

Other new downtown business districts formed in the 1980s—a fish-processing industry, flower wholesalers, and a fashion district—creating a fascinating array of small, pastel-colored stucco facilities under the bright California sky. As Los Angeles slipped into recession in the early 1990s, Central City East enjoyed one of the best growth rates in the city—and achieved it against enormous odds. Residents of the sidewalk encampments defecated on the new enterprises' doorsteps, set up heroin-shooting galleries outside, and jeered owners' efforts to clean up the sidewalks. Only the most intrepid employees were willing to work there. Many prospective hires, arriving for job interviews, simply drove on by.

The city government did little to nurture these pioneering entrepreneurs and usually opposed their interests in favor of the burgeoning homelessness complex. Periodically, the anguish of Central City East's employers and workers would inspire a local police captain to try to bring order to the streets, but the efforts always proved short-lived.

In 1987, for example, Police Chief Daryl Gates announced plans to enforce the city's defunct ordinance against sleeping, lying, or sitting on the sidewalk, setting off a firestorm within Mayor Tom Bradley's administration and outside of it. Actor Martin Sheen penned an op-ed for the *Los Angeles Times* yoking the sidewalk law to America's "useless nuclear arsenal" and worldwide starvation. Gates received "stinging letters," he says, from the West Side, Los Angeles's sylvan enclave for Hollywood moguls and other titans. "I told the writers, 'If you want the homeless to pitch a tent, I'll give them your address. If you're so anxious, let them camp in Brentwood.'" No one took him up on the suggestion.

Gates's enforcement effort resulted in a 20 percent crime drop in the first month and a total cessation of homicides over two months—a "world record for us," according to a local commander. The city had passed out housing vouchers to anyone who would take them and created a tent city where people could get assistance with jobs (almost no one accepted the job offers). Nevertheless, the sidewalk policing initiative fell before elite opinion. Lawlessness returned to Skid Row.

* * *

A pattern in the advocates' efforts soon emerged: the more the government and philanthropy spent on helping the homeless, the louder the charge that nothing was being done. By now, public and private entities have spent $350 million on homeless housing downtown without quieting the activists.

In 1999, the doyenne of downtown homeless agitators, Alice Callaghan, picketed the opening of a Skid Row drop-in center providing people with showers, a place to sit or lie down, and various services that would start them on the path to rehabilitation. Callaghan, an ex-nun and ordained Episcopal priest, likened the 24-hour facility to an "internment camp." The problem? A drop-in center reinforces the idea that "anyone still on the street is on the street by choice and not because of a lack of options," she told *Mother Jones* magazine in 2001. "The language of rehab and programs and community is the velvet glove on a puritanical and punitive fist," she added.

The exertions of the homelessness industry long ago passed into the realm of the surreal. Estela Lopez, director of Skid Row's business improvement district, the Central City East Association (CCEA), had to negotiate in a judge's chambers the arcane question of whether feces in a plastic bag constitute "property." Defending the property label were lawyers from the prestigious law firm Morrison & Foerster, who, along with the ACLU, had sued CCEA over its efforts to remove encampment detritus from the sidewalks in front of members' businesses.

On Skid Row, such efforts at cleanliness take on titanic significance. In 2006, CCEA concluded that its usual street sweeping couldn't keep up with

the area's filth and disease. To help business owners fulfill their legal obligation to keep the sidewalks in front of their properties clean, the association
would hire a power-cleaning truck to wash the pavement. (The resulting
runoff was anticipated to be so toxic that CCEA also paid to vacuum it up
before it poured into the storm drains.) The association sent out notices for
two days in advance, asking encampment residents to pack their possessions
up during the operation, after which they would be free to return to the same
spot on the sidewalk.

Abuse! cried the advocates, who showed up en masse to protest. Sidewalk
cleaning was another tactic, they said, in the "criminalization of homelessness," a ubiquitous slogan used to discredit any effort to apply rules and laws
evenhandedly in areas colonized by vagrants. A member of the Los Angeles
Catholic Worker movement lay down under the cleaning truck to block its
advance. "If you see street cleaning in any other neighborhood, you don't
see [a] police presence," groused Becky Dennison of the Los Angeles Community Action Network (LA CAN). Dennison is right: police don't routinely
accompany street cleaners elsewhere. But only on Skid Row have psychotic
drug addicts, whom the police have been prevented from removing to safer
quarters, been known to attack the workers.

When Police Chief William Bratton took control of the LAPD in late 2002,
vowing to clean crime out of Skid Row through the application of Broken
Windows policing, the ACLU launched a litigation war to stop him. For the
advocates, the stakes had never been higher. A few developers had started
converting empty office buildings in adjacent areas of downtown to lofts;
the activists seized on this revitalization of Los Angeles's historical core as
proof that the evil capitalists were seeking to afflict the poor. In March 2003,
the ACLU filed a lawsuit against the department's efforts to track down the
hundreds of violent parole violators and absconders in Skid Row encampments who were driving up violent crime. And in an even more ambitious
lawsuit, *Jones* v. *City of Los Angeles*, the ACLU charged that application of
the city's ordinance against sleeping or lying on the sidewalk violated the
Eighth Amendment's ban on cruel and unusual punishment. The majority of
a Ninth Circuit Court of Appeals panel agreed in April 2006, and the police
halted their mostly desultory efforts to enforce the sidewalk law. The ACLU
handed out leaflets on the *Jones* decision to encampment residents, some of
whom waved them tauntingly in police officers' faces. Skid Row got worse
than anyone could have imagined.

* * *

Enter Andrew Smith. He had become captain of Central Division, the
police jurisdiction responsible for Skid Row, in April 2005, determined to
"change the culture of chaos," as he put it. Smith had no doubt that the

anarchy did not represent an unavoidable consequence of poverty, as the advocates alleged. "People were here because they chose not to conform to ordinary standards of behavior and the laws of the land," he says.

Smith's ambitions required a lot of additional officers. The area represented the "granddaddy of all order maintenance problems," says Chief Bratton. The department's perennial manpower shortage, however, as well as the ongoing litigation over police power, forced Smith to put his plans on hold. Instead, he organized a demonstration project for Main Street, where a homeless colony was strangling a nascent commercial and residential rebirth. Smith assigned existing officers to foot beats, put up security cameras, and started enforcing the narcotics laws and, to a very limited extent, the ordinance against sleeping on the sidewalk. The encampments disappeared; legitimate street life arose in its place.

The advocates struck back. Officer Lenny Davis walks Main Street; like all Skid Row cops, he often has a shadow. LA CAN, the most radical antipolice outfit on Skid Row, sends out its members to film the police. Davis never knows when a videographer will trail him, or when a specious complaint, filed by someone coached by the activists, might hit him. "Our back is against the wall," he says in frustration. "We don't know what to do to make them stop making complaints." Yet despite thousands of hours of accumulated tape, LA CAN has yet to publicize any footage showing the police abuse that it and the ACLU allege is so common.

Finally, in September 2006, Smith got the additional officers he needed. A graphic series on Skid Row by a *Los Angeles Times* columnist in late 2005 and a widely publicized video of a hospital ambulance abandoning a mentally ill patient to the streets gave Bratton the political cover to assign an entire graduating class of 50 new recruits to the area. Crucial support came from the city attorney and the local councilwoman, both of whom bucked Los Angeles political traditions to fight for sanity in Central City East. Mayor Antonio Villaraigosa broke with his own past as president of the ACLU of Southern California to back the cleanup. Even though the ACLU litigation was still tying the city up in legal knots, Chief Bratton signaled the go-ahead for the Safer City Initiative (SCI).

* * *

Four mornings a week, Safer City squads blanket Skid Row's most intractable blocks. Much of their effort targets quality-of-life issues—discouraging public drinking and littering, stopping sales of counterfeit merchandise, nabbing illegal dumpers. "The key to SCI is perception," Smith says. "Do people feel comfortable coming down here? We talk to the homeless and ask them what still needs to be done." When SCI began, the sanitation department was picking up six tons of trash dumped illegally on the streets every day; by August 2007, that amount was down to two tons. Some of that garbage comes from misguided do-gooders, who hourly drive into the neighborhood to un-load bags of clothing and unneeded food onto the sidewalk before making as fast a getaway as possible. "If I see one more plate of salad next to someone's turd, I'll kill someone," laments a City Hall aide who has worked to clean up the area.

Because of the *Jones* litigation, the police department allows nighttime encampments but asks people to pack up their belongings in the morning. Despite the brouhaha over sidewalk enforcement, the department has ar-rested only a handful of the most recalcitrant campers who set up in front of restaurants or new businesses and refuse to leave. Every one of those ar-restees—if he has no recent history of violence—gets the option of shelter and services as an alternative to jail, as is true of every other misdemeanor of-fender on Skid Row. But few of them qualify, since most have violent records; even fewer accept the services; and a vanishingly small number complete the 21-day alternative to jail time.

Yet the mere possibility of enforcement has had a major effect. In Septem-ber 2006, there were 1,876 people sleeping on the street and 518 tents; in early June 2007, there were 700 people and 315 tents. "We've broken the back of the problem," says Bratton. "We're controlling behavior with the ability just to move people along. You need to interrupt the cycle where they never leave and collect mountains of stuff in a very short time." The police no longer find dead bodies in the tents, rotting unnoticed for days or weeks.

Measured by crime statistics alone, the Safer City Initiative's results have been remarkable. Major felonies on Skid Row plummeted 42 percent in the first half of 2007, the largest decrease in all of Los Angeles. There were 241 fewer victims of violent crime in that period. In downtown as a whole, the murder rate dropped over 75 percent. This crime drop has coincided with the decline in the street population, suggesting that the encampment dwell-ers weren't engaged exclusively in "life-sustaining activities," as the majority in the *Jones* decision foolishly put it. But other markers of social progress have improved as well. Drug overdose and natural deaths were down over 50 percent through June 2007; emergency medical incidents requiring EMS response were down 17 percent.

The Safer City Initiative has also worked with stepped-up narcotics en-forcement. The increased arrests under SCI allowed the police to move up the organization chart of the ruthless Fifth and Hill heroin gang, which operated out of Skid Row; SCI cameras caught the license numbers of Fifth and Hill middlemen, leading to the crucial March 2007 takedown of gang kingpins.

* * *

Though the advocates refuse to budge from their untruths about police abuse of the homeless, the homeless themselves know better. If the Safer City Initiative were in fact the travesty that the elite cop-haters claim, the reception that Commander Smith and his officers get when they travel the streets of Skid Row would be far different from the love fest that currently greets them.

As Smith drives down Fifth Street, a toothless man shouts out: "Hey, man!" and walks up to Smith's squad car to give him a fist-to-fist handshake. "Where are you?" the elderly alcoholic asks. "I'm everywhere, Larry," Smith responds. Larry mumbles something about Smith's recent promotion from captain to commander, and concludes, "Way to go, Smith!" Farther down the block, another bedraggled man leaves his post at a wall and accosts Smith: "How's your father doing?" he asks. Smith spots another acquaintance. "Mr. Jackson! Hello, Mr. Jackson. How many watches you got on?" Mr. Jackson presents his scrawny wrist: "I got on four," he replies proudly. You can't get far on Skid Row without encountering a young woman with sunburned cheeks, pale eyes, and deeply chapped lips, who spends her days circling the area. She flags Smith's car down. "Hey, how you been?" she asks, slurring her words. The two engage in a surreal exchange about the woman's pet white mouse, which she concludes by volunteering: "I'm going to stay on drugs for a while."

There are several things to notice about Smith's interactions. First, many of his greeters should be receiving mental health care but are too ill to seek it. The police would love to secure them that assistance but cannot, thanks to the advocates' ongoing campaign against involuntary commitment. In fact, when officers call an ambulance to help deranged and severely ill people get physical care, chances are that LA CAN's cameras will switch on, accompanied by charges of "harassing the homeless." Second, unlike the advocates, Smith knows the names of the homeless, because he has spent so much time trying to improve their lot by enforcing standards of behavior and getting rid of the criminals in their midst. Third, if Smith's officers were acting thuggishly, Smith wouldn't enjoy such a procession of goodwill.

But no need to work from inferences. It's easy enough to observe the cops themselves doing their work. Deon Joseph has devoted the last nine years of his life to fighting the forces of lawlessness on Skid Row, a battle he records eloquently on the LAPD blog. As this massively muscled, low-key officer ambles down San Julian Street, once the heart of Skid Row decadence, he encounters a pretty young woman with a bike. "I've been avoiding you," she says sheepishly. Joseph had put her into a housing program, but she absconded. "When I was in the program, it added value to my life. I had a TV, a DVD player, but I got bored." Joseph inquires if she has drugs on her and asks to see her fingertips, which tell whether someone is using crack cocaine or selling it. "I'm going to give you a second chance," he says. "If you see me on the street—and this is real—don't be afraid to holler on me, because I know people make mistakes."

A string of elderly ladies in wheelchairs are drinking out of paper bags. In response to Joseph's question about the contents of her bag, a senior citizen with three nose rings replies: "I ain't drinking no beer, I'm drinking whisky. You caught me slippin'." Joseph takes a beer from a man's hand and pours it out. "There's no drinking in public on my block. It's how I keep crime down." The drinkers accept this intervention without protest.

* * *

The people who would most benefit from observing this complex web of formal authority and personal connectedness are L.A.'s liberal judges, who demonstrate complete ignorance about how the police operate in a community like Skid Row. Officers' rapport with addicts and the mentally ill has no counterpart in the anticop bar and its supporters. Only the police are out there every day, trying to nudge people who have fallen out of normal society back into it, and putting themselves (and their families) at risk of infectious disease in doing so. The cops know the rhythms of the sidewalk: that people lying there in 110-degree heat are selling dope, or crashing from a cocaine binge, or drinking, not enduring the unjust conditions of poverty.

Officer Joseph passed out hundreds of flyers for work at a Long Beach plant. A mere four people sought jobs there; the rest preferred to stay on welfare. Still, he's currently negotiating with the owners of a massive downtown development project, L.A. Live, for additional job offers. Joseph spends hours away from his family writing police reports to educate judges and district attorneys about the connections between street disorder and crime. "I put in everything I know, and then in several minutes they plead it out," he says wearily.

As the Safer City Initiative progresses, the advocates of disorder are running scared. "Today, Skid Row's streets are strangely empty," opined Ramona Ripston, the executive director of the ACLU of Southern California, in April 2007. Actually, what was "strange" was the chaos that had engulfed them just months previously. And so the homeless activists are preparing what they hope will be the deathblow to SCI and to the Broken Windows theory behind it.

For this final push, the unreality of antipolice propagandizing has reached record levels. A new lawsuit against the police filed by Carol Sobel, an attorney who has made a career of suing the police for the ACLU and the National Lawyers Guild, charges that low-income Skid Row residents have become prisoners in their own homes because of a police "war" against them. Sheer nonsense. It was the drug carnival before SCI that held Skid Row's law-abiding tenants hostage in their apartments; the dismantling of that free-for-all has liberated the hardworking poor, the elderly, and the infirm to use the area's public spaces. And many of the people who remain on the streets want more policing, not less. Jimmy, a middle-aged convict from Alabama with a self-confessed "violent temper," says he has "seen a lot of things change" since getting out of prison in 2003 for attempted murder. As he stands on San Julian Street with a group of other loafers on a hot August afternoon, he observes: "There's less crime, women are not getting harassed the way they used to." But Jimmy has some advice for the police: "They need to be here in the middle of the month; they are missing some things that are going on." As for Sobel's charge that no one dares use the streets for fear of the police, the most cursory tour through Skid Row reveals that, though the worst of the encampments are gone, plenty of people—like Jimmy—feel perfectly safe to loiter all day and night on the sidewalks.

A parallel ACLU lawsuit repeats the false claim that the police have a policy of stopping and violently searching people for no reason at all. One of the area's fiercest police foes has unwittingly refuted this claim. Casey Horan, director of a facility for the mentally ill, told the *Los Angeles Times* in August 2006 that 90 percent of the people on the street were engaging in misdemeanor crime. Far from harassing innocent people, in other words, the police ignore the vast majority of violations on Skid Row, which occur nonstop. The accusations against the police that the ACLU solicited for its suit from street people, often unnamed, are absurd on their face. They are contradicted in the record by numerous other homeless individuals and service providers testifying to compassionate, lawful police behavior. "The LAPD contacts me several times a day," says a six-year resident of the Gladys Street sidewalk. "They ask me how I'm doing and if I am okay. They are my friends and they are good to me." Yet a federal judge, Dean Pregerson, has already ruled provisionally in favor of the ACLU on the flimsiest of grounds.

* * *

What may be the most lethal assault on Skid Row policing, however, is only now revving up. For months, UCLA law professor Gary Blasi pelted Commander Smith with demands for all e-mails, transcripts, and supervisory notes relating to SCI, as well as for reams of police data. (The demands stopped only when Smith told Blasi that he'd have to come to Central Division and make copies of the material himself, because officers were spending too much time on his requests.) Blasi is preparing to charge that the enforcement of misdemeanor laws on Skid Row is discriminatory and ineffective. A centerpiece of his argument is that, as of summer 2007, SCI squads had made only 16 arrests for violent crime. Therefore, Blasi's reasoning goes, they're not targeting real crime but merely trying to "ethnically cleanse" downtown to make way for gentrification.

Blasi's complaint strikes at the heart of the Broken Windows theory, for he is attacking the validity of going after low-level lawlessness, such as public drinking or graffiti, to reduce crime and the fear of crime. For the advocates, observes Chief Bratton, "any arrest that isn't for a felony is per se harassment." But the enforcement of laws relating to civil behavior—mostly through warnings, rather than arrests or citations—has been essential to undercutting the identity of Skid Row as a place beyond ordinary rules of human conduct. Says Officer Joseph: "The idea that because people were homeless, they had a right to break 'minor' laws . . . has led to nothing but death, disease, and despair." Equally important, misdemeanor enforcement has driven away drug dealers, who can no longer hang out all day, littering and jaywalking.

Sadly, the influential are listening to Blasi. *Los Angeles Times* columnist Steve Lopez, whose 2005 series on Skid Row galvanized the city, wrote a Blasi-inspired column in August 2007 denouncing the enforcement of jaywalking laws on Skid Row. Lopez quoted President George W. Bush's homelessness "czar," Philip Mangano, who ludicrously called Safer City "shameful," based on no knowledge of Skid Row or of the police's efforts to salvage it. Blasi's research has also made waves among Mayor Villaraigosa's aides at City Hall. L.A.'s crime drop—including that of Skid Row—stands as the sole accomplishment of the scandal-plagued mayor's administration, but Villaraigosa's advocate roots may yet prove a stronger lure.

* * *

The city's policymakers should be under no illusions: if they dismantle the Safer City Initiative, the only people they'll help are drug dealers and other street criminals. SCI has improved the lot of Central City East's workers, of course, but the greatest beneficiaries have been the homeless. "The police have really improved things," explains street habitant Kharo Brown. "The crack is thinning out. It is getting really hard to find. Crack doesn't have a conscience. These people do crazy things on crack"—including attacking Brown. More subtly, Commander Smith and his officers have changed the area's culture. In 2006, for instance, when volunteers delivered Christmas food baskets to every poor SRO tenant, street residents didn't harass them.

The Safer City Initiative is about not poverty but behavior. "I don't care if 125 people are hanging out on San Julian if they are obeying the law," says Deon Joseph. Nor is it about lack of housing. The advocates will deny to their last breath the reality of "shelter resistance"—that is, the refusal of vast numbers of the homeless to take advantage of shelter and other housing options. The advocates have crafted a host of logical sophistries to dismiss the phenomenon, which anyone can test for himself by offering the homeless a place for the night or by asking the formerly homeless why they didn't get off the streets. Here's what you'll hear: "I didn't want help because I didn't want to conform to the rules," in the words of Ken Williams, who came from Long Beach to Skid Row a decade ago to indulge his crack and alcohol habit.

The inevitable next lawsuit will be a terrible waste of resources. "It's unending," says a city attorney. "We don't have 500 attorneys to put on these ACLU attacks." Regardless of the outcome of the suit, it will slow down the progress made to date. "Every time we get sued, it sets us back," says Joseph. "It makes officers unsure of what they can do and creates confusion where criminals fester."

Skid Row is hardly a paradise. There are still sights that you would never see elsewhere in the city; apart from the devoted businesses, it remains in some ways a world apart. Spend time there and you start to wonder which is real: the world of responsibilities fulfilled and discipline adhered to, or the world where you can watch months and years go by from a perch on the pavement. Yet the overall improvement of Skid Row is one of the greatest vindications to date of the power of policing to improve lives. It would be a tragedy if the advocates succeeded in reversing that success.

[2007]

15

The LAPD Remade

How William Bratton's Police Force Drove Crime Down—and Won Over Los Angeles's Minorities

John Buntin

IT STARTED AS A ROUTINE 911 CALL. Someone in South Gate, a working-class city in Los Angeles County, had seen a group of young black males who appeared to be breaking into a neighbor's house. When the South Gate police arrived at the scene, they blocked the street with their patrol cars. Three teenagers ran out of the house, jumped into their own car, and rammed through the barricade. The kids headed for the freeway, first speeding south toward Long Beach on the 710 and then turning west onto the 105. By now, Los Angeles County Sheriff's deputies and California Highway Patrol officers had joined the pursuit.

Moments later, the suspects' car caught fire. They pulled over, leaped out of the car, and scrambled down the highway embankment. To the north was the Watts section of South L.A.; to the south, Compton. It was here that the three teenagers made a serious mistake: they ran north into Imperial Courts, a 500-unit public-housing development controlled by one of Watts's oldest street gangs, the PJ Crips. The suspects themselves were members of a rival gang, the Bounty Hunter Bloods.

Sheriff's deputies caught one of the Bloods before he could vanish into the maze of two-story apartment blocks that make up Imperial Courts. Another suspect got away. Deputies spotted the third ducking into one of the apartment buildings. They were preparing to go in when Phil Tingirides, the Los Angeles Police Department captain responsible for Southeast Division, arrived on the scene. Tingirides didn't like what he saw. Entering seemed an unwise tactic; in fact, LAPD guidelines called for the use of a Special Weapons and Tactics (SWAT) team. Tingirides was also disturbed by the atmosphere developing among the assembled group of roughly 15 spectators, including the suspect's mother, sisters, and brothers. Almost as soon as she had arrived, upset and worried, the mother had gotten into it with one of the deputies, who began upbraiding her for raising a gangbanger. Meanwhile, Tingirides noticed, one of the brothers had started an argument with a group of PJs nearby.

Any cop who'd worked the public-housing developments of Watts during the 1980s and 1990s had seen it happen: the gang skirmish that escalates to a shooting; the crowd that turns on the cops. But not this time. Tingirides interrupted the deputy's harangue, saying, "Hey, I got this." Then he introduced himself to the mother and the sisters as a cop and a parent. "Your priority needs to be getting your son out of here safe," he said. He explained what had happened. This was news to the mother, who had simply gotten a call from her son saying that the cops were chasing him for no reason. These things can happen, Tingirides said. Disgusted at the way Tingirides was talking about a hard-core gangbanger, the deputy left. Tingirides and the mother then went over to the brother, who was still arguing with the PJs. Mom and the highway patrol pulled him aside. "Once she understood what had happened and had someone talking to her as a person and a fellow parent, it totally changed her demeanor and dynamic," says Tingirides.

The crowd was losing interest. So were the deputies. Tingirides told them that LAPD guidelines prohibited an attempt to make an entry. Fine, they said; in that case, we're handing this off to you. The deputies pulled back. And then the suspect emerged. His brother had called him on his cell phone and explained the situation. South Gate police took him into custody. The crowd dispersed. "There was never any element of hostility toward our department at all," Tingirides says.

For more than half a century, many African-American Angelenos and more than a few Latinos considered the LAPD an oppressor—"an occupation force," in the words of former Urban League president John Mack. That is no longer the case. Over the past decade, the department has transformed itself radically, along with its relations with local minorities. Nor has the police department become popular by sacrificing public safety: violent crime in Los Angeles has been falling for years. How the LAPD's reconciliation with L.A.'s minorities came about may be the most important untold story in the world of policing. What makes the reconciliation even more remarkable is that its architect was the same man who had already transformed the New York City Police Department: William Bratton.

* * *

The LAPD has a long history of strained relations with Los Angeles's minority communities. During the early 1960s, Chief William Parker publicly took issue with the civil rights movement while turning a blind eye to his officers' sometimes brutal conduct in black and Latino neighborhoods. Almost every week, African-American newspapers published horror stories of black Angelenos stopped, verbally abused, unlawfully detained, or beaten by the police. Even many law-abiding black Angelenos feared maltreatment. Parker investigated the people who filed complaints against the department more enthusiastically than he investigated the officers being complained about. He declined to criticize Bull Connor's tactics in Birmingham and insisted that race riots could never occur in Los Angeles.

He was wrong. In 1965, Watts and much of South L.A. went up in flames after a highway-patrol stop gone bad. Far from damaging Parker's reputation, the Watts riots seemed to give credence to his increasingly apocalyptic warnings about California's future, and he emerged from the riots the most popular figure in California—the white community's "security blanket," as *Los Angeles Times* publisher Otis Chandler called him. Parker died in office in 1966, but his legacy—a deeply conservative, fiercely independent police department—lived on. In 1977, his protégé Daryl Gates took over the LAPD. Gates dismantled an early community-policing initiative developed by his immediate predecessor and focused instead on such innovations as SWAT teams. Under his tenure, the LAPD managed to patrol a sprawling, 468-square-mile city with a force less than half the size of the NYPD, relative to the population of each city.

Then, in the mid-1980s, crack cocaine arrived in Los Angeles. With the drugs came money. With the money came cars, guns, and a fierce scramble for markets. Neighborhoods long known for violence suddenly became killing fields. In response, Gates launched Operation Hammer. Hundreds of cops swarmed through black and Latino neighborhoods, usually at the beginning of the weekend. The goal was to make arrests. To do so, every law was strictly enforced. Over the course of a typical weekend, police would pick up 1,000 to 2,000 people, jail them, and impound their cars. Come Monday morning, the courts would dismiss all but a few dozen charges. Residents would go to the impound yards to retrieve their cars; often, they'd been damaged, and not infrequently, rims and stereos went missing.

"They were pissed, really angry," recalls Lieutenant Fred Booker, an African-American and the son of South Carolina sharecroppers. He had joined the LAPD in 1972. "Who were they angry at? The police department. Relations with the police was nonexistent. Anger and frustration with the department was overwhelming." The anger reached a boiling point in 1992, when the officers involved in the beating of Rodney King were unexpectedly acquitted, and South Los Angeles erupted in looting and violence. Instead of suppressing the criminal activity, the LAPD withdrew. It took nearly a week to restore order.

This time, the public didn't rally around its police chief. Gates retired, and voters approved an amendment to the city charter that replaced the chief's life tenure with a limit of two five-year terms. Other changes increased the powers of the Board of Police Commissioners, whose members, appointed by the mayor, oversaw the chief. And now the chief would be appointed not by the board but by the mayor, subject to the city council's approval.

His authority enhanced, Mayor Tom Bradley chose former Philadelphia police commissioner Willie Williams to head the department. He was the first African-American chief in the department's history and the first chief appointed from outside the LAPD's ranks since 1949. But his tenure was brief and overshadowed by reports, which proved true, that a Las Vegas casino had given him free rooms and other perks. In 1997, Mayor Richard Riordan replaced Williams with an LAPD veteran, Bernard Parks, who was also black. Parks made some noteworthy reforms, improving the way police treated suspects in high-crime neighborhoods and instituting a system that, for the first time, gave commanders a comprehensive account of complaints filed against every officer. But his administration, too, suffered from scandal—allegations that gang officers in the Rampart Division had stolen drugs from evidence lockers and framed suspects. In 2001, after a long investigation by the U.S. Department of Justice, city officials negotiated a consent decree that put the LAPD under the supervision of a federal judge.

At the same time, violent crime was starting to increase, reversing a trend that had begun in the mid-1990s. In 2002, Mayor James Hahn announced that he was selecting Bill Bratton as the city's next police chief.

* * *

It wasn't self-evident that New York mayor Rudy Giuliani's first police commissioner was the best candidate to reduce crime and bridge L.A.'s "black-blue" divide. But Bratton's entire life had prepared him for the assignment. His parents were high school sweethearts who had grown up together in the projects of Charlestown, Massachusetts. By the time Bill was born in 1947, they had moved to the Boston neighborhood of Dorchester, where they lived down the street from a police station. One of Bratton's earliest memories is watching patrolmen march out of the station, two abreast, and load themselves into the open-backed blue wagons that delivered them to their posts. From an early age, he wanted to be a cop.

But the Boston Police Department required applicants to be at least 21 years old. Bratton couldn't afford college, so after high school, he joined the army, became an MP, and was sent to Vietnam, where he spent three years walking the perimeter of various military bases with a German shepherd. He returned to Boston in 1969 and became a policeman the following year.

His first assignment was in Mattapan, which bordered Dorchester to the south. When Bratton was growing up, Mattapan had been predominantly Jewish, but now it was mostly African-American and one of the toughest districts in Boston, a dumping ground for new recruits with no pull in the department—in other words, for people like Bratton. There, he got a firsthand look at the complexities of race and policing. One evening, he and his partner were ordered to park their cruiser in front of the house of an elderly Jewish woman, a holdout from the tidal wave of demographic change that had swept over the neighborhood. Some black kids had been throwing bricks through her windows. As dusk was falling, a black teenager came walking down the street. Nothing about the kid suggested trouble; in fact, he reminded Bratton of his best friend from basic training. Bratton's partner thought otherwise. He got out of the car and planted himself in the middle of the sidewalk, arms crossed. The kid tried to walk around him. The officer stepped in front of him. "Excuse me," the teen said. "I want to get by."

"Cross the street," responded Bratton's partner. "You can't walk here."

"What do you mean, I can't walk here?" the teen said. Soon the two were going at each other, voices rising. Eventually, the boy complied, and as he walked away, Bratton asked his partner why he'd confronted him in the first place. "Fuck those niggers," his partner said loudly, so that the kid could hear him.

Tensions got hotter. In 1974, U.S. federal district judge Arthur Garrity ordered the Boston school district—but not the suburban jurisdictions that surrounded the city, such as Wellesley, the judge's hometown—to engage in busing to end segregation. The order set off protests throughout the city, but close-knit, Irish-American South Boston emerged as the locus of resistance. Confrontations with the police became increasingly common. On Father's Day 1977, white fathers marched on South Boston High School, which was defended by a small contingent of police officers, including Bratton. What the police had expected to be a standoff turned into an assault. The mob surged toward the gate to the school, destroying police cars and hurling rocks and bottles at the officers.

Bratton suddenly found himself standing next to Police Commissioner Robert diGrazia. "Good afternoon, Sergeant Bratton," diGrazia said cheerfully, acting for all the world as though the two men had just bumped into each other strolling through the Public Garden. (At this point, Bratton was already famous in the department for persuading an armed bank robber with a hostage to surrender.) "You know," the commissioner continued as projectiles flew through the air, "we've been talking about a new initiative to bring some of you young sergeants into headquarters to work on my staff and get a feel for the place. Would you be interested in coming up?"

"I would love it!" Bratton said. The idea of working in the commissioner's office must have seemed particularly appealing at that moment.

* * *

Not long after Bratton's transfer to headquarters, he was asked to take over an initiative called the Boston-Fenway Program. Prostitution, drug dealing, and drug use were increasing in a part of town that housed such institutions as the Museum of Fine Arts, Symphony Hall, Boston University, and Fenway Park, home of the Boston Red Sox. Suburban arts patrons had become afraid to visit; Boston University had started hinting that it might eventually have no choice but to move to the suburbs. The Boston-Fenway Program was supposed to combat the growing disorder. At its core were neighborhood panels in which 15 or so local leaders talked with the police—including regular patrol officers, a novel arrangement at the time.

At first, Bratton focused on what he saw as serious crime. He was meticulous about tracking crime—his penchant for crime maps earned him the nickname "Lord of the Dots"—and the maps clearly identified rape, burglary, assaults, muggings, robberies, and auto theft as the most pressing problems. In the South End, for instance, police were worried about a string of robberies. But at the community meetings, Bratton kept hearing about different concerns: prostitution, after-hours clubs, loud parties, and public drinking. The sore spot in the South End was dirty streets: street sweepers couldn't clean them because of illegally parked cars, and though the scofflaws got tickets, they rarely got towed. So after one complaint-filled meeting, Bratton decided to do what the community wanted. For days, police officers wrote tickets and towed cars.

In the process, something unexpected happened. While out writing tickets, one of the cops started chatting with a resident about the South End burglaries. It turned out that the resident had seen someone suspicious around the time of a recent break-in. The officer handed the tip to detectives, who arrested the offender and ended the burglary spree. Bratton had learned an important lesson: addressing public concerns about disorder could prevent more serious crimes.

Others were intuiting that connection, too. In New York City, Deputy Mayor Herb Sturz had begun to urge police to target disorder in midtown Manhattan. In 1980, sociologist Nathan Glazer argued that graffiti in New York City's subway system sent a message that the trains carried "uncontrollable predators" and, by sending that message, encouraged those predators to appear. Two years later, the connection between disorder and danger became still more coherent with the publication in *The Atlantic Monthly* of "Broken Windows: The Police and Neighborhood Safety," by James Q. Wilson and

George Kelling. The article advanced two arguments: that small problems left unaddressed tended to give rise to bigger problems; and that cops walking the beat, whom modern police administrators viewed as relics of the past, were in fact engaged in the vital task of maintaining order and enforcing quality-of-life issues.

Though the article caused a sensation among policymakers and the public, criminologists weren't interested in exploring the Broken Windows theory. In 1983, the National Institute of Justice prepared to fund an experimental assessment of the proposition that reducing disorder could reduce crime. At the last minute, the project was rejected. Not until 1990 would a police department test the theory on a large scale. The test took place under the most adverse circumstances imaginable: in the New York City subway system. And the experimenter was Bill Bratton, who—after successful stints running police departments for the Massachusetts Bay Transit Authority and Massachusetts's Metropolitan District Commission—had just been hired as the new chief of the New York City Transit Police.

* * *

In his previous positions, Bratton had begun to develop what he thought of as a doctor's kit for damaged police departments. For example, he thought that morale was important. So when he arrived in New York, he improved both the transit police's uniforms (adding commando-style sweaters) and weapons (issuing modern Glocks, a distinct improvement on the old revolvers). Bratton also upgraded the department's radio system, so that the transit cops could communicate underground.

But the most celebrated aspect of Bratton's tenure as transit chief was his embrace of the Broken Windows theory. Along with Kelling, who was working as a consultant for the transit police, he emphasized catching fare beaters. The transit cops who, following his orders, started arresting turnstile jumpers made a surprising discovery: one in seven was wanted on an outstanding warrant, and one in 21 was carrying a weapon. In short, enforcing the law was also an excellent way to arrest felons and fugitives, which in turn drove down crime rates and public fear. Bratton's subway successes vindicated Broken Windows as a policing strategy and put Bratton on track to become Rudy Giuliani's commissioner of the NYPD in 1994.

It also created a problem that bedevils the NYPD to this day: a widespread tendency to confuse Broken Windows with "zero tolerance" policing. The British press has been particularly zealous about describing the NYPD's approach as "zero tolerance." It isn't. "Broken Windows has always been a negotiated sense of order in a community, in which you negotiate with residents about what is appropriate behavior in an area," says Kelling. "If you tell your cops, 'We are going to go in and practice zero tolerance for all minor crimes,' you are inviting a mess of trouble." The idea that authorities alone, without community involvement, should implement a zero-tolerance policy toward anything more than the most limited problems of crime or disorder disturbs Kelling greatly. Both he and Bratton view it as the single most misunderstood legacy of their time in New York.

Their concern isn't academic or theoretical: there *was* a place where observers could have watched the effect of zero-tolerance policing, had they cared to look for it. That place was South Los Angeles, where Daryl Gates's Operation Hammer was shattering relations between the police and minority communities. One of the officers working Operation Hammer was Charlie Beck, who today is chief of the LAPD, having succeeded Bratton in 2009. Like most officers, Beck supported the department's tough approach. Then came the Rodney King riots. "All the strategies that tore down willing cooperation made a lot less sense after those nights," he says.

* * *

As the NYPD's commissioner, Bratton famously presided over an unprecedented crime drop while developing such innovations as Compstat, the department's computerized crime-tracking system. By the time he resigned in 1996, he was the most lauded lawman in the world. But when he arrived in Los Angeles in 2002, he had his work cut out for him. Violent crime was rising; the number of homicides was on track to exceed 600 for the first time since 1996. (The city would ultimately register 654 homicides that year.) The police department was still operating under federal oversight after the Rampart scandal. The relationship between the LAPD and Los Angeles's minority communities, particularly the African-American community, was poisonous.

And Bratton's doctor's kit looked nearly empty. For one thing, L.A. had just 9,000 cops on staff—about 27 per 10,000 residents, far fewer than New York City's 53 and Chicago's 49—making it hard to cover the large city. Bratton wanted to expand the force to 12,000 officers. In the past, he had typically looked for an incident that would mobilize the public to demand more spending on public safety. In New York City, it had been the murder of Brian Watkins, a tourist from Utah in town for the U.S. Open; in Boston, it had been the accidental slaying in a gang beef of 12-year-old Tiffany Moore, struck with three bullets while sitting on her front stoop in Dorchester. In Los Angeles, Bratton focused on 14-year-old Clive Jackson, a basketball player and honors student who had steered clear of the gangs in his South L.A. neighborhood and been murdered by a 17-year-old gangbanger anyway. Bratton was determined to use the incident to rally the city for more resources. His press conference made the front page of the *Los Angeles Times*, but in a matter of days, the story died. L.A. was apparently too big and sprawling to elicit the communal responses that had occurred in Boston and New York.

The LAPD's size was a problem in another way. In New York, Bratton had moved quickly to replace the top brass with more aggressive chiefs, forcing four of the department's five senior commanders to resign in his first week on the job. The LAPD simply wasn't big enough for such a sweeping turnover. Also, Bratton's expertise was in turning around demoralized police departments. The LAPD, by contrast, was parochial and proud. When Bratton decided to import Compstat from New York, for example, the LAPD brass were hostile to the consultant whom he hired to run the process, former NYPD chief of department Louis Anemone.

So with limited resources, Bratton decided to focus on a handful of high-priority areas: Hollywood, Baldwin Village, the San Fernando Valley, MacArthur Park, and Skid Row downtown. He also brought Broken Windows policing to Los Angeles and called in Kelling to guide the effort. Because the LAPD had a history of enforcing minor ordinances, such as the law against jaywalking, Broken Windows didn't generate the pushback in L.A. that it had in New York (with the notable exception of Skid Row, where the LAPD's actions led to a lawsuit by the American Civil Liberties Union of Southern California; see the previous chapter).

At the same time, Bratton continued Bernard Parks's efforts to soften the hard edges of certain LAPD practices: making suspects kneel on the street with their hands behind their heads, for example, and "proning out," making them stand spread-eagled against a wall to be searched. "We were still every bit as assertive," says Bratton, "but we were cutting back on some of the practices, such as the proning, such as the kneeling, while at the same time working on officer behavior." Captains were now required to respond in person to homicides. Dead bodies were treated with greater respect.

Bratton worked hard, too, at building relationships in the black community. In his early years as chief, he made a point of responding in person to many homicides. He also courted the city's African-American leadership, many of whom had made their names suing the LAPD. He started with two of the department's most outspoken critics, the Urban League's John Mack and civil rights attorney Connie Rice. Even before he was selected as police chief, Bratton paid a courtesy call on Mack, quizzing him for two hours about his thoughts on the department. And Bratton asked Rice, who had repeatedly sued the LAPD on issues as varied as its use of dogs to its treatment of minority officers, to conduct a new investigation of the allegations surrounding misconduct at the Rampart Division.

Bratton also hired Gerry Chaleff—a noted criminal-defense lawyer and former president of the Board of Police Commissioners who was working for the city on matters related to the consent decree—to serve as commanding officer of the department's consent-decree bureau. Bratton stationed Chaleff next to his own office, an important sign of status in the hierarchy-conscious LAPD. By publicly embracing the consent decree, Bratton sought to demonstrate to both the department and the city his commitment to change. One difference between the current NYPD and the LAPD, suggests Bratton, is that the NYPD's very successes have meant that it hasn't had to explain itself. "Because of the consent decree," in contrast, the LAPD "had to explain itself every step of the way."

* * *

The greatest change that Bratton made was in the composition of the LAPD. When he scanned the 106 officers with the rank of captain or higher for talent, he found a cadre of officers with deep roots in the department who were nonetheless committed to fundamental change. Among their number was Charlie Beck. Bratton quickly spotted Beck's aptitude and tapped him for a series of increasingly challenging assignments, such as cleaning up Skid Row and revitalizing the Rampart Division in the wake of the corruption scandal.

Another promoted officer was Pat Gannon, a white-haired Irish-American cop from the Harbor Division whom Bratton made the commander of the 77th Street Division, the epicenter of gang crime in L.A. Within a month of Gannon's arrival, a shooting war erupted. Despite requesting and receiving 200 additional officers to flood the area, Gannon couldn't stop the cycle of retaliation. But he knew that he had to do something. Bratton's new Compstat didn't merely track crime; it also held precinct commanders accountable for crime surges in their areas. In the old LAPD, headquarters would roll out impressive-sounding programs with beautiful charts and brochures that were sometimes "really light on substance," Gannon recollects. Bratton communicated something different: "In the 77th, my job was to reduce crime. My job was to figure out different ways to make that happen in a structure where I was accountable for that."

This was highly motivating—so motivating that Gannon did something desperate. He turned to an acquaintance from his days in the Harbor Division who was a gang intervention worker. Since at least the time of the Rodney King riots, gang interventionists had worked the streets of South and East L.A. Most were onetime gang members, so the police viewed them suspiciously, not without reason. But Gannon had watched this intervention worker shut down gang feuds simply by providing gang members with accurate information. The interventionist agreed to introduce himself to the players in South L.A., provided Gannon himself was willing to show up—alone, in civilian clothes, and at the place of their choosing. Gannon agreed. After two meetings in which discussion focused on the misdeeds of the LAPD, Gannon pushed back, telling the group that the shooting war between the Rolling 60s and the Inglewood Family needed to end. The shooting stopped.

Gannon's success caught Beck's attention. In 2006, when Beck became deputy chief, he introduced himself to Bo Taylor, one of the city's most prominent gang interventionists. When Taylor mentioned that he was hosting a meeting of gang interventionists at his house, Beck decided to stop by. The group was startled to have an LAPD deputy chief just show up—in civilian clothes, no less—and even more startled to have him stay for several hours, listening and talking. Eventually, Beck, Taylor, and Connie Rice agreed that the city should develop a curriculum for gang intervention workers and provide training and credentials for them. They found a willing partner in Mayor Antonio Villaraigosa, who in 2008 established a new office to train and fund intervention workers.

* * *

Bratton's ability to convert the department's fiercest detractors into partners, his knack for promoting talented officers, and his method of holding them accountable led to fundamental changes in perception. By 2009, surveys showed that 83 percent of Angelenos believed that the LAPD was doing a good or an excellent job, up from 71 percent two years earlier. The percentage of residents saying that the police in their communities treated members of all racial and ethnic groups fairly "almost all the time" or "most of the time" rose from 44 percent in 2005 to 51 percent in 2009. When asked to assess personal experiences, a majority of every racial and ethnic group in Los Angeles reported that most LAPD officers treated them, their friends, and their family with respect. Bratton accomplished this while driving crime down dramatically—especially violent crime. Its rate during his final year in L.A. was 54 percent lower than it had been during his predecessor's final year. In July 2009, a federal judge lifted the consent decree that had saddled the LAPD since the Rampart scandal. Two months later, Bratton announced that, after seven years in Los Angeles, he was resigning and would return to New York to serve as chairman of Kroll, a security consulting firm.

The safety spree has continued since Bratton's departure, thanks to an LAPD leadership that "has changed fundamentally—to the bone," as Rice says. Under Beck, violent crime has fallen an additional 26 percent. By the end of 2012, in all likelihood, Los Angeles will have seen two consecutive years of double-digit reductions in gang-related crime. Beck is proud of those statistics, but there's another that he's equally proud of: though the LAPD today has nearly 2,200 more officers than it did in 1992, it arrests just two-thirds the number of people it did then. Some senior commanders now work on *not* arresting certain types of people, such as juveniles, for whom a conviction is effectively the beginning of a criminal career.

It's hard to document the precise effects of the LAPD's reconciliation with the black and Latino communities, but the department's brass unanimously support it. "Based on my experience, unequivocally I will tell you it works," says Bob Green, who runs operations in South L.A. "Shootings are down, violent crime is down, and I don't have the aggravated relations that I have had in the past." The numbers bear him out: crime in Los Angeles has fallen to the levels that New York City enjoys, or even lower, by some measures.

In August 2010, federal law enforcement authorities led a massive raid on the Pueblo del Rio housing development, a stronghold of the Pueblo Bishop Bloods. Doors were kicked down, guns were brandished, and dozens of residents were arrested. Roughly 1,000 officers, federal and local, were involved (a sign of how big L.A.'s gang problems remain). Some Pueblo del Rio residents were upset by the size of the raid. The following day, Guillermo Cespedes, Los Angeles's deputy mayor for gang reduction and youth development, attended a community meeting. "So here I am, cornered in this meeting, thinking I'm going to get chewed out for being part of the assault. And it was just the opposite," he says. "What the community was demanding is, 'We need to talk to LAPD. We don't trust what the feds are telling us.'" And not only did residents want to talk to the cops; "they wanted to have meetings with specific captains that they had relationships with."

* * *

Perhaps the most dramatic transformation has occurred in Watts. Stretched along the northern edge of the Imperial Highway is the largest cluster of public-housing developments west of the Mississippi River. The three largest—Imperial Courts, Nickerson Gardens, and Jordan Downs—were built in the early 1950s, during the vogue for public housing that followed World War II. Though intended to serve as transitional housing, the developments instead became multigenerational communities. In the 1970s, violent gangs took control of each development: Imperial Courts and Jordan Downs fell under the control of the PJ Crips and the Grape Street Crips, respectively, while Nickerson Gardens gave birth to the Bounty Hunter Bloods.

Beck worked gangs in the Watts projects in the late 1970s and 1980s. "It was a surreally brutal time," he says. When crack arrived, things got even worse. Police attempts to open a substation in Imperial Courts were repeatedly thwarted by vandalism. After the department's ninth attempt, the substation was firebombed.

The LAPD presence in Watts is very different today. Every Monday morning, one of the two police captains responsible for the area sits down for two hours with members of the Watts gang task force, a group that consists of community members, gang intervention workers, and others—many of them the mothers and grandmothers of serious gang players. The police never get tips about unsolved crimes, to the great frustration of many detectives. But the meetings do serve as an opportunity to circulate information and to build relationships that shut down situations that might otherwise spiral out of control, such as the peaceful arrest of the burglar that occurred in the spring of 2012 with Captain Tingirides' help.

A week after that arrest, Tingirides attended the Monday meeting and reported on other things the police had done—and things they hadn't. There had been a foot chase through Imperial Courts, he said; the person running had even fired shots at the police, but instead of shooting back, the officers had managed to subdue the runner without using lethal force. The audience applauded. Tingirides also mentioned that some officers had participated in a cleanup at Nickerson Gardens—a place where, not long ago, gang members had routinely fired on LAPD cruisers with assault rifles. Tingirides and his wife, an African-American sergeant who grew up across the street from Nickerson Gardens, had participated. At one point, Tingirides told the room, a neighborhood kid asked his wife what she was digging with. It was a shovel—a tool that the kid didn't recognize. The room fell silent.

The LAPD's improved relations in Watts permit more aggressive policing where the circumstances warrant it, as recently happened in Gonzaque Village, one of the smaller projects there. Gonzaque Village, like Watts as a whole, is divided between Latinos (who now constitute a majority) and African-Americans. But unlike most developments, where a single gang has established control, Gonzaque Village is contested by two rival gangs, the Hacienda Village Bloods and the Hacienda Boys. The Hacienda Village Bloods are mostly black; the Hacienda Boys are mostly Latino.

In April 2012, a Blood put a bullet into the head of a Hacienda Boy. Police officers were promptly deployed in Gonzaque Village. The next day, the Hacienda Boys reciprocated, shooting a Blood in the neck. The LAPD transferred even more officers into the development (a course of action that it explained at the next Monday meeting of the Watts gang task force). The following afternoon, I went out with Captain Jeff Bert to check on his officers. After stopping to talk with a sergeant who was supervising the deployment, we got back into the captain's car. No sooner had we driven 100 yards than we saw a black teenager exit one of the units and cut diagonally across a yard, heading toward the back of the patrol car that we had just left.

It was early afternoon on a warm day, but the hood on the kid's sweatshirt was up. His gait was funny, too, as if he had something shoved into the waistband of his pants—something like a gun. The teen made a beeline toward the officers. "I've got to stop this guy," Bert said. Furtive movements, officer self-defense. It was exactly the kind of stop that a ban on the stop-and-frisk tactic, such as the one advocated by the *New York Times* editorial board, would prohibit.

Bert walked over to the kid. He identified himself, explained that there had been some recent shootings in the neighborhood—indeed, a car with a bullet hole above the back left tire was jacked up for repairs just across the street—and asked the youth to lift his shirt. Bert frisked him. Nothing. The kid continued on his way.

A bad stop? Considering the active gang war under way in Gonzaque Village, surely not. Deploying officers in consultation with local community leaders isn't racial profiling. It's the epitome of community policing. "I call them part police officer, part social worker," says Mack. "They're cops with hearts. I think this is some groundbreaking stuff."

* * *

Groundbreaking stuff may be just what police departments across the nation need. Since 1994, the United States has experienced a 40 percent crime decline. By all accounts, today's cops are more professional, more effective, and less corrupt than ever. Yet public opinion surveys show that public confidence in the police hasn't risen, especially among blacks. A 2009 Pew Research Center study found that just 14 percent of African-Americans said that they had a great deal of confidence in the proposition that local police officers treated blacks and whites equally, compared with 38 percent of whites.

A National Academy of Sciences panel has called the discrepancy between cops' performance and reputation "the paradox of American policing." If police forces around the country want to solve that paradox, they should take lessons from the LAPD—and from the man who fixed it.

[2013]

16

The Sidewalks of San Francisco

Can the City by the Bay Reclaim Public Space from Aggressive Vagrants?

Heather Mac Donald

THE HOMELESSNESS INDUSTRY HAS PULLED off some impressive feats of rebranding over the years—most notably, turning street vagrancy into a consequence of unaffordable housing, rather than of addiction and mental illness. But for sheer audacity, nothing tops the alchemy that homelessness advocates and their government sponsors are currently attempting in San Francisco. The sidewalks of the Haight-Ashbury district have been colonized by aggressive, migratory youths who travel up and down the West Coast panhandling for drug and booze money. Homelessness, Inc. is trying to portray these voluntary vagabonds as the latest victims of inadequate government housing programs, hoping to defeat an ordinance against sitting and lying on public sidewalks that the Haight community has generated.

The outcome of the industry's rebranding campaign—and of the Haight's competing effort to restore order—will be known in November 2010, when San Franciscans vote on the proposed sit-lie law. That vote will reveal whether San Francisco is ready to join the many other cities that view civilized public space as essential to urban life.

* * *

Four filthy targets of Homelessness, Inc.'s current relabeling effort sprawl across the sidewalk on Haight Street, accosting pedestrians. "Can you spare some change and shit? Will you take me home with you?" Cory, a slender, dark-haired young man from Ventura, California, cockily asks passersby. "Dude, do you have any food?" His two female companions, Zombie and Eeyore, swig from a bottle of pricey Tejava tea and pass a smoke while lying on

Illustration by Arnold Roth.

a blanket surrounded by a fortress of backpacks, bedrolls, and scrawled signs asking for money. Vincent, a fourth "traveler," as the Haight Street punks call themselves, stares dully into space. All four sport bandannas around their necks—to ward off freight-train exhaust as they pass through tunnels, they explain—as well as biker's gloves and a large assortment of tattoos and metal hardware. The girls wear necklaces and bracelets of plastic disks and other hip found objects; their baggy tank tops and stockings are stylishly torn.

A petite Asian woman passes the group and smilingly hands Cory the remains of a submarine sandwich. Suddenly, all four are on their feet, tearing at the sub. As Zombie stuffs the bread into her mouth, partly chewed chunks fall back out onto the ground.

Such juvenile hobos see themselves as on a "mission," though they're hard-pressed to define it. Sometimes they follow rock bands, and other times more mysterious imperatives, between Seattle, Portland, Santa Cruz, Berkeley, Venice Beach, and San Diego. Some are runaways; some are college dropouts; others are years older. Eeyore says she got kicked out of her Riverside, California, home at 14 because she was "a punk and an asshole."

Of all the destinations on the "traveler" circuit, the Haight carries a particular attraction to the young panhandlers, thanks to the Summer of Love. Starting in late 1965, waves of teens from across the country began pouring into what was then a ramshackle, blue-collar neighborhood of pastel Victorian houses and low-rent businesses, drawn to the emergent drug culture and its promised liberation from the bourgeois values of self-discipline and hard work. "The time has come to be free," a local flyer proclaimed. "Be FREE. Do your thing. Be what you are. Do it. Now." This insipid philosophy was eventually co-opted by consumer capitalism, while the hippie ethos gave way to punk, daisy chains to piercing, acid to meth, and mindless utopianism to mindless nihilism. In the Haight itself, national chain stores like American Apparel, McDonald's, and Ben & Jerry's found a place next to the head shops, tie-dye boutiques, and check-cashing outlets. But the kids kept coming.

The defining characteristic of all these "travelers" seems to be an acute sense of entitlement. "If you can afford this shit on Haight Street, then goddamn, you can probably afford to kick down $20 [to a panhandler] and it won't fucking hurt your wallet," a smooth-faced blond boy from Spartanburg, South Carolina, defiantly tells the camera in *The Haight Street Kids*, a documentary by Stanford University's art department. I ask the group on the blanket: Why should people give you money? "They got a dollar and I don't," Cory replies. Why don't you work? "We do work," retorts Eeyore. "I carry around this heavy backpack. We wake up at 7 AM and work all day. It's hard work." She's referring to begging and drinking. She adds judiciously: "Okay, my liver hates me, but I like the idea of street performance. We're trying to get a dollar for beer." More specifically, they're aiming for two Millers and a Colt 45 at the moment, explains Zombie. Aren't you embarrassed to be begging? "I'm not begging, I'm just asking for money," Cory says, seemingly convinced of the difference. How much do you make? "In San Francisco, you don't get much—maybe $30 to $40 a day," says Eeyore. "When you're traveling, you can make about $100 on freeway off-ramps."

What more conventional people consider "employment" is, in the eyes of the street punk, something conferred gratuitously. "People see you, they're like, 'Get a job.' You're like, 'Okay, pay me, hire me. You know, *do* something!'" a boy complains on a promotional video made by Larkin Street Youth Services, a local organization that serves "homeless" youth. Meantime, welfare will do just fine. A strapping young redhead trudging down Haight Street with a bedroll and a large backpack explains the convenience of his electronic food-stamp card, which he can use to pick up his benefits wherever he happens to be—whether in Eugene, Oregon, where he started his freight-train route last Halloween, or in California.

Over the last several years, the Haight's vagrant population has grown more territorial and violent, residents and merchants say. Pit bulls are a frequent fashion accessory, threatening and sometimes injuring passersby. In July 2010, two pit bulls bred by the residents of an encampment in nearby Golden Gate Park tore into three pedestrians, biting a 71-year-old woman to the bone and wounding her two companions. In October 2009, one of three punks sitting on a blanket with dogs spat on a 14-month-old baby when its mother rejected their demand for change. The vagrants carry knives and Mace; people who ask them to move risk getting jumped.

Merchants trying to clean up feces and urine left by the alcohol-besotted youth are sometimes harassed and attacked. Kent Uyehara, the proprietor of a skateboard shop in the Haight, has gotten into fistfights with vagrants when he tells them that they can't sell marijuana in front of his store. "They start it, but if they say 'F you,' we're going to say 'F you' back," he says matter-of-factly. Business owners, already struggling to stay afloat in the weak economy, worry that shoppers will avoid their stores or the entire neighborhood, rather than navigate around packs of drunken youths on the sidewalk.

* * *

By late 2009, community frustration with the gutter punks' rising aggressiveness had led the Haight's police captain, Teri Barrett, to propose a new law that would ban sitting or lying on city sidewalks from 7 AM to 11 PM. Under current policies, an officer can ask someone sprawled across a sidewalk to move only if he observes a pedestrian being substantially obstructed *and* if that pedestrian will sign a complaint and testify in court against the sidewalk sprawler. Few pedestrians are willing to do so; as for the merchants themselves, they fear retaliation. After the manager of a boutique selling "Goth" clothing installed outdoor cameras and called the police about the vagrants outside her store, the vagrants threw live birds, their wings flapping wildly, in a cashier's face.

Barrett's proposed ordinance against sidewalk colonization would remove the current requirement of a civilian victim and allow a police officer to take action on his own. The officer would first have to warn someone sitting or lying on a sidewalk that he was violating the law; only if that person refused to move could the officer issue a citation against him.

Both Mayor Gavin Newsom and San Francisco's new police chief endorsed the proposed law, later named "Civil Sidewalks." It is similar to ordinances adopted in Seattle, Berkeley, Portland, Santa Cruz, and Palo Alto, all cities with impeccable "progressive" credentials. The police have issued few citations under those laws; as in San Francisco, their main purpose is to give officers the authority to ask squatters to move along and to prevent the hostile occupation of public space.

* * *

The homelessness industry instantly mobilized against the Civil Sidewalks law. Its first tactic was to assimilate the gutter punks into the "homelessness" paradigm, so that they could be slotted into the industry's road-tested narrative about the casualties of a heartless free-market economy. "Homelessness, at its core, is an economic issue," intoned the Coalition on Homelessness, San Francisco's most powerful homelessness advocacy group, in a report criticizing the proposed law. "People are homeless because they cannot afford rent." Even applied to the wizened shopping-cart pushers of the traditional "homeless" population, this simplistic statement is deeply misleading. But applied to the able-bodied Haight vagrants, it is simply ludicrous, entailing a cascading series of misrepresentations regarding the role of choice in youth street culture. The Haight punks may not be able to afford rent, but that is because they choose to do no work and mooch off those who do. Further, they are not *looking* for housing. They have no intention of settling down in San Francisco or anywhere else. The affordability or unaffordability of rent is thus irrelevant to their condition.

Shoehorning the street kids into the homeless category requires ignoring their own "voices," ordinarily a big no-no among "progressives" when it comes to official victims of capitalism and other oppressions. They are not homeless, the "travelers" insist, and they look down on those who are. "When you stop traveling and stay on the street, you become a home bum," Eeyore says. A stringy, middle-aged alcoholic buzzes around Eeyore and her

Illustration by Arnold Roth.

companions' blanket, offering incoherent sallies. Asked if the older guy is an acquaintance, Cory scoffs, "He's just some crazy that wandered up," in between more pitches for food and change.

If the "travelers" feel no affinity for the white winos of the Haight and Golden Gate Park, they keep themselves even farther from the largely black street population of the Tenderloin, a drug-infested downtown neighborhood of single-room-occupancy buildings that is San Francisco's other major locus of public disorder. "I don't hang out in the Tenderloin because I don't feel like smoking crack," Cory says primly. Such scruples suggest a keen sense of self-preservation, notes Kent Uyehara. "These kids couldn't handle the Tenderloin," he says. "The local drug dealers won't tolerate hippie punks interrupting their operations; they'd get beaten up or shot."

Trouble in the Tenderloin

Police officers in the Tenderloin are as eager for a sit-lie law as their colleagues in the Haight are. The Tenderloin is the smallest police precinct in the city, but it has the highest number of parolees and sex offenders and the highest rate of violent crime. It's also right next to Union Square, San Francisco's central tourist area. Tourists walking through the Tenderloin to its few remaining theaters have been mugged; those waiting for the cable car at the bottom of Powell Street are routinely accosted by panhandlers. The city's persistent failure to dent the disorder has kept the area, along with the adjacent Market Street Corridor, in thrall to crime and blight for years, as have strict laws protecting single-room-occupancy buildings from acquisition and development. Police officials and local entrepreneurs speak wistfully of the transformation of New York's Times Square, and they still hope that it could happen here.

Whereas street sitters in the Haight are usually engaged in various forms of drug consumption, many in the Tenderloin are in sales. Asked how he would use the proposed sit-lie ordinance, Officer Adam Green responds, "I'd ask these ladies to move on," referring to a group of women sitting on folding chairs on the sidewalk. Green's "ladies" are most likely holding drugs for the dealers milling around a few paces down the block. "It's a very sophisticated game," Green explains. "They know it's harder for us to search women. We try to prevent people from congregating, because that's when we get our drive-by shootings." (A few weeks later, an Oakland man wearing body armor was gunned down in the Tenderloin in a cascade of 16 bullets, saved from death only by his foresight in putting on his bulletproof vest before entering the area.) Other sidewalk sitters serve as lookouts against the cops.

Green and his partner, Officer Ed Saenz, recognize some of the dealers waiting for customers down the street from an arrest they made yesterday. "That guy in the blue hat was giving us a lot of lip. It would also be nice if people actually went to jail without being immediately released."

A second category of Tenderloin sidewalk occupants represents what the Haight kids will become if they continue their "traveling" lifestyle. A middle-aged woman with bright red hair and smeared lipstick, a leopard-skin jacket, green-painted nails, and red-and-black striped stockings is passed out on the sidewalk, behind a miniature pyramid of nine Milk Duds. Saenz radios for an ambulance while Green grabs her ear. "Wake up, Kelly! How much did you drink today?" After prolonged shaking, she rouses herself, grimacing and shaking her head: "Just a little bitty one." "She's got caramel tunnel syndrome," the officers joke, referring to the candy used by alcoholics to prevent their blood sugar from dropping precipitously. Allowed to sit on the sidewalk all day, alcoholics like Kelly often become victims of robbery and assault when they doze off.

A reed-thin black man with a grizzled beard and sore-infested legs barely manages to sit upright on the curb in front of Kelly. He's far from his usual post at Union Square, the officers note. They had given him a citation a few hours earlier for drinking in public, which the Coalition on Homelessness will make sure is dismissed in court; now his inebriation has progressed even further. A fire truck drives up to take the two drunks to the city's free detox center; 80 percent of the fire department's runs are devoted to picking up drunks or providing other emergency services, at huge taxpayer expense. Sometimes the officers themselves provide the rides to the detox center or a hospital. "We're like paramedics," observes Green. "C'mon, Joe, your ride's here," Saenz says encouragingly. "Give it your best!"

Though the police fervently hope that under the data-driven policing of Chief George Gascón, the Tenderloin will show the same capacity for renewal as Manhattan's once-crime-ridden neighborhoods, parts of San Francisco's populace seem as indifferent to violent crime as they are to public disorder. In August 2010, a German schoolteacher visiting San Francisco to celebrate her wedding anniversary and 50th birthday was killed in crossfire outside a dance party in the Tenderloin, a block from her hotel. Public reaction to the shooting was strangely muted, probably in part because of political correctness and the sense that the victims in these periodic club shootings are usually other gangbangers. Perhaps, too, such public passivity in the face of crime owes to the city's lack of a tabloid newspaper; in New York, such grisly events, which were common in the early 1990s, sparked widespread outrage in no small part because papers like the *New York Post* made them front-page news.

Whatever the reason, a proposed Starbucks or other chain store in a favorite neighborhood seems to provoke more organized indignation among affluent San Franciscans than a random killing. This hierarchy of concern may partly explain why San Francisco's violent crime rate was higher than that of Los Angeles or New York in 2008.

An unintentionally hilarious letter to the *San Francisco Chronicle* in January 2010 revealed just why the homelessness-industrial complex is so desperate to claim the Haight infestation for itself: government contracts. "The majority of the youth on the streets and in the park are in the Haight seeking support to address the issues that have led them there," wrote the executive director of Larkin Street Youth Services in criticizing the sit-lie proposal. "Funding to help these youths through outreach, case management, education and employment has been severely cut over the past two years. . . . Rather than rallying in anger, a better use of our time is to focus on helping youths exit the streets so they can find work and housing and become contributing members of the community." Translation: Homelessness, Inc. wants more money.

Larkin Street's analysis of why people hang out in the Haight is as wildly inaccurate as the Coalition's fingering of unaffordable rent. Few, if any, of these vagrants are "in the Haight seeking support to address the issues that have led them there," unless "support" means money for booze and drugs. To the contrary, the "youth" are there to party, en route to their next way station. As a platinum blonde boozily announces in *The Haight Street Kids*: "I love this city, love your fucking life." A tall youth draped around her adds: "It's awesome for traveling kids to stop in when they need a break."

Predictably, the offer of services and housing—which San Francisco's round-the-clock outreach workers constantly put before the Haight Street vagrants—is usually turned down. As for becoming "contributing members of the community," that's definitely not on the agenda, either. Asked what he saw for himself in the future, a "traveler" in the Stanford documentary rolls his eyes, smiles nervously, and shakes his head for nearly a minute before replying: "A hot dog, there's definitely a hot dog in my future."

But a social-services empire has grown up around the street vagrants; its members' livelihood depends on a large putative "client" population, even if the clients aren't interested in their services. Enforcing laws designed to ensure safe and accessible public spaces is the most effective means of changing behavior, which is why the sit-lie law is such a threat to Homelessness, Inc. San Francisco has poured billions of dollars into nonprofit groups and subsidized housing over nearly three decades; the street population perceptibly wanes and becomes less aggressive only during those intermittent periods when the city summons the will to enforce common norms of public behavior.

In March 2010, Santa Cruz's mayor testified to the San Francisco Board of Supervisors (the city is also a county) about Santa Cruz's own sit-lie law. The ordinance had a "major impact on making sidewalks passable," Mayor Mike Rotkin said, by "sending a message that it was not acceptable to claim turf and live on the sidewalk all day." After years of ineffectual social-services spending, Santa Cruz's vagrant youth population started acting more civilly a mere couple of weeks after the ordinance passed. Such results are why San Francisco's advocates must prevent these instructive experiments in law enforcement from happening in the first place.

* * *

The homelessness industry's second tactic was to demonize Civil Sidewalks supporters as motivated by hatred toward the poor. "This issue makes me sick to my stomach," the head of the Coalition on Homelessness, Jennifer Friedenbach, told a supervisors' meeting in May 2010. "It makes me sick because we're putting into place another law that promotes hatred and that will codify economic profiling. Giving tickets for being destitute is not what a civilized society engages in." Mary Howe, executive director of the Homeless Youth Alliance, a needle-exchange program in the Haight, testified at the same hearing that it was "disgusting that there was not more compassion where there is not enough affordable housing."

Needless to say, the sit-lie law says nothing about economic status; what it "profiles" is not wealth but behavior. The Haight Street vagrants colonize the sidewalk all day not because they are poor but because doing so is the essence of their "traveling" lifestyle. And a resident or store owner afflicted by punks threatening passersby in front of his home or business is indifferent to how much money is in their pockets; he's even indifferent to the constant panhandling. He only wants a passageway open and welcoming to all. "I don't care if they ask for change," says Arthur Evans, a self-described former hippie from Greenwich Village who has lived in the neighborhood for 35 years. "It's okay if they loiter and make a bit of noise. But I don't feel safe walking down the Haight at night any more."

The statement from the Homeless Youth Alliance's director about "affordable housing" is the usual non sequitur: the gutter punks are not looking for housing, whether temporary or permanent. Every night, about 100 beds in the city's shelter system remain vacant, though outreach workers are always trying to get people to use them. As for permanent housing, you're not going to be able to afford rent at any level if you opt out of working or studying. And while some of the street colonists may come from truly impoverished backgrounds—though such a fact is irrelevant to the validity of the proposed law—others do not. Two blondes in "The Haight Street Interviews," a YouTube video, explain that they "got to escape the whole private school mentality" by starting to follow punk bands in seventh grade.

* * *

Finally, the homelessness advocates pulled out their trump card: associating supporters of the Civil Sidewalks law with "business interests." San Francisco "progressives" regard businessmen as aliens within the body politic whose main function is to provide an inexhaustible well of funds to transfer to the city's social-services empire. If it weren't for vigilant politicians, however, the interlopers would constantly seek to duck this ever-growing civic obligation. "If these corporations pay their fair share," supervisor John Avalos explained in 2009 when introducing a new business tax, "we can generate millions that will go towards keeping health clinics, youth and senior services, and jobs safe for San Franciscans." (The contradiction between raising business taxes and keeping jobs safe was lost on Avalos.)

So the sit-lie opponents portrayed the law as the brainchild of the rapacious profit seekers, even though the Haight's residents were as instrumental in its genesis as local merchants were. "I've heard we should pander to business," a member of the Coalition on Homelessness told the supervisors in May 2010. "To that I say: San Francisco is not a theme park for tourists. If they want a squeaky-clean world, they should go to Six Flags and pay for the privilege." Tourists who can't get by someone on the sidewalk, she continued, "need to develop some spine and say 'excuse me.'" (Those on the sidewalk can't be expected to say "excuse me" for blocking everyone else.)

* * *

Such cluelessness about the challenges of creating a business and staying afloat is typical of advocates everywhere, as is the aristocratic assumption that San Franciscans will always enjoy an endless supply of tourist dollars, no matter the street conditions. What makes San Francisco unique is that so many of its elected officials have just as limited an understanding of civil society. And no one embodies this contempt for the private sector more than supervisor Chris Daly, a youthful-looking former activist now representing the Tenderloin.

Daly's signature blend of pomposity and childishness was on full display in the hearing on the sit-lie law, during which he condescended to an assistant chief of police, the mayor's public-safety advisor, a small-business owner, and the Chamber of Commerce. He fulfilled the spirit, if not the letter, of his earlier pledge to use the f-word at every board meeting, a tradition for which he had already laid ample groundwork during past foulmouthed public tantrums. "You can sugarcoat shit, but that doesn't make it ice cream," he said, in reference to the proposed law. But his most distinguishing touch was to see the law as all about himself and his fellow "progressives." In Daly's fantasy narrative, the bill's real purpose was to unseat the board's progressive bloc by creating a "wedge issue" that would mobilize moderate and conservative voters in the November election. The desire of residents and proprietors across the city for passable, open public spaces, in Daly's view, was a front orchestrated by the nefarious Chamber of Commerce. Maintaining this story line, for which no shred of evidence exists, required Daly to dismiss the testimony of mothers worried about walking their children to school and of struggling managers who told of losing customers unwilling to navigate the human mess in front of their stores.

The unexpected twists and turns of Daly's monologues, not to mention their length, may put a listener in mind of a certain obsolete Caribbean dictator. In the middle of his opening harangue against the sit-lie law, he interjected, for no apparent reason: "My name is Chris Daly. I'm a homeless advocate." Having caught everyone's attention with this oddly timed piece of information, he went on: "I was elected ten years ago talking about affordable housing and I'm still talking about it. We're lying if we say that measures like this will get us there. We need radical changes in budget priorities. . . . We need to move money from the sacred cows of fire and police to housing and special needs."

Leaving aside the eternal irrelevance of "affordable housing" to the Haight gutter punks, the notion that San Francisco has been stiffing welfare spending in favor of fire and police is ludicrous. In the 2009 fiscal year, the city spent $175 million on homelessness, compared with a $442 million police budget. That's $26,865 in services for each of the city's 6,514 "homeless" persons, the majority of whom are housed in city-subsidized lodgings, compared with $52 per San Franciscan on police protection. (Including such indirect services for the homeless as paramedic calls and psychiatric services for inmates would bring the per-capita rate much higher.) The rest of San Francisco's massive social-services spending, including health care and welfare, was nearly $3 billion in 2009, compared with a combined police and fire budget of $720 million. (The fire department could, in any case, be considered part of the city's service empire, since most of its runs are for non-fire-related emergency services, often for passed-out vagrants.)

* * *

The weirdest argument against the sit-lie law marshaled by Daly and his allies at the May 2010 supervisors' meeting was that the new measure was not even necessary, since the police already had the legal authority to move people along who were sitting on the sidewalk. Why the police would go to the trouble of seeking a new ordinance when they could just use an existing one was never explained—nor was the incongruity of the progressives' arguing for the existence and use of a power that they fiercely oppose.

At issue in the supervisors' odd claim is the requirement of a civilian complainant under the existing law. Police officials and city attorneys testified that under the current ordinance, judges would not entertain a prosecution unless a civilian victim of sidewalk obstruction had done the unlikely and come forward. (And as Santa Cruz's mayor had testified in the supervisors' earlier meeting, quality-of-life laws requiring third-party complainants are "completely ineffective.") Daly and fellow supervisors David Campos and Ross Mirkarimi, however, hammered city witnesses on the fact that the current sidewalk obstruction law does not *explicitly* state that a civilian victim and complainant is needed. True, but the courts have inferred that requirement in interpreting the statute—and judicial practice is just as controlling an authority.

The progressives' obsessive statutory nit-picking deflects attention from certain key but unstated facts. First, the board's leftists seem not to understand—or else simply reject—the concept of public order. Campos badgered an assistant police chief about his statement that the sit-lie law's purpose was to "protect neighborhood safety and vitality." Such an idea apparently flummoxed Campos: "What exactly do you mean by 'neighborhood vitality'? What conduct hurts it?" he asked. One trip to the Haight should be enough to answer that question. Campos then took up the hairsplitting strategy: "Activities when you are standing up can also hurt 'neighborhood vitality.' So what is the conduct you are trying to stop?" The fact that a law does not target all negative behavior does not mean that stopping *some* negative behavior is illegitimate. San Francisco does not hesitate to ban discrimination against gays just because other groups might independently face discrimination.

Second, the progressives reject Broken Windows theory—the idea that an environment where low-level offenses are pervasive is likely to breed higher-level offenses—notwithstanding the universal experience of law enforcement officials that allowing people to flout public norms and to take over public space all day, often drinking, leads to more serious crimes.

* * *

The supervisors voted in June 2010 against the sit-lie law eight to three, though the public had backed it by a 71 to 24 percent margin in an earlier 2010 poll. (In the Haight itself, support for the law, though strong, is not unanimous: one merchant has called for a boycott of businesses that endorse the measure, which he sees as the advance wedge of "gentrification.") The supervisors' vote reflects both a recent change and longer-term trends in San Francisco's politics and culture.

Since 2000, San Francisco has held district elections for supervisors, replacing the traditional citywide franchise. It now takes fewer votes and a far smaller campaign chest to get elected; local nonprofit social-services groups and unions man get-out-the-vote drives that easily push their preferred candidates into city hall. The resulting boards have made even their liberal 1990s predecessors look moderate (though those earlier boards were as much a product of Mayor Willie Brown's vacancy appointments as they were of at-large elections). Developers "bleed money to non-profits of the supervisors' choosing," according to the *San Francisco Weekly*. During budget negotiations in 2009, the board used a barely legal maneuver to restore cut funds to specific social-services groups in their districts, including one that provided a festive "Ladies' Night" for prostitutes. This action violated the intent of a law that the supervisors fund only government departments, not specific non-profit grantees, reported the *San Francisco Public Press*.

The tight alliance between politicians and service providers within Homelessness, Inc. has not gone unnoticed by city residents. At the May 2010 hearing on the sit-lie law, a petite young black woman mocked the progressives' claim that they were "fighting for the [homeless] population." "You people in the social-service mafia make money off this population," she retorted, "and then go home to neighborhoods where people are not loitering, puking, and pissing outside your door 24 hours a day. We don't need you here; we need accountability for low-income residents who go to work and don't do drugs 24/7."

But the supervisors' contempt for the economic engine that makes government social-services spending possible also stems from changes in the city's political culture that long predate district elections. Hard as it is to believe today, San Francisco once understood that entrepreneurial energy was essential to urban vitality. After World War II, San Francisco aspired to rival Manhattan as a world-class center of finance and commerce, positioning itself as the gateway city to the Pacific Rim. A progrowth coalition of mayors, downtown business leaders, and unions launched transportation and other development projects to create the conditions for economic opportunity, writes San Francisco State University professor Richard DeLeon in *Left Coast City*. Voters consistently defeated antidevelopment measures. In the late

1970s, refugees from New York's blackouts, crime, and budgetary disasters found in Frisco a city that still "knew how," in William Howard Taft's phrase.

By the mid-1980s, however, the progrowth coalition had collapsed. The fatal pressures upon it included the loss of such longtime city fathers as industrialist J. D. Zellerbach and banker Charles Blyth, a backlash against the perceived overbuilding of downtown, and the emergence of a new white-collar population with the affluence to value lifestyle over economic growth, DeLeon observes. The passage in 1986 of the most restrictive antigrowth measure of any big city in the country marked the city's transformation. Henceforth, San Francisco would be characterized by a progressivism "concerned with consumption more than production [and] residence more than workplace," writes DeLeon—one that has inured itself to threats of private-sector disinvestment. The city's political elites also developed a taste for identity politics and useless symbolic gestures, especially regarding foreign policy. Public order and economic viability took a backseat to the rapid expansion of municipal unions and the government-subsidized social-services sector.

* * *

The fate of various sit-lie ordinances over the years limns San Francisco's political evolution. In 1968, at hippie high tide, a unanimous board of supervisors passed a law banning sitting and lying on city streets and sidewalks. The board had no trouble understanding the Haight-Ashbury Merchants and Improvement Association's plea that "it's time that our sidewalks were free to walk again."

By 1994, however, Mayor Frank Jordan could not get a narrower sit-lie law past the board of supervisors or the voters (the ACLU had long since eviscerated the 1968 ordinance in the courts). Though the city was already spending $50 million on homeless services and $55 million on welfare for able-bodied single adults (many of whom chose to live on the street and spend their generous checks on drugs and booze rather than rent), the supervisors embraced the line that the proposed sit-lie law "criminalized poverty." Homelessness, Inc. was already a key player in San Francisco politics. After the supervisors rejected the sit-lie law, Jordan placed it on the ballot. In an election year of resurgent leftism that saw the loss of San Francisco's last Republican supervisor, voters were nevertheless much more narrowly divided on the measure than the board was, rejecting it by barely a 2 percent margin.

Between 1994 and today, little permanent progress has been made in the public discourse regarding civil order. San Francisco seems doomed to repeat a one-step-forward-two-steps-back approach to the maintenance of safe and civil streets. Jordan, a former San Francisco police chief, had been elected in 1991 to clean up the city from the chaos tolerated by Mayor Art Agnos, a social worker and well-connected state assemblyman. Jordan crafted thought-ful initiatives that balanced assistance to vagrants with misdemeanor enforce-ment, an approach he dubbed "Matrix."

The homelessness industry found a ready champion against Jordan in for-mer California assembly speaker Willie Brown, one of the most charismatic and powerful politicians in recent California history. Brown promised that he would end Matrix if elected mayor, and upon taking office in 1996, he proved true to his word. Embracing the advocates' mantra that homelessness was a housing and welfare problem, Brown vowed to end it within 100 days. In-stead, within less than a year, he had declared the problem unsolvable. "When I came into office I assumed that making services available would and could cause a reversal of the situation for most people on the streets," Brown said. "I was wrong. . . . There are some people who just don't want to live inside, and there's nothing you can do with them. They are the hobos of the world. They don't want help." As for Homelessness, Inc., Brown said that he would henceforth "ignore" the advocates. "They have their own political agenda," he observed. "They don't know what's going on" in the streets.

Throughout his eight years as mayor, Brown sporadically revived Jordan's quality-of-life law enforcement strategies, usually sub rosa, when the public clamor against needle-infested parkland or refuse-infested plazas grew too loud. The advocates denounced each short-lived initiative as the product of downtown business interests and lambasted Brown as a traitor. A 1996 ef-fort in the Haight to reduce its vagrant youth population collapsed when the youth turned down the offered housing and jobs and the district attorney decided that he couldn't be bothered to prosecute the public-order arrests that the police were bringing in.

From the early 1990s to 2002, spending on vagrancy rose 50 percent, with nothing to show for it. Voters in 2002 rated homelessness as the city's most pressing problem, as they had for years and would continue to do throughout the decade. In another déjà-vu moment, then-supervisor Gavin Newsom, a restaurateur and Brown protégé, resuscitated one of Jordan's most inno-vative ideas: requiring single, able-bodied welfare recipients to use part of their welfare check for housing. Newsom took his proposed Care Not Cash program directly to the public, which voted it in by 60 percent in 2002. The usual machinations followed: a judge overturned the law, and the board then passed a rival, less demanding, measure sponsored by Chris Daly.

Newsom's revenge was to ride Care Not Cash into the mayor's office, win-ning the election in 2003 on his support for tough love. In 2004, the California Supreme Court reinstated Care Not Cash; since then, the number of homeless adults collecting cash welfare has dropped 86 percent. Newsom's reprise of the Jordan playbook continued with a ballot initiative to counter aggressive panhandling (since emasculated by the pro bono defense bar) and, after goading, support for the sit-lie law. In late 2009, a Haight activist fighting for the Civil Sidewalks ordinance observed sarcastically to a local TV reporter that there had been more sightings of the late Jerry Garcia in the Haight than of Newsom, who lives on the tony hilltop a few blocks above the besieged street. Soon thereafter, Newsom publicly acknowledged the Haight disorder and embraced the Civil Sidewalks ordinance.

* * *

Perhaps the lock of Homelessness, Inc. on San Francisco's politics will be broken in November 2010, when citizens will vote on the sit-lie law in a referendum.[1] It is auspicious that the current push for civil sidewalks is coming from the Haight, long viewed as the epicenter of San Francisco's progressive movement. In 1987, antidevelopment radicals there burned down a Thrifty drugstore during construction. Mayor Agnos then refused to meet with Thrifty's president, a moment that epitomized the city's indifference to private enterprise and even the rule of law when it conflicted with the higher prerogatives of progressive political correctness. Now a majority of Haight residents are clamoring for surcease from the intimidation and lawlessness that Homelessness, Inc. declares is the price that a city must pay until every last tax dollar is turned over to itself.

Of course, a victory for the Civil Sidewalks law at the ballot box will not end the matter. San Franciscans have been voting for sensible order-maintenance policies for decades, only to see the supervisors and the courts thwart their will. But there are other hopeful signs of a possible sea change in the city's most counterproductive tendencies. The public defender, unabashedly left-wing on many matters, has put a wide-ranging public-pension-reform measure on the November ballot;[2] a moderate supervisor has sponsored another ballot initiative to eliminate the most egregious transit-union protections.[3] Both measures gleaned a record-breaking number of qualifying signatures, despite the city's traditional inclination to rubber-stamp the demands of municipal-service unions. However, if Newsom's current bid for California lieutenant governor is successful, which would allow the supervisors to appoint his replacement, all bets regarding the implementation of the sit-lie law are off.[4]

Not relying on their possible king-making power, the progressives are fighting back against the sit-lie law at the ballot box. Supervisor Mirkarimi, who represents the Haight, has authored an initiative requiring the police department to engage in "community policing"—specifically, foot patrols—in an effort to draw votes from the sit-lie measure. Mirkarimi, who has pushed foot patrols for years as a foil to what he disparagingly calls "L.A.-style policing," claims that mandating more cops on the beat will resolve whatever disorder problems the Haight may face, thus obviating the need for an allegedly rights-trampling measure like the sit-lie law. If the intention behind Mirkarimi's measure was not clear enough, board of supervisors president David Chiu has added an amendment to it, holding that if the foot-patrol initiative wins with a larger majority than the sit-lie law, out goes the sit-lie law.

The idea that the supervisors have the expertise to dictate police deployment and strategy is laughable, as police chief George Gascón has said. It is also dangerous, since Mirkarimi's foot-patrol requirement could interfere with the department's ability to deploy officers to the city's highest-crime areas, even as Gascón's data-driven policing—"L.A.-style policing," in fact— is just kicking in. But the foot-patrol measure also fails as an alternative to the sit-lie law, since officers walking the beat lack the authority to do anything about the disorder they confront, absent a cooperating victim.

* * *

San Francisco's magical topography has allowed it to indulge in antiurban policies for decades. Even as sector after sector of its economic base has peeled off under the pressure of high taxes, ignorant regulations, and government-inflated housing costs, tourists have kept pumping billions into the city's coffers. Homelessness, Inc. could disparage these visitors, as well as the workers and entrepreneurs who tried to meet their needs, confident that the bay, the islands, the light, and the city's unique architecture would keep the tourist tax dollars—$21.5 million a day in 2009—pouring down.

Such self-indulgence is particularly foolish in a recession. But the sit-lie law is about more than business viability, however important such viability is to a city's lifeblood and energy. It is also about the most basic rules of civilized society, which hold that public spaces should be shared by the public, not monopolized by the disorderly few.

[2010]

Notes

1. The measure, known as Proposition L, passed, 54.3 percent to 45.7 percent.

2. That measure, known as Proposition B, lost, 43.04 percent to 56.96 percent. In 2011, a similar measure, Proposition D—known as "Son of B"—lost, 66.55 percent to 33.45 percent.

3. Voters approved Proposition G, which eliminated pay guarantees for municipal workers, 64.94 percent to 35.06 percent.

4. Newsom was elected easily. Newsom's successor, Ed Lee, has applied the law inconsistently. Though the problems remain in the Haight and elsewhere, Lee used the sit-lie law to instruct police to remove tents that Occupy Wall Street protesters had set up in Justin Herman Plaza.

V

IMMIGRATION DILEMMAS

17

The Rainbow Coalition Evaporates

Black Anger Grows as Illegal Immigrants Transform Urban Neighborhoods

Steven Malanga

TERRY ANDERSON IS ANGRY. From his KRLA-AM radio perch in Los Angeles, the black talk-show host thunders, "I have gone on the streets and talked to people at random here in the black community, and they all ask me the same question: 'Why are our politicians and leaders letting this happen?'" What's got Anderson—motto: "If You Ain't Mad, You Ain't Payin' Attention"—so worked up isn't the Jena Six or nooses on Columbia University doorknobs; it's the illegal immigrants who allegedly murdered three Newark college students in August 2007. And when he excoriates politicians for "letting this happen," he's directing his fire at Congressional Black Caucus members who support open borders and amnesty for illegal aliens. "Massive illegal immigration has been devastating to my community," Anderson, a former auto mechanic and longtime South Central Los Angeles resident, tells listeners. "Black Americans are hit the hardest."

Though blacks have long worried that the country's growing foreign-born population, especially its swelling rolls of illegal immigrants, harmed their economic prospects, they have also followed their political leadership in backing liberal immigration policies. Now, however, as new waves of immigration inundate historically African-American neighborhoods, black opinion is hardening against the influx. "We will not lay down and take this any longer," says Anderson.[1] If he's right, it could upend the political calculus on immigration.

* * *

Black unease about immigration goes back a long way. In the 1870s, former slave Frederick Douglass warned that immigrants were displacing free blacks in the labor market. Twenty-five years later, Booker T. Washington exhorted America's industrialists to "cast down your bucket" not among new immigrants but "among the eight million Negros . . . who have without strikes and labor wars tilled your fields, cleared your forests, builded your railroads and cities." Blacks supported federal legislation in 1882 that restricted Chinese immigration to the United States. They favored the immigration reform acts of the 1920s, which limited European immigration, and also urged restrictions on Mexican workers: "If the million Mexicans who have entered the country have not displaced Negro workers, whom have they displaced?" asked black journalist George Schuyler in 1928.

But the 1960s brought a big change in the views of black political leaders, especially after President Lyndon B. Johnson and congressional supporters of liberalizing immigration claimed the mantle of the civil rights movement for their reforms, which became law in 1965 and resulted in a 60 percent increase in legal immigration over the subsequent decade. Martin Luther King, Jr. believed that blacks and poor immigrants had much in common and could become political allies, which was why, in the run-up to the immigration bill's passage, he endorsed the idea of letting Cubans fleeing Castro settle in Miami. Jesse Jackson would later herald the imminent arrival of a mighty "black-brown" or "rainbow" coalition that would—or so he claimed—propel him to the 1984 Democratic presidential nomination. As it turned out, Jackson failed to win much Hispanic support, which mostly lined up behind Walter Mondale. But Jackson's dream continued to spread among black politicians, including those in the Congressional Black Caucus, which became one of Washington's most vocal groups opposing immigration restrictions.

Black leaders' liberal views clearly helped soften anti-immigration attitudes within the African-American community. A 1986 *New York Times* poll found that a larger percentage of blacks than of whites believed that immigrants took jobs from Americans—but it also found blacks less likely than whites to favor immigration restrictions. In the California vote on Proposition 187, a 1994 ballot initiative that banned government benefits for illegals, blacks split nearly in half on the measure, while whites heavily supported it and Latinos opposed it. "Even confronted with evidence that immigrants are taking jobs from them, some blacks would say, 'These are people who are fighting for their rights like us,'" says Carol Swain, a Vanderbilt University political scientist and editor of the 2007 book *Debating Immigration.*

But as immigration reignited as a national issue in 2006, ambivalence has increasingly given way to opposition to current policies—and even to anger. When Earl Ofari Hutchinson, a columnist for BlackNews.com, wrote a series of pieces sympathizing with illegal aliens, the volume of hostile mail that poured in from other blacks shocked him. Illegal immigration has sizzled as a topic on African-American stations like satellite radio XM's "The Power," with most callers demanding more immigration restrictions. African-American bloggers have excoriated black politicians who favor liberal immigration policies. "In the realm of pandering black elites, there is no more notorious public figure than [Texas] Congresswoman Sheila Jackson-Lee," wrote Elizabeth Wright in the online newsletter *Issues & Views*. "According to Jackson-Lee, those blacks who forcefully oppose mass immigration are simply naive and are being 'baited' [by white opponents of immigration] into taking such negative positions."

Recent polling data reveal the shift. Though a 2006 Pew Center national survey showed some of the same ambivalence among blacks toward immigrants, it also found that in several urban areas where blacks and Latinos were living together, blacks were more likely to say that immigrants were taking jobs from Americans and also more likely to favor cutting America's current immigration levels.

* * *

What's behind the anger, as the Pew data hint, is the rapid change that legal and illegal Hispanic immigration is bringing to longtime black locales. Places like South Los Angeles and Compton, California, have transformed, virtually overnight, into majority-Latino communities. Huge numbers of new immigrants have also surged beyond newcomer magnets California and New York to reach fast-growing southern states like North Carolina and Georgia, bringing change to communities where blacks had gained economic and political power after years of struggle against Jim Crow laws. Since 1990, North Carolina's Hispanic population has exploded from 76,726 people to nearly 600,000, the majority of them ethnically Mexican. In Georgia, the Hispanic population grew nearly sevenfold, to almost 700,000, from 1990 to 2006.

This Latino "tsunami," as Los Angeles–based Hispanic-American writer Nicolás Vaca calls it, has intensified the well-founded feeling among blacks that they're losing economic ground to immigrants. True, early research, conducted in the wake of the big immigration reforms of the 1960s, suggested that the arrival of newcomers had little adverse impact on blacks—one study found that every 10 percent increase in immigration cut black wages by only 0.3 percent. But as the immigrant population has in some places grown six or seven times larger over the last four decades, the downward pull has become a vortex. A study by Harvard economist George Borjas and colleagues from the University of Chicago and the University of California estimates that immigration accounted for a 7.4 percentage-point decline in the employment rate of unskilled black males between 1980 and 2000. Even for black males with high school diplomas, immigration shrank employment by nearly 3 percentage points. While immigration hurts black and white low-wage workers, the authors note, the effect is three times as large on blacks because immigrants are more likely to compete directly with them for jobs.

A case study of Los Angeles janitorial services cited in a Government Accounting Office report captures the enormity of the shift. It began in the late 1970s, as several small firms began hiring Mexican janitors at low pay, prompting building owners to drop contracts with the companies that employed blacks in favor of the cheaper upstarts. As the immigrant-dominated firms grabbed more business, industry wages slipped from a peak of $6.58 an hour in 1983 to $5.63 an hour in 1985. The number of black janitors in L.A. plummeted from about 2,500 in the late 1970s to only 600 by 1985. Today, the city's janitorial industry, like apparel manufacturing and hotel services, is almost entirely immigrant.

Former mechanic Anderson felt the effects of low-wage immigrant competition in his old line of work. "I used to sell parts to body shops, and I knew Americans who were making $20 an hour repairing dented fenders," he says. "Now, 95 percent of South Central L.A. body-shop jobs are held by recent immigrants making $7 or $8 an hour." Says Joe Hicks, former chair of Los Angeles's Human Relations Commission and now head of the nonprofit Community Advocates: "It's hard to find a black face on a construction site or in a fast-food restaurant around here any more. People from the black community have noticed."

* * *

As the Hispanic population has expanded in formerly black areas, Latinos have also vied more intensely with blacks for affirmative-action slots, public-sector jobs, and political power. In one notable late-1990s case that presaged future confrontations, Hispanic leaders in South L.A. launched an official complaint that blacks made up the overwhelming majority of the county hospital's staff. A federal agency then forced the hospital to hire more Latinos, provoking bitterness among local blacks. More recently, in Compton—where Hispanics have replaced blacks as the largest ethnic group, but where blacks continue to dominate local politics—Latinos have been grumbling that they don't hold as many jobs in the public schools as they should, given their numbers.

This battle over quotas for public-sector jobs is a glaring example of how immigration is turning the race-based policies of the last 40 years, originally designed to help blacks, against them. For African-American leaders like Claud Anderson, head of the Harvest Institute, the turnabout represents a betrayal of the civil rights movement: only blacks deserve quotas. "When did our government ever exclude immigrants or deny them their constitutional rights, as they did African-Americans?" he asks. But for other blacks, the demands of Latinos and Asians that government set-aside programs include them are further evidence that racial preferences were misguided in the first place. "Blacks who support skin color privileges now will be singing a different tune later once government starts discriminating against them once again, this time in favor of Hispanics," writes columnist and blogger La Shawn Barber.

* * *

The Latino influx into formerly black-majority urban neighborhoods has sparked deadlier kinds of conflict. While most violent crime in these areas is still black-on-black or Latino-on-Latino, interethnic violence is mounting, and in some locales, much of it—perhaps surprisingly, given high overall black crime rates—is Hispanic-on-black. In the heavily mixed-race community of Harbor Gateway in Los Angeles, for example, Latinos now commit five times more violent crimes against blacks than vice versa. Countywide numbers are just as startling. Though blacks make up just 9 percent of L.A. County's population, they were the victims of 59 percent of all racially motivated attacks in 2006, while Latinos committed 52 percent of all racially motivated attacks.

Gangbanging is responsible for much of the carnage. Greater Los Angeles is now home to some 500 Mexican gangs—compared with some 200 black ones—and they've aggressively tried to push blacks out of mixed-race neighborhoods. More than just turf wars, the Latinos' violence has included attacks against law-abiding African-Americans with no gang involvement; a horrifying example was the December 2006 murder of 14-year-old Cheryl Green by Mexican gang members in Harbor Gateway, a brutal crime designed to terrorize local blacks. Three years earlier, the same gang had killed a black man because he dared to patronize a local store that they considered "for Hispanics only." Meantime, federal authorities have indicted members of another Los Angeles–based Latino gang, Florencia 13, for random shootings of blacks in South L.A. The indictment chillingly accuses a gang leader of giving members instructions on how to find blacks to shoot.

"This all began in local high schools back in the early 1990s, but it wasn't noticed by many people then," says sociologist Alex Alonso, an expert in Los Angeles gangs. "When blacks and Latinos started sharing high schools, they fought, at first because they refused to celebrate each other's ethnic holidays. Since then, the fighting has made its way into the streets and the gangs." Alonso, who runs an online forum where gang members can vent, says that Latino-black relations are one of the hottest topics. Typical is this remark from a forum member: "Black folks in L.A. better wake up and realize that the 'myth' of the brown minority brother and sister, being black folks' latent brothers and sisters in the struggle . . . is a wet dream. If black folks don't soon realize this in L.A., unite and come together for their own survival—then it will be blacks walking around with their heads up their asses . . . asking: 'What happened???'"

The violent neighborhood confrontations initially received little media attention outside Southern California. But the murder in the summer of 2007 of three black, college-bound students in Newark, New Jersey—allegedly by several illegal Hispanic immigrants, including a Peruvian with a criminal record named Jose Carranza—sparked widespread national coverage and a heated debate within the black community. The Reverend Jesse Lee Peterson, a conservative radio host and columnist, called the Newark killings and the California violence "a wake-up call" for blacks. Reflecting the new mood, Terry Anderson, the Los Angeles talk-show host, challenged black leaders like Jesse Jackson and Al Sharpton to speak out. "If you make one simple change, and change Jose Carranza to a white man," said Anderson, "I will guarantee you that [Sharpton and Jackson] would be screaming and marching in the streets."

* * *

Many blacks are also uncomfortable with the more prosaic cultural changes that accompany rapid immigration. Akbar Shabazz, a telecommunications consultant, moved out of Gwinnett County, a middle-class Atlanta suburb with a large African-American population, after a huge influx of foreign-born Spanish speakers suddenly created a bilingual culture in the public schools, as well as such overcrowding that some schools had to hold classes in trailers. Since 1990, Gwinnett's foreign-born population has increased tenfold, to about 185,000—now making up about 25 percent of the total population. "There were so many students speaking Spanish in my daughter's kindergarten class that she felt isolated," says Shabazz, who has joined a group of blacks supporting immigration restrictions.

Some observers, aware of the historical irony, have even begun talking about "black flight" from Latino migration. In Los Angeles, for instance, the black population has declined by some 123,000 in the last 15 years, while the Hispanic population has increased by more than 450,000. "Black communities are being transformed, and it isn't going down so well," says Joe Hicks.

Blacks may also be starting to realize that many Latinos hold intensely negative stereotypes about them. In a 2006 study that ten academic researchers conducted of various racial groups' attitudes in Durham, North Carolina, 59 percent of Latino immigrants said that few or no blacks were hardworking, and 57 percent said that few or no blacks could be trusted. By contrast, only

9 percent of whites said that blacks weren't hardworking, and only 10 percent said that they couldn't be trusted. Interestingly, the survey found that blacks were broadly well-disposed toward Hispanics, though how long that will be true remains to be seen.

The rising tensions between African-Americans and Hispanics render the old hopes of a black-brown coalition chimerical. "In studies," says Frank Morris, former dean of graduate studies at Morgan State University, "immigrants actually tend to say they think of themselves more like whites in America than like blacks, which is one reason why a black-brown political coalition has never existed anywhere except in the minds of black political leaders." Morris, the former head of the Congressional Black Caucus Foundation, says that elected black leaders have sought to join forces with Hispanics not out of true common concerns but out of fear that demographic changes will leave them vulnerable to challenges from Latino pols. A research paper published by Morris and University of Maryland professor James Gimpel estimates that Hispanic candidates could win as many as six seats that blacks currently hold in the U.S. House of Representatives. Latino politicians understand that their own gains will come largely at the expense of black candidates. When black California congresswoman Juanita Millender-McDonald died suddenly in 2007, the Congressional Hispanic Caucus targeted her seat, realizing that her district was 57 percent Latino. The effort, which angered members of the Congressional Black Caucus, failed. But Hispanic congressman Joe Baca justified it: "It's time we have one of our own that speaks on our behalf," he said.

Nicolás Vaca, the writer, dismisses the notion that African-Americans and Latinos are natural allies. "A divide exists between Blacks and Latinos that no amount of camouflage can hide," he writes in his book *The Presumed Alliance*. Vaca says that the split has been evident for years, though largely ignored by the media and political leaders. He contends, for instance, that the 1992 Los Angeles riots, sparked by the LAPD's beating of Rodney King, became on the ground a black-brown confrontation in which the majority of businesses destroyed were Latino. At the same time, Vaca argues, Latinos believe that, since they had nothing to do with black oppression in America, they owe blacks nothing and "come to the table with a clear conscience."

* * *

Such talk could portend problems for the Democratic Party, where Hispanics and African-Americans are two crucial constituencies. Courting the growing Hispanic vote, virtually all the top Democratic leaders in Washington support liberal immigration policies, including some form of amnesty. So far, the party has been able to embrace amnesty without threatening its traditional lock on black votes. Republicans are missing an opportunity, thinks

Vanderbilt's Swain. "Some Republicans have positions on immigration that would resonate in the black community, but only a few have tried to take advantage of black anger on immigration," she says.

For Swain, white members of Congress who favor restrictions on low-wage immigration may be representing black interests better than the Congressional Black Caucus does. Many blacks, she believes, now recognize that former political allies like the Democratic Party, white liberals, and unions have abandoned them in favor of immigrants, who represent the newest leftist cause—and that the black political leadership isn't doing anything about it.

Black politicians, noticing the growing anger within their communities, have started to shun the immigration debate. Major civil rights organizations didn't participate in the 2007 Latino marches and protests in favor of amnesty. At the Congressional Black Caucus's annual legislative conference in September of that year, no sessions tackled immigration, despite the issue's national prominence. And when Sheila Jackson-Lee proposed her liberal immigration-reform bill in 2006, only nine of the CBC's 43 members cosponsored it.

Black politicians would influence the direction of future immigration debates merely by sitting them out. Back in 1994, when initial polls showed that well over 60 percent of California blacks backed Proposition 187, African-American politicians and civil rights leaders began an intense campaign to change their minds, ultimately cutting black support for the proposition by 15 to 20 percentage points. But in the current environment, with discontent growing among many black voters, it's unlikely that many African-American politicians would be as willing to undertake a similar campaign. As Earl Ofari Hutchinson recently acknowledged, "Black leaders are looking over their shoulders."

Blacks could play a far more decisive role, though, if their political leaders felt threatened enough to pursue tougher immigration policies actively. Such a move wouldn't be unprecedented. In the late 1980s, blacks reacted bitterly when Congress proposed an amnesty for illegals. The pressure that they put on black representatives prompted the Congressional Black Caucus to ensure that the immigration bill that eventually passed included tough sanctions against employers who knowingly hired undocumented workers, though court challenges eventually watered them down. Today, black America appears to be in the throes of a more profound shift in attitudes—one that could make the African-American voter a crucial part of the immigration debate.

[2008]

Note

1. Anderson died of pancreatic cancer on July 8, 2010.

18

The Demographic Revolution

If the Upward Mobility of the Impending Hispanic Majority Doesn't Improve, the State's Economic Future Is in Peril

Heather Mac Donald

CALIFORNIA IS IN THE MIDDLE of a far-reaching demographic shift: Hispanics, who already constitute a majority of the state's schoolchildren, will be a majority of its workforce and of its population in a few decades. This is an even more momentous development than it seems. Unless Hispanics' upward mobility improves, the state risks becoming more polarized economically and more reliant on a large government safety net. And as California goes, so goes the nation, whose own Hispanic population shift is just a generation or two behind.

The scale and speed of the Golden State's ethnic transformation are unprecedented. In the 1960s, Los Angeles was the most Anglo-Saxon of the nation's ten largest cities; today, Latinos make up nearly half of the county's residents and one-third of its voting-age population. A full 55 percent of Los Angeles County's child population has immigrant parents. California's schools have the nation's largest concentration of "English learners," students from homes where a language other than English is regularly spoken. From 2000 to 2010, the state's Hispanic population grew 28 percent, to reach 37.6 percent of all residents, almost equal to the shrinking white population's 40 percent. Nearly half of all California births today are Hispanic. The signs of the change are everywhere—from the commercial strips throughout the state catering to Spanish-speaking customers, to the flea markets and illegal vendors in such areas as MacArthur Park in Los Angeles, to the growing reach of the Spanish-language media.

The poor Mexican immigrants who have fueled the transformation—84 percent of the state's Hispanics have Mexican origins—bring an admirable work ethic and a respect for authority too often lacking in America's native-born population. Many of their children and grandchildren have started thriving businesses and assumed positions of civic and economic leadership. But a sizable portion of Mexican, as well as Central American, immigrants, however hardworking, lack the social capital to inoculate their children reliably against America's contagious underclass culture. The resulting dysfunction is holding them back and may hold California back as well.

* * *

Three members of the Crazy Little Stoners, a small but violent drug-dealing gang, are hanging out on a ficus-lined residential street in Santa Ana, America's largest predominantly Spanish-speaking city (located in what was once solidly Republican Orange County). A white truck filled with members of a local graffiti crew slowly pulls up to check out their gang affiliation; since CLS and the taggers are not at war, the truck passes on.

Salvador, 16, Casimiro, 16, and Michael, 15, joined CLS three years ago and promptly racked up serious criminal records, including convictions for armed robbery and burglary that would have sent them to state prison had they not been juveniles. Casimiro, in red love beads and baggy shorts, is a short, self-consciously cocky tough ("I've got people doing my homework 'cause I show 'em my fist," he brags); he faces 20 years if caught again. Salvador, the most articulate of the three, has a nine-and-a-half-year suspended sentence hanging over him. Michael has been kicked out of school for fighting and now attends an alternative school—but not for long, all evidence suggests. "They don't teach us nothing; I didn't know how boring it would be," he says sullenly. Salvador claims that their long suspended prison terms have taught them a lesson and that they're "done" with the criminal life; now they just want to make steady money with a job, he says.

The family situations of these young gangbangers are typical of California's lower-class Hispanic population, characterized by high rates of single parenthood, teen pregnancy, and welfare use. Michael's unmarried mother is on welfare. The mother of Salvador's 16-year-old girlfriend recently sent her to Washington State to keep her away from him—too late, since she is already pregnant. "If she has the kid, I'll stop messing around and take care of it," he says. Salvador's father was arrested for drug possession and deported after serving time in the Orange County jail; he is presently planning his return. Casimiro claims that his parents tolerate his gang activities: "I be going to parks and I be like, I was like kind of nervous in the beginning but I was like, 'Get used to it,' but they were cool with it," he says. Perhaps Casimiro is accurately conveying his family's attitudes toward his gangbanging; social workers in Santa Ana and Los Angeles tell of multigenerational gang families in which the fathers smoke pot and take meth with their children. Equally likely, however, is that Casimiro's parents oppose criminality but cannot keep him away from the streets.

If any of these Crazy Little Stoners is going to turn his life around, Salvador seems to have the greatest chance, based on his ability to make steady eye contact and engage with an interlocutor. He "thinks about" going to college, he says, adding, without irony, that he likes studying criminal justice for "what it teaches you about the world." Some children do, in fact, put aside their gang affiliations after their first encounters with the law; others muddle through their young adult years in a dim, semi-criminal limbo. As I take leave of the group, Casimiro asks casually, "You got a dollar?"—already displaying the entitlement mentality of a Haight-Ashbury or Venice Beach gutter punk (see chapter 16, "The Sidewalks of San Francisco").

A more plausible candidate for bourgeois respectability may be found on a street corner not far from the CLS hangout. Jessica, a plump 11th-grader in a low-cut black tank top, has just exited from Cesar Chavez High School, a fashionably industrial edifice, during the last week of remedial summer classes. Her family, too, demonstrates the ravages of underclass culture, including "multiple partner fertility": her 23-year-old brother, 18-year-old sister, and 14-year-old brother have different fathers from her own. Jessica's father shows up occasionally from Riverside, but she doesn't know if he works or not. Jessica's mother, never married, was born in the U.S. but raised in Mexico. She now works as a security guard but has ceded child-rearing to Jessica's grandmother. Both parents have roots in Santa Ana's largest and oldest gang, F Troop.

Self-contained and cautious, Jessica says that she has learned from other people's mistakes just by watching. She takes a jaundiced view of her classmates: "Most students don't do the work." (Her own favorite class is earth science.) As for the pregnant girls, "I'm sure that they knew what they were doing." Since the sixth grade, she has been picking up various wind instruments, including the bass clarinet and the sax, and she plays in the marching band. "It's something to keep us off the streets 'n' stuff," she observes coolly of this last endeavor. Her older siblings don't provide much inspiration: her brother has been amassing low-level police citations but is otherwise "doing nothing," she tells me, and her sister barely passed the watered-down California high school exit exam. But as to her future, "it's on me," she says. "It's up to me to do something."

* * *

Jon Pederson works as a pastor in the Willard area of Santa Ana, a formerly middle-class neighborhood of stucco apartment blocks whose balconies now sport bright blue tarps and small satellite dishes. Participation in gangs and drug culture is rising in the second and third generation of Hispanic immigrants, he observes. "It's a perfect storm. When a family comes from Mexico, both parents need to work to survive; their ability to monitor their child's life is limited." Families take in boarders, often kin, who sometimes rape and impregnate the young daughters. "Daddy hunger" in girls raised by single mothers is expressed in promiscuity, Pederson says; the boys, meanwhile, channel their anger into gang life. Nearly 53 percent of all Hispanic births in California are now out of wedlock, and Hispanics have the highest teen birthrate of all ethnic groups. Pederson saw similar patterns as a missionary in Central America: teen pregnancy, single-parent families with six or eight serial fathers, and high poverty rates.

Routine domestic violence is another Third World import, especially from Mexico. More than a quarter of the 911 calls to the Santa Ana Police Department are for domestic violence, reports Kevin Brown, a former Santa Ana cop who now serves on an antigang intervention team. "Children are seeing it at home—they're living the experience," he says.

* * *

The complicated reality of Hispanic family life in California—often straddling the legitimate and the criminal worlds, displaying both a dogged determination to work and poor decision making that interferes with upward mobility—helps explain why the state's Hispanic population has made only modest progress up the educational ladder. Most parents want their children to flourish, yet they may not grasp the study habits necessary for academic success or may view an eighth-grade education as sufficient for finding work. Julian Rodriguez, a Santa Ana gang detective, recalls a case several years ago in which two parents had taken their 14-year-old daughter out of school to care for their new baby—a classic display of "Old World values," he says.

A significant portion of Hispanic children lag cognitively, a problem that led David Figueroa Ortega, the Mexican consul general of Los Angeles, to sound an alarm: "Our children, when they arrive in primary school, sometimes arrive behind in skills. They don't have sufficient training to keep up with the rest of the group." Nationally, 42 percent of Latino children entering kindergarten are in the lowest quartile of reading preparedness, compared with 18 percent of white children, reports UCLA education professor Patricia Gándara in her 2009 book *The Latino Education Crisis*. By eighth grade, 43 percent of whites and 47 percent of Asians nationally are proficient or better in reading, compared with only 19 percent of Latino students.

Many of California's Hispanic students who have been schooled in the U.S. for all their lives and are orally fluent in English remain classified as English learners in high school because they have made so little academic progress. In the Long Beach Unified School District, for example, nearly nine-tenths of English learners entering high school have been in a U.S. school at least since first grade. The lack of progress isn't due to bilingual education: Long Beach got rid of its last bilingual program in 1998, and the current ninth-grade English learners have been in English-only classrooms all their lives. Some come from families that immigrated to the U.S. two or three generations ago.

True, Hispanics' cognitive skills have been improving over the last decade; the percentage of Hispanic eighth-graders deemed proficient in math and reading on the California Standards Tests doubled from 2004 to 2010. But the gap between Hispanics' performance and that of whites and Asians narrowed only modestly, since white and Asian scores rose as well. Latino students' rate of B.A. completion from the University of California and California State University is the lowest of all student groups and has slightly declined in recent years, reports the Institute for Higher Education Leadership and Policy at California State University in Sacramento. The state spends vast sums each year trying to get more Hispanics into college and to keep them there—$100 million in 2009, for instance, on the education of full-time community-college students who dropped out after their first year, according to the American Institutes for Research. (Facilitating transfers from community college is a favored strategy for increasing Hispanic enrollment in four-year colleges.)

Hispanic underperformance contributes to California's dismal educational statistics. Only Mississippi had as large a percentage of its eighth-grade students reading at the "below basic" level on the 2011 National Assessment of Educational Progress (NAEP); in eighth-grade math, California came in third, after Alabama and Mississippi, in the percentage of students scoring "below basic." Only 56 percent of ninth-graders graduate in four years in Los Angeles; statewide, only two-thirds do.

* * *

Since the 1980s, California's economic growth has been powered by skilled labor. Silicon Valley, for example, added jobs at a rate of 3.2 percent for the year beginning in November 2010, despite the economic slump. If current labor-market trends continue, 41 percent of California's workers will need a B.A. by 2025, according to the Public Policy Institute of California (PPIC). But California already has trouble finding skilled employees. Because it can't produce all the skilled workers that it needs, it imports them: in 2006, for example, 33 percent of all college-educated California workers had been born in other states and 31 percent had been born abroad, PPIC says. Moreover, since 2000, more college graduates have been exiting California than entering. California will need to attract almost 160,000 college-educated workers annually for 20 years in a row to meet the projected demand, PPIC estimates—three times the number who have been arriving from elsewhere since 2000.

Unfortunately, though Hispanics will make up 40 percent of the state's working-age population by 2020, just 12 percent of them are projected to have bachelor's degrees by then, up from 10 percent in 2006. Moreover, their fields of academic concentration are not where the most economically fertile growth will probably occur. At California State University in 2008, just 1.7 percent of master's degree students in computer science were Mexican-American, as were just 3.6 percent of students in engineering master's programs. The largest percentage of Mexican-American enrollment in M.A. programs was in education—40 percent—despite (or perhaps because of) Mexican-Americans' low test scores.

The future mismatch between labor supply and demand is likely to raise wages for college-educated workers, while a glut of workers with a high school diploma or less will depress wages on the low end and contribute to an increased demand for government services, especially among the less educated Hispanic population. U.S.-born Hispanic households in California already use welfare programs (such as cash welfare, food stamps, and housing assistance) at twice the rate of U.S.-born non-Hispanic households, according to an analysis of the March 2011 Current Population Survey by the Center for Immigration Studies. Welfare use by immigrants is higher still. In 2008–09, the fraction of households using some form of welfare was 82 percent for households headed by an illegal immigrant and 61 percent for households headed by a legal immigrant.

Higher rates of Hispanic poverty drive this disparity in welfare consumption. Hispanics made up nearly 60 percent of California's poor in 2010, despite being less than 38 percent of the population. Nearly one-quarter of all Hispanics in California are poor, compared with a little over one-tenth of non-Hispanics. Nationally, the poverty rate of Hispanic adults drops from 25.5 percent in the first generation—the immigrant generation, that is—to 17 percent in the second but rises to 19 percent in the third, according to a Center for Immigration Studies analysis. (The poverty rate for white adults is 9 percent.) That frustrating third-generation economic stall repeats the pattern in high school graduation and college completion rates as well.

* * *

Hispanics' reliance on the government safety net helps explain their ongoing support for the Democratic Party. Indeed, liberal spending policies are a more important consideration for Hispanic voters than ethnic identification or the so-called values issues that they are often said to favor. "What Republicans mean by 'family values' and what Hispanics mean are two completely different things," says John Echeveste, founder of the oldest Latino marketing firm in Southern California and a player in California Latino politics. "We are a very compassionate people; we care about other people and understand that government has a role to play in helping people." That Democratic allegiance was on display in the 2010 race for lieutenant governor, when Hispanics favored San Francisco mayor Gavin Newsom, the epitome of an elite tax-and-spend liberal, over the Hispanic Republican incumbent, Abel Maldonado, despite Newsom's unilateral legalization of gay marriage in San Francisco in 2004. *La Opinión*, California's largest Spanish-language newspaper, cited Newsom's "good progressive platform" in endorsing him. In the 2010 race for state attorney general, Hispanic voters helped give the victory to liberal San Francisco district attorney Kamala Harris, who was running against Los Angeles district attorney Steve Cooley, a law-and-order moderate—even in Cooley's own backyard of L.A.

Republican political consultants routinely argue that California's Hispanics were driven from their natural Republican home by a 1994 voter initiative—backed by then-governor Pete Wilson, a Republican—denying most government benefits to illegal aliens. But it would be almost impossible today to find a Hispanic immigrant who has even heard of Proposition 187. Jim Tolle, pastor of one of the largest Hispanic churches in Southern California, La Iglesia En El Camino, says that his congregation knows nothing about Prop. 187. The fact is that Hispanic skepticism toward the Republican Party derives as much from its perceived economic biases as from Republicans' opposition to illegal immigration and amnesty. A March 2011 poll by Moore Information asked California's Latino voters why they had an unfavorable view of the Republican Party. The two top reasons were that the party favored only the rich and that Republicans were selfish and out for themselves; Republican positions on immigration law were cited less often.

Hispanics' low rates of naturalization and civic participation have depressed their political influence below their population numbers. Nearly 40 percent of Latino adults are ineligible to vote, according to Lisa Garcia Bedolla, an education professor at UC Berkeley. But Hispanics' representation in the state legislature has been growing even faster than their population numbers, and a string of recent speakers in the state assembly have been Hispanic. The Latino Caucus has already made its mark on higher education, putting constant pressure on the University of California to admit more Hispanic students or face draconian budget cuts. "If campuses don't capitulate, you'll get killed. The Latino Caucus will march with torches," says John Moores, a former chairman of the UC Board of Regents. Moores resigned the chairmanship "in disgust," he says, at his inability to restore color-blind admissions to the system.

Such a push for meritocratic admissions shouldn't even be necessary, given the 1996 voter initiative banning racial preferences in state government, including the university systems. The UC and CSU systems, however, quickly devised stratagems for evading Proposition 209—and even those schemes haven't gone far enough for the Latino Caucus. "Minority students are not getting an equal shake in our state, and as an elected official I'm going to do everything in my power to change that," declared caucus member Ed Hernandez in September 2011, as his pet project, a bill to give campuses the official go-ahead to restore open racial preferences in admissions, once again landed on the governor's desk. Governor Arnold Schwarzenegger had vetoed the bill in the past, and Governor Jerry Brown, to his credit, did so again, citing its patent unconstitutionality. Hernandez and the caucus can console themselves with the fact that UC's "holistic" and "comprehensive" admissions gambits are accomplishing sub rosa much of what the bill aimed to make official.

The caucus did score a major legislative victory in 2011. The University of California, California State University, and the community-college system already grant in-state tuition to illegal aliens. (Back in 2003, when then–UC regent Ward Connerly asked university officials why illegal aliens should get a $12,000 annual tuition break when, say, a citizen from Washington State did not, they answered: Our budget will be cut if we don't go along.) In October 2011, however, Brown signed a bill going even further and granting illegal aliens taxpayer-funded tuition assistance and fee waivers. The so-called California Dream Act was not a popular bill, except among Latinos: 55 percent of voters opposed the law, and only 30 percent of whites supported it, but 79 percent of Latinos approved of it. In one generation, observes CSU San Jose political scientist Larry Gerston, California has gone from outlawing affirmative action and banning nonessential government services to illegal aliens to granting them free tuition subsidies, a change that "speaks to the growing pressure of Latinos on the legislative process."

Even as Hispanics are gathering clout in Sacramento, the immigrant populations of some small, almost entirely Latino, cities in the Los Angeles basin have been politically passive toward local governance. As a result, the city councils and managers of Bell, Maywood, La Puente, and other localities, unchecked by their residents, have engaged in rampant self-dealing, virtually bankrupting those cities' governments (see chapter 10, "How the Road to Bell Was Paved").

Such extreme civic miscarriages will diminish as Latinos become further integrated into American society. And there may be advantages to an increasingly Latino-populated state legislature, which may prove less prone to job-killing regulation than one led by white liberals.

* * *

But the cost of government services for the Hispanic poor is not likely to abate soon—a serious problem for a state suffering budget woes. The most expensive of those services is education, which is increasingly dominated by enormous programs to try to close the achievement gap; Santa Ana's Willard Intermediate School, for example, where Pastor Pederson once taught, is on the receiving end of a $35 million state transformation grant. As for health-care spending, Los Angeles has become the HMO to the world, says County Supervisor Mike Antonovich, who recommends establishing medical centers south of the Mexican border to remove the health-care incentive for illegal immigration. Crime perpetrated by Latinos burdens communities and tax-payers as well. Though the Hispanic crime rate is generally less than half the black crime rate, it is still several times the rate of crime among whites. Four out of ten state prisoners were Hispanic in 2008.

Poor Hispanics don't pay in taxes what they cost in state expenditures. And with rising Latino political power, California's welfare policies will probably become even more redistributionist, predicts CSU San Jose's Gerston—at least if Latinos remain poor, their drop-out rates don't improve, and they don't feel they can climb the economic ladder. A 1996 study for Pepperdine University found that Latinos in Southern California achieved middle-class status by pooling wages from three or more workers in a single household, rather than through an "education-based meritocratic formula—as is more common with Asians and Jews." While such a collective work ethic is praise-worthy, it is limited as a strategy for further upward mobility.

Of course, California's budget problems have plenty of causes unrelated to its growing Hispanic population. One, a 1999 law that contributed to the current pension crisis for public employees by granting them retroactive pension in-creases of up to 50 percent, was pushed through by the teachers' and state prison guards' unions, which aren't dominated by Hispanics. Nevertheless, the im-minent Hispanic majority will surely put additional fiscal pressure on the state.

* * *

Certain policies may help avoid a future of growing income inequality and social decline. One is to stop the emigration of California's best talent. The state should meet the demand for college-educated workers by making itself attractive to the highly educated, not by trying to dragoon all students into college. California cannot hope to retain the entrepreneurs it still has and to attract others unless it radically revamps its business climate and lowers its taxes (a course made more difficult, though, by the demands on government social services imposed by the growing Hispanic population). Congress could help California stay globally competitive by letting foreign-born Ph.D. stu-dents in science and technology automatically obtain green cards to work in the U.S. after completing their degrees (see chapter 28, "The Silicon Lining").

California should also create a robust vocational-education system. The fashionable prejudice against vocational education will end up bankrupting the school and college systems by forcing students into academically oriented classrooms that hold no interest for them and for which they are not quali-fied. Further, the blue-collar skilled trades are desperate for workers and pay much better than many a service-sector job. Only 55 percent of Hispanic male students graduated from California high schools in 2007, reports the Califor-nia Dropout Research Project; many of the dropouts would undoubtedly have welcomed the opportunity to learn a trade. At the same time, California must stop decimating what remains of its manufacturing sector with business-killing regulations (see chapter 5, "The Long Stall").

And Washington should institute an immigration pause for low-skilled immigrants. In 1970, the average Southern California Latino spoke only English and had assimilated to Anglo culture, according to the Pepperdine study. Since then, even though California's Hispanic population has expanded outside its traditional enclaves and spread across the state and nation, the acculturation process has slowed. In 1988, when accountant and entrepreneur Martha de la Torre began *El Clasificado*, a free Spanish classified-advertising newspaper, she assumed that the demand for Spanish-language publications would last only a couple of decades; instead, the market for *El Clasificado* has grown far beyond its original base in Los Angeles, even as similar English-language publications have gone bankrupt. "I'm surprised by how people in some communities try not to change," she observes. Teachers, service employees, police officers, and ordinary private-sector workers report that many California residents now expect to be addressed in Spanish.

The reason for this assimilation reversal is our de facto open-borders policy, argues Michael Saragosa, a public-relations consultant who oversaw Latino outreach for Meg Whitman's 2010 gubernatorial campaign. "We need to allow people who are already here to grow into the American Dream over generations," he says. "That can't happen when they have a steady flow of people behind them." Illegal immigration, which did not drop in California during the recession, should be reduced, and legal immigration should be reoriented toward high-skilled immigrants rather than the family members of existing immigrants.

Empresarios

It doesn't get any more assimilated than this: for his daughter's third birthday party, Alex Guerrero, who lives in a wealthy equestrian suburb of Los Angeles, rented a miniature horse dressed as a pink unicorn to entertain his daughter's young guests. Guerrero is part of a highly successful, upwardly mobile cohort of California Latinos who manipulate symbols for a living, manage other employees, and start businesses. An informal survey suggests that the children of South Americans and Cubans are overrepresented among them.

Guerrero's parents emigrated in 1966 from Colombia. His father, who had worked as a railroad porter in Colombia, changed sheets at Los Angeles's Beverly Wilshire hotel, while his mother, who had run a hair salon out of her garage in Colombia, worked as a seamstress. "Our parents instilled in us that we had to go to college," he says. Guerrero graduated from USC with a business degree and worked in Latin American marketing for a record company before joining a friend's construction firm as an executive vice president in charge of finance.

Jose Villa, who has a Harvard B.A. in economics and a Wharton M.B.A., owns a multicultural advertising agency, Sensis. His father had been a salesman for Colgate-Palmolive in Cuba before fleeing the country in the 1960s; in Los Angeles, his father worked in a factory alongside mostly Mexican immigrants, but eventually moved into life insurance and then real estate. Many of Villa's classmates in the San Fernando Valley who spoke Spanish at home didn't necessarily get the same relentless message of upward mobility from their parents that he received. "With Cubans, there's a lot of emphasis on education and moving ahead—you have to be a doctor or an engineer or you're an embarrassment to the family." (Despite the trendy multiculti focus of his business, Villa is building a website with some Hispanic colleagues to honor the libertarian Guatemalan economist Manuel Ayau. Another libertarian economist, Robert Barro, was Villa's most important influence at Harvard, he says.)

Martha de la Torre, an accounting major at Loyola Marymount University, worked for Arthur Young on a portfolio of businesses targeting the Hispanic market before starting her newspaper, *El Clasificado*. One-third of de la Torre's Hispanic colleagues at Arthur Young were Ecuadoran-Americans like herself. "My parents were determined that their children would go to college," she says. "We had to write the alphabet by age five."

To be sure, there are plenty of highly successful Mexican-American businessmen, but they appear—based, again, on a nonscientific sample—to belong disproportionately to an older generation, whose parents were more likely to have emigrated legally than today's Mexican arrivals. Likewise, South Americans, Cubans, and Spaniards generally had to buy a plane ticket and obtain a visa to enter the U.S., and thus brought more social capital with them. "If you emigrate from a really poor community," speculates Guerrero, "maybe a roof over your head is enough."

The entrepreneurial spirit is not particularly strong among California's Mexican farm laborers, according to George Lugo, a grower in Temecula who flamboyantly hawks his cantaloupes and watermelons at the Irvine Farmers Market. "There's not many workers moving into ownership positions, not at all," Lugo says (an observation corroborated by the low number of Mexican owners at Southern California farmers' markets).

"If you talk to people who farm anywhere in California, they'll tell you that their workers don't have much aspirations of upward mobility. They like what they do, and when we have a good strawberry crop, you've never seen a bigger smile on someone's face that says: 'This is mine.' But they don't want to be owners and have the responsibility of dealing with government overseers and time management. My guys say to me: 'Go do some paperwork'; they know what to do on the farm and they do it."

The reluctance to be mired in California's huge regulatory apparatus is more than understandable. But those farmworkers are not always preparing their children for more promising work. Lugo organizes study sessions for the children of his workers: "I try to foster in them that they have to get good at something other than farming." Lugo calls some of the children in his tutoring group his "spark plugs" because of their curiosity about the world and their eagerness to discover something that he doesn't know. But he says that if he weren't overseeing their schooling, they wouldn't get the same message about education.

* * *

Pastor Tolle says that he feels "both hope and consternation" when he contemplates his congregation, the majority of whom are illegal immigrants. Though the grounds for concern are obvious, there are numerous reasons for hope as well. The most striking thing about the teens I spoke to in Santa Ana—even those with criminal records—was that they were *nice* kids, despite Casimiro's thuggish braggadocio and Michael's sullen disengagement. The students filing out of Cesar Chavez High School toward the bus stop were orderly; there was little chance that they would start walking on the tops of parked cars, as sometimes happens in Philadelphia or Brooklyn. Though it is taboo to say so, the greatest advantage possessed by the Mexican-American poor and middle class is that they are not burdened with the anger and resentments that afflict parts of black society.

Jose Cruz, head of the Literacy Council of San Diego, is just one of the thousands of Mexican-Americans in California who exemplify the grounds for hope. His father, born in Mexico but raised in the U.S., was a chef; his mother, born in Texas but raised in Mexico, pressed shirts. "My parents were steady workers; they didn't make a big deal of it," he says. "They taught me and my siblings: Go to work every day. Do what you are told. And never question your boss, a police officer, or a teacher." If California's Hispanics can better avoid single parenthood and school failure, that reverence for work and authority could become one of the state's biggest assets.

[2012]

VI

Education

19

The Worst Union in America

How the California Teachers Association Betrayed the Schools and Crippled the State

Troy Senik

IN 1962, AS TENSIONS RAN HIGH BETWEEN school districts and unions across the country, members of the National Education Association gathered in Denver for the organization's 100th annual convention. Among the speakers was Arthur F. Corey, executive director of the California Teachers Association (CTA). "The strike as a weapon for teachers is inappropriate, unprofessional, illegal, outmoded, and ineffective," Corey told the crowd. "You can't go out on an illegal strike one day and expect to go back to your classroom and teach good citizenship the next."

Fast-forward nearly 50 years, to May 2011, when the CTA—now the single most powerful special interest in California—organized a "State of Emergency" week to agitate for higher taxes in one of the most overtaxed states in the nation. A CTA document suggested dozens of ways for teachers to protest, including following state legislators incessantly, attempting to close major transportation arteries, and boycotting companies, such as Microsoft, that backed education reform. The week's centerpiece was an occupation of the state capitol by hundreds of teachers and student sympathizers from the California State University system, who clogged the building's hallways and refused to leave. Police arrested nearly 100 demonstrators for trespassing, including then–CTA president David Sanchez. The protesting teachers had left their jobs behind, even though their students were undergoing important statewide tests that week. With the passage of 50 years, the CTA's notions of "good citizenship" had vanished.

So had high-quality public education in California. Seen as a national leader in the classroom during the 1950s and 1960s, the country's largest

Illustration by Sean Delonas.

state is today a laggard, competing with the likes of Mississippi and Washington, D.C., at the bottom of national rankings. The Golden State's education tailspin has been blamed on everything from class sizes to the property-tax restrictions enforced by Proposition 13 to an influx of Spanish-speaking students. But no portrait of the system's downfall would be complete without a depiction of the CTA, a political behemoth that blocks meaningful education reform, protects failing and even criminal educators, and inflates teacher pay and benefits to unsustainable levels.

* * *

The CTA began its transformation in September 1975, when Governor Jerry Brown signed the Rodda Act, which allowed California teachers to bargain collectively. Within 18 months, 600 of the 1,000 local CTA chapters moved to collective bargaining. As the union's power grew, its ranks nearly doubled, from 170,000 in the late 1970s to approximately 325,000 today. By following the union's directions and voting in blocs in low-turnout school-board elections, teachers were able to handpick their own supervisors—a system that private-sector unionized workers would envy. Further, the organization that had once forsworn the strike began taking to the picket lines. Today, the CTA boasts that it has launched more than 170 strikes in the years since Rodda's passage.

The CTA's most important resource, however, isn't a pool of workers ready to strike; it's a fat bank account fed by mandatory dues that can run more than $1,000 per member. In 2009, the union's income was more than $186 million, all of it tax-exempt. The CTA doesn't need its members' consent to spend this money on politicking, whether that's making campaign contributions or running advocacy campaigns to obstruct reform. According to figures from the California Fair Political Practices Commission (a public institution) in 2010, the CTA had spent more than $210 million over the previous decade on political campaigning—more than any other donor in the state. In fact, the CTA outspent the pharmaceutical industry, the oil industry, and the tobacco industry *combined*.

All this money has helped the union rack up an imposing number of victories. The first major win came in 1988, with the passage of Proposition 98. That initiative compelled California to spend more than 40 percent of its annual budget on education in grades K–12 and community college. The spending quota eliminated schools' incentive to get value out of every dollar: since funding was locked in, there was no need to make things run cost-effectively. Thanks to union influence on local school boards, much of the extra money—about $450 million a year—went straight into teachers' salaries. Prop. 98's malign effects weren't limited to education, however: by essentially making public school funding an entitlement rather than a matter of discretionary spending, it hastened California's erosion of fiscal discipline. In recent years, estimates of mandatory spending's share of the state's budget have run as high as 85 percent, making it highly difficult for the legislature to confront the severe budget crises of the past decade.

In 1991, the CTA took to the ramparts again to combat Proposition 174, a ballot initiative that would have made California a national leader in school choice by giving families universal access to school vouchers. When initiative supporters began circulating the petitions necessary to get it onto the ballot, some CTA members tried to intimidate petition signers physically. The union also encouraged people to sign the petition multiple times in order to throw the process into chaos. "There are some proposals so evil that they should never go before the voters," explained D. A. Weber, the CTA's president. One of the consultants who organized the petitions testified in a court declaration at the time that people with union ties had offered him $400,000 to refrain from distributing them. Another claimed that a CTA member had tried to run him off the road after a debate on school choice (see chapter 1, "The Beholden State").

Weber and his followers weren't successful in keeping the proposition off the ballot, but they did manage to delay it for two years, giving themselves time to organize a counteroffensive. They ran ads, recalls Ken Khachigian, the former White House speechwriter who headed the Yes on 174 campaign, "claiming that a witches' coven would be eligible for the voucher funds and [could] set up a school of its own." They threatened to field challengers against political candidates who supported school choice. They bullied members of the business community who contributed money to the provoucher effort. When In-N-Out Burger donated $25,000 to support Prop. 174, for instance, the CTA threatened to press schools to drop contracts with the company.

In 1993, Prop. 174 finally came to a statewide vote. The union had persuaded March Fong Eu, the CTA-endorsed secretary of state, to alter the proposition's heading on the ballot from PARENTAL CHOICE to EDUCATION VOUCHERS—a change in wording that cost Prop. 174 ten points in the polls, according to Myron Lieberman in his 1997 book *The Teacher Unions*. The initiative, which had originally enjoyed 2–1 support among California voters, managed to garner only a little over 30 percent of the vote. Prop. 174's backers had been outspent by a factor of eight, with the CTA alone dropping $12.5 million on the opposition campaign.

* * *

As the CTA's power grew, it learned that it could extract policy concessions simply by employing its aggressive PR machine. In 1996, with the state's budget in surplus, the CTA spent $1 million on an ad campaign touting the virtues of reduced class sizes in kindergarten through third grade. Feeling the heat from the campaign, Republican governor Pete Wilson signed a measure providing subsidies to schools with classes of 20 children or fewer. The program was a disaster: it failed to improve educational outcomes, and the need

Illustration by Sean Delonas.

to hire many new teachers quickly, to handle all the smaller classes, reduced the quality of teachers throughout the state. The program cost California nearly $2 billion per year at its high-water mark, becoming the most expensive education-reform initiative in the state's history. But it worked out well for the CTA, whose ranks and coffers were swelled by all those new teachers.

The union's steady supply of cash allowed it to continue its quest for political dominance unabated. In 1998, it spent nearly $7 million to defeat Proposition 8—which would have used student performance as a criterion for teacher reviews and would have required educators to pass credentialing examinations in their disciplines—and more than $2 million in a failed attempt to block Proposition 227, which eliminated bilingual education in public schools. In 2002, the union spent $26 million to defeat Proposition 38, another school voucher proposal. And in 2005, with a special election called by Governor Arnold Schwarzenegger looming, the CTA came up with a colossal $58 million—even going so far as to mortgage its Sacramento headquarters—to defeat initiatives that would have capped the growth of state spending, made it easier to fire underperforming teachers, and ensured "paycheck protection," which compels unions to get their members' consent before using dues for political purposes.

Cannily, the CTA also funds a wide array of liberal causes unrelated to education, with the goal of spreading around enough cash to prevent dissent from the Left. Among these causes: implementing a single-payer health-care system in California, blocking photo-identification requirements for voters, and limiting restraints on the government's power of eminent domain. The CTA was the single biggest financial opponent of another Proposition 8, the controversial 2008 proposal to ban gay marriage, ponying up $1.3 million to fight an initiative that eventually won 52.2 percent of the vote. The union has also become the biggest donor to the California Democratic Party. From 2003 to 2012, the CTA spent nearly $102 million on political contributions; 0.08 percent of that money went to Republicans.

* * *

At the same time that the union was becoming the largest financial force in California politics, it was developing an equally powerful ground game, stifling reform efforts at the local level. Consider the case of Locke High School in the poverty-stricken Los Angeles neighborhood of Watts. Founded in response to the area's 1967 riots, Locke was intended to provide a quality education to the neighborhood's almost universally minority students. For years, it failed: in 2006, with a student body that was 65 percent Hispanic and 35 percent African-American, the school sent just 5 percent of its graduates to four-year colleges, and the drop-out rate was nearly 51 percent.

Shortly before Locke reached this nadir, the school hired a reform-minded principal, Frank Wells, who was determined to revive the school's fortunes. Just a few days after he arrived, a group of rival gangs got into a dust-up; Wells expelled 80 of the students involved. In the new atmosphere of discipline, Locke dropped "from first in the number of campus crime reports in

LAUSD [Los Angeles Unified School District] to thirteenth," writes Donna Foote in *Relentless Pursuit: A Year in the Trenches with Teach for America.* Test scores and college acceptance also began to rise, Foote reports.

But trouble arose with the union when Wells began requiring Locke teachers to present weekly lesson plans. The local CTA affiliate—United Teachers Los Angeles—filed a grievance against him and was soon urging his removal. The last straw was Wells's effort to convert Locke into an independent charter school, where teachers would operate under severely restricted union contracts. In May 2007, the district removed Wells from his job. He was escorted from his office by three police officers and an associate superintendent of schools, all on the basis of union allegations that he had let teachers use classroom time to sign a petition to turn Locke into a charter. Wells called the allegations "a total fabrication," and the signature gatherers backed him up. The LAUSD reassigned him to a district office, where he was paid $600 a day to sit in a cubicle and do nothing.

Luckily for Locke students, the union's rearguard action came too late. In 2007, the Los Angeles Board of Education voted 5–2 to hand Locke High School to Green Dot, a charter school operator. Four years later, as the final class of Locke students who had attended the school prior to its transformation received their diplomas, the school's graduation rate was 68 percent, and over 56 percent of Locke graduates were headed for higher education.

* * *

One of the most noticeable changes at Locke has ramifications statewide: when Green Dot took over, it required all teachers to reapply for their jobs. It hired back only about one-third of them. That approach is unimaginable in the rest of the state's public schools, where a teaching job is essentially a lifetime sinecure. A tiny 0.03 percent of California teachers are dismissed after three or more years on the job. In the past decade, the LAUSD—home to 33,000 teachers—has dismissed only four. Even when teachers are fired, it's seldom because of their classroom performance: a 2009 exposé by the *Los Angeles Times* found that only 20 percent of successful dismissals in the state had anything to do with teaching ability. Most terminations involved teachers behaving either obscenely or criminally. The National Council on Teacher Quality, a Washington-based education-reform organization, gave California a D-minus on its teacher-firing policies in its 2010 national report card.

Responsibility for this sorry situation goes largely to the CTA, which has won concessions that make firing a teacher so difficult that educators can usually keep their jobs for any offense that doesn't cross into outright criminality. With the cost of the proceedings regularly running near half a million dollars, many districts choose to shuffle problem employees around rather than try to fire them.

Illustration by Sean Delonas.

Even outright offenses are no guarantee of removal, thanks to CTA in-fluence. When a fired teacher appeals his case beyond the school board, it goes to the Commission on Professional Competence—two of whose three members are also teachers, one of them chosen by the educator whose case is being heard. The CTA has stacked this process as well by bargaining to require evidentiary standards equal to those used in civil-court procedures and coaching the teachers on the panels. One veteran school-district lawyer calls the appeals process "one of the most complicated civil legal matters anywhere." As the *Times* noted, "The district wanted to fire a high school teacher who kept a stash of pornography, marijuana and vials with cocaine residue at school, but [the Commission on Professional Competence] balked, suggesting that firing was too harsh." The commission was also the reason that, as the newspaper continued, the district was "unsuccessful in firing a male middle school teacher spotted lying on top of a female colleague in the metal shop"; the district had failed to "prove that the two were having sex."

Another regulatory body dominated by CTA influence is the state's Commission on Teacher Credentialing (CTC), the institution responsible for removing the credentials of misbehaving teachers. A report released in 2011 by California state auditor Elaine Howle found that the commission had a backlog of approximately 12,600 cases, with responses sometimes taking as long as three years. Because the CTC—which was created by an act sponsored by the CTA—is made up of members appointed by the governor, the CTA is able to bring its political pressure to bear on determining the commission's makeup. In September 2011, for instance, one of Governor Jerry Brown's appointments to the CTC was Kathy Harris, who had previously been a CTA lobbyist to the body.

* * *

The CTA's most recent crusade for job security made clear that the union was prepared to jeopardize the financial future of California's schools. In 2011, it vigorously pushed (and Governor Brown hastily signed) Assembly Bill 114, which prevented any teacher layoffs or program cuts in the coming fiscal year and removed the requirement that school districts present balanced budget plans. The bill also forced public schools to prepare budget estimates that didn't take into account the state's downturn in revenues—meaning that schools could budget for activities even though there wasn't money to pay for them. Since then, state officials have forecast that revenues for the 2012 fiscal year will be $3.2 *billion* lower than they were when the schools were making their budgets. Eventually, accommodations to reality will have to be made—at which time the CTA will, of course, use them to plead hardship.

Such pleas seem impudent coming from the highest-paid teachers in the nation, with an average annual salary of $68,000. For a bit of perspective, if two California teachers get married (not an unusual occurrence) and each makes the average salary, their combined annual income would be $136,000, nearly $80,000 more than what the state's median household pulls down. That's for an average annual workload of 180 days, only two-thirds of the average total in the private sector. Don't forget retirement benefits: after 30 years, a California teacher may retire with a pension equal to about 75 percent of his working salary. That pension averages more than $51,000 a year—more than *working* teachers earn in more than half the states in the nation. And that's just an average; from 2005 to 2011, the number of education employees pulling down more than $100,000 a year in pensions skyrocketed from 700 to 5,400.

With the state's economy in tumult, however, prospects for the teachers' retirement fund look grim. The California State Teachers' Retirement System (CalSTRS) is now officially estimated to have about $56 billion in liabilities and about 30 years left before it runs dry, though many outside analysts think that those numbers are too optimistic. A report by the Legislative Analyst's Office in November 2011 estimated that restoring full funding to CalSTRS would require finding an extra $3.9 billion a year for at least 30 years.

* * *

If California is to generate the economic growth necessary to mitigate its coming fiscal reckoning, it will need to retain its historical role as a leading site for innovation and entrepreneurship. But that won't be possible if its next generation of would-be entrepreneurs attends one of the Golden State's many mediocre or failing schools. And what little economic dynamism is left in California will be impeded if the union gets its way and the state keeps increasing its already weighty tax burden.

Meaningful change probably won't come from elected officials, at least for now. The CTA's size, financial resources, and influence with the state's regnant Democratic Party are enough to kill most pieces of hostile legislation. For years, school reformers fantasized about a transformative figure who could shift the balance of power from the union through force of charisma and personality, taking his case directly to the people. Yet when that figure seemed to emerge in Governor Arnold Schwarzenegger, even he proved unable to alter the status quo, with his 2005 ballot initiatives to reform tenure, school financing, and political spending by unions all going down to decisive defeat. It's unlikely that salvation will come from Governor Brown, either. The man who originally opened the door for the CTA's collective bargaining has remained an ally of the union, firing four proreform members of the state board of education in his first few days in office and appointing a new group that included Patricia Ann Rucker, the CTA's top lobbyist. Brown also avoided including any changes to CalSTRS in his October 2011 announcement of proposed pension reforms, probably because he had learned Schwarzenegger's lesson that irking the CTA can lead to the demise of a broader agenda.

Parents, however, are starting to revolt against CTA orthodoxy. Unlike elected officials, parents—who want nothing more than a good education for their kids—are hard for the union to demonize. In early 2010, a Los Angeles–based nonprofit called Parent Revolution shocked California's pundit class by getting the state legislature to pass the nation's first "parent trigger" law, which lets parents at failing schools force districts to undertake certain reforms, including converting schools into independent charters (see chapter 22, "Triggering School Reform."). The law caps the number of schools eligible for reform at 75, but if early results are successful, it will become hard for Californians to avoid comparing thriving charter schools with failing traditional ones.

The CTA is fighting back, of course. In 2010, when 61 percent of parents at McKinley Elementary School in the blighted L.A. neighborhood of Compton opted to pull the trigger, the CTA claimed that "parents were never given the full picture . . . [or] informed of the great progress already being made"— despite the fact that McKinley's performance was ranked beneath nearly all other inner-city schools in the state. Several Hispanic parents in the district also said that members of the union had threatened to report them to immigration authorities if they signed the petition. Eventually, the Compton Unified school board—heavily lobbied by the CTA—dismissed the petition signatures, with no discussion, as "insufficient" on a handful of technicalities, such as missing dates and typos. Though the union's power had proved too much for the McKinley parents, an enterprising charter school operator opened two new campuses in the neighborhood anyway.

Institutions like Locke High School, Green Dot, Parent Revolution, and the Compton charters are glimmers of hope for California's public school system. Despite their inferior resources, they have fought the CTA not by participating in direct political conflict but by undermining the union's moral standing. These organizations reframe the education question in starkly humanitarian terms: In the California public school system, are anyone's interests more important than the students'? It was a question that the CTA itself might have asked back when teachers entered the classroom to "teach good citizenship."

[2012]

20

The Bilingual Ban That Worked

Rising Test Scores Vindicate English Immersion in California—But Hispanics Are Still Struggling

Heather Mac Donald

IN 1998, CALIFORNIANS VOTED TO PASS Proposition 227, the "English for the Children Act," and dismantle the state's bilingual-education industry. The results, according to California's education establishment, were not supposed to look like this: button-cute Hispanic pupils at a Santa Ana elementary school boasting about their English skills to a visitor; those same pupils cheerfully calling out to their principal on their way to lunch, "Hi, Miss Champion!"; and a statewide increase in English proficiency among all Hispanic students.

Instead, warned legions of educrats, eliminating bilingual education in California would demoralize Hispanic students and widen the achievement gap. Unless Hispanic children were taught in Spanish, the bilingual advocates moaned, they would be unable to learn English or to succeed in other academic subjects.

California's electorate has been proved right: Hispanic test scores on a range of subjects have risen since Prop. 227 became law. But while the curtailment of California's bilingual-education industry has removed a significant barrier to Hispanic assimilation, the persistence of a Hispanic academic underclass suggests the need for further reform.

* * *

The counterintuitive linguistic claims behind bilingual education were always a fig leaf covering a political agenda. The 1960s Chicano rights movement ("Chicano" refers to Mexican-Americans) asserted that the American tradition of assimilation was destroying not just Mexican-American identity but also Mexican-American students' capacity to learn. Teaching these students in English rather than in Spanish hurt their self-esteem and pride in their culture, Chicano activists alleged; hence the high drop-out rates, poor academic performance, and gang involvement that characterized so many Mexican-American students in the Southwest. Manuel Ramirez III, currently a psychology professor at the University of Texas at Austin, argued that bilingual education was necessary to ensure "the academic survival of Chicano children and the political and economic strength of the Chicano community." The role of American schools, according to this nascent ideology, became the preservation of the Spanish language and Mexican culture for Mexican-origin U.S. residents.

Novel linguistic theories arose to buttress this political platform. Children could not learn a second language well unless they were already fully literate in their native tongue, the newly minted bilingual-ed proponents argued. To teach English to a five-year-old who spoke Spanish at home, you had to instruct him in Spanish for several more years, until he had mastered Spanish grammar and spelling. "Young children are not language sponges," asserts McGill University psychology professor Fred Genesee, defying centuries of parental observation. Even more surprisingly, the advocates suddenly discovered that the ability to learn a second language improved with age—news to every adult who has struggled through do-it-yourself language recordings.

Such ad hoc justifications rested on shaky scientific ground. Psycholinguistics research supports what generations of immigrants experienced firsthand: the younger you are when you tackle a second language, the greater your chances of achieving full proficiency. Children who learn a second language early in life may even process it in the same parts of the brain that process their first language, an advantage lost as they age.

Only one justification for bilingual education made possible sense. The bilingual theorists maintained that children should be taught academic content—physics, say, or history—in their home language, lest they fall behind their peers in their knowledge of subject matter. But this argument applied most forcefully where bilingual education has always been the rarest: in high school, where, one would hope, teachers use relatively sophisticated concepts. In the earliest grades, however, where bilingual education has always been concentrated, academic content is predominantly learning a language—how to read and write B-A-T, for example. Moreover, most Hispanic children who show up in American elementary school have subpar Spanish skills to begin with, so teaching them in Spanish does not provide a large advantage over English in conveying knowledge about language—or anything else.

* * *

The bilingual-education crusade also contained patent inequities that never seemed to trouble its advocates. If teaching a nonnative speaker in his home tongue was such a boon—if it was, as many argued, a civil right—bilingual education should have been provided to every minority-language group, not just to Hispanics, who have been almost the exclusive beneficiaries of the practice. If instructing non-English-speaking students in English was destructive, it would damage a school's sole Pashto speaker just as much as its Hispanic majority. But minority rights, usually the proud battle cry of self-styled progressives, invariably crumpled before brute political power when it came to bilingual ed. "If it could benefit 82 percent of the kids, you don't have to offer it to everyone," says Robert Linquanti, a project director for the government-supported research organization WestEd.

Nor did bilingual-education proponents pause long before counterevidence. In 1965, just as the movement was getting under way in the United States, the Canadian province of Quebec decided that not enough Quebecois children were learning French. It instituted the most efficient method for overcoming that deficit: immersion. Young English-speaking students started spending their school days in all-French classes, emerging into English teaching only after having absorbed French. By all accounts, the immersion schools have been successful. And no wonder: the simple insight of immersion is that the more one practices a new language, the better one learns it. Students at America's most prestigious language academy, the Middlebury Language Schools, pledge not to speak a word of English once the program begins, even if they are beginners in their target languages. "If you go back to speaking English, the English patterns will reassert themselves and interfere with acquisition of the new grammatical patterns," explains Middlebury vice president Michael Geisler.

McGill professor Genesee—who opposed Prop. 227 in 1998, when he was directing the education school at the University of California at Davis—hates it when proponents of English immersion in America point to the success of French immersion in Quebec. The English-speaking Quebecois don't risk losing English, Genesee says, since it remains the predominant Canadian tongue and is a "high-prestige language."

Whereas if you start American Hispanics off in English, Genesee maintains, "they won't want to speak Spanish" because it is a "stigmatized, low-prestige language." Genesee's argument exposes the enduring influence of Chicano political activism on academic bilingual theory. Hispanic students do risk losing their home tongue when taught in the majority language. Such linguistic oblivion has beset second- and third-generation immigrants throughout American history—not because of the relative status of their home languages but simply because of the power of language immersion and the magnetic force of the public culture. But bilingual-ed proponents know that most Americans don't view preserving immigrants' home tongues as a school responsibility. So they publicly promote bilingual education as a pedagogically superior way to teach Hispanics English and other academic subjects, even as they privately embrace the practice as a means for ensuring that Hispanic students preserve their Spanish.

The early Chicano activists sought the "replacement of assimilationist ideals . . . with cultural pluralism," writes University of Houston history professor Guadalupe San Miguel, Jr. in his book *Contested Policy*. Bilingual education was the activists' primary weapon in fighting assimilation because, as they rightly understood, English-language teaching is a powerful tool for encouraging assimilation. In a country as diverse as the United States, fluency in the common tongue is an essential bond among citizens, and the experience of learning it alongside classmates of different ethnic origins reinforces the message that Americans share a common culture. Bilingual-ed proponents often accuse immersion advocates of opposing multilingualism or wanting to stamp out Spanish. This is nonsense. But it is true that maintaining students' home language for the sake of strengthened ethnic identity is no part of a school's mandate. Its primary language duty, rather, is to ensure that citizens can understand one another and participate in democracy.

* * *

Despite its conceptual contradictions, bilingual education spread inexorably through the federal and state education bureaucracies. The National Education Association, undoubtedly whiffing a jobs bonanza for its unionized members, produced a report in 1966 arguing that teaching Hispanic children in English hurt their self-esteem and led to underachievement. In 1968, Congress passed the Bilingual Education Act, which provided federal funds for bilingual teaching. When not enough school districts applied for the funds, advocacy groups sued, claiming that the districts were violating Hispanic children's civil rights. The federal Department of Education agreed, issuing rules in 1975 that penalized schools for not establishing bilingual programs for their non-English-speaking students. Though the Reagan administration cut back on several bilingual-education mandates from the Ford and Carter years, the federal bilingual bureaucracy remained firmly entrenched for decades.

In California, which contains the vast majority of the country's so-called English learners—students from homes where a language other than English is regularly spoken—the rise of the bilingual machine was swift and decisive. The 1976 Chacon-Moscone Bilingual-Bicultural Education Act declared that bilingual education was the right of every English learner. Elementary schools had to provide native-language instruction if they enrolled a certain number of English learners; bilingual education in the lower grades became the default mode for anyone with a Hispanic surname. (Hispanics have always dominated the "English learner" category. In California, they make up 85 percent of all English learners; the next-largest language group—Vietnamese—constitutes just 2.4 percent.)

Even after Governor George Deukmejian refused to reauthorize the Chacon-Moscone bill in 1987, the bilingual establishment in Sacramento continued to enforce the law's mandates. The state's department of education sponsored numerous conferences and reports alleging that bilingual education was necessary for Hispanic success and showered an additional $5,000 a year on bilingual teachers. Administrators and teachers in heavily Hispanic areas often saw themselves as part of the Chicano empowerment movement. "You weren't worthwhile if you didn't speak Spanish," recalls a Santa Ana teacher. "The attitude was: 'No one should teach our kids but native language speakers.'"

Bilingual-education theory posits a carefully calibrated, multiyear transition from all-Spanish to all-English classes, with the proportion of each language changing every year. An exacting realization of that theory with highly qualified teachers would likely not do irremediable harm—precisely because children *are* language sponges. But the reality of bilingual education in California was very different. Many low-skilled native Spanish speakers were lured into the education profession by the generous stipends available to bilingual teachers, but they didn't speak English well enough to make the transition into English teaching. English instruction, when it happened at all, was haphazard and unsystematic, recalls Jane Barboza, director of Student Support Services for the Green Dot Charter Schools. "It was left to the end of the day or to the playground. You'd sing 'Old MacDonald,' accompanied by a guitar," she says. Jose Hernandez, the elementary education coordinator for District Six in the Los Angeles Unified School District, admits: "We never implemented bilingual education with the idea of moving kids into English; we weren't great at delivering the dual-language aspect of it."

* * *

Such problems were not lost on parents. In 1996, a group of them in the Ninth Street Elementary School in downtown L.A. tried to remove their children from all-Spanish classes and place them in English immersion. When their letters and petitions produced no response, 63 families, organized by poverty advocate Alice Callaghan, pulled their children out of classes in protest. The school was jeopardizing their children's futures by not teaching them English, these poor Central American garment workers maintained.

Case in point: after six years in Ninth Street's "bilingual" program, reported Jill Stewart in *New Times LA*, a fifth-grader wrote the following passage for his English class: "I my parens per mi in dis shool en I so feol essayrin too old in the shool my border o reri can grier das mony putni gire and I sisairin aliro sceer." (In fairness to bilingual education, whole-language theory should probably share the blame for that gibberish. Whole language, then dominant in California schools, holds that children should not be instructed—and by *no* means corrected—in phonics, grammar, or spelling.)

The Ninth Street boycott caught the attention of Silicon Valley software entrepreneur Ron Unz. Stunned to learn that schools were imprisoning children in Spanish classes against their parents' will, Unz, along with Santa Ana teacher Gloria Mata Tuchman, drafted a ballot initiative that mandated that all children be taught "overwhelmingly" in English and integrated into mainstream classes, following one year of specialized English instruction. Waivers for bilingual education would be granted only on an individual basis, following a parental request and a school certification that the child had "special . . . needs" that made a bilingual setting more appropriate. Unz could not refrain from an ironic jab at bilingual theory: "All children in California public schools shall be taught English by being taught in English," announced the English for the Children Act.

The national bilingual-education establishment reacted with fury. Unz was a nativist who wanted to eradicate Spanish and drive out immigrants, it charged. Dismantling bilingual education would put "generations at risk," as the title of a 1998 educrat conference convened by the University of California at Riverside proclaimed. Joseph Jaramillo, staff attorney for the Mexican American Legal Defense and Educational Fund, told the *Los Angeles Times* that the proposition "would send many California schools into crisis because they would be stripped of the very tools necessary to bring children into the mainstream."

The establishment pointed to studies that showed that bilingual education produced better results than English immersion—and it still points to them whenever challenged. But according to Russell Gersten, an expert in educational-research design, most evaluations in the bilingual-ed field are "poorly constructed and utterly unpersuasive, consisting of makeshift, descriptive research open to multiple interpretations." Manhattan Institute senior fellow Jay Greene conducted a meta-analysis of the extant studies in 1998. After winnowing out the vast majority on quality grounds, he found a slight edge to bilingual education in conveying academic content. But the programs he reviewed were irrelevant to California's version of bilingual education, Greene says: "Most were highly resource-intensive pilot programs from the 1960s that resembled French écoles or Jewish day schools. They attracted high-quality teachers and were accountable for results." Further-more, most comparisons of bilingual and immersion methods have an inher-ent bias, since bilingual regimes exempt the lowest-performing English learn-ers from taking tests in English until the teacher deems them ready, whereas immersion regimes test a far greater percentage of English learners.

The establishment marshaled President Bill Clinton and California's politi-cal elite from both parties against Prop. 227. Unions lined up in opposition. The California Teachers Association contributed $2.1 million to defeat the initiative; the American Federation of Labor also pitched in. Jerrold Peren-chio, chair of Spanish-language media conglomerate Univision, gave $1.5 million, perhaps out of a sincere belief that bilingual education was the best means of teaching his audience English. All told, those opposed to 227 spent close to $5 million, while the pro-227 forces spent less than $1 million, most of it from Unz's own account.

The vote wasn't even close. The initiative passed, 61 to 39 percent. Though preelection polls showed 60 percent of Latinos supporting Prop. 227, only 37 percent voted for it in the end. Many may have been moved at the last minute by claims that the measure was anti-immigrant.

Lawsuits to invalidate or water down 227 began the day after the vote and have continued ever since. Outside the courthouse, efforts to torpedo the ini-tiative were hardly more subtle. The Los Angeles County Office of Education ruled that teaching "overwhelmingly in English" meant teaching in English for 51 percent of the school day; the Riverside and Vista school districts made that 60 percent. Soliciting waivers from parents to put their children back into bilingual classes became so successful a crusade in some districts that the bilingual teaching load barely budged.

* * *

The bureaucratic resistance wasn't able to suppress the good news, how-ever. In Los Angeles, young Hispanic pupils placed in immersion were ab-sorbing spoken English far more quickly than expected and were starting to read and write in English as well, their teachers told the *Los Angeles Times*. The Oceanside School District, on the Pacific coast north of San Diego, be-came the emblem for the new English immersion. Superintendent Kenneth Noonan, a former bilingual teacher himself and cofounder of the California Association of Bilingual Education, had opposed Prop. 227, but once it passed, he determined that Oceanside would follow the law to the letter. He applied the criteria for granting bilingual waivers strictly and ended up creat-ing no Spanish-taught classes. He then sat back with considerable trepidation and waited. "Trained bilingual teachers started calling me," he says. "'You've got to see what's happening down here,' they said. I thought: 'I guess it's true, the sky has fallen.'" But when Noonan visited their classrooms, he found that these new converts to immersion were "glowing with a sense of success."

The first four months were difficult, Noonan recalls, but then the students took off. Second-grade test scores in reading rose nearly 100 percent in two years—with the average student moving from California's 13th percentile to its 24th—after staying flat for years. These accomplishments didn't stop protesters from holding candlelight vigils outside the Oceanside school board's offices and from filing federal and state civil rights complaints challenging the district's strict waiver policies. Those complaints were eventually rejected.

Oceanside and its inland neighbor, the Vista Unified School District, formed a natural experiment of sorts. Advocates in Vista actively solicited waivers, and Vista officials granted them to everyone who asked, so that half the eligible students remained in bilingual education. Oceanside's test-score increases from 1998 to 2000 were at least double those of Vista in nearly every grade, reported the *New York Times*, despite the districts' similar English-learner populations—low-income, largely agricultural Spanish speakers. Critics dismissed Oceanside's test-score gains as nothing remarkable. But today, the Vista Unified School District has shrunk its bilingual program to minimal proportions, and its coordinator of English-language development—Matt Doyle, another former bilingual teacher—speaks like an immersion true believer: "Almost all our students come at such an early age that it's the perfect opportunity to develop English."

Two broad observations about the aftermath of Prop. 227 are incontestable. First: despite desperate efforts at stonewalling by bilingual diehards within school bureaucracies, the incidence of bilingual education in California has dropped precipitously—from enrolling 30 percent of the state's English learners to enrolling 4 percent. (Bilingual proponents love to cite the "low" 30 percent figure as proof that the 1998 reform was unnecessary—but that figure includes all grades from kindergarten through 12th. Bilingual ed was always concentrated heavily in the elementary grades and rare in high school; in some districts, nearly all young Hispanic pupils were enrolled in it.)

Second: California's English learners have made steady progress on a range of tests since 1998. That progress is all the more impressive since school districts can no longer keep their lowest-performing English learners out of the testing process. In 1998, 29 percent of school districts submitted under half of their English learners to the statewide reading and writing test; today, close to 100 percent of the state's English learners participate. Despite this, the performance of English learners has improved significantly, from 10 percent scoring "proficient" or "advanced" (the top two categories) in 2003 to 20 percent in 2009. Similarly, on the English proficiency test given to nonnative speakers, the fraction of English learners scoring as "early advanced" or "advanced" (the top two categories) has increased from 25 percent in 2001, when the test was first administered, to 39 percent in 2009. If the critics of Prop. 227 have the burden of proof to substantiate their warnings of catastrophe, they clearly haven't met it.

* * *

But the bilingual advocates have a number of ways—some valid, others specious—to dismiss or complicate the significance of these broad trends. Drawing unassailable, detailed statistical conclusions about the consequences of 227 may be impossible, given a host of shortcomings in the data. If you wanted to devise conditions that would make it impossible to resolve definitively the immersion-versus-bilingual-ed debate, California's school policies are what you would create.

The largest obstacle is California's failure to keep longitudinal information on students. Thanks to pressure from teachers' unions, the state cannot track a cohort of students or a single student over time. (Such a capacity would be necessary if California were to start awarding teachers merit pay, a bane of unions.) From one year to the next, all data about a specific student—his test scores, say, or whether he was taught in English or Spanish—disappears. Further, even if you could track students' progress, you would have to account for the fact that students who enrolled in bilingual education after 227 have tended to enter school with weaker language skills than immersion students. This means that test scores that appear to show a clear advantage to immersion—in 2009, for example, only 19 percent of bilingual-ed students scored "advanced" or "early advanced" on the English-proficiency test, compared with 43 percent of immersion students—can be dismissed by bilingual advocates as comparing apples with oranges.

Second, all the tests currently used to measure students' skills were implemented after 227, and all have been changed or replaced at least once since they were first developed. No test spans the pre- and post-227 period.

Finally, after 227, California and the federal government introduced educational and accountability reforms that changed how schools interacted with students. California began measuring schools' performance through test results in 1999 and progressively developed more sophisticated means for holding schools accountable. Soon thereafter, the state developed standards for what children should learn in each grade. And it began shifting from whole-language ideology toward phonics instruction for teaching reading. In 2002, the federal No Child Left Behind Act (NCLB) imposed even more stringent demands on schools, requiring that they improve the test scores of black and Hispanic students and English learners; the result was an intense focus on English learners, accompanied by new programs and funding. Bilingual proponents argue that English learners' rising test scores in the 2000s reflect these other developments, not the switch to English instruction.

One cannot defeat that claim statistically, since no control group exists *not* taught under the new federal and state standards. But a key fact weakens the bilingual advocates' case: school districts have cut back on their waivered bilingual programs in order to meet their annual test-score targets. In 2006, for example, the Lennox School District, near the Los Angeles International Airport, announced that its persistent designation under NCLB as under-performing had prompted it to stop promiscuously handing out waivers for bilingual education. To bilingual backers, among them the California Association of Bilingual Education, this change of policy—repeated elsewhere throughout Southern California—illustrated how destructive NCLB was. But the schools may know something about the efficacy of bilingual education that the advocates do not. This grassroots move to English immersion was a repudiation of the claim that the best way to teach nonnative speakers English skills is to teach them in Spanish.

The schools that have abandoned bilingual education have not regretted it. Every school that has done so in Los Angeles's District 6 has improved its rating on California's 800-point Academic Performance Index at least 150 points, says district elementary coordinator Hernandez.

* * *

The bilingual industry also argues that Prop. 227 has failed in its mission because the gap between English learners and native English speakers on statewide reading and math tests hasn't closed. "The 227 advocates weren't saying: 'Children aren't learning English'; they were saying: 'Look at their reading and math scores: they're failing,'" asserts Shelly Spiegel-Coleman, director of Californians Together, the state's most powerful bilingual-education advocacy group. But Spiegel-Coleman is engaging in revisionist history here. Unz and others were clearly decrying Hispanic students' lack of English proficiency. Moreover, the distinction between learning English and showing proficiency in reading and math is undoubtedly far subtler than most voters realized.

But the "persistent test-score gap" argument has a more fundamental flaw. California defines English learners as students who are less than fluent in English *and* who occupy the bottom rungs of reading and math achievement. To be reclassified out of English-learner status, a student must score well not just on the test of English proficiency but also on statewide reading and math tests. As soon as a student becomes more capable academically, he leaves the English-learner pool and enters a new category: Reclassified Fluent English Proficient, or RFEP. By fiat, then, the English-learner pool contains only the weakest students, whereas the native-speaker pool contains the entire range of students, from the highest achievers to the lowest. Eliminating the gap between English learners and native speakers (known as "English only" students) is logically impossible. A fairer test of how English learners are performing in relation to English-only speakers would combine English learners and RFEP students into one category and compare them with the English-only students. Yet this the state does not do.

The test-score gap between English learners and English-only students is so large that even narrowing it significantly would take Herculean efforts. In 2003, recall, 10 percent of English learners scored "proficient" or above in a statewide reading and writing test. By 2009, 20 percent of them did, a 100 percent improvement. During the same time, English-only students improved their performance on the same test only 32 percent, from 44 percent proficient or above to 58. The gap between the two groups nevertheless grew from 34 to 38 percentage points, because gains in the English-only category started from such a higher base level than those of the English learners.

* * *

Notwithstanding the complexities and inadequacies of the data and the persistence of the achievement gap, the steady advance of English learners on both English proficiency and academic tests vindicates Prop. 227. Had the near-elimination of bilingual education been the disaster that the bilingual advocates predicted, the state and federal accountability measures that they now tout as responsible for English learners' improvement could not have made up for the loss of bilingual instruction.

Prop. 227 changed the debate in California; widespread bilingual education is no longer on the agenda. To be sure, some die-hard districts are quietly trying to increase Spanish-language classes without attracting attention, but they are in the minority. In public, the bilingual industry finds itself reduced to fighting rearguard actions, such as demanding NCLB tests in Spanish or separate textbooks (in English) for English learners. Californians Together does not even mention bilingual education in the statement of purpose posted on its website. Asked if students should be back in Spanish classes, Spiegel-Coleman demurs: "I'm not suggesting that teaching them in Spanish would solve the problems."

And the transformation in the classroom has to be seen to be believed. It is extraordinary, for example, to observe elementary school teachers in Santa Ana, once a bastion of bilingual education, talking to their young Hispanic students exclusively in English about the Great Wall of China. It is just as extraordinary to see those students eagerly raising their hands to read English workbooks aloud in class. The main sign that the students are not native

English speakers is an occasional reminder about past-tense formation or the pronunciation of word endings, but plenty of English-only speakers in the state need such assistance, too. Schools are not universally following the time frame set out in Prop. 227: a year of separate instruction in English followed by integration with English-only students. In some schools, English learners remain cloistered for a longer period. But regardless of classroom composition, English learners *are* being taught "overwhelmingly in English," which is the most important goal of 227.

Self-esteem seems fine. "I didn't know how to speak English in first grade," says a husky fourth-grade boy at Adams Elementary School in Santa Ana. "I just figured out at the end of the year and talked all English." The boy's classmates, who are sitting next to him at a picnic table under a pepper tree for lunch, jostle to get in on the interview. They are fluent in schoolyard insults. "He's a special ed!" one boy says of another. "I am not a special ed, you liar!" retorts the target. The fifth-grade girls at a table nearby complain that the boys are lazy. A slender girl has recently arrived from Mexico. Her translator for that day, a tiny blue-eyed girl named Lily, drapes her arm lovingly around the new immigrant and will sit next to her in all their classes, explaining what the teacher is saying. The pair and their fellow pupils amble back into the school after lunch, any signs of psychological distress well concealed. No one reports unhappiness at speaking English in class; on the contrary, they brag that it's easy.

* * *

Such students are clearly better off liberated from California's inept version of bilingual education. But though test scores have risen, the educational situation for Hispanics remains troubling. Bilingual ed has come and gone, but the conditions that provided the pretext for it—Hispanics' low academic achievement, high drop-out rates, and gang involvement—live on.

The academic problems afflicting many so-called English learners do not necessarily result from speaking Spanish at home. Students who were born here, who speak little or no Spanish, and who have been taught in English all their lives continue to be designated English learners in middle and high school because of poor test scores. They sound fluent in English, yet may read at a second-grade level. Their vocabulary is highly constricted. As a result, the term "English learner" has taken on an unofficial new meaning: a student who knows English but whose academic skills are extremely low. (Indeed, the state bureaucracy has started referring to some black students whose academic struggles resemble those of Hispanic English learners as "standard English learners.") A 2006 report by the National Literacy Panel concluded that the literacy problems of many officially designated English learners reflect "underlying processing deficits," such as "difficulties with phonological awareness and working memory," rather than language-minority status. The math skills of long-term English learners are as shaky as their reading and writing abilities, also suggesting that their academic shortcomings stem from something other than hearing a second language at home.

It is easy to find such students in Southern California: at ease in spoken English but at sea in what the education profession calls "academic English"—the conventions of writing, logic, and argument. A 17-year-old with lustrous auburn hair hanging below his shoulders and several lip studs is performing skateboard tricks outside Locke High School in Watts. Though his father's family is exclusively Spanish-speaking, he speaks with the intonations of a black rapper and avoids Spanish. "Spanish is hard, man!" he explains. He failed ninth-grade English: "I didn't do the homework; I'm not a baby no more." Manny, a ninth-grader in Santa Ana, remains designated an English learner even though he has never been taught in Spanish and was born in the United States. He failed English last year, he says, "because I would mess on some problem; I didn't do my work."

California schools could do far more to improve the performance of such students. Progressive pedagogy continues to handicap their chances of academic mastery. Though the California school system has, in theory, renounced whole-language ideology in favor of phonics instruction, long-term English learners' phonemic awareness remains weak, high school teachers say. Grammar is not taught systematically or explicitly enough. Separating students by ability levels is taboo, so English learners and RFEP students with academic potential stay tethered to the low performers.

I observed some excellent teaching in Southern California classrooms. Santa Ana High School's Brian Lilly stands out for his enthusiastic presentation of the joys of grammar ("Do you see how useful prepositional phrases are, people? They add detail to sentences") and for his carefully controlled colloquies with students (the antithesis of progressive "student-centered learning"). Yet in other classrooms, I saw mindless collaborative learning exercises and lethargic traditional instruction, with teachers mechanically copying phrases into their PowerPoint projectors or asking students to alphabetize vocabulary lists.

The culture that many Hispanic students bring to school, especially as they age, also hinders progress. Many high school teachers have a sense of futility about assigning homework. "I give them silent reading time in class because they're not reading at home," a teacher at Los Angeles's Oscar De La Hoya Animo charter school tells me. Some students who unself-consciously speak English in elementary school start using Spanish again in middle and high school. Gangbangers use Spanish in class to issue threats in teacher-proof code; other students take up Spanish again as an assertion of Hispanic identity.

Under pressure from the No Child Left Behind Act, California school districts have ramped up for another costly assault on the English-learner test-score gap—sending specialists to work with middle school students, establishing separate academies for Hispanic males, and increasing outreach to parents. Whether those efforts will achieve the act's goal of closing the achievement gap remains to be seen.

The fact remains, however, that the English for the Children Act has swept away a misguided drag on assimilation and routed a once-powerful educrat interest group. The significant rise in English learners' test scores since 1998 demonstrates that bilingual education is not necessary for Hispanic progress. Proposition 227 represents a triumph of common sense over one of the more counterintuitive pedagogical theories to emerge from the 1960s political agitation.

[2009]

21

The Union's Occupation

United Teachers Los Angeles
Wages Its Own War on "The 1 Percent"

Ben Boychuk

UNTIL RECENTLY, IT'S BEEN TOUGH to pinpoint precisely where Occupy Los Angeles ends and public-employee union activism begins. For weeks, a large contingent of teachers' union activists mingled among the several hundred progressive malcontents encamped on the north lawn of Los Angeles City Hall. But the emergence of a new movement—"Occupy LAUSD"—will just about obliterate any distinctions between the two groups. In early October 2011, 500 Los Angeles Unified School District teachers marched about a mile to demonstrate in front of their district's headquarters. A few dozen hard-core activists joined them, camping out for five days before ending the "occupation" with a large union pep rally.

Truth is, parents and taxpayers—to say nothing of thousands of hardworking teachers—have plenty to gripe about. L.A. Unified is a picture of dysfunction, bureaucratic bloat, and massive waste. The second-largest school district in the United States, the LAUSD has a $7 billion budget and enrolls ("educates" isn't quite the word) about 600,000 students. The district is home to both the glistening, half-billion-dollar Robert F. Kennedy Community Schools complex, opened in 2010 on the former site of the Ambassador Hotel (where Kennedy was assassinated in 1968), and Locke High School, one of the worst-performing high schools in California. Only 55 percent of LAUSD students graduate from high school after four years. The district is hindered, in large part, by its 350-page contract with United Teachers Los Angeles (UTLA), which enshrines seniority over quality and leaves younger, talented teachers most vulnerable to pink slips. Yet as Los Angeles education blogger Anthony Krinsky notes, despite three consecutive years of layoffs, "we have more teachers per student than we had 5 years ago, 10 years ago, 15 years ago, and 20 years ago." For all the manpower, student performance remains stagnant.

But the demonstrations at 4th Street and South Beaudry Avenue had little to do with those concerns. For Occupy LAUSD, all the district's problems could be solved with more money, more teachers, and less student testing. It's no coincidence that the Occupy leaders were all top officials with UTLA, which represents 40,000 LAUSD teachers, or that the marches and rallies preceded preliminary contract negotiations. What's more, Occupy LAUSD got backing from the California Teachers Association (CTA), the California Federation of Teachers, and dozens of local teachers' unions around the state. The CTA is the most powerful lobbying organization in Sacramento; it has spent more than $210 million in the past decade on lobbying, supporting liberal causes and Democratic candidates almost exclusively (see chapter 19). The CTA's state council authorized expending $8 million on the 2012 elections, a figure that's likely to rise.[1]

Unlike the Occupy Wall Street protesters, whose consensus-driven committees offered an inchoate list of complaints and a hodgepodge of utopian remedies, Occupy LAUSD has issued demands easy to divine. They are precisely the same demands that UTLA has made for months, with derisive references to the rapacious "percent" tacked on to align the union's public-relations campaign with the Occupy zeitgeist. Foremost among the demands is the union's insistence that district officials use a $55 million budget surplus to rehire up to 1,200 laid-off teachers. One teachers' union activist—writing for the *Socialist Worker*, no less—summarized the larger goals of the occupation: "Tax the 1 percent to fully fund our schools; keep our schools public—by the 99 percent, for the 99 percent; and democratic community-based schools, not corporate Wall Street reform."

District officials reacted to the union-led occupation with frustration and dismay. Superintendent John Deasy, a reliable liberal, professed his bewilderment at the protests in front of his office. "Occupy LAUSD is both misinformed and contrary to the spirit and intent of Occupy Wall Street, Occupy L.A., and the other laudable movements for economic justice that have sprung up around the country and the world over the last month," Deasy said in a statement. "It is an insult for these protesters to equate a school district that during the past four years has experienced a $2 billion loss . . . in state and federal funding, with policies and institutions that have systematically hurt the poor and middle class." Deasy's befuddlement may have been confounded further by Occupy LAUSD's response. "It is hard for him to understand what the 99 percent movement is really about because he represents the worst of the 1 percent," said Jose Lara, a board member of UTLA and chief spokesman for Occupy LAUSD.

For people like Lara, "the 1 percent" consists of people such as Microsoft's Bill Gates and Los Angeles real-estate mogul Eli Broad, both of whom support charter schools and contribute heavily to education-reform efforts. References to "keeping schools public" and rejecting "corporate Wall Street reform" are code for long-standing union opposition to school choice and suspicion of private philanthropy. Gates and Broad come up again and again in union talking points. "We reject the premise that the 1 percent billionaires—Bill Gates and Eli Broad—should be allowed to seize our public schools by buying seats on school boards that dismantle our schools, lay off thousands of teachers, and then award dozens of public schools to private charters, while denying teachers collective bargaining rights," reads an October 2011 UTLA press release outlining the themes of Occupy LAUSD's closing rally.

Beyond union rabble-rousing ahead of what's sure to be a contentious contract negotiation, Occupy LAUSD highlights a stark and widening disagreement about what American public education should be. With their billion-dollar endowments, Gates and Broad are powerful players among an ideologically diverse coalition of reformers that includes conservative Republicans, Milton Friedman libertarians, and urban Democrats. But Gates and Broad are hardly the prime movers or the last word in education reform—a point that UTLA and its left-wing union allies refuse to concede. In general, reformers hold that public education should teach students how to be autonomous, knowledgeable, and self-governing citizens. The *how* and the *where* matter less than the *what*. So reformers advocate empowering parents with a range of options, whether they're charters or "virtual schools" or opportunity scholarships aimed primarily (but not exclusively) at lower-income families. Traditional public schools should compete with alternative models. Excellent teachers should be rewarded with higher pay. Bad teachers should be eased out of the system.

When Deasy took office in the summer of 2011, he laid out a handful of proposed contract changes, including more school-site flexibility with hiring, overhauling tenure rules, and experimenting with merit pay. Occupy LAUSD opposes every one of those ideas. For the occupiers, public education means tax-funded schools operated by union-organized administrators and teachers with little testing and accountability and no choice. Seen in that light, Occupy LAUSD is less radical than reactionary.

Note

1. In fact, the union spent more than $21 million to defeat Proposition 32, a ballot initiative that would have banned unions and corporations from using money deducted from members' or employees' paychecks for political purposes, and barred direct contributions from unions and corporations to candidates or their campaign committees. In addition, the CTA contributed $11.4 million to Governor Jerry Brown's campaign to raise income and sales taxes.

22

Triggering School Reform

Parents Push for Their
Legal Rights to Better Schools, but
the Education Establishment Pushes Back

Ben Boychuk

WON'T BACK DOWN, A MAJOR HOLLYWOOD motion picture that came and went in late 2012, was supposed to be popular culture's coming-out party for school reform. Starring Maggie Gyllenhaal and Academy Award winners Viola Davis and Holly Hunter, the film portrayed the plight of a single mom and a teacher battling to turn around a failing school in the face of bureaucratic intransigence and teachers' union obstructionism. To the disappointment of its producers, not to mention thousands of school-reform activists around the country, *Won't Back Down* bombed. Though set in Pittsburgh, the film was based loosely on the melancholy experience of parents in Compton, California and more recently in the Southern California desert town of Adelanto—where, earlier in the year, a Hollywood happy ending appeared far out of parents' reach.

But in the kind of third-act turnaround that screenwriters love, Adelanto's blue-collar parents didn't blink when confronting a stubborn school board that tried to dismiss their efforts to remake a struggling elementary school. Instead, they went to court and won. On October 12, 2012, San Bernardino County Superior Court Judge John Vander Feer ruled that the Adelanto Elementary School District must let parents proceed with plans to convert Desert Trails Elementary School into a charter school, starting with the 2013 school year. Vander Feer's decision reinforced a July 18 ruling, which barred the district from using an eleventh-hour "rescission" campaign to pressure parents to withdraw support from the charter-conversion effort.

Adelanto serves both as vindication for California's first-in-the-nation parent empowerment law—also known as the "parent trigger"—and as a model for parent-activists around the state and nation to emulate. The *Wall Street Journal* in 2010 called the parent trigger "the radical school reform law you've never heard of." That's starting to change, as lawmakers in other states debate similar measures and parents in some of the worst-performing school districts in the Golden State learn how to wield the law.

* * *

Under California's parent-trigger law, if at least half of eligible parents at a persistently failing school sign a petition, the school district must undertake one of several prescribed "intervention models." The district can close the school and let students enroll in a higher-performing public school nearby; convert the school into a charter school, which would operate with greater autonomy from local and state regulations; or implement the "turnaround" and "transformation" requirements set forth under Race to the Top, the Obama administration's education-reform program, which could involve replacing staff, extending school hours, and revising the curriculum. Parents have the first choice of which intervention model to use. If a district determines that it cannot carry out the particular reform that parents want, officials must adopt one of the others. Ignoring the petition is not an option.

By a margin of one vote in each house, California's Democratic-dominated state legislature narrowly passed the law in January 2010 as part of the state's effort to win a piece of the $4.35 billion in federal funding for Race to the Top. California didn't get any money, but the landmark law remains on the books. Seven other states now have some version of it, and legislatures in 20 others were considering similar laws in early 2013.

California's law caps at 75 the number of schools subject to the parent trigger statewide, even though at least 1,300 out of California's 9,000 public schools would qualify—that is, they have missed federally mandated Average Yearly Progress goals for four consecutive years, as established under the 2002 No Child Left Behind law. Adelanto's Desert Trails Elementary, which serves about 650 mostly black and Latino students in kindergarten through sixth grade, hadn't met California's reading or math standards for nearly seven years when Doreen Diaz and six other parents got together in early 2011 to form a "parent union," which they registered as a nonprofit organization with California's secretary of state. In 2012, when the Desert Trails Parent Union petitioned the Adelanto Elementary School District to hand the school over to a charter school operator, Desert Trails ranked among the worst-performing elementary schools in San Bernardino County and resided in the bottom 10 percent of schools in the state, according to the California Department of Education. Just 34 percent of Desert Trails students were proficient in reading and 46 percent in math, state statistics showed. Worse, the school's Academic

Performance Index (API) ranking fell from 712 to 699 in 2012. A school with an API score below 800—a measure the state calculates by taking students' standardized test scores and comparing them with students sharing similar demographic and academic characteristics—is considered failing.

Adelanto parents say they tried to work with school and district officials to improve Desert Trails, only to be rebuffed again and again. "The goal of a great school for our children is primary," Diaz wrote to Adelanto superintendent Darin Brawley. "The preference to keep the school within the District and teachers covered by the contract is secondary." Holly Odenbaugh, a Desert Trails parent whose daughter started kindergarten in 2011, said she learned how bad the situation was on the first day of classes. "The teacher told me it wasn't worth it for her to come to school anymore," Odenbaugh recalled. She wondered what she was getting her daughter into. Odenbaugh was among a dozen parents who met on November 21, 2011, with Adelanto assistant superintendent Ross Swearingen. They presented a lengthy list of demands for reform, which included giving the principal control over budgeting and hiring. The district rejected them all.

With that, the Desert Trails petition drive began in earnest. About 100 parents rallied on January 12, 2012, at a park adjacent to the school before delivering several thick binders full of signed petitions in a red Radio Flyer wagon to Desert Trails principal David Mobley, who had only been on the job three months. At an impromptu gathering of reporters in the teachers' lounge, the soft-spoken Mobley said he believed that parents, teachers, and district officials were "all working toward the same ends." But he said he worried the parent-trigger law could divert limited resources away from schools toward litigation. "We should be spending money improving education for kids, not tying things up in court," Mobley said. He didn't know how right he was.

Diaz, a mother of three and an active PTA member until she cofounded the parent union, said she had become frustrated and disillusioned with the school district's empty promises to reform the failing school. In letters to the school district and at the January rally, parents detailed allegations of bullying, poorly maintained facilities, and indifferent instructors. When district officials flatly rejected the parents' detailed proposal for overhauling Desert Trails, they realized any chance of collaboration was hopeless. "I can't just sit here and hope they're going to get it right," Diaz said a few weeks after parents submitted their petitions and found themselves facing a wall of opposition not only from Adelanto district officials, but also from the California Teachers Association. "It's been more than six years now. They haven't done anything yet. What makes me think they're going to do something now?"

The parents' eventual win in Adelanto was hard-fought. It took nearly a year to reach a resolution and required outside assistance, including pro bono legal representation from Kirkland & Ellis, one of the nation's biggest law firms. Almost immediately after parents submitted their petitions with signatures from about 70 percent of Desert Trails' parents, strangers began appearing at parents' homes with a petition of their own. This one called on the Adelanto school district to reject the Desert Trails Parent Union charter conversion. These same strangers showed up at school at pickup time, rapping on parents' car windows, urging them to sign the rescission petition—and making it difficult for them to drive away if they refused. It didn't take long for the DTPU to figure out that the strangers were operatives from the California Teachers Association.

One month after Diaz and her fellow parents submitted their signatures, the Adelanto school board rejected their petition, claiming they hadn't met the 50 percent threshold. The Desert Trails Parent Union had submitted 466 parent signatures, representing 70 percent of the 665 students enrolled. But at the school board's February meeting, district officials claimed 97 signatures were either invalid or had been rescinded by parents—despite clear language stating such changes were not allowed. The five-member Adelanto Elementary School District board voted unanimously to deny the parents' petition, which Superintendent Brawley said fell 16 signatures short of what the law required.

Diaz and her compatriots expected trouble, but they hadn't expected this. Fortunately, they had training and aid from the Los Angeles-based Parent Revolution, a liberal activist group led by Ben Austin, a former Clinton administration staffer and advisor to former Los Angeles mayor Richard Riordan. Parent Revolution, in fact, was instrumental in persuading the Los Angeles Unified School District in 2008 to create a "proto" parent-trigger rule for a limited number of failing schools, and it worked with state senator Gloria Romero on writing the state law in late 2009. Though they regularly profess solidarity with the labor movement, Austin and his team had run up against teachers' union opposition for years and had become accustomed to the kinds of dirty tricks and intimidation on display in the desert.

Each side accused the other of bad faith and lies (often in all-capital letters and exclamation points). Adelanto school officials and opponents of the parent-trigger petition repeatedly claimed that Parent Revolution's organizers and Desert Trails parents circulated two different petitions, calling it a "bait and switch" on parents who didn't necessarily want a charter school. Gabe Rose, Parent Revolution's assistant executive director, said the Adelanto parents leveraged the trigger law to "force the district to the bargaining table." As Rose explained, "The parents weren't getting anywhere with the district until they collected these signatures"; he suggested that the parents could have withdrawn the petition if district officials and the local teachers' union agreed to make concessions on curriculum, school hours, hiring, and budgeting.

But those changes would have required the Adelanto District Teachers' Association to waive its current collective bargaining agreement with the school district, a concession the union flatly refused to make. "The union can waive the contract or the school will become a community charter. Either way, the parents win," Rose said.

* * *

For a time, however, it appeared that the Desert Trails story would end much as it had for parents at McKinley Elementary School in Compton. If Adelanto is the feel-good saga of the parent-trigger movement, then Compton is the cautionary tale. At first glance, the stories seem similar. On December 7, 2010, dozens of enthusiastic parents delivered petitions to the Compton Unified School District office. Aided by professional community organizers from Parent Revolution, the mostly black and Latino parents spent months collecting signatures from 61 percent of McKinley's parents. Like Desert Trails, the school cried out for reform. Ranked among the bottom 10 percent of California schools, McKinley had met its yearly goals only once since 2003. Not that the rest of Compton Unified district was much better. A state audit released in July 2010 portrayed a district mired in dysfunction, where school personnel routinely "exhibit a lack of civility and respect" for parents and "the focus . . . is primarily on adult issues and not on student needs." And like the Adelanto parents, the McKinley group wanted to convert the school into an independently managed charter.

District apologists, however, opposed applying the parent trigger to McKinley, pointing to its API score of 684, a 26-point improvement over 2009—still well below the 800-point threshold separating success from failure. "The parent trigger law was never intended to apply to a school making gains like these," claimed the Compton Education Association, the local teachers' union, in a written statement. In a unanimous vote on February 22, 2012, Compton's school board denied the McKinley parents' petition on the thinnest of pretexts: some of the signatures may not have been valid; a few signatures were duplicated; the petition had some embarrassing typographical errors; and parents didn't attach supporting documentation properly. For want of a staple—and other minor technicalities spelled out in a seven-page staff report made public only a few minutes before the public meeting began—the school board deemed the petition "insufficient." There was no discussion. "The district reviewed the petition not to verify the signatures, but to disqualify them," said Jeff Senik, a Kirkland & Ellis attorney representing the Compton parents, who filed a lawsuit against the trustees.

But even before the McKinley parents submitted their petition, Compton officials' "lack of civility and respect" was on full display. Two parents filed formal complaints in January with the U.S. Department of Education's Office of Civil Rights, claiming their children had been threatened and intimidated by some teachers because of the parents' support for the petition drive. Once the petition was filed, the district escalated its campaign of misinformation and intimidation. Abetted by state and local teachers' union members, as well as the local PTA, Compton district officials charged that parents had been badgered or tricked into signing the petition. About 10 parents withdrew their signatures as a result. In a tactic repeated in Adelanto almost a year later, Compton district surrogates claimed parents were dupes for "private charter corporations." Parent Revolution, in fact, did get its start as a community-organizing offshoot of Green Dot Charter Schools, a nonprofit organization that runs over a dozen charters in the Los Angeles area. But the McKinley parents chose Celerity Education Group as their charter-management organization, not Green Dot. For charter-school critics, though, these are distinctions without a difference.

When Compton Unified couldn't persuade enough parents to withdraw their signatures, officials became even more coercive. In late January 2011, officials informed parents that they would need to appear at the district office for a "short interview" and sign a form verifying their petition signatures. Otherwise, the officials said, the signatures would be disqualified. In their lawsuit, parents called the district's ultimatum "burdensome and intrusive." Los Angeles Superior Court Judge Anthony Mohr agreed and granted a temporary restraining order against the district, barring officials from requiring parents to verify their signatures in person but stopping short of suspending the verification process entirely.

A series of court victories gave McKinley parents reason to believe they would prevail. Mohr rebuked Compton school trustees for violating the parents' First Amendment rights and ordered a recertification of the petitions. Incredibly, district officials responded to Mohr's order by announcing that they could not verify *any* of the signatures. "Staff cannot be assured that in all instances the signatures are legitimate and/or the persons executing the document maintained educational rights to do so," the district concluded in a five-page finding. The McKinley parents expected Mohr to return with an even harsher judgment against Compton Unified. But to their surprise, the judge dealt their case a fatal blow by invalidating the petitions because they lacked a date box required by state law. "The court is aware of the pain, frustration, and perhaps educational disadvantages this ruling may cause," a sympathetic Mohr wrote in a May 18 ruling. "However, the court believes the law compels this result." Mohr's decision was a discouraging setback to other parents who might have sought relief under the parent-trigger law. After all, McKinley's parents had pro bono legal aid from two of the top U.S. law firms—in addition to representation from Kirkland & Ellis, lawyers from Gibson Dunn & Crutcher vetted their petitions. If those parents couldn't prevail with that caliber of legal firepower, what chance would other families have?

* * *

The parent trigger's opponents tried to exploit the Compton fiasco to eviscerate the law. One problem with California's law, for its friends and enemies alike, is its brevity. At less than 600 words, the statute contains few nitty-gritty details about how the parent trigger should work in practice. The legislature left it to the Board of Education to spell out tedious but essential points, such as how petitions must be formatted, who would be qualified to sign, how quickly a school district must act on a valid petition, and how parents may appeal adverse district rulings. Sensing an opportunity, the CTA, the California School Boards Association, the state Parent Teachers Association, and other education-establishment groups demanded that the state board set extensive verification rules for parent signatures—including mandated public meetings where school district officials would control the agenda, along with onerous supermajority requirements for petitions that Democrats would otherwise reject as undemocratic. As Parent Revolution's Austin put it, "the parent trigger law is about empowering parents, not about empowering bureaucracies to find technicalities to disenfranchise parents and defend an indefensible status quo."

The state board passed temporary, "emergency" regulations in 2010 and was poised to approve permanent regulations at the beginning of 2011, until new governor Jerry Brown intervened. Less than a day after taking the oath of office on January 3, 2011, Brown sacked seven members of the 11-person board. Apart from being appointed by Brown's predecessor, Arnold Schwarzenegger, the ousted board members had something else in common: all were vocal supporters of the parent trigger. Out went the business-minded reformers—almost all Democrats critical of the education status quo. They included Ted Mitchell, president and CEO of NewSchools Venture Fund, and Parent Revolution's Austin. Taking their place were more conventional Democrats, reflecting the constituencies that helped return Brown to the governor's office after a 28-year hiatus: Carl Cohn, the former superintendent of Long Beach Unified School District; James Ramos, chairman of the San Manuel Band of Mission Indians in Southern California; and Patricia Ann Rucker, chief lobbyist for the CTA. Michael Kirst, an emeritus professor from Stanford who advised Brown on education during the 2010 gubernatorial campaign, replaced Mitchell as board president.

Also in the mix was newly elected California superintendent of public instruction Tom Torlakson, whose job includes carrying out the policies the board sets but who also has a prominent voice in setting the policies. As a state assemblyman from the East Bay town of Antioch, Torlakson—a former California Federation of Teachers executive—voted against Romero's parent-trigger legislation "on philosophical grounds." Torlakson explained he didn't believe parents should have so much power over a vital public asset. Torlakson and his chief deputy, Richard Zeiger, told state board members at their February 2011 meeting that the draft version of permanent rules for the parent trigger may not align with state law. "The law is difficult," Zeiger said. "It's vague where you want specificity, and specific where you would want a little more flexibility."

The board endorsed Torlakson's solution, which was to rewrite the parent-trigger law. Such "cleanup" legislation is not uncommon; the problem was the people doing the cleaning up. The new bill's lead author was Santa Monica Democratic assemblywoman Julia Brownley. As initially written, Brownley's bill would have made what the legislative counsel's summary called "technical, non-substantive changes" to the parent-empowerment law. But Brownley was no friend of parent empowerment. She previously offered a watered-down version of the parent trigger in 2010 that would have given parents the right to petition not for a school overhaul, but only for a hearing to air their grievances before district officials. As Compton and Adelanto parents discovered, merely airing grievances before an intransigent bureaucracy was a futile exercise. An amended version of Brownley's Assembly Bill 203 would have restricted the eligibility of parents to sign petitions and required a school board to consider testimony from parents opposed to petitions in reaching decisions about reforms. Though the assembly education committee eventually stripped those provisions, parent-trigger supporters worried they would reappear later.

Austin argued that the legislature shouldn't revise a law that barely had a chance to work. "At this stage, it is too early to determine what, if any, changes are necessary for this new pilot program," he told legislators. "And it is premature to propose legislative 'fixes' to the parent empowerment law while it is still being reviewed at both the executive and judicial levels." The original law's author was even blunter. "Let's not call it 'cleanup legislation,'" Gloria Romero said. "They're going to try to repeal the law."

Brownley's bill eventually passed, but to the surprise of partisans on both sides of the parent-trigger debate, Governor Brown vetoed the bill. If opponents couldn't effectively repeal the parent-trigger law, might they be able put a regulatory lock on it? As the state board pondered enabling regulations in early 2011, the CTA argued that teachers should have a veto. At issue was whether half of the faculty at a "triggered" school must ratify a parent petition seeking a charter-school conversion. The union argued that California's

1992 charter school law requires teachers to sign off on a charter conversion; the 2010 parent-empowerment act did not amend that provision. But parent-trigger supporters countered that the union's argument made no sense. "Our thinking is the parent empowerment law lets parents do something they couldn't otherwise do," explained Colin Miller, vice president for policy at the California Charter Schools Association. "If the regulations impose both petition processes, we're actually creating a harder process."

When the final regulations emerged in July 2011, the state board denied the CTA its veto. Kirst dismissed last-minute objections from CTA lobbyists over the charter-conversion rules. "It's called the parent empowerment act, not the teacher empowerment act, for a reason," he said. The final regulations included a requirement that school districts targeted for transformation hold "at least two public hearings to notify staff, parents, and the community of the school's designation and to seek input from staff, parents, and the community regarding the option or options most suitable for the school." Another rule specified that "signature gatherers, students, school site staff, [district] staff, community members, and parents and legal guardians shall be free from harassment, threats, and intimidation related to circulation or signature of a petition." But as Adelanto parents would discover, the rules don't spell out penalties or remedies for such behavior.

The Adelanto experience—like the ill-fated Compton effort before it— shows just how tricky the petition process can be. Though the state board's enabling regulations may have clarified the law, they didn't make parents' task much easier. The Desert Trails Parent Union still encountered harassment and intimidation, and though district officials complied with the state's mandated timetable for evaluating the parents' petitions, they initially disregarded the law's requirement to abide by the parents' preferred remedy.

*   *   *

But Adelanto set two crucial precedents for the parent-trigger law that should make future petition drives less onerous. First, trigger opponents no longer will be permitted to mount any sort of "rescission campaigns." In Compton, school officials and teachers' union activists shamelessly hassled parents to withdraw their signatures, telling them they'd been duped by outsiders and warning parents with questionable legal status in the United States that they could be deported. San Bernardino County Superior Court Judge Steve Malone ordered Adelanto school officials to disregard the CTA's efforts to mount a counter-petition drive and let Desert Trails parents begin evaluating charter school proposals.

Second, school officials won't be able to ignore the law's clear language. Adelanto officials tried to wiggle out of Malone's order, citing a provision of the law stating that a district "shall implement the option requested by the parents unless . . . the local educational agency makes a finding in writing stating the reason it cannot implement the specific recommended option and instead designates in writing which of the other options described in this section. . . ." In effect—as Judge Vander Feer would rule—the district trustees tried to run out the clock on parents, claiming they could not be expected to permit an outside charter-management group to take over Desert Trails just a few days before the school year was scheduled to begin. In lieu of the charter school the parents wanted, the board voted to create a "community advisory council" comprised of parents, teachers, administrators, and community members—a remedy not specified in the law or state regulations.

At least one Adelanto trustee left little doubt that the board never intended to abide by Malone's order. "There's a lot of things I'm willing to do," said trustee Jermaine Wright at the board's August meeting. "And if I'm found in contempt of court, I brought my own handcuffs"—which he dramatically produced and dropped on the table with a great *thunk.* "Take me away today. I don't care." To some parents' chagrin, Vander Feer didn't find Wright or any other school board members in contempt. Instead, he ruled that the district's "community advisory council" scheme didn't comply with the law and said the parents would have their charter school.

* * *

As the Compton and Adelanto experiences show, a worthwhile parent-empowerment law minimizes bureaucratic imposition and offers protection against harassment from district officials and their surrogates. Districts should be held to tight deadlines for evaluating parent petitions, and signature verifications should be straightforward and unobtrusive. Given the institutional advantages school districts already hold over parents, it's hard to see why parent groups should be forced to be *more* transparent than school-district employees. For example, if parents must file notice that they're engaged in a petition drive to convert, reform, or close a school, they deserve access to the data and resources a district or its union surrogates might use to oppose such an effort. As for claims that parents are merely pawns for a "corporate charter" agenda, Desert Trails Parent Union member Joe Morales makes clear that parents go into this with their eyes open. "We knew what we were doing," he said. "No one was strung along. We made the plans, we made the decisions as a group and as a committee. Nobody needed to tell us what was going wrong."

Above all, parents need clarity. Education "experts" often discuss policy using mind-numbing terminology indecipherable to lay people. They have a vested interest in everything except whether kids succeed. By itself, the parent trigger might not turn around low-performing schools, but the law can help reframe the way parents and policymakers approach education reform. It cuts through bureaucratic jargon and gives parents a powerful means of bringing about change.

On January 8, 2013—four days shy of a year since Desert Trails parents delivered their petitions, and nearly two years since the parents' union formed—the Adelanto school board approved the Desert Trails charter-school plan. Parents hugged and wept. It was a Hollywood happy ending.

How about a sequel? On January 17, 2013, a group of 100 parents delivered 358 signatures to the office of John Deasy, superintendent of the Los Angeles Unified School District, the second-largest school district in the United States and the parent trigger's birthplace. Their goal: to convert L.A.'s failing 24th Street Elementary School into an independent charter. Deasy promised the district's full cooperation with parents; even the head of the local teachers' union pledged restraint.

"Today was a new chapter in this movement," Ben Austin told the *Los Angeles Times*. "It was a paradigm shift in changing the way that parents, educators and administrators talk about [the] parent trigger." After years of hard fighting, parent empowerment appears to be here to stay.

[2013]

23

Grading the Teachers

Value-Added Teacher Evaluations Are a Useful Accountability Tool

Larry Sand

CALIFORNIA'S PUBLIC SCHOOL TEACHERS are the highest paid in the country, earning well over $60,000 a year on average, along with generous health-insurance and pension plans. Their salaries and benefits are funded with taxes paid by all of us—workers, consumers, homeowners, and businesses large and small. It's useful to think of taxpayers as owners of our troubled public education franchise, which has a statewide high school drop-out rate of about 30 percent. And for many of those who do graduate from high school and go on to college, remediation is essential. Value-added teacher evaluation—a method that estimates the contribution that teachers make to student test-score gains—is a concept whose time has most definitely come. Californians are entitled to know precisely who is and isn't delivering the goods for their children.

In May 2011, the *Los Angeles Times* published a much-anticipated follow-up to its pathbreaking 2010 investigation, which ranked 6,000 third-, fourth-, and fifth-grade teachers based on their students' progress on standardized tests year after year. The updated rankings included data for more than 11,500 teachers. Using the California Public Records Act, *Times* reporters Jason Felch, Jason Song, and Doug Smith obtained student math and language arts scores for the Los Angeles Unified School District from 2003 through 2009. The newspaper commissioned Richard Budden, a senior economist and education researcher with the Santa Monica–based RAND Corporation, to analyze the data. Using the value-added technique, he converted the scores into percentile ratings, and then divided them into five equal categories from "least effective" to "most effective."

The *Times* stories exposed that what currently passes for teacher evaluation in California is useless. Currently, a principal or other administrator may visit a class several times (usually with a warning given long in advance), stay a few minutes, scribble down some notes, and leave. Union contracts generally spell out strict protocols about which administrator can perform the observations and when and how many times a teacher may be observed. The contracts also discourage unsatisfactory ratings by forcing principals to navigate a nightmarish labyrinth of costly and time-consuming documentation. Thanks to this ineffective process, more than 99 percent of all teachers receive satisfactory ratings, and after just two years in the classroom achieve tenure—essentially a job for life.

Value-added evaluations offer a better way of assessing a teacher's strengths and weaknesses in the classroom. Though student math and English scores had been readily available to the school district and the teachers' union for years, nobody did anything with them. Not only did the *Times* make the effort to get the scores and categorize them; the paper also published the data along with teachers' names. In doing so, the *Times* incurred the wrath of United Teachers Los Angeles president A. J. Duffy, who accused the paper of "teacher bashing" and immediately called for its boycott. Undaunted by the union's bullying, the *Times* spent the next nine months showing the benefits of value-added teacher evaluations. The paper reported: "Highly effective teachers routinely propel students from below grade level to advanced in a single year. There is a substantial gap at year's end between students whose teachers were in the top 10 percent in effectiveness and the bottom 10 percent. The fortunate students ranked 17 percentile points higher in English and 25 points higher in math." The *Times* also pointed out that more than 8,000 students were stuck in classes with a bottom-rung teacher for at least two years in a row. Studies have shown that two consecutive years with a bad teacher can leave students so far behind that they will never catch up.

Value-added isn't new, but the technique has gained greater acceptance in recent years as a way of evaluating teachers. Louisiana, Texas, and North Carolina have incorporated value-added into their teacher evaluation rules. Hoover Institution senior fellow and economist Eric Hanushek claims that while value-added analysis isn't perfect, it's "the best tool we have available to zero in on the impact of the individual teacher on student achievement gains. Using it, we can begin to distinguish between the best teachers and the worst, so we can begin rewarding the best while learning from their successes and improving—or removing—the worst." Ideally, education reformers would like to see value-added measures used along with principals' and outside experts' observations, student portfolios, and parent input to reach a well-rounded evaluation.

As a result of the *Times* reports and the ensuing controversy, John Deasy, Los Angeles Unified's new superintendent, felt compelled to develop an evaluation process of his own. His idea was to get teachers and administrators to participate in the plan, which includes a value-added assessment. Under Deasy's proposal, 900 teachers—all of whom volunteered—would be offered a $1,250 stipend and other perks to participate. In short order, UTLA sought a court injunction to block the plan, claiming unfair labor practices because union bosses were not consulted. A superior-court judge denied the union's complaint in May 2011, and the voluntary program will go forth as planned, barring any other legal roadblocks by the union.[1]

The teachers' union's problem with Deasy's pilot program extends beyond a mere lack of consultation. Teachers' unions dislike all forms of substantive teacher evaluation, viewing any kind of official differentiation among teachers as encouraging competition, which sows envy and thus undermines solidarity. Yet objective evaluations show that some teachers really are more effective than others. To concede as much exposes the union to serious difficulties. Suppose, for example, that the more effective teachers suddenly feel entitled to greater compensation than their less competent peers? And when a school district faces a budget crunch, why shouldn't the more effective teachers be spared pink slips? A seniority system that elevates clock-watchers and ignores teacher quality hardly seems fair to adults or kids.

To make value-added evaluations public only adds insult to injury. The union argues that the *Times* wrongly trumpeted the results because the public cannot see the whole picture of a teacher's worth. But the *Times*, to its credit, advertised that any teacher who so chose could leave a comment next to his or her score. Shortly after the first *Times* story appeared in 2010, National Education Association president Dennis Van Roekel tried to dismiss value-added evaluations with a sports analogy. A .250 hitter in baseball, Van Roekel said, may possess other talents that a .350 hitter does not. He's right, of course. But take Van Roekel's analogy one step further. Every day during the baseball season, anyone can pick up a daily newspaper or check the Internet and find out all kinds of things about baseball players—their batting average, errors, home runs, strikeouts, and so forth. The publication of the teachers' value-added scores is no more "teacher bashing" than the publication of hitters' statistics is "batter bashing."

[2011]

Note

1. In December 2012, Deasy and the UTLA agreed to a new contract that overhauls the teacher evaluation system and includes student test scores in the process, but notably does not use "value-added" in the calculation. Los Angeles mayor Antonio Villaraigosa called the deal a "major concession" by the district but supported it because "overall it was a step forward from what we had before."

24

UC Two

Can a School Obsessed with Diversity Survive?

Heather Mac Donald

IN THE SUMMER OF 2012, as the University of California reeled from one piece of bad budget news to another, a veteran political columnist sounded an alarm. Cuts in state funding were jeopardizing the university's mission of preserving the "cultural legacy essential to any great society," Peter Schrag warned in the *Sacramento Bee*:

> Would we know who we are without knowing our common history and culture, without knowing Madison and Jefferson and Melville and Dickinson and Hawthorne; without Shakespeare, Milton and Chaucer; without Dante and Cervantes; without Charlotte Bronte and Jane Austen; without Goethe and Moliere; without Confucius, Buddha, Gandhi and Martin Luther King Jr.; without Mozart, Rembrandt and Michelangelo; without the Old Testament; without the Gospels; without Plato and Aristotle, without Homer and Sophocles and Euripides, without Tolstoy and Dostoyevsky; without Gabriel Garcia Marquez and Toni Morrison?

Schrag's appeal to the value of humanistic study was unimpeachable. It just happened to be laughably ignorant about the condition of such study at the University of California. Stingy state taxpayers aren't endangering the transmission of great literature, philosophy, and art; the university itself is. No UC administrator would dare to invoke Schrag's list of mostly white, mostly male thinkers as an essential element of a UC education; no UC campus has sought to ensure that its undergraduates get any exposure to even one of Schrag's seminal thinkers (with the possible exception of Toni Morrison), much less to America's founding ideas or history.

Schrag isn't the only Californian ignorant about UC's priorities. The public is told that the university needs more state money to stay competitive in the sciences, but not that the greatest threat to scientific excellence comes from the university's obsession with "diversity" hiring. The public knows about tuition increases, but not about the unstoppable growth in the university's bureaucracy. Taxpayers may have heard about larger class sizes, but not about the sacrosanct status of faculty teaching loads. Before the public decides how much more money to pour into the system, it needs a far better understanding of how UC spends the $22 billion it already commands.

* * *

The first University of California campus opened at Berkeley in 1873, fulfilling a mandate of California's 1849 constitution that the state establish a public university for the "promotion of literature, the arts and sciences." Expectations for this new endeavor were high; Governor Henry Haight had predicted that the campus would "soon become a great light-house of education and learning on this Coast, and a pride and glory" of the state.

He was right. Over the next 140 years, as nine more campuses were added, the university would prove an engine for economic growth and a source of human progress. UC owns more research patents than any other university system in the country. Its engineers helped achieve California's mid-century dominance in aerospace and electronics; its agronomists aided the state's fecund farms and vineyards. The nuclear technology developed by UC scientists and their students secured America's Cold War preeminence (while provoking one of the country's most cataclysmic student protest movements). UC's physical infrastructure is a precious asset in its own right. Anyone can wander its trellised gardens and groves of native and exotic trees, or browse its library stacks and superb research collections.

But by the early 1960s, UC was already exhibiting many of the problems that afflict it today. The bureaucracy had mushroomed, both at the flagship Berkeley campus and at the Office of the President, the central administrative unit that oversees the entire UC system. Nathan Glazer, who taught sociology at Berkeley at the time, wrote in *Commentary* in 1965: "Everyone—arriving faculty members, arriving deans, visiting authorities—is astonished by the size" of the two administrations. Glazer noted the emergence of a new professional class: full-time college administrators who specialized in student affairs, had never taught, and had little contact with the faculty. The result of this bureaucratic explosion reminded Glazer of the federal government: "Organization piled upon organization, reaching to a mysterious empyrean height."

At Berkeley, as federal research money flooded into the campus, the faculty were losing interest in undergraduate teaching, observed Clark Kerr, UC's president and a former Berkeley chancellor. (Kerr once famously quipped that a chancellor's job was to provide "parking for the faculty, sex for the students, and athletics for the alumni.") Back in the 1930s, responsibility for introductory freshman courses had been the highest honor that a Berkeley professor could receive, Kerr wrote in his memoirs; 30 years later, the faculty shunted off such obligations whenever possible to teaching assistants, who by 1964 made up nearly half the Berkeley teaching corps.

Most presciently, Kerr noted that Berkeley had split into two parts: Berkeley One, an important academic institution with a continuous lineage back to the nineteenth century; and Berkeley Two, a recent political upstart centered on the antiwar, antiauthority Free Speech Movement that had occupied Sproul Plaza in 1964. Berkeley Two was as connected to the city's left-wing political class and to its growing colony of "street people" as it was to the traditional academic life of the campus. In fact, the two Berkeleys had few points of overlap.

* * *

Today, echoing Kerr, we can say there are two Universities of California: UC One, a serious university system centered on the sciences (though with representatives throughout the disciplines) and still characterized by rigorous meritocratic standards; and UC Two, a profoundly unserious institution dedicated to the all-consuming crusade against phantom racism and sexism that goes by the name of "diversity." Unlike Berkeley Two in Kerr's Day, UC Two reaches to the topmost echelon of the university, where it poses a real threat to the integrity of its high-achieving counterpart.

It's impossible to overstate the extent to which the diversity ideology has encroached upon UC's collective psyche and mission. No administrator, no regent, no academic dean or chair can open his mouth for long without professing fealty to diversity. It is the one constant in every university endeavor; it impinges on hiring, distorts the curriculum, and sucks up vast amounts of faculty time and taxpayer resources. The university's budget problems have not touched it. In September 2012, for instance, as the university system faced the threat of another $250 million in state funding cuts on top of the $1 billion lost since 2007, UC San Diego hired its first vice chancellor for equity, diversity, and inclusion. This new diversocrat would pull in a starting salary of $250,000, plus a relocation allowance of $60,000, a temporary housing allowance of $13,500, and the reimbursement of all moving expenses. (A pricey but appropriately "diverse" female-owned executive search firm had found this latest diversity accretion.) In May 2011, UCLA named a professional bureaucrat with a master's degree in student affairs administration as its first assistant dean for "campus climate," tasked with "maintaining the campus as a safe, welcoming, respectful place," in the words of UCLA's assistant vice chancellor and dean of students. In December 2010, UC San Francisco appointed its first vice chancellor of diversity and outreach—with a starting salary of $270,000—to create a "diverse and inclusive environment," announced UC San Francisco chancellor Susan Desmond-Hellmann. Each of these new posts is wildly redundant with the armies of diversity functionaries already larding UC's bloated bureaucracy.

UC Two's worldview rests on the belief that certain racial and ethnic groups face ongoing bias, both in America and throughout the university. In 2010, UCLA encapsulated this conviction in a "Principle of Community" (one of eight) approved by the Chancellor's Advisory Group on Diversity (since renamed the UCLA Council on Diversity and Inclusion, in the usual churn of rebranding to which such bodies are subject). Principle Eight reads: "We acknowledge that modern societies carry historical and divisive biases based on race, ethnicity, gender, age, disability, sexual orientation and religion, and we seek to promote awareness and understanding through education and research and to mediate and resolve conflicts that arise from these biases in our communities."

The idea that a salient—if not the most salient—feature of "modern societies" is their "divisive biases" is ludicrously unhistorical. No culture has been more blandly indifferent than modern Western society to the individual and group characteristics that can still lead to death and warfare elsewhere. There is also no place that more actively celebrates the characteristics that still handicap people outside the West than the modern American campus. And yet when UC Two's administrators and professors look around their domains, they see a landscape riven by the discrimination that it is their duty to extirpate.

* * *

Thus it was that UC San Diego's electrical and computer engineering department found itself facing a mandate from campus administrators to hire a fourth female professor in early 2012. The possibility of a new hire had opened up—a rare opportunity in the current budget climate—and after winnowing down hundreds of applicants, the department put forward its top candidates for on-campus interviews. Scandalously, all were male. Word came down from on high that a female applicant who hadn't even been close to making the initial cut must be interviewed. So she was, and she got mediocre reviews. The powers-that-be then spoke again: her candidacy must be brought to a departmental vote. In an unprecedented assertion of secrecy, the department chair refused to disclose the vote's outcome and insisted on a second ballot. After that second vote, the authorities finally gave up, and both vote counts remain secret.

An electrical and computer engineering professor explains what was at stake. "We pride ourselves on being the best," he says. "The faculty know that absolute ranking is critical. No one had ever considered this woman a star." You would think that UC's administrators would value this fierce desire for excellence, especially in a time of limited resources. Thanks to its commitment to hiring only "the best," San Diego's electrical and computer engineering department has made leading contributions to circuit design, digital coding, and information theory.

Maria Sobek, UC Santa Barbara's associate vice chancellor for diversity, equity, and academic policy and a professor of Chicana and Chicano studies, provides a window into how UC Two thinks about its mission. If a faculty hiring committee selects only white male finalists for an opening, the dean will suggest "bringing in some women to look them over," Sobek says. These female candidates, she says, "may be borderline, but they are all qualified." And *voilà!* "It turns out [the hiring committees] really like the candidates and hire them, even if they may not have looked so good on paper." This process has "energized" the faculty to hire the woman, says Sobek. She adds that diversity interventions get "more positive responses" from humanities and social-sciences professors than from scientists.

Leave aside Sobek's amusing suggestion that the faculty just happen to discover that they "really like" the diversity candidate whom the administration has forced on them. More disturbing is the subversion of the usual hiring standard from "most qualified" to "qualified enough." UC Two sets the hiring bar low enough to scoop in some female or minority candidates, and then declares that anyone above that bar is "qualified enough" to trump the most qualified candidate, if that candidate is a white or Asian male. This is a formula for mediocrity.

Sometimes, UC Two can't manage to lower hiring standards enough to scoop in a "diverse" candidate. In that case, it simply creates a special hiring category outside the normal channels. In September 2012, after the meritocratic revolt in UC San Diego's electrical and computer engineering department, the engineering school announced that it would hire an "excellence" candidate, the school's Orwellian term for faculty who, it claims, will contribute to diversity and who by some odd coincidence always happen to be female or an underrepresented minority. UC San Diego's Division of Physical Sciences followed suit the next month, listing two tenure-track positions for professors who could "shape and expand the University's diversity initiatives." If the division had any specific scientific expertise in mind, the job listing made no mention of it.

* * *

Every campus has legions of diversity enforcers like Sobek. In 2010, as a $637 million cut in state funding closed some facilities temporarily and forced

UC faculty and staff to take up to three and a half weeks of unpaid leave, Mark Yudof, the president of the entire university system, found enough time to announce the formation of a presidential Advisory Council on Campus Climate, Culture and Inclusion. It would be supported by five working groups of faculty and administrators: the Faculty Diversity Working Group, the Diversity Structure Group, the Safety and Engagement Group, the Lesbian, Gay, Bisexual and Transgender Group, and the Metrics and Assessment Group. Needless to say, this new burst of committee activity replicated a long line of presidential diversity initiatives, such as the 2006 President's Task Force on Faculty Diversity and the president's annual Accountability Sub-Report on Diversity.

These earlier efforts must have failed to eradicate the threats that large subsets of students and faculty face. Yudof promised that his new council and its satellite working groups would address, yet again, the "challenges in enhancing and sustaining a tolerant, inclusive environment on each of the university's 10 campuses . . . so that every single member of the UC community feels welcome, comfortable and safe." Of course, under traditional measures of safety, UC's campuses rate extremely high, but more subtle dangers apparently lurk for women and certain minorities.

In April 2012, one of Yudof's five working groups disgorged its first set of recommendations for creating a "safe" and "healthy" climate for UC's beleaguered minorities, even as the university's regents, who theoretically govern the school, debated whether to raise tuition yet again to cover the latest budget shortfall. The Faculty Diversity Working Group called for hiring quotas, which it calls "cluster hiring," and more diversity bureaucrats, among nine other measures. (California's pesky constitutional ban on taking race and gender into account in public hiring, which took effect after voters approved Proposition 209 in 1996, has long since lost any power over UC behavior and rhetoric.)

You would think that an institution ostensibly dedicated to reason would have documented the widespread bias against women and minorities before creating such a costly apparatus for fighting that alleged epidemic. I ask Dianne Klein, the spokesman for UC's Office of the President, whether Yudof or other members of his office were aware of any faculty candidates rejected by hiring committees because of their race or sex. Or perhaps Yudof's office knew of highly qualified minority or female faculty candidates simply *overlooked* in a search process because the hiring committee was insufficiently committed to diversity outreach? Klein ducks both questions: "Such personnel matters are confidential and so we can't comment on your question about job candidates."

Does UC Santa Barbara's associate vice chancellor for diversity, equity, and academic policy know of such victims of faculty bias? "It's hard to prove that qualified women haven't been hired," says Sobek. But "people don't feel comfortable working with people who don't look like them and tend to hire people that look like them." Doesn't the high proportion of Asian professors in UC's science departments and medical schools suggest that UC's white faculty *are* comfortable working with people who don't look like them? "Oh, Asians are discriminated against, too," replies Sobek. "They face a glass ceiling. People think that maybe Asians are not good enough to run a university." Sobek's own university, UC Santa Barbara, has an Asian chancellor, but never mind.

Bureaucratic overseers are not enough to purge the faculty of its alleged narrow-mindedness; the faculty must be retrained from within. Every three years, representatives from departmental hiring committees at UCLA must attend a seminar on "unconscious bias" in order to be deemed fit for making hiring decisions. In 2012, a Berkeley department in the social sciences was informed that a female professor from outside the department would be sitting on its hiring committee, since its record of hiring women was unsatisfactory. Only after protest did UC Two's administrators back down.

* * *

In September 2012, even as he warned of financial ruin if voters didn't approve Governor Jerry Brown's $6 billion tax hike in November, Yudof announced another diversity boondoggle. The university was embarking on the nation's largest-ever survey of "campus climate," at a cost of $662,000 (enough to cover four years of tuition for more than a dozen undergraduates). The system-wide climate survey was, of course, drearily repetitive. Individual campus "climate councils" had been conducting "climate checks" for years, and an existing UC survey already asked each undergrad if he felt that his racial and ethnic group was "respected on campus." Nevertheless, with the university facing a possible quarter-billion-dollar cut in state funding, Yudof and his legions of diversity councils and work groups felt that now was the moment to act on the 2007 recommendations of the little-remembered "Regents' Study Group on University Diversity (Work Team on Campus Climate)" and of the "Staff Diversity Council."

Yudof's many campus-climate pronouncements are rife with the scary epidemiological language typical of this diversity subspecialty. "Now is a time when many of our most marginalized and vulnerable populations are most at risk," he wrote in July 2011, informing the campus chancellors that despite the budget crisis, planning for the "comprehensive and systematic campus climate assessment" was under way. Yudof didn't specify what these "marginalized and vulnerable populations" were "at risk" of, or why they would be at even *greater* risk now that the financial challenges facing the university had worsened.

If UC One were launching a half-million-dollar survey of the incidence of bubonic plague, say, among its students, faculty, and staff, it would have assembled enough instances of infection to justify the survey. It might even have formulated a testable hypothesis regarding the main vectors of infection. But UC Two's campus-climate rhetoric promiscuously invokes the need for "safe spaces" and havens from "risk" without ever identifying either the actual victims of its unsafe climates or their tormentors. These unsavory individuals must be out there, of course; otherwise, UC's "marginalized and vulnerable populations" wouldn't require such costly interventions. It would be useful if UC Two provided some examples. Who are these people and where do they hide? Further, the presence of such bigots means that UC's hiring and admissions policies must be seriously flawed. Where are the flaws and what does UC intend to do about them?

* * *

Time for a reality check. UC's campuses are among the most welcoming and inclusive social environments known to man. They are filled with civilized, pacific professors who want to do their research and maybe a little teaching and who have nothing but goodwill for history's oppressed groups. The campuses are filled, too, with docile administrators whose only purpose is swaddling students in services and fending off imaginary threats to those students' fragile identities. For their part, said students want to make friends and connections, maybe do a little learning, and get a degree. Race, ethnicity, and other official varieties of "identity" would be a nonissue for almost all of them if the adults on campus would stop harping on the subject. If Yudof and the regents, who enthusiastically back every diversity initiative that UC's administrators can dream up, don't know that, they are profoundly out of touch with the institution that they pretend to manage.

Your average UC student is unimpressed by UC Two's campus-climate initiatives. "That's ridiculous!" guffaws Tuanh, a UCLA senior majoring in psychobiology, when asked about UCLA's new campus-climate dean. But then, Tuanh is a first-generation Vietnamese-American from the San Gabriel Valley; perhaps, as a member of a successful minority group, she doesn't count as "marginalized and vulnerable," however poor her parents. Vanessa, a black UCLA junior from Long Beach, is closer to the kind of student whom Yudof and UCLA's administrators have in mind. But Vanessa is perplexed when told about the campus-climate dean. "I don't understand what that person would do," she says. "The school definitely takes racism seriously." Are your professors open to you? "I've never felt that a professor here didn't care about me succeeding." Perhaps things are worse on other campuses? Not at UC Irvine. Ade, a 24-year-old Nigerian finishing up his economics B.A. there, says that he's found no hostility on campus: "Everyone was welcoming and willing to try to get to know me."

UC One's faculty, too, are unenthusiastic about the campus-climate initiatives. Yudof's office tried to boost participation rates in the latest "inclusion survey" by raffling off two $5,000 faculty-research grants and two $5,000 graduate-student stipends to people answering merely half of the survey questions. (Whether such a raffle is the best way to allocate scarce research dollars is debatable.) Yudof also offered respondents a shot at five $2,000 professional-development grants and 24 iPads. Some campuses have thrown in their own incentives: UC San Francisco provided ten lucky raffle winners the opportunity to have lunch with the local vice chancellor for diversity and outreach and handed out 50 gift certificates worth $50 apiece. Despite these goodies, most people ignored the survey. After extending its deadline by nearly two months, UC San Francisco had reached only a 40 percent response rate. Most professors and grad students apparently have better things to do than answer grammatically challenged questions about whether they have "personally experienced any exclusionary (e.g., shunned, ignored), intimidating, offensive and/or hostile conduct (harassing behavior) at UC."

True, every so often an oafish student at UC, as at campuses across the country, stages a tasteless incident to rile the enforcers of political correctness. In 2010, a group of UC San Diego frat students sent out an invitation for an off-campus party with a crude ghetto theme; a black comedian later claimed responsibility for the event, which came to be known as the Compton Cookout. The inevitable student protests triggered the usual ballooning of UC Two's diversity bureaucracy, along with handwringing, from the UC president's office on down, about how hostile the university is to nonwhite students.

In a more rational world, the adults on campus might respond to such provocations by putting them in perspective—condemning the juvenile pranks but pointing out their insignificance compared with the resources and opportunities available to *all* students. If the adults were particularly courageous, they might even add that a minority student's best response to such pygmies is to crush them with his own success. Acing a chemistry exam does magnitudes more for minority empowerment, the straight-talking administrator might say, than sitting in at the dean's office demanding more "resources" for the Black Student Union. Such a message, however, would put UC Two out of business.

⁂ ⁂ ⁂

UC Two's pressures on the curriculum are almost as constant as the growth of the diversity bureaucracy. Consider Berkeley's sole curricular requirement. The campus's administration and faculty can think of only one thing that all its undergraduates need to know in order to have received a world-class education: how racial and ethnic groups interact in America. Every undergraduate must take a course that addresses "theoretical or analytical issues relevant to understanding race, culture, and ethnicity in American society" and that takes "substantial account of groups drawn from at least three of the following: African Americans, indigenous peoples of the United States, Asian Americans, Chicano/Latino Americans, and European Americans." In decades past, "progressives" would have grouped Americans in quite different categories, such as labor, capital, and landowners, or bankers, farmers, and railroad owners. Historians might have suggested Northerners, Southerners, and Westerners, or city dwellers, suburbanites, and rural residents. Might the interplay of inventors, entrepreneurs, and industrialists, say, or of scientists, architects, and patrons, be as fruitful a way of looking at American life as the distribution of skin color? Not in UC Two.

Naturally, this "American Cultures" requirement is run by Berkeley's ever-expanding Division of Equity and Inclusion. Berkeley students can fulfill the requirement with such blatantly politicized courses as "Gender, Race, Nation, and Health," offered by the gender and women's studies department, which provides students with "feminist perspectives on health care disparities" while considering gender "in dynamic interaction with race, ethnicity, sexuality, immigration status, religion, nation, age, and disability." Another possibility is "Lives of Struggle: Minorities in a Majority Culture," from the African-American studies department, which examines "the many forms that the struggle of minorities can assume." It is a given that to be a member of one of the course's favored "three minority aggregates"—"African Americans, Asian Americans (so called), and Chicano/Latino Americans"—means having to struggle against the oppressive American majority.

In 2010, the UCLA administration and a group of faculty restarted a campaign to require all undergraduates to take a set of courses explicitly dedicated to group identity. UCLA's existing "general-education" smorgasbord, from which students must select a number of courses in order to graduate, already contained plenty of the narcissistic identity and resentment offerings so dear to UC Two, such as "Critical Perspectives on Trauma, Gender, and Power" and "Anthropology of Gender Variance Across Cultures from Third Gender to Transgender." Yet that menu did not sufficiently guarantee exposure to race-based thinking to satisfy the UC Two power structure.

So even though UCLA's faculty had previously rejected a "diversity" general-education requirement in 2005, the administration and its faculty allies simply repackaged it under a new title, with an updated rationale. The new requirement would give meaning, they said, to that ponderous Eighth Principle of Community that the Chancellor's Advisory Group on Diversity had just approved. After the usual profligate expenditure of committee time, the faculty voted down the repackaged diversity requirement in May 2012, recognizing the burdens that any new general-education mandate puts on both students and faculty. UCLA chancellor Gene Block issued a lachrymose rebuke: "I'm deeply disappointed that the proposed new general education requirement was not approved and I'm especially disappointed for the many students who worked with such passion to make the case for a change in curriculum." As a consolation prize to UC Two, Block promised to set his administrators to work creating more courses on "diversity and community conflict issues."

* * *

UC Two captured the admissions process long ago. Ever since the passage of Proposition 209 banned racial discrimination at public institutions, UC's faculty and administrators have worked overtime to find supposedly race-neutral alternatives to outright quotas. Admissions officials now use "holistic" review to pick students, an opaque procedure designed to import proxies for race into the selection process, among other stratagems.

Vanessa, the UCLA junior, shows how drastically UC administrators violate the intention of Prop. 209. If she were white or Asian, her chances of being accepted into UCLA would have been close to zero. The average three-part SAT score of UCLA's 2012 freshman admits was 2042, out of a possible total of 2400. Vanessa's score was 1300, well below even the mediocre national average of 1500. Her academic performance has been exactly what her SATs would predict. She wants to double-major in psychology and gender studies, but she received a D-minus in psychological statistics, a prerequisite for enrolling in the psychology major. "I tried so hard; I don't understand why my grades didn't reflect how hard I was working," she says. "But I was always hard on myself and never gave myself enough credit." Apparently, Vanessa thinks that she suffers from a self-esteem, rather than a skills, deficit. On her second attempt at psychological statistics, she got a C, enough (for now) to continue in the major. "It's all I can ask for," she says. If UCLA's psychology major requires strong quantitative ability, however, Vanessa stands a good chance of ending up a gender studies major and nothing else.

Vanessa is a case study in a powerful critique of racial preferences known as "mismatch theory," pioneered by Richard Sander, a UCLA law professor. Sander and other economists have shown, through unrebutted empirical analysis, that college students admitted with academic qualifications drastically lower than those of their peers will learn less and face a much higher chance of dropping out of science and other rigorous majors. Had Vanessa gone to a school where her fellow students shared her skill level, she would be likelier to finish her psychology degree in good standing, because classroom instruction would be pitched to her academic needs. The leaders of UC Two, however, don't just ignore Sander's work; they press on relentlessly in their crusade to reinstate explicit racial quotas at UC. In 2012, Yudof and UC's ten chancellors found the time to submit an amicus brief to the U.S. Supreme Court in *Fisher* v. *Texas*, bellyaching about the crippling effect of Prop. 209 on the university's "diversity" and urging the court to reaffirm college-admissions preferences.

The admission of underprepared students generates another huge hunk of UC Two's ever-expanding bureaucracy, which devotes extensive resources to supporting "diverse" students as they try to complete their degrees. Take UC's vice president for student affairs, Judy Sakaki, who has traveled a career path typical of the "support-services" administrator, untouched by any traditional academic expertise or teaching experience. Sakaki started as an outreach and retention counselor in the Educational Opportunity Program at California State University, Hayward, and then became special assistant to the president for educational equity. She moved to UC Davis as vice chancellor of the division of student affairs and eventually landed in the UC president's office, where, according to her official biography, she continues to pursue her decades-long involvement in "issues of access and equity." She earns more than $255,000 a year.

Sakaki has dozens of counterparts on individual campuses. UCLA's $300 million Division of Undergraduate Affairs, with nary a professor in sight, is a typical support-services accretion, stuffed with "retention" specialists and initiatives for "advancing student engagement in diversity." (The division, which labels itself UCLA's "campus-wide advocate for undergraduate education," hosts non-diversity-related programs as well, intended to demonstrate that the university really *does* care about undergraduate education, despite complaints that its main interest lies in nabbing faculty research grants.) It is now assumed that being the first member of your family to go to college requires a bureaucracy to see you through, even though thousands of beneficiaries of the first G.I. Bill managed to graduate without any contact from a specially dedicated associate vice provost. So did the children of East European Jews who flooded into the City College of New York in the 1930s and 1940s. So do the children of Chinese laborers today who get science degrees both in China and abroad. Yet UC Two and other colleges have molded a construct, the "first-generation college student," and declared it in need of services—though it is simply a surrogate for "student admitted with uncompetitive scores from a family culture with low social capital."

It's unclear how much these retention bureaucracies actually accomplish. What *has* improved minority graduation rates, though UC Two hates to admit it, is Prop. 209. Graduation rates for underrepresented minorities in the pre–Prop. 209 era, when the university openly used racial preferences, languished far behind those of whites and Asians; it was only when Prop. 209 reduced the number of students admitted with large achievement gaps that minority graduation rates improved.

* * *

The costs of all these bureaucratic functions add up. From the 1997–1998 school year to 2008–2009, as the UC student population grew 33 percent and tenure-track faculty grew 25 percent, the number of senior administrators grew 125 percent, according to the Committee on Planning and Budget of UC's Academic Senate. The ratio of senior managers to professors climbed from 1 to 2.1 to near-parity of 1 to 1.1. University officials argue that hospitals and research functions drive such administrative expansion. But the rate of growth of non–medical center administrators was also 125 percent, and more senior professionals were added outside the research and grants-management area than inside it.

It's true that UC isn't wholly responsible for its own engorgement, since politicians promiscuously impose frivolous mandates that produce more red tape. In October 2011, for example, Governor Brown signed a bill requiring the university to provide the opportunity for students, staff, and faculty to announce their sexual orientation and "gender identity" on all UC forms. A hurricane of committee meetings ensued to develop the proper compliance procedures.

But most of UC's bureaucratic bulk is self-generated, and the recent budget turmoil hasn't dented that growth. In 2011, Berkeley's $200,000-a-year vice chancellor for equity and inclusion presided over an already princely staff of 17; by 2012, his realm had ballooned to 24. In September 2012, UC San Francisco's vice chancellor of diversity and outreach opened a new Multicultural Resource Center, complete with its own staff, timed to coincide with Celebrate Diversity Month.

And expanding its own bureaucracy isn't the only way that UC Two likes to spend money. In September 2012, UC San Diego chancellor Pradeep Khosla announced that every employee would get two hours of paid leave to celebrate California Native American Day, a gesture that under the most conservative salary assumptions could cost well over $1 million. In the same month, the vice provost of UCLA's four ethnic-studies departments announced that five professors would get paid leave to pursue "transformative interdisciplinary research" regarding "intersectional exchanges and cultural fusion"—at a time when the loss of faculty through attrition has led to more crowded classrooms and fewer course offerings. (Yes, UCLA's ethnic-studies departments boast their own vice provost; the position may be UC Two's most stunning sinecure.) In August 2012, UCLA's Center for Labor Research and Education announced that it would create the "National Dream University," an online school exclusively for illegal aliens, where they would become involved in "social justice movements" and learn about labor organizing. Only after negative publicity from right-wing media outlets did UC cancel the program, while leaving open the possibility of reconstituting it at a future date.

* * *

UC Two's constant accretion of trivialities makes it difficult to take its leaders' protestations of penury seriously. Yudof likes to stress that the state's contribution to the University of California's 2012 budget ($2.27 billion out of a total UC budget of $22 billion) is only 10 percent higher, in non-inflation-adjusted dollars, than it was in 1990, even as enrollment has grown 51 percent and UC has added a tenth campus. To Yudof, that equation signals crisis. It would be just as easy to argue, though, that UC must be doing just fine with the money that the state is giving it. Otherwise, why would it have added that new campus, not to mention reams of new bureaucrats?

Indeed, for an institution not known for its celebrations of capitalism, the university shows a robber-baron-like appetite for growth. The system announced plans to add a fifth law school in 2006, notwithstanding abundant evidence that California's 25 existing law schools were generating more than enough lawyers to meet any conceivable future demand. Initial rationalizations for the new law school focused on its planned location—at UC Riverside, in the less affluent and allegedly law-school-deficient Inland Empire east of Los Angeles. But even that insufficient justification evaporated when movers and shakers in Orange County persuaded the regents to site the school at well-endowed UC Irvine, next door to wealthy Newport Beach. Following the opening of Irvine's law school in 2009, California's glut of lawyers and law schools has only worsened, leading another UC law school (at UC San Francisco) to cut enrollment by 20 percent in 2012.

UC's tenth campus, UC Merced, which opened in 2005, is just as emblematic of the system's reflexive expansion, which is driven by politics and what former regent Ward Connerly calls "crony academics." Hispanic advocates and legislators pushed the idea that a costly research university in California's agricultural Central Valley was an ethnic entitlement—notwithstanding the fact that UC's existing nine research institutions were already more than the state's GDP or population could justify, according to Steve Weiner, the former executive director of the Accrediting Commission for Senior Colleges and Universities. And now that the Merced campus exists, UC's socialist ethos requires redistributing scarce resources to it from the flagship campuses, in pursuit of the chimerical goal of raising it to the caliber of Berkeley, UCLA, or UC San Diego.

Smaller-scale construction projects continue as well. UC Irvine's business school is getting an opulent new home, though its existing facility—an arcaded sandstone bungalow nestled among willowy eucalyptus—is perfectly serviceable. The new building will have white-noise cancellation technology, as well as Apple TV and iPads in every classroom. Like the new law school and the new UC campus, this doesn't paint a portrait of a university starved for funds.

Even UC's much-lamented rise in tuition masks a more complicated picture than is usually acknowledged. Tuition has trebled over the last decade to about $12,000 and now covers 49 percent of the cost of an undergraduate education, compared with 13 percent in 1990, according to the UC Faculty Senate. For the first time in UC's history, students are contributing more to their education than the state is. But contrary to received wisdom, tuition increases have not reduced "access." The number of students attending UC whose family income is $50,000 or less rose 61 percent from 1999 to 2009; such students now make up 34 percent of enrollment, according to the *Los Angeles Times*. Students whose families earn up to $80,000 pay no tuition at all, a tuition break that extends even to illegal aliens.

It is certainly true that state funding has not kept up with enrollment growth, leading UC to freeze much faculty hiring and eliminate courses. But UC's leaders continue to expect the state to bail them out. They shilled heavily for Governor Brown's successful November 2012 ballot measure to raise approximately $6 billion a year in new taxes, calling it the only alternative to avoiding further tuition increases and cuts in core functions. Given the still-perilous condition of the state's finances, however, the chance that taxpayer funding will be restored to the level to which UC feels entitled is zero.

* * *

If the university doesn't engage in internal reform, the primary victim will be UC One, that still-powerful engine of learning and progress. The first necessary reform: axing the diversity infrastructure. UC Two has yet to produce a scintilla of proof that faculty or administrator bias is holding professors or students back. Accordingly, every vice chancellor, assistant dean, and associate provost for equity, inclusion, and multicultural awareness should be fired and his staff sent home. Faculty committees dedicated to ameliorating the effects of phantom racism, sexism, and homophobia should be disbanded and the time previously wasted on such senseless pursuits redirected to the classroom. Campus climate checks, sensitivity training, annual diversity subreports—all should go. Hiring committees should be liberated from the thrall of diversity mandates; UC's administrators should notify department chairs that they will henceforth be treated like adults and trusted to choose the very best candidates they can find. Federal and state regulators, unfortunately, will still require the compiling of "diversity" data, but staff time dedicated to such mandates should be kept to a minimum.

UC should also start honoring California's constitution and eliminate race and gender preferences in faculty appointments and student admissions. The evidence is clear: admitting students on the basis of skin color rather than skills hurts their chances for academic success. And by jettisoning double standards in student selection, UC can significantly shrink its support-services bureaucracy.

Some useful reforms at UC are only loosely related to its obsession with "diversity." For example, one of the university's reigning fictions is that it is a unified system of equal campuses, efficiently managed from the Office of the President. That conceit is false and results in enormous waste. The campuses should be cut free from central oversight to the greatest extent possible and allowed to govern themselves, including setting their own tuition. Local boards should oversee the campuses, as recommended in a 2012 paper by Berkeley's outgoing chancellor, Robert Birgeneau; its provost, George Breslauer; and researcher Judson King. The regents "want to do the right thing and they behave as if they know what's going on," says Larry Hershman, who oversaw UC's budget from 1978 to 2004, "but they can't possibly understand the details of a $22 billion budget." (In fairness to the regents, UC's budget is opaque to all but the deepest insiders, and UC's administrators have a history of deliberately keeping the regents in the dark about such matters as cushy executive pay packages.) John Moores, an entrepreneur and owner of the San Diego Padres, served as chairman of the regents in the 2000s. "I cannot imagine less oversight over an organization that size," he says. "Our meeting agendas, which were controlled by the administration, were set up to celebrate the university's various (and generally well-deserved) achievements. But there was never anything that looked like regental oversight."

The behemoth Office of the President should be put on a starvation diet. With a budget of well over a quarter-billion dollars and a staff of more than 1,500 people, it is the equivalent of a small college—without faculty or students. It "absorbs a staggering amount of money," says UCLA astronomer Matt Malkan, "but no one can figure out what it actually does except consume the research overheads from our grants." Administrators at the stronger campuses chafe under its make-work demands. The Office of the President "messes in things that it has no knowledge of," says former UCLA chancellor Charles Young. The office is the main engine of UC's socialist redistribution mechanism, however, so while the flagship campuses are eager to jettison it, the weaker ones see it as protection against market forces.

A 2007 effort to reorganize the office achieved little, and postrecession personnel cuts, achieved in part by foisting its administrators on local campuses, have been window dressing. (Asked for the job titles that have been recently eliminated and those that remain, spokesman Dianne Klein responds: "Such information isn't readily available.") Ongoing decentralization efforts have stalled. UC San Francisco and UCLA's business school have sought to become more financially self-supporting but have been blocked by howls about "privatization."

* * *

So far, UC's students have borne the brunt of the system's budget problems. Whenever the state legislature sends UC less money than it thinks it deserves, its response is to increase tuition. By comparison, the faculty have been relatively unharmed, aside from the occasional salary freeze. Faculty positions have been eliminated through attrition, but the professors who remain haven't been asked to teach more to make up for the loss—so students face more crowded classrooms and greater difficulty enrolling in the courses needed for their major.

Despite the rapid growth in the bureaucracy, the faculty is still the largest single fixed cost at UC (as at other research universities); asking them to teach more is an obvious way to increase productivity in the face of reduced funding. The average teaching load at UC is four one-quarter courses a year; some professors work out deals that allow them to teach even less. By contrast, at California State University—also public but less prestigious than UC—the faculty may teach four lecture courses a semester and are paid about half as much as at UC.

Some professors readily acknowledge that they have "the best deal in the world," in the words of Berkeley political scientist Jack Citrin. Some, however, threaten to decamp at the mere mention of more time in the undergraduate classroom, and the regents and UC administration appear to back them in their opposition. Complicating the already thorny question of the proper balance between research and teaching is the widespread conflation of the sciences and the humanities. In the hard sciences, the line between teaching and research is less sharp. A graduate student who works in a professor's audiology lab is learning from him no less than if the professor were lecturing before him; the professor is teaching even as he does research. But the faculty member who churns out another paper on de-gendered constructions of postcolonial sexuality is probably doing it solo.

Even in the sciences, however, there may come a point of diminishing returns to investment. "No one has ever asked the fundamental question: 'How much research should Californians be supporting at UC?'" Steve Weiner observes. The assumption, he says, has always been that there can never be enough research, and therefore that each of the ten campuses should become world-class research institutions, with faculties equally absolved from teaching duties. That assumption will have to change.

The university could further save on faculty costs by encouraging students to take introductory courses at a community college or online. (Governor Brown began pushing UC in this direction, as well as toward higher faculty course loads, in early 2013.) If it's true that undergraduates at a research university benefit from being taught by professors at the cutting edge of knowledge, they do so mostly in the final stages of their degree. Industrial-strength freshman courses don't require instruction by the author of a field's standard textbook. A 20-year-old Chinese engineering major at UC Irvine, paying $30,000 a year in nonresident tuition, says ruefully: "It's too late now, but had I known more, I would have started out at a junior college."

As for tuition, all UC students should contribute something toward their education, no matter their income level. And students' tuition money should fund their own education, not other students'. Currently, one-third of all tuition supports financial aid. This cross-subsidy drives up the price for those paying their own way. Instead, financial aid should be funded directly by the legislature (or by donors), so that decisions about how much aid to offer are transparent and taxpayers know the cost of their subsidy.

* * *

The UC undergraduates whom I met in 2012 were serious, self-directed, and mature. But they are ill-served by a system that devotes so many resources to political trivia. UC Two's diversity obsessions have no place in an institution dedicated to the development of knowledge. No one today asks whether the Berkeley physics laboratory that developed the cyclotron contained a sufficient quota of women and underrepresented minorities; the beneficiaries of nuclear medicine are simply happy to be treated.

The retirement of President Yudof in summer 2013 provides an opportunity for an overdue course correction. Unfortunately, it is doubtful that anyone will seize it. Every potential countervailing force to UC Two has already been captured by UC Two's own ideology. The California legislature is as strong an advocate for specious social-justice crusades as any vice chancellor for equity and inclusion. The regents have been unanimous cheerleaders for "diversity" and will run all presidential candidates through a predictable gauntlet of diversity interrogation. For more than a decade, the federal government has used its grant-making power to demand color- and gender-driven hiring in the sciences. UC One's passion for discovery and learning will fuel it for a long time yet, but it has already been severely weakened by UC Two.

[2013]

VII
THE CULTURE

25

The Lost Art of War

Hollywood's Anti-American War Films Don't Measure Up to the Glories of Its Patriotic Era

Andrew Klavan

HOLLYWOOD HAS GONE BACK TO WAR. And this time, it's appalling. Throughout the autumn of 2007, the film industry released movies about America's battle against global jihad. With one exception—the competent actioner *The Kingdom*—each of these movies distorted an urgent, ongoing historical enterprise through the lens of a filmmaker's unthinking leftism. *Redacted*, *Rendition*, *In the Valley of Elah*, and *Lions for Lambs* characterize our soldiers and government agents as rapists, madmen, murderers, torturers of the innocent, or simply victims caught up in a venal and bloodthirsty American foreign policy. All this at the very moment when our real-life soldiers and agents are risking, and sometimes losing, their lives fighting the most hateful and cancerous worldview since Nazism.

But I guess that's showbiz.

Needless to say, it wasn't always thus. During World War II, Hollywood stars like James Stewart and directors like Frank Capra enlisted in the military to combat dictators as willingly as Sean Penn and Michael Moore now tootle down to Venezuela and Cuba to embrace them. More to the point, yesteryear's studio heads—many of them conservative Republicans—worked in cooperation with a Democratic administration to produce top-notch entertainment supporting the war effort. The result was not only rousing combat tales like 1943's *Sahara, Bataan,* and *Action in the North Atlantic*—all still watchable today—but also some of the finest motion pictures ever made: 1942's *Casablanca* and *Mrs. Miniver*, for instance, and the terrific yet all-but-forgotten *They Were Expendable* (1945). It was one of the film industry's finest hours.

Much has changed in Hollywood since then. The fall of the business-driven studio system has freed creative types to make more personal films, just as the internationalization of markets and multiple methods of distribution protect them from the financial consequences of alienating the nation's mainstream. If their anti-American labor of love bombs in Peoria, their investors will probably still make their money back in Europe and on the DVDs.

Beyond that, however, the movie business merely provides the most glamorous example of a greater change throughout our creative and intellectual communities: a decades-long drift toward an idiot radicalism. Movie artists—like all artists except the most original—are the products of the atmosphere of fashionable opinion that surrounds and sustains them. They may play at being heroes who speak truth to power, but the real powers in their lives are the elites who feed them praise, awards, and jobs. To them, the filmmakers speak nothing but slavish agreement.

Because of this, Hollywood war films past and present reflect the political philosophy not just of a small lotusland enclave but of a large segment of our culture-making classes. The changing ways that these films portray the internal experience of the warrior, along with the change in their overall depiction of the nation and its guardians, are signs of deeper developments with unnerving ramifications.

* * *

Movies about the inner experience of war frequently revolve around the relationship of a young soldier to a battle-hardened father figure. Such films underwent a violent transformation between World War II and the aftermath of Vietnam. The 1949 film *Sands of Iwo Jima*, directed by Allan Dwan, is a good benchmark against which to measure that transition. The picture follows John Wayne's hardboiled marine sergeant John Stryker as he prepares his men for the Iwo assault. John Agar plays the sensitive private Peter Conway, who resentfully identifies Stryker with his own tough marine-colonel father. But as Conway learns, only Stryker's unyielding warrior ethos will keep him alive in the fighting to come. At the same time, this ethos exacts a brutal price. Away from his duties, Stryker is a self-pitying drunk, lamenting the wife who left him. During battle, he finds his humanity repeatedly compromised. In one grim scene, Stryker keeps Conway and his other men safe by forcing them to lie low as a comrade dies in the field, calling for help.

After a sniper fells Stryker on Iwo Jima, his men listen solemnly as Conway reads the sergeant's unfinished letter to his estranged son. Through this letter, Conway, now a warrior himself, is finally able to see Stryker—and so his own father—in his full humanity. At that moment, the famous flag raising takes place, perhaps a bit of 1950s Freudianism linking the coming of manhood to the guarding of the nation. Conway speaks Stryker's signature line—"Saddle up!"—and leads his comrades back into battle to the tune of the Marines' Hymn.

It's nice mythic stuff, corny but still stirring. And in its old-fashioned way, it manages to explore not just the physical but also the spiritual sacrifice of becoming a warrior. As he takes on his father's warrior role, the son learns his father's terrible secret: that in defending his home, he becomes estranged from it; in defending his values, he has to contravene them; in defending civilization and peace, he has to steep himself in uncivilized violence.

If you want to see the exact moment at which the movies' approach toward those tragic truths began to shift, watch the opening scene of *Patton* (1970). George C. Scott, in his Oscar turn as the indomitable general, rises from the base of an enormous American flag to recite his famous speech to the troops: "No bastard ever won a war by dying for his country. He won it by making the other poor dumb bastard die for his country."

This is the warrior's initiation distilled, a battle-hardened veteran introducing untried men to their brutal roles as guardians of the nation. The camera angle places us in the position of Patton's troops. There, we find our reactions caught between two points of view. The Vietnam-era filmmakers—including screenwriter Francis Ford Coppola—clearly intended to imbue the scene with grim irony. Their very next cut takes us to vultures overlooking a battlefield where indifferent natives strip the American dead. But the speech itself is so powerful that, in memory, the viewer edits the irony out. All anyone remembers is that general, that speech, that flag.

* * *

The moment thus stands as a pivot point between competing visions: on the one hand, *Sands of Iwo Jima*; on the other, the best films dealing with a soldier's initiation into the Vietnam War. In these later films, the sacrifice of a man's gentler self to the needs of his warrior role is no longer necessary and inspiring. Instead, it has become an unbearable doubling, even a kind of spiritual death.

Platoon (1986) is Oliver Stone's Oscar-winning, fictionalized account of his own Vietnam service, a powerful and anguished vision by a man who volunteered for combat duty and won medals for valor. Stone's stand-in is Private Chris Taylor, played by Charlie Sheen. Taylor describes himself as a "child born of . . . two fathers": a scarred, heartless killer, Sergeant Bob Barnes (Tom Berenger); and a Christlike stoner, Sergeant Elias Grodin (Willem Dafoe). After Grodin reports Barnes for committing atrocities in a Vietnamese village, Barnes murders him in the field to shut him up. With no one else to testify against him, Barnes seems above justice, as free as a force of nature. "Are you smoking this shit so's to escape from reality?" he sneers at Grodin's drug-taking disciples. "Me, I don't need this shit. I *am* reality." It's the father's warrior initiation speech broken free of its guardian context. Barnes doesn't kill to preserve the peace and freedom of the nation. He does it because that's the Hobbesian state of things.

This puts Taylor in the essential warrior bind. In order to be like Grodin in defending righteousness, he feels that he has to become like Barnes—has to kill Barnes as cold-bloodedly as Barnes killed Grodin. Like Conway in *Sands of Iwo Jima*, Taylor must set aside gentleness for the greater good. But for Taylor, it's not a necessary emotional sacrifice for the sake of the nation; it's a tormenting psychomachy almost unrelated to the mission of the war. It leaves him broken and sobbing as he heads for home. "We did not fight the enemy, we fought ourselves," he says. "And the enemy was in us."

Stanley Kubrick's *Full Metal Jacket* (1987)—a less personal, more artificial film—at first externalizes this inner conflict between the warrior's brutal and gentle selves. The first half of the movie follows an intelligent and observant private called "Joker" (Matthew Modine) through basic training on Parris Island. The double nature of the human heart is represented, on the one hand, by the comically bellicose Drill Instructor Hartman (wonderfully played by R. Lee Ermey) and, on the other, by a sweet-natured idiot nicknamed Private Pyle (the much underrated Vincent D'Onofrio). After Joker and the other recruits reject Pyle and assault him, the gentle fool goes mad and kills both the DI and himself—a cataclysmic end to the struggle between the two men, and symbolic of the violent suppression of Joker's internal struggle as well.

The second half of the film, which takes place in Vietnam, bears this reading out. Now a detached, sarcastic military journalist, Joker ironically represents what he calls the "duality of man" by wearing a peace button on his lapel and the words BORN TO KILL scrawled across his helmet. But when he leaves his journalistic post and joins a patrol during the Tet Offensive, his detachment finally fails him. In the end, he is forced to execute a teenage girl, a sniper. It's an act of both mercy and brutality that represents the final annihilation of even this twisted remnant of his *anima*. His soul must die in order for him to stay alive.

What has changed between *Sands of Iwo Jima* and the Vietnam films is, of course, the context. In *Sands*, Stryker's internal sacrifice—not to mention the sacrifice of his life—is tragically noble because it contributes to the freedom of a good and grateful nation. The Vietnam films reject the worthiness of the sacrifice precisely because they reject the worthiness of the nation. They do this, however, in two very different ways.

Stone, with his kooky left-wing paranoia, has become a bugbear of conservatives, but his deeply felt and tormented examination of his war service deserves respect. Like *Platoon*, Stone's *Born on the Fourth of July* (1989), based on the autobiography of paralyzed antiwar veteran Ron Kovic, details the experience of a war that was rejected by the culture-making vanguard and so stripped of its glory. A conservative viewer can easily interpret the film as the tale of a man seduced into left-wing lunacy by his need to find a celebratory context for his sacrifice—a context supplied by the antiwar Left. Nonetheless, the director's ultimate message is clear. "We love the people of America," says Tom Cruise as Kovic, "but when it comes to the government . . . [they're] a bunch of corrupt, greedy racists and robbers."

The expatriate Kubrick's rejection of America is far more complete, and so his attitude toward the warrior sacrifice is utterly contemptuous. *Full Metal Jacket* ends with Joker and his comrades marching through a landscape of fire, singing the Mickey Mouse Club theme song. In becoming warriors, they have made the world a living hell, in service of a shallow, artificial culture.

Whether through Stone's tortured paranoia or Kubrick's cultural self-hatred, the Vietnam films' bitter vision of the warrior's initiation went hand in hand with Hollywood's increasingly negative depiction of America. That depiction depended partly on the filmmakers' specific rejection of Vietnam-era policies. But it was shaped, informed, and encouraged by a larger phenomenon: the intellectuals' turning away from nationalism itself.

* * *

Antinationalism has a long pedigree in Western art and thought, so to track its development in Hollywood war movies, we now have to double back, before Vietnam and World II, to even earlier films.

Through much of the nineteenth and early twentieth centuries, with nationalism at its height in Europe, Western artists routinely depicted war as purifying and ennobling. With World War I, that idea became increasingly insupportable. A generation of young men had been wiped out for reasons that remain murky even today, slaughtered in their millions by a technology that seemed to eliminate any trace of martial sublimity.

The dominant artistic reaction was a rejection of nationalist sacrifice. It was best summed up by Wilfred Owen's famous poem "Dulce et Decorum Est," which sneers at "the old lie" that it is sweet and fitting to die for one's country. Between the world wars, Hollywood took up that antinationalist theme in one of its earliest talkies, 1930's *All Quiet on the Western Front*. The film won an Oscar for best picture and remains an extraordinary movie to this day. In this story of German soldiers in the trenches, based on Erich Maria Remarque's fine novel, every father figure who fills young men with dreams of "some desperate glory," to use Owen's phrase, is a blustering fool, a militaristic buffoon, or a secret coward. The war is nothing but senseless death.

Key to this depiction is one scene that remains a staple of the war-movie genre: battle-weary soldiers sitting together and discussing the greater mission. These scenes almost invariably ring false—statements by the artists intruding on the art—but they're telling nonetheless.

"How do they start a war?" one soldier asks in *All Quiet.*

"One country offends another," a second says.

"Oh, well, if that's it, I shouldn't be here at all. I don't feel offended."

Here, the concerns of the individual—and, by extension, the concerns of the People—are different from, and even antithetical to, the concerns of the nation. In the wake of this devastating conflict, that pretty much became the left-wing line. Nationalism had caused the war; therefore cosmopolitanism, and a stateless commitment to the People, would end war altogether.

* * *

The trouble with cosmopolitanism, as George Orwell pointed out, is that no one is willing to fight and die for it. When warlike racial nationalism resurged in the 1930s, only an answering "atavistic emotion of patriotism," as Orwell wrote, could embolden people to stand against it.

Though European intellectuals and their left-wing American acolytes are loath to admit it, the U.S. had already provided an excellent new rationale for that emotion. Our founding redefined nationhood along social-contract lines that Europeans can still only theorize about. Our love of nation at its best was ethical, not ethnic. Our patriotism was loyalty not to race, or even to tradition, but to ideals of individual liberty and republican self-governance.

The films of World War II often reflect just that sort of patriotism. Yes, there's plenty of pure jingo, not to mention racial slurs so nonchalant that they're now hilarious: the enemies are always krauts or dagos or—my personal favorite from *Fighting Seabees*—"Tojo and his bug-eyed monkeys." But many World War II films emphasize what America stands for. The ceaseless Hollywood roll calls of Spinellis, O'Haras, Dombrowskis, and Steins highlight the *e pluribus unum* of it all: an ethnically diverse nation unified by democratic ideals. Those ideals were embodied by the characters themselves—by their rough, easygoing demeanor, their friendly interaction over ethnic and class lines, and their suspicion of fascist strongmen. Mussolini "kinda thinks he's God, don't he?" says a cynical Humphrey Bogart in *Sahara.* "Someday that guy's gonna blow up and bust."

Most people love their homeland, but these movies understood that, for Americans, the democratic ethos constituted the substance of that land. It was that substance that was worth fighting and dying for, even when the battle was lost. As a doomed soldier remarks in *Bataan*, "It don't matter much where a man dies, as long as he dies for freedom." Hold your breath and wait for a modern filmmaker to say that about Vietnam or Iraq.

* * *

Largely, Hollywood films continued to reflect American-style patriotism through the 1950s and 1960s. But with the doubts and dissensions of the Vietnam era, the antinationalist agenda that governed Europe's intelligentsia after World War I reached our shores full force and became, by corollary, anti-Americanism. And as respect for America as a worthy nation waned among the elite, so, too, did respect for America's guardians. Instead of a movie hero, the warrior became the self-serious militaristic buffoon of such antiwar films as Kubrick's *Dr. Strangelove* (1964) and Robert Altman's *MASH*, which lost the 1970 Oscar to *Patton*. *MASH*'s blood-laced depiction of countercultural army surgeons stitching up the wounded in the Korean War is frequently offset by a PA announcer's apathetic reading of heroic ad copy for old war movies: "Tell it to the marines, those lovable lugs with wonderful mugs." And the chief foil for the picture's hippie-like heroes is the pompous patriot and religious hypocrite Frank Burns, played by Robert Duvall.

Duvall, probably the best film actor of his generation, would bring that caricature to a stunning apotheosis in Francis Ford Coppola's *Apocalypse Now*. An adaptation of Joseph Conrad's *Heart of Darkness* set in Vietnam, *Apocalypse Now* has as much to do with the real war as Coppola's *The Godfather* has to do with the real Mafia. But as *The Godfather* brilliantly dramatizes the director's ideas about assimilation and capitalism, so *Apocalypse Now* plays out his notions about America's role in the world. It's a nightmare vision. American warriors are the extension of a clueless, violent, and imperialist culture. A rain of napalm burns away pristine jungles so that indigenous primitives can be replaced by Yank thugs drooling over *Playboy* bunnies in spangled cowboy suits. The supreme manifestation of this fantasy is Duvall's aptly named Lieutenant Colonel Bill Kilgore, a madman who wipes out an entire village merely to clear the beach for a famous surfer likewise aptly named L. B. Johnson. In a film that denigrates the nation and its culture, the patriot warrior can only appear absurd.

* * *

Liberals often argue that in criticizing American actions and culture, artists are actually defending American principles by holding the nation to its own standards. That argument would make sense in an atmosphere of contending visions that showed both America's greatness and its imperfections. But when the arts purvey only a consistently antipatriotic and antimilitary message, it seems clear that they have in fact detached the ethos from the country that embodies it. In doing so, American artists are adopting European-style cosmopolitanism, which leaves them virtually incapable of depicting warriors as heroes. "International society has ideas to defend—ideas of universal justice—but little actual ground," the political thinker Robert Kaplan has written. "And without ground to defend, it has little need of heroes."

The full implications of our artists' growing cosmopolitanism become painfully vivid when modern filmmakers attempt to impose their view on World War II, the gold standard for the Good War. The 1996 Oscar winner, *The English Patient*, based on Michael Ondaatje's novel, provides an unintentional dramatization of how high ideals, untethered from their territory, drift away into a dreamy blue of narcissistic hedonism.

The English Patient is such a visually beautiful film that the mind has to overcome the eye in order to comprehend its moral emptiness. Ralph Fiennes plays a Hungarian count, László Almásy, a man too fine for nationhood. Employed to map the Sahara, he flies high above the earth in his plane, disdaining borders and any concept of ownership. As war threatens, he begins a passionate affair with another man's wife, Katharine, played by Kristin Scott Thomas. At the story's climax, László must find a plane to rescue the wounded Katharine from a cave in the desert. He procures one from the Nazis in exchange for his strategic maps. When it's pointed out to him that thousands of people might've died because of his treachery, he responds, "Thousands of people did die. They were just different people." In any case, he reaches Katharine too late. She dies after writing in her journal, "We [individuals] are the real countries. Not the boundaries drawn on maps with the names of powerful men."

Pause here a moment and think back to 1942's *Casablanca*, an Oscar winner surely as great as any film of the studio era. In its depiction of a man coming out of disengagement and self-pity to embrace a larger cause, it provides one of the most moving climaxes in cinematic history. Humphrey Bogart's cabaret owner Rick Blaine makes the warrior's classic sacrifice, giving up the love of his life in order to join the fight for freedom. "I'm no good at being noble," he famously tells Ingrid Bergman's Ilsa, "but it doesn't take much to see that the problems of three little people don't amount to a hill of beans in this crazy world." It's a scene that still makes viewers cry.

The English Patient is the anti-*Casablanca*. Here, the problems of this crazy world don't amount to a hill of beans when there's some hot lovin' to be done. It doesn't matter which people die, which nation wins. There are no values, no issues of human ideals, human liberty, or self-governance. There are merely "boundaries drawn on maps with the names of powerful men." So here's that intelligence you wanted, Mr. Hitler, and excuse me while I get it on.

The film's real value lies in its unintentional depiction of the way a high-minded cosmopolitanism results not in the universal good that it espouses but in selfishness and evil. And since that's the movie's secret story—two selfish people ditching their national obligations in pursuit of sensual fulfillment—it remains, for all its flights of high romance, one of the coldest, least affecting love stories ever screened. There's a *Seinfeld* episode in which Elaine, forced to sit through the film, yells at the screen, "Stop telling your boring stories about the desert and die already!" That gets it just about right.

* * *

For the most part, that *English Patient* logic, the logic of lofty cosmopolitanism that is, in fact, the deadly logic of radical selfishness, continues to prevail in Hollywood when filmmakers confront the actual presence of war. But there was a brief end-of-millennium period when patriotism, and the respect for the military that goes with it, began cautiously to appear in American movies again. Post–Cold War revelations showed that Americans were the good guys after all, a liberal president presided over healthy economic times, and it seemed to the inattentive that we might never again have to deal with any real wars. It was then, in 1998, that at least one great director felt secure enough to make a major motion picture that tried to recapture the lost ideal of patriotic sacrifice.

Despite its virtually perfect cast, 1998's *Saving Private Ryan* is no classic. It is marred by two of director Steven Spielberg's most prominent traits: sentimentalism and a tendency to turn characters into archetypes. These (related) traits served the director well in great films like *Jaws*, *E.T.*, and *Raiders of the Lost Ark*. But they render even his most lauded historical epics mawkish and intellectually shallow.

Still, *Ryan* is an important war movie for two reasons. First, Spielberg is, as *Jaws* author Peter Benchley once bitchily remarked, the nation's "greatest second-unit director"—that is, the guy assigned by the *chief* director to handle action scenes. *Ryan* opens with a D-day sequence that is epoch-making in its realism, rendering every battle scene before it obsolete and every one after it derivative.

Second, the movie is a sincere attempt by a great post-Vietnam director to recapture the American argument for the warrior. After the invasion sequence, the film goes through the usual scenes of dehumanizing combat—including, as in *Sands of Iwo Jima*, the one in which the men have to remain in hiding while their wounded comrade dies. But each scene is soon followed by another showing why the brutal warrior attitude makes sense under the circumstances: a German soldier mercifully left alive returns to wreak havoc; a child taken in out of tenderness nearly gets everyone killed. There are no self-serious patriots here, only businesslike citizen soldiers doing what has to be done. The final sweeping pan up from a field of soldiers' graves to a fluttering American flag makes it clear: these soldiers fought and died not as the instrument of princes but as free men defending a nation that was an extension of themselves.

Here, as in the war movies of the 1940s and 1950s, American values are embodied in the men who fight for them. The American way is most effectively dramatized in the person of Captain John Miller, through Tom Hanks's awe-inspiring genius for communicating the complexities of decency. A former schoolteacher, Miller suppresses his gentler peacetime character and forces himself into the role of warrior with discipline and self-knowledge. In direct contrast with the Nazi foe, he leads not through militaristic worship of rank but by example and simple worth. He is the exemplar of the Democratic Man.

Shot down in battle, Miller whispers his last words to the rescued Private Ryan: "Earn this. Earn it." The words touch off the film's embarrassingly maudlin final sequence, in which an older Ryan, representing all America, weeps at Miller's grave, wondering if he's been good enough to have earned his salvation.

* * *

As ham-handed as *Ryan*'s moral lesson may be, it also seems irrefutable. The warrior's sacrifice finds its purpose in the defense of the nation, and the nation, in turn, owes him glorious memory and the preservation of the values for which it stands.

Perhaps, if the post–Cold War peace had lasted longer, this thought would have become more acceptable to our artistic elite. *Black Hawk Down*, a movie of martial valor, though released after 9/11, was in the pipeline beforehand; perhaps it would have become part of a larger movement. In time, American artists and intellectuals might have felt secure enough to wonder if European aversion to the nation was merely a symptom of a civilization on the wane, irrelevant to us. Perhaps even Vietnam would have begun to seem not an ill-advised European-style colonial venture but, like Bataan, a lost battle in a larger ethical struggle. It don't matter where a man dies, as long as he dies for freedom.

But, of course, the peace didn't last. With 9/11 violently awaking us to the fact of ongoing global jihad, real war came again. And not merely war, but a war that made nonsense out of cherished cosmopolitan left-wing doctrines like multiculturalism and moral relativism. Rather than face the obvious failures of their philosophy, intellectual and creative elites retreated into their present high-sounding but secretly selfish antinational moralizing.

* * *

It was Clint Eastwood, of all people, who went beyond even *The English Patient* in attempting to reexamine World War II in the new cosmopolitan light. As both actor and director, Eastwood is an American classic—I would say so even if he hadn't once filmed a novel of mine. But his 2006 double feature about the battle of Iwo Jima, *Flags of Our Fathers* and *Letters from Iwo Jima*, is a masterpiece of moral confusion. American heroism is deemphasized, Japanese courage underscored. Americans are shown committing atrocities, Japanese nobly holding out so that "our children can live for one more day." They were all just people, that's the idea; all just doing their duty, fighting for their countries. Which is surely true, but so what? World War II wasn't a Yankees–Red Sox game. It actually mattered, in the end, which country you fought for and who won. Sure, individuals and nations are universally flawed, and all have fallen short of the glory of God, but the ideas and values for which those individuals and nations stand tend to guide them in better or worse directions and so are more or less worth defending. America's liberty and toleration: yes. Japan's imperialist tyranny: not so much.

Eastwood said that he wanted his films to expose the "futility of war." But war is dreadful, not futile—there's a big difference. These films create the illusion of war's futility through the ultimate act of cosmopolitanism: they delete the knowledge of good and evil. True, the Bible tells us that we lived in a peaceful paradise before we acquired that knowledge. But the Bible likewise tells us that the way back there is barred by a sword of fire.

* * *

So we return to the antiwar films of autumn 2007. It seems odd to compare these with the powerful and influential pictures discussed above. It's not just that these new movies failed at the box office: a film's popularity, like a war's popularity, is no fair measure of its worth. Each of these movies is also emotionally ineffective and intellectually stale. Together, however, they're indicative of the philosophical cage in which our creative community has trapped itself.

In *Redacted, Rendition, In the Valley of Elah,* and *Lions for Lambs*—as in more successful thrillers like *Shooter* and *The Bourne Ultimatum*—virtually every act of the American administration is corrupt or sinister, and every patriot is a cynically misused fool. Every warrior, therefore, is either evil himself or, more often, a victim of evil, destined for meaningless destruction or soul-death and insanity. These movies' anti-American attitudes strike me not as the products of original vision and reflection but rather as the tired expressions of inherited prejudices. The films work the way that prejudice works, anyway: by taking extraordinary incidents and individuals and extrapolating general principles from them.

Redacted is the worst example. Politically repellent, emotionally dishonest, artistically incompetent, and, at 90 minutes, about an hour too long, the film shows American soldiers raping a 15-year-old Iraqi girl and slaughtering her family. Writer and director Brian De Palma, a vastly overrated hack, used the same trope in his so-so 1989 Vietnam film, *Casualties of War*, which tells you exactly how far his thinking has progressed. The other three films take a more earnest, if smarmy, approach, smothering our fighters in loving pity, but the principle of extrapolation is the same. In *Lions for Lambs*, patriotic youngsters are sent to die for a wartime scheme meant to advance a cynical conservative politician's career. In *Rendition*, the CIA ships off a wholly innocent man to a foreign country to be tortured for information that he doesn't have. And *In the Valley of Elah* has enough murderously loony posttraumatic veterans to make up a sort of nutcase rifle battalion. Put on a uniform, serve in Iraq, and zappo, you're kill-crazy forever.

If these stories were representative rather than exceptional, *In the Valley of Elah* would have at least half an excuse for its disgraceful and infantile final shot, which shows the American flag flown upside down as a token of our terrible distress. But the stories—even though some are based on fact—are not representative at all. The overwhelming impression that reporters with our fighters in the Middle East send back is of professionalism, valor, and continued faith in the mission. These movies, as the *Wall Street Journal*'s Peggy Noonan pointed out, simply select modern images that remind them of the old Vietnam-era films and rehash them to support their outmoded political points of view.

Locked in an echo chamber of fashionable leftism, our filmmakers have lost the ability to question those discredited assumptions. Only in fantasy war films—films like Spielberg's undervalued *War of the Worlds*, Michael Bay's amusing *Transformers*, or Peter Jackson's wonderful *Lord of the Rings* trilogy—does the truth of our present situation emerge. Here, filmmakers don't have to confront the deathblow that radical Islam deals to the logic of leftist ideology. They can portray evil without giving it a human face and affirm our values without paying too particular a tribute to the nation in which those values become flesh. The warrior's sacrifice makes sense again, martial virtues can be openly honored, and those who protect us are given back their glory.

* * *

That glory, however, is not the stuff of fantasy alone. The threat of global jihad is all too real, and the stakes are all too high. Liberty, tolerance, the harmony of conflicting voices—these things didn't materialize suddenly out of the glowing heart of human decency. People thought of them, fought and died to establish them, not in the ether, but on solid ground. That ground has to be defended or the values themselves will die. The warriors willing to do this difficult work deserve to have their heroism acknowledged in our living thoughts and through our living arts. We should hear their voices every day, saying: Earn this. Earn it.

[2008]

26

Radical Graffiti Chic

*Sponsored by L.A.'s Aristocracy, a Museum of
Contemporary Art Show Celebrates Vandalism*

Heather Mac Donald

D RIVE BEHIND THE GEFFEN CONTEMPORARY, an art museum in downtown Los Angeles, and you will notice that it has painted over the graffiti
scrawled on its back wall. Ordinarily, that wouldn't be surprising; the Geffen's
neighbors also maintain constant vigilance against graffiti vandalism. But
beginning in April 2011, the Geffen—a satellite of L.A.'s Museum of Contemporary Art—will host what MOCA proudly bills as America's first major
museum survey of "street art," a euphemism for graffiti. Graffiti, it turns out,
is something that MOCA celebrates only on other people's property, not on
its own.

MOCA's exhibit, *Art in the Streets*, is the inaugural show of its new director, Jeffrey Deitch, a former New York gallery owner and art agent. Deitch's
now-shuttered Soho gallery showcased vandal-anarchist wannabes whose
performance pieces and installations purported to strike a blow against establishment values and capitalism, even as Deitch himself made millions serving
art collectors whose fortunes rested on capitalism and its underpinning in
bourgeois values. MOCA's show (which will also survey skateboard culture)
raises such inconsistencies to a new level of shamelessness. Not only would
MOCA never tolerate uninvited graffiti on its walls (indeed, it doesn't even
permit visitors to use a pen for note-taking *within* its walls, an affectation unknown in most of the world's greatest museums); none of its trustees would
allow their Westside mansions or offices to be adorned with graffiti, either.

Even this two-facedness pales beside the hypocrisy of the graffiti vandals
themselves, who wage war on property rights until presented with the opportunity to sell their work or license it to a corporation. At that point, they

— 271 —

grab all the profits they can stuff into their bank accounts. Lost in this anti-bourgeois posturing is the likely result of the museum's graffiti glorification: a renewed commitment to graffiti by Los Angeles's ghetto youth, who will learn that the city's power class views graffiti not as a crime but as art worthy of curation. The victims will be the law-abiding residents of the city's most graffiti-afflicted neighborhoods and, for those who care, the vandals themselves.

* * *

MOCA's practice of removing graffiti from its premises represents cutting-edge urban policy; too bad its curatorial philosophy isn't equally up-to-date. Graffiti is the bane of cities. A neighborhood that has succumbed to graffiti telegraphs to the world that social and parental control there has broken down. Potential customers shun graffiti-ridden commercial strips if they can; so do most merchants, fearing shoplifting and robberies. Law-abiding residents avoid graffiti-blighted public parks, driven away by the spirit-killing ugliness of graffiti as much as by its criminality.

There is no clearer example of the power of graffiti to corrode a public space than the fall and rebirth of New York's subways. Starting in the late 1960s, an epidemic of graffiti vandalism hit the New York transit system, covering every subway with "tags" (runic lettering of the vandal's nickname) and large, colored murals known as "pieces." Mayor John Lindsay, an unequivocal champion of the urban poor, detested graffiti with a white-hot passion, but he was unable to stem the cancer. The city's failure to control graffiti signaled that the thugs had won. Passengers fled the subways and kept going, right out of the city. To the nation, the graffiti onslaught marked New York's seemingly irreversible descent into anarchy.

Yet in the late 1980s, the city vanquished the subterranean blight by refusing to allow scarred cars onto the tracks. That victory was a necessary precondition for the Big Apple's renewal in the following decade; it was the first sign in years that New York could govern itself. Riders flooded back—by 2006, 2 million more passengers each day than in the 1980s. The subway's rising ridership was a barometer of the city's rising fortunes.

Not everyone welcomed the conquest of subway graffiti. From its inception, New York's tagging epidemic spawned a coterie of elite propagandists, who typically embraced graffiti not despite but because of its criminal nature. "You hit your name and maybe something in the whole scheme of the system gives a death rattle," hopefully wrote Norman Mailer, graffiti's most flamboyant publicist, in 1973. A glossy book of subway photographs by Henry Chalfant and Martha Cooper, published in 1984, became known as the graffiti movement's "Bible" for having inspired youth and adults the world over to deface property. (MOCA's show will honor Chalfant and Cooper.) Such propaganda could reach absurd levels of pomposity. Mailer suggested that Puerto Rican graffitists were criticizing modern architecture (why they attacked Beaux Arts structures with equal zeal was not explained); journalist Richard Goldstein imagined Parisian vandals as budding deconstructionists, hip to the "decenteredness" of the "floating signifier." By the time Chalfant and Cooper's *Subway Art* was reissued in a fancy 25th anniversary edition, complete with a glowing blurb from Jeffrey Deitch, the graffiti-glorification industry was in high gear, counting thousands of books, magazines, documentaries, gallery shows, and websites dedicated to giving taggers the facile notoriety that they craved.

* * *

The two guest curators of *Art in the Streets*, Roger Gastman and Aaron Rose, are longtime members of this graffiti-glorification industry; both have produced documentaries on "street art." Gastman's film, *Infamy*, profiles (among several other taggers) what it calls "an industry-standard classic" of the graffiti subculture: a gangly, fast-talking young hustler named Earsnot. Understand Earsnot, and you understand everything you need to know about the world that MOCA deems worthy of celebration.

Earsnot is a member of Irak, an infamous New York City tagging crew. Only a graffiti ignoramus would think that "Irak" is a political reference; rather, it is a play on "I rack," that is, I steal. (Stealing is so entrenched a practice among graffiti vandals that a line of spray paint designed exclusively for graffiti, Montana Colors, is sold only by mail order. The company is underwriting *Art in the Streets*.) Earsnot, who sports flashy platinum mouth bling, justifies his crew's name every day. The camera follows him as he shoplifts a silver Magic Marker from a New York hardware store ("You need to be fucking David Copperfield to get a couple of Magic Markers out of this store," he grouses), calmly tries it out on three mailboxes, and then petulantly complains about the quality of the merchandise: "This marker is such shit." Earsnot has a strict code of what he will not deign to purchase. "I will not pay for Gore-Tex, chicken cutlets, steaks, or meat," he announces self-righteously. "If I pay for something, I feel really stupid about it—I could've racked that shit." As the camera lovingly chronicles his tagging spree across Manhattan, he shares his personal philosophy: "I like it especially when I can see the cops and I'm catching my tag and I'm like, 'I can see where you are so I'm not getting caught.' You want to fucking break the law and there's nothing you can fucking do. I'm going to be fucking bad. You can make the laws; it doesn't mean everyone will follow them."

Far from being appalled by Earsnot, *Infamy*'s creators are clearly charmed by him. The documentary's publicity materials highlight his mockery of his hardworking victims and revel in his crew's lawbreaking. Irak's "motto is 'Every night is New Year's Eve,' and their days and nights are a sea of graffiti, drugs, theft, and rolling like kings into the best nightclubs and parties," reports the film's advertising copy. "Each day as the crew wakes up, they're all broke again, so they head to the shops and boutiques of New York—where Black kids such as Earsnot are usually followed by watchful staff—and still manage to commit grand larceny without a problem." Cool! Of course, *Infamy*'s producers would deem those watchful staffers racist, though the documentary provides solid justification for their concern, in Earsnot's case.

Earsnot's amoral sense of entitlement is at the core of graffiti culture. One of Deitch's favorite graffiti vandals, Saber, defiantly tells the camera in *Infamy*: "I write graffiti, and you gotta deal with it." (Saber's fame comes from having painted on the Los Angeles river channel the largest graffiti moniker ever recorded.)

* * *

Though infantile solipsism drives the graffiti phenomenon, its perpetrators often dress up their disregard for others as grand political gesture. Naturally, they turn to that tired trope of privileged Western leftists: the evil of business. The standard line among graffitists and their fans is that because big, bad corporations advertise, vandals have the right to deface other people's property. British cult hero Banksy writes in his glossy coffee-table book *Wall and Piece* ($23 on Amazon): "The people who truly deface our neighborhoods are the companies that scrawl giant slogans across buildings and buses trying to make us feel inadequate unless we buy their stuff. They expect to be able to shout their message in your face from every available surface but you're never allowed to answer back. Well, they started the fight and the wall is the weapon of choice to hit them back."

Leave aside the fact that corporations buy advertising space in a fair exchange, whereas the graffiti vandal commandeers others' rights. Leave aside, too, that graffiti is scrawled as often on public as on private property. The real puzzle of Banksy's left-wing platitudes is how defacing a civic monument, say (Banksy has tagged the base of an already cruelly assaulted Mercury in Barcelona, as *Wall and Piece* proudly documents), hurts Def Jam Recordings when it advertises the latest Kanye West album on the Sunset Strip. Banksy apparently feels that his name and his stencils are so compelling that they weaken corporate power wherever they are found.

Barry McGee, long in the Deitch orbit, is another political philosopher manqué. *Beautiful Losers*, the documentary made by MOCA's second guest curator, Aaron Rose, shows the 40-something McGee adding his tag, TWIST, to severely scarred walls and stairwells. The film then settles down to an interview with the pensive master. As McGee pushes a stick and pebbles around on a patch of bare dirt, his eyes averted from the camera and covered with a loose shock of hair, he disburdens himself of the following gem: "I think the basic tag, and tagging, and tagging on private, like, you know, on private property, I like to think of it as something that's, like, really political and, you know, as antagonistic, but it's not really that antagonistic. If it's antagonistic, you know, get rid of it, like, with a roller, but I think the act in itself is antagonistic."

The late graffiti vandal Dash Snow, a pathetic, self-destructive heir to the de Menil fortune and a colleague of Earsnot's in the Irak crew, was asked in a Web video what he believed in. "I don't believe in the laws or the system by any means. I try not to obey them at any time," the strikingly beautiful faker mumbled in response, unable to make eye contact with the interviewer. Snow won notoriety for his "Hamster Nest" extravaganzas, wherein he and a collaborator would trash a hotel room by opening all the taps, pulling the curtains off their rods, and shredding dozens of phone books while ingesting industrial quantities of drugs. Snow also showed his disregard for "the laws" and "the system" by dribbling newspaper photographs of police officers with his own semen. Jeffrey Deitch managed to commission this visionary to re-create a Hamster Nest in his gallery before Snow died, at age 27, of a drug overdose.

Shepard Fairey, who became widely known for the ubiquitous HOPE poster that he designed to support Barack Obama's presidential campaign, was already famous in the graffiti world for slapping stickers with an image of an old World Wrestling Federation character and the command OBEY over various city surfaces. Fairey, who will be contributing what he calls "graphic re-illustrations of my outdoor work" to the MOCA show, also invokes commercial advertising to justify the defacement of public and private property. In a rambling 1990 manifesto, he noted that some people had tried to peel his OBEY stickers off mailboxes and lampposts, viewing them as an "eyesore and an act of petty vandalism." Such unenlightened actions were "ironic," he wrote, "considering the number of commercial graphic images everyone in American society is assaulted with daily."

As for Jeffrey Deitch himself, the petite, tightly wound "gallerist" is a far more cautious speaker than the graffiti vandals he patronizes, affecting an almost Warhol-like blankness. His chic suits and self-designed round glasses contrast sharply with the jeans, T-shirts, and baseball caps favored by his downtown poseurs. Yet beneath that Zegna blazer beats the heart of a Deadhead, he wants us to know. *Art Forum* interviewed him in 2010 in anticipation of his move to Los Angeles. "I'm a child of 1960s idealism, where we really believed that art and a progressive attitude toward life could change consciousness," he told the magazine. He particularly valued the late Keith Haring, a graffitist and poster artist, for "warning us about subversive forces in the military, government, business—entities we needed to keep fighting against."

* * *

So what happens when these critics of corporate power and bourgeois values see an opportunity for profit? They turn into grasping capitalists. Earsnot's Irak crew "now offers its services as fashion and lifestyle consultants, along with their IRAK NY clothing line," report the *Infamy* producers. Banksy's stencils have pulled in hundreds of thousands of pounds at Sotheby's auctions. Saber, who declares in an interview with the graffiti journal *Arrested Motion* that "there is no room for empathy when there is a motive for profit," has sold his designs to Levi's, Hyundai, and Harley-Davidson. Other graffiti thugs featured in *Infamy* have contracts with Nike, Guinness, Foot Locker, and Calvin Klein, all of which have been wont to "scrawl giant slogans across buildings and buses trying to make us feel inadequate unless we buy their stuff." Snow managed to choke down his contempt for "the system" long enough to suck up the proceeds from the sales of his works to the Greek investor Dakis Joannou, an important Deitch client, and the art dealer Charles Saatchi, among others.

Fairey had already been busily leveraging his obey-sticker notoriety into lines of clothing and collectibles (as well as continuing to vandalize property) when he struck it rich with the Obama poster. The Associated Press sued him for appropriating its Obama photograph without permission. So unwilling was Fairey to share any of his wealth with the AP that he knowingly perjured himself in court and submitted false images to cover up his use of the photo. He finally settled for having to pay an undisclosed sum in January 2011, stating primly, "I respect the work of photographers"—but only, it seems, when a lawsuit forces him to.[1]

Art in the Streets cocurator Gastman also runs a publicity agency, R. Rock Enterprises (RRE), whose website boasts in fawning marketing-speak: "Our artists can design cutting-edge graphics and logos for brands seeking to communicate with a progressive, art-savvy audience. [RRE] has a wide range of clients, from major corporations to independent small businesses." Could Gastman be producing—gasp!—corporate advertising? The same Gastman who approvingly quotes a Philadelphia vandal: "Graffiti to me was war with the establishment—bombing corporate and government, big-money stuff"?

Deitch outdoes all these rebels in his savvy exploitation of property rights. Early in his career, he "shamelessly" ingratiated himself with the superrich, he informed *The New Yorker* in 2007. By 1988, he was making as much as

Citibank's CEO. Today, as he yachts around the Greek isles with his industrialist clients and generates fat commission fees for procuring the identical stable of big-name hucksters (Jeff Koons, Damien Hirst, Takashi Murakami) for billionaires' art collections, his income undoubtedly makes those early returns look puny.

Deitch intends to turn MOCA's museum store into a corporate showcase, notwithstanding the antibusiness play acting of his "street art" retinue: "We are looking at a rapidly changing landscape where many advertisers don't want conventional print or television ads," he told *Art Forum*. "They want to connect with the community in a more interesting way, and there is subsequently great potential for museums to work with sponsors, for partnerships with luxury and consumer brands."

Not to fear: "transgressive" is still one of the highest compliments that Deitch can bestow. For one of his New York dinner parties, he commissioned a performance piece in which unclothed gay Austrians urinated into one another's hats while standing on a scaffold above the dinner guests. The work was "spectacular, perverse, uplifting, beautifully horrifying, and deeply transgressive," Deitch told *The New Yorker*. The desperation of the art impresario to find anything that can still "transgress" in the endless post-Duchamp era is a piteous thing.

Jeffrey's Poodle

If you'd like further proof of the hunger for status and wealth that lies beneath the antiestablishment pose of graffiti vandals, look no further than their toadying to powerful patrons. In December 2010, Jeffrey Deitch ordered that a mural on the outside of the Geffen Contemporary that he had commissioned for *Art in the Streets* be painted over. (This mural, by the Italian "street artist" Blu, was separate from the nondescript graffiti tags that are regularly erased from the Geffen's back wall.) The mural's dollar-bill-draped soldiers' coffins were inappropriate, Deitch said, given the Geffen's proximity to a Veterans Affairs hospital and to a memorial to Japanese-American soldiers.

The graffiti blogosphere angrily accused Deitch of "censorship." Shepard Fairey, however, sprang to Deitch's defense with an obsequiousness that would make a courtier at Versailles look like a paragon of principle. "I'm not a fan of censorship but that is why I, and many of the other artists of the show, chose to engage in street art for its democracy and lack of bureaucracy," Fairey oozed in a prepared statement. "However, a museum is a different context with different concerns. . . . Street

art or graffiti purists are welcome to pursue their art on the streets as
they always have without censorship. I think that though MOCA wants
to honor the cultural impact of the graffiti/street art movement, it only
exists in its purst form in the streets from which it arose."

Fairey has strung one non sequitur after another here. The fact that
"street artists" can continue vandalizing their usual haunts does not
make Deitch's alleged "censorship" acceptable. Presumably, Fairey
would not have accepted the argument that George W. Bush could have
thrown Cindy Sheehan in prison because other war protesters were still
at large. Further, "street artists" take up graffiti not to defy "censorship"
heroically, as Fairey implies (graffiti, after all, is painted over far more
frequently than commissioned artwork), but because they want the
thrill of breaking the law.

Of course, Deitch could be legitimately defended on the ground that
he was not, in fact, censoring anything. Censorship is what happens
when the government exercises monopolistic coercion over citizen
expression. Private patrons, by contrast, have no obligation to preserve
the work that they have commissioned. But that argument would put
Fairey at odds with the contemporary art establishment, which claims
free-speech martyrdom every time a private institution rejects its work.

The most hilarious aspect of Fairey's statement, however, is the no-
blesse oblige with which he "welcomes" graffitists to continue defacing
other people's property. Who is Fairey to issue such an invitation? As
for his pretentious claim that graffiti is "democratic," he has obviously
never asked a property owner whether his vote was taken in the matter
of being vandalized. For Fairey, "democracy" means being able to take
what you want from someone else, without consequences.

Other prominent "street artists" under Deitch's wing simply went
mute after the mural effacement. "They're being silent because they
don't want to jeopardize the opportunity to be in the exhibit," street
muralist and gallery owner Alex Poli, Jr. told the *Los Angeles Times*. So
much for courage in standing up to the Man.

Even before Deitch arrived in Los Angeles, the "street art" community was bowing and scraping. "Jeffrey is a phenomenal businessman,"
cocurator Aaron Rose said to the magazine *Fast Company* in January
2010. This may be the first time that a member of the graffiti establishment has used the term "businessman" as an honorific.

* * *

How much serious thought had Deitch given to graffiti before bestowing MOCA's imprimatur upon it? Available evidence suggests: zero. Deitch's understanding of the impact of graffiti on civic life is as superficial as that of the perpetual adolescents whose posturing he bankrolls. I spoke with him in January 2011, after a screening at MOCA of a documentary about a kitschy underground cartoonist, Robert Williams. Middle-aged art-world groupies in tight miniskirts, black boots, and bright red lipstick buzzed around Deitch, taking pictures, while Deitch, in a tan suit and open collar, projected cool impassivity. "What is the message you hope to send with the graffiti show?" I asked. "To take this really seriously," he replied. "What about the fact that graffiti appropriates someone's property?" "I'm not going to be moralistic about it." Deitch means "moralistic" as a put-down; one wonders whether, if his luxury car were stolen, he would consider it "moralistic" to call the police.

Property owners bring graffiti on themselves, according to Deitch. "You'll be blasted if you use roll-down gates or if you don't keep your property up and be welcoming," he asserted. Nonsense. Graffitists don't distinguish among "welcoming" and "unwelcoming" proprietors; they hit the most eye-catching, status-producing target, or simply whatever is at hand, such as the Geffen Contemporary. Moreover, that Deitch would fault a struggling store owner in a crime-plagued area for using roll-down gates suggests just how clueless he is about the world beyond Spring Street in Soho and Melrose Avenue in Los Angeles.

The assertion that graffiti is retribution for irresponsible proprietor behavior is inconsistent with Deitch's decision to celebrate graffiti with a museum exhibit. If graffiti were a positive urban art form, it would not allegedly be inflicted as punishment for poor community relations; it would be conferred like a *Good Housekeeping* seal of approval. Deitch's ascription of fault to graffiti's victims at least suggests a slight pricking of conscience about his glorification of graffiti—unfortunately, not one strong enough to stop the exhibit.

Certain inescapable implications follow from the decision to mount a graffiti show in a museum. Deitch has clearly confronted none of them. The city and county of Los Angeles annually spend over $30 million on graffiti abatement, a sum that does not include law enforcement and court time, private outlays, or the hidden costs of fear and lost neighborhood vitality. The city could save a lot of money by suspending its graffiti-eradication efforts. "Should it?" I asked Deitch. "I don't know," he responded. This will not do. If graffiti is a boon, the city should not waste its money trying to paint it over. If the city is right to paint over graffiti, why is Deitch promoting it?

To be sure, some graffiti murals are visually striking, showing an intuitive understanding of graphic design (though their representational iconography is usually pure adolescent male wish-fulfillment, featuring drug paraphernalia, cartoon characters, T&A, space guns, and alien invaders). In theory, it might be possible to mount a show that acknowledged the occasionally compelling formal elements of wall-painting without legitimating a crime. Such an exhibit would include only authorized murals, whether past or present, and would unequivocally condemn taking someone else's property without permission. No graffiti propaganda has ever abided by such limits; the MOCA show will not, either.

And for good reason. What defines graffiti is its "commitment to vandalizing property," as Richard Goldstein wrote in his catalog essay for a 2009 graffiti show at the Fondation Cartier in Paris. "To be a graffiti writer, you have to hold down your fucking name," one of Gastman's subjects explains in *Infamy*. "Graffiti belongs illegally. It does not belong on canvas but on a building or a train."

* * *

Deitch's lack of serious thought regarding graffiti has a long pedigree. In 2000, Barry McGee and two other graffiti vandals created a mock-up of a ghetto street inside Deitch's Soho gallery, Deitch Projects. A few thousand people showed up for the opening-night party. "It turned out," Deitch told *Art Forum*, "that Barry had brought some friends along to 'get the word out,' tagging the neighborhood." McGee's friends used what Deitch appreciatively called "an entire countercultural communication system of tags on doorways and stickers on mailboxes." It didn't occur to Deitch to ask: What about the property owners who were not consulted about this "countercultural communication system"? Who will remove the tags and stickers? To Deitch, the nameless, faceless property owner is out of sight, and hence out of mind.

McGee's installation at Deitch Projects, called "Street Market," was a harbinger of the sensibility that Deitch is bringing to *Art in the Streets*—and it is fitting, therefore, that MOCA will reproduce the installation. As McGee and his two fellow "artists" were assembling their mock-up check-cashing business, liquor store, and bodega inside Deitch Projects, officers from the New York Police Department arrested one of them and an assistant to McGee outside the gallery on outstanding warrants for graffiti vandalism. "Artist" Todd James had painted his tag on a middle school in the Bronx the previous year. The assistant, Josh Lazcano, had defaced a building south of Chinatown.

It is beyond comprehension how a 28-year-old, as James was in 1999, could be so juvenile as to deface a school. The only thing Deitch found shocking, however, was the police's effrontery in accosting his "artists." "This is unprecedented," he fumed to the *New York Times*. "I have never, never in my experience known artists to be arrested while they're putting up a serious museum exhibit in a leading gallery." Apparently, the owner of a "leading gallery" can confer immunity from the law upon anyone in his orbit.

Deitch's Disneyesque barrio gave New Yorkers who would never dream of getting off the subway north of 96th Street that delightful frisson of proximity to the underclass, just as the graffiti cult provides affluent viewers with the sense that they are in touch with authentic ghetto culture. Of course, anyone who did occasionally visit East Harlem in 2000 would have known that, by then, the most immediate risk facing a stranger from midtown was difficulty in locating a Starbucks. A visitor would also have observed that trucks in the barrio do not lie on their sides in the middle of the street, as portrayed in "Street Market."

But those overturned trucks may have been inspired by nostalgia for the good old days of New York lawlessness, before Mayor Rudolph Giuliani's conquest of crime in the 1990s. When Steve Powers, one of the graffitists behind the "Street Market" installation, arrived in New York in 1989, the first thing he saw was a "cop car totally burned out and every trash can in Tompkins Square Park on fire," he says in *Beautiful Losers*. "And I was like, 'I could like this, this is what I'm talking about!'" Such anarchist sympathies did not, of course, inhibit Powers from selling his "work" for tens of thousands of dollars at Deitch Projects in 2000.

A target audience for *Art in the Streets* is black and Hispanic teenagers, whom the museum expects to crowd the Geffen Contemporary. The museum is planning on doing outreach to Los Angeles schools, Deitch said, presumably as insurance in case the teenagers don't come.

It would have been useful if Deitch had spent time talking with garden-variety ghetto graffitists. Curiously, the vast majority of graffiti thugs who have gained art-world notoriety are white and middle-class. One would never think of accusing the art world of racism, of course. Still, that skew means that wealthy graffiti patrons like Deitch may not be fully informed about what a graffiti lifestyle means to a black or Hispanic boy raised by a single parent in a marginal neighborhood. Deitch could find out easily enough by traveling less than a mile and a half from his exquisite office on Bunker Hill to Homeboy Industries, a gang-intervention agency just east of downtown.

What Deitch would learn from Homeboy Industries' Latino clientele is that the "cholo" graffiti in MOCA's show blights young minority lives. Every midnight hour that a child spends tagging or "piecing" is an hour not spent studying or sleeping—the former activity, enabled by the latter, crucial to escaping the barrio. Ivan Gonzalez, a 35-year-old in a checked shirt, baseball cap, and black hipster glasses, started tagging in eighth grade in Gardena, a small city in Los Angeles County near Compton. He dropped out of school in the 11th grade and has never held a job for more than a year. "It all coincided together," he says. "The drugs, the tagging, the stealing. To be out at night, I'd be all high on meth to go writing." Gonzalez would ditch school the next day, too tired to attend classes. He continued tagging with the Graffiti Bandits Krew for the next two decades, finally serving a four-year prison sentence for vandalism. Asked if he would advise a 16-year-old to study or to write graffiti, Gonzalez replies: "Study, especially if you have drawing talent. My friends are now either in prison or doing things I no longer want to do."

Carlos Mesa, a squat 30-year-old with crucifix necklaces, a shaved head, and tattoos on his arms and neck, tells a similar story. He was once a book-worm, he says. "I loved getting good grades, but one guy changed it all." Mesa followed his mentor into Graffiti 'N' Drugs, a tagging crew based in tiny Pico Rivera, south of Los Angeles, and started ditching school every day. After going to two or three periods to get credit for attendance, he would take off to "mark spots" all over the Southland. "We were marking so many spots, we got known," he recalls. "It feels good. People let us know that we were recognized." This reputation came with the usual price. Mesa dropped out of high school to pursue an obsession that continued—as is typical with graffiti vandals—into adulthood. In 2004, he led the police on a high-speed car chase through the streets of Whittier, another small community in the Los Angeles basin, after they spotted him tagging. Luckily, it was late at night and he didn't hit anyone, he says, but he spent 16 months in prison for the escapade. Prison taught him a few lessons: "In prison, you don't got a friend. The people you've been destroying all these walls with, they can't even write you a letter." Mesa says that he doesn't want his sons, whom he is raising as a single father, to follow in his footsteps. I ask him how he plans to prevent them from doing so. "I would show them the outcome of my life."

The violence that afflicts minority neighborhoods is frequently tied to the graffiti cult. Graffiti apologists insist on the distinction between "bad" graffiti produced by gangs and "good" graffiti produced by tagging crews, allegedly dedicated solely to tagging. The distinction is phony. "The line between tag-ging and gangbanging is very thin now," says Gonzalez. "Young taggers today are not hesitant to carry guns and shoot people like everyone else." And when cops bust a large tagging crew, they usually find fugitives wanted on outstand-ing warrants for car theft, assault, and drug trafficking. Both Mesa and Gon-zalez have been shot at by rivals; many of Mesa's graffiti partners, including the captain of Graffiti 'N' Drugs, have been killed. Mesa's oft-battered jaw structure is held together by a set of metal braces.

One can only wish good luck to those barrio parents who want to keep their children out of the tagging and gang lifestyle once word gets out that a fancy downtown museum is honoring graffiti with a major exhibit. Children who deduce from *Art in the Streets* that graffiti is a route to fame and contracts with Nike will have about as realistic an understanding of their career odds as boys who think they don't have to study because jobs await them in the NBA.

* * *

The ultimate responsibility for *Art in the Streets* lies with MOCA's buzz-hungry trustees. They knew exactly whom they were getting in Jeffrey Deitch, who had a reputation for promoting "street art." But when Deitch first proposed a graffiti exhibit, any adult with the slightest awareness of urban issues should have felt at least a twinge of ambivalence. A conscientious trustee might have asked himself: "If I woke up one morning and found that my home had become the site of 'street art,' would I be delighted by this windfall or furious at the assault on my property? Would I call the Art Historical Society to register this addition to my home, or the cops and a painting service?" In case the answer is not obvious, let's listen to the taggers themselves. "I've never written on my own house," says Gonzalez. "And I wouldn't like it if someone else did it on my house." Mesa finds my question about whether he would tolerate graffiti on his home silly. "Why would you want to fuck up your own area?" he asks me. "That's why you go out and mess up other people's cities."

Assuming that the conscientious trustee concludes that he would not welcome a surprise gift of "street art," he might then ponder: "Where do I think that unauthorized graffiti *is* appropriate—on the walls of MOCA? On Disney Hall, the Frank Gehry–designed concert hall across Grand Avenue from MOCA? Or simply on some struggling Laundromat on Cesar Chavez Avenue in East Los Angeles?" If none of the above, why is the museum promoting it?

MOCA's trustees include hugely successful executives from Hollywood, real estate, and finance. Their wealth was made possible by the rule of law, which allows them to take risks and make investments, knowing that their contractual and property rights are secure. Banksy claims that "crime against property is not real crime." Do the trustees agree? If someone were to vandalize the trustees' intangible property—plundering their hedge-fund accounts, say—they would sic their attorneys and the feds on the thieves in a heartbeat. But the defacement of physical property is a crime that affects the poorest property owners far more than the wealthiest. Identifying with the victims of graffiti may thus be difficult for MOCA's moguls.

Nevertheless, one of MOCA's trustees in particular should try, since he is the direct beneficiary of the most important graffiti-eradication project in history. Darren Star is the creator and executive producer of the blockbuster TV show *Sex and the City*, which premiered on cable in 1998. *Sex and the City* would never have been conceived had New York not defeated subway graffiti. Without that success, New York would have continued its spiral of decline—and it sure wouldn't have provided the backdrop for a sex comedy in which single women clomp through the city in their Manolo Blahniks at 2 AM seeking their next conquest. The final elimination of subway graffiti in 1989 was the precondition for the reincarnation of New York in the 1990s as the embodiment of urban cool. No New York rebirth, no *Sex and the City*, no fortune for Darren Star. Star—who lives in Beverly Hills, a neighborhood not known for graffiti—wouldn't comment about *Art in the Streets*.

Other MOCA trustees have benefited almost as obviously from the New York renaissance. As New York restored order first to its subways, then to the rest of the city, the value of the trustees' property shot up. Charles S. Cohen owns the D&D Center in Manhattan, a design center catering to the most upscale interior decorators, as well as the similarly targeted Pacific Design Center in Los Angeles. Edward Minskoff owns a luxury residential and commercial development in Tribeca that boasts a Whole Foods Market, a Bed Bath & Beyond, and a Bank of America. These are just the sort of tenants that graffiti ideology designates for targeting, at least until the tagger gets an offer to illustrate a new line of bath towels or organic salsa. Billionaire paper-company mogul Peter Brant lives in Greenwich, Connecticut, but occupies a Soho office with a Prada store at ground level. It is unlikely that either the Prada store or the stables sheltering Brant's polo ponies would tolerate graffiti. Steven Mnuchin, founder of a New York hedge fund, put his Park Avenue apartment on the market, presumably graffiti-free, for $37.5 million in 2009. None of these New York–centered trustees would speak about the MOCA show, either.

Graffiti is equally remote from the lives of MOCA's Los Angeles–based trustees. Cochair David Johnson's film-production company (dedicated to "socially and politically relevant film and television") is located on the most prime and immaculate piece of Santa Monica real estate, Ocean Avenue. MOCA's other cochair, soap-opera producer and writer Maria Arena Bell, lives in Bel Air, whose wooded roads and hidden estates are patrolled 24 hours a day by private guards. Someone spray-painting a security gate or street sign in Bel Air would last maybe a minute before being apprehended by guard dogs, a groundskeeper, or Bel Air's private security. Timothy Leiweke is president of Los Angeles's Staples Center sports arena and the adjacent L.A. Live, a downtown entertainment and residential complex. If any of the urban youths visiting *Art in the Streets* decide to try out the new designs they've learned on L.A. Live's Ritz-Carlton, they won't get far.

And then there's founding member and life trustee Eli Broad, the billionaire home builder who bailed MOCA out of impending bankruptcy in 2008 and who, it's safe to assume, can exercise considerable influence over programming decisions. Broad has constantly lauded Deitch's commitment to "populist"—read: minority-targeted and pop-culture-based—shows. When asked for an opinion of Deitch's inaugural "populist" show, though, Broad suddenly pled ignorance. "That is not something that he would comment on," his assistant told me. "He didn't feel that he had enough background; other trustees are more appropriate." Broad has undoubtedly not given a moment's thought to how MOCA's glamorization of "cholo" graffiti can be reconciled with his philanthropic efforts to close the academic achievement gap.

Many graffiti apologists claim that inner-city children have no other outlets for artistic expression than vandalizing property. The claim is ridiculous: a box of 16 watercolors at Target costs $1.99, while paper and pencil, the basis of all achievement in the visual arts, are no more expensive. But if this is the MOCA trustees' thinking, there are far better ways for them to support the artistic potential in the barrio. They could redirect some of their millions to the Youth Orchestra of Los Angeles, the local version of the Venezuelan music program for the poor that nurtured conductor Gustavo Dudamel, who is electrifying L.A. audiences at Disney Hall. Or they could donate to MOCA's next-door neighbor, the Colburn School, a music conservatory and performing-arts school. The Colburn already provides early-childhood arts education but could undoubtedly expand its reach with increased philanthropic help.

* * *

What unites the players in MOCA's graffiti show is self-indulgence. The graffiti vandal combines the moral instincts of a two-year-old with the physical capacities of an adult: when he sees a "spot" that he wants to "mark," he simply takes it. Jeffrey Deitch and his trustees can toy with the "outlaw vibe" (as Aaron Rose euphemistically puts it) of graffiti, knowing full well that their own carefully ordered lives will be untouched.

The inner city is not so protected. *Art in the Streets* will earn MOCA accolades from the already standard-free art world, but it will only increase the struggles of Los Angeles's poor communities to enjoy a modicum of the security and order that the wealthy take for granted.

[2011]

Note

1. In February 2012, Fairey pleaded guilty to criminal contempt and admitted to destroying and fabricating evidence related to the AP lawsuit. In September, he was sentenced to two years' probation and fined $25,000.

27

Tom Wolfe's California

In the Golden State, the Great Writer First Chronicled the Social Changes That Would Transform America

Michael Anton

Tom Wolfe is most identified with New York City, for good reason. He has lived and worked in Manhattan since the early 1960s, and New York dominates his writing the way London looms for Dickens. But Wolfe has never been afraid to venture from his home turf—his 2012 novel *Back to Blood*, an exploration of Miami, is a case in point—and his true literary second home is California. Over the course of his career, Wolfe has devoted more pages to the Golden State than to any setting other than Gotham. In his early years, from the mid-1960s through the early 1970s, the ratio was almost one-to-one. More to the point, the core insights on which he built his career—the devolution of style to the masses, status as a replacement for social class, the "happiness explosion" in postwar America—all first came to him in California. Even books in which the state figures not at all are informed by Wolfe's observations of the West. Without California, there would be no Wolfe as we know him—no *Bonfire*, no *Right Stuff*, no Radical Chic or Me Decade, none of the blockbuster titles or era-defining phrases that made him world-famous.

And without Wolfe, we would not understand California—or the California-ized modern world. At the time of his most frequent visits, the state was undergoing a profound change, one that affects it to this day and whose every aspect has been exported throughout the country and the globe. Both have become much more like California over the last 40 years, even as California has drifted away from its old self, and Wolfe has chronicled and explained it all.

* * *

It started by accident. Wolfe was working for the *New York Herald Tribune*, which, along with eight other local papers, shut down for 114 days during the 1962–63 newspaper strike. He had recently written about a custom car show—phoned it in, by his own admission—but he knew there was more to the story. Temporarily without an income, he pitched a story about the custom car scene to *Esquire*. "Really, I needed to make some money," Wolfe tells me. "You could draw a per diem from the newspaper writers' guild, but it was a pittance. I was in bad shape," he chuckles. *Esquire* bit and sent the 32-year-old on his first visit to the West—to Southern California, epicenter of the subculture.

Wolfe saw plenty on that trip, from Santa Monica to North Hollywood to Maywood, from the gardens and suburbs of mid-1960s Southern California to its dung heaps. He saw so much that he didn't know what to make of it all. Returning to New York in despair, he told *Esquire* that he couldn't write the piece. Well, they said, we already have the art laid in, so we have to do something; type up your notes and send them over. "Can you imagine anything more humiliating than being told, 'Type up your notes, we'll have a *real* writer do the piece'?" Wolfe asks. He stayed up all night writing a 49-page memo—which *Esquire* printed nearly verbatim.

It's a great tale, but, one fears, too cute to be strictly true. I ask him about it point-blank. "Oh, yes, that's exactly what happened," he says. "I wrote it like a letter, to an audience of literally one person"—*Esquire* managing editor Byron Dobell—"with all these block phrases and asides. But at some point in the middle of the night, I started to think it might actually be pretty good."

That piece—"The Kandy-Kolored Tangerine-Flake Streamline Baby"— represents the first time that Wolfe truly understood and was able to formulate the big idea that would transform him from an above-average feature writer into the premier cultural chronicler of our age. Those inhabiting the custom car scene were not rich, certainly not upper-class, and not prominent—indeed, they were almost invisible to society at large. Wolfe described his initial attempt to write the story as a cheap dismissal: "Don't worry, these people are nothing." He realized in California that he had been wrong. These people were something, and *very* influential within their own circles, which were far larger than anyone on the outside had hitherto noticed.

"Max Weber," Wolfe tells me, "was the first to argue that social classes were dying everywhere—except, in his time, in England—and being replaced by what he called 'status groups'" The term improves in Wolfean English: "Southern California, I found, was a veritable paradise of statuspheres," he wrote in 1968. Beyond the customizers and drag racers, there were surfers, cruisers, teenyboppers, beboppers, strippers, bikers, beats, heads, and, of course, hippies. Each sphere started off self-contained but increasingly encroached on, and influenced, the wider world.

"Practically every style recorded in art history is the result of the same thing—a lot of attention to form plus the money to make monuments to it," Wolfe wrote in the introduction to his first book. "But throughout history, everywhere this kind of thing took place, China, Egypt, France under the Bourbons, every place, it has been something the aristocracy was responsible for. What has happened in the United States since World War II, however, has broken that pattern. The war created money. It made massive infusions of money into every level of society. Suddenly classes of people whose styles of life had been practically invisible had the money to build monuments to their own styles." If Wolfe's oeuvre has an overarching theme, this is it.

* * *

After the strike ended, the *Herald Tribune* created *New York*, a Sunday magazine to compete with *The New Yorker* and *The New York Times Magazine*. Impressed by the *Esquire* piece, the new magazine's editor, Clay Felker, assigned Wolfe a series, *The New Life Out There*—"out there" meaning California. "There was a real provincialism about the title, like that famous Saul Steinberg *New Yorker* cover"—the one showing New York City in great detail and the rest of the country as a comically tiny sliver—"as if the West Coast were some exotic frontier," Wolfe laughs. Between 1963 and 1970, he made frequent trips to California and lived in San Francisco for nearly a year. His visits tapered off after that, but he never stopped going there, both for research trips and for book tours.

His California texts may be sorted into three tranches. The first consists of the early essays, most of them written for *New York* and later collected into books. Then there are sections of later works not primarily set in California, chiefly *The Right Stuff*—his 1979 treatment of the first American astronauts— and his Atlanta-set novel *A Man in Full* (1998). The third tranche and the linchpin of the oeuvre is *The Electric Kool-Aid Acid Test* (1968)—Wolfe's "nonfiction novel" about the counterculture, his longest treatment of California by far, and the most important book about the state since Helen Hunt Jackson's *Ramona* of 1884.

Jackson had set out to do for the mission Indians what Harriet Beecher Stowe had done for the slaves. It didn't work out that way, but readers were mesmerized by her descriptions of the salubrious climate, bounteous landscape, and relaxed culture. *Ramona*, which defined California's image for more than half a century, is at once a romance, a protest tract, and a travel brochure packaged into an enduring myth. The California that Tom Wolfe describes, though, is real, right down to the dirt clods in the unpaved, chain-link-fenced parking lots of windswept, sunbaked, industrial Contra Costa County. That it often seems too fantastical to be true is testament as much to the wacky character of the state as to Wolfe's choice of particular subjects. Wolfe's focus in California is almost exclusively on the middle class, from the strip malls of North Hollywood at the low end to the beaches of La Jolla at the upper. But the thing about California's middle class, especially at the time Wolfe began his investigations, is that it's weird.

* * *

A chicken-or-egg question I have always pondered is: Are celebrities driven by a rare inner weirdness that pushes them to seek fame, or is there something weird in all of us that only fully reveals itself if we become able to indulge ourselves? Think of Michael Jackson, who moved from Gary, Indiana, to Encino in 1970 at 11, built his Neverland Ranch in the Santa Ynez Mountains, and died in the Holmby Hills at 50. Wolfe's exploration of California's middle class answers this question.

There is, in California, an inherent strangeness that has always attracted loners, dreamers, and outliers. Hemmed in on all sides by mountains, forests, deserts, and the sea, California is an island in every sense but the literal, with its own distinct climate, air, soil, flora, and fauna. Geographically and culturally, California is a world unto itself.

The first white man to lay eyes on it was the Portuguese explorer Juan Rodriguez Cabrillo, who anchored in San Diego Bay on September 28, 1542. More than 200 years passed before anyone returned; this time, it was a party of religious ascetics bent on saving souls. The first settlement they built, Mission San Diego de Alcalá, was 1,500 miles from the colonial capital of Mexico City, a four-month trek on foot through treacherous desert. Over the next 50 years, the Franciscan friars managed to crawl their way north, one mission at a time, 21 in all, each a day's walk from the next. And walking was necessary, at least northbound. The prevailing winds on the coast blow from the north-northwest, and the California Current streams south virtually every day of the year. Sailing "downhill" is, to this day, a breeze and a blast; north is a miserable business. Rather than beating relentlessly upwind, the Spanish in Mexico would head to their more important possession, the Philippines, all the way across the Pacific, and recross the ocean to visit California on the return trip. Well before the term was invented to describe Australia in the age of sail, California was afflicted by the "tyranny of distance." Only the mildness of the weather and the abundance of the land mitigated what was, in every other respect, a hard, lonely life. Naturally, it drew a certain kind of man—and they were all men.

The Gold Rush drew a different type of man. (Though this time, 10 percent of the migrants were women, many of them disreputable.) Religious fanaticism gave way to greed, lust, treachery, and vaulting ambition to have it all. The 49ers were Herculean workers but more interested in enjoying the trappings of civilization than in building one. That task fell to the farmers, grocers, carpenters, merchants, entrepreneurs, and other skilled tradesmen who followed to make a living and build fortunes on the miners' lucre and on their failures. This combination of eminent practicality and pie-in-the-sky fabulism still shapes the character of the state.

Once the gold was gone, yet another kind of man began to arrive. One might say that these men formed California's first significant cohort of stable adults: low-church Protestants from the Midwest and Great Plains who started coming even before World War I and mostly settled in the Southland and in the Santa Clara Valley. The next war, the war that "created money," brought the second, and last, wave of adults to California. They came to build the arsenal of democracy or passed through San Francisco or San Diego on their way to fight in the Pacific. Hundreds of thousands decided to settle in California. Millions more joined them to partake in arguably the greatest and longest economic boom in human history.

These people, now revered as the "greatest generation," built modern California. Wolfe's essay "Two Young Men Who Went West," the finest short history of the early Silicon Valley ever written, details the cultural baggage that Intel cofounder Robert Noyce brought with him to California from Grinnell, Iowa, after the war:

> Noyce was like a great many bright young men and women from Dissenting Protestant families in the Middle West after the Second World War. They had been raised as Baptists, Methodists, Congregationalists, Presbyterians, United Brethren, whatever. They had been led through the Church door and prodded toward religion, but it had never come alive for them. Sundays made their skulls feel like dried-out husks. So they slowly walked away from the church and silently, without so much as a growl of rebellion, congratulated themselves on their independence of mind and headed into another way of life. Only decades later, in most cases, would they discover how, absentmindedly, inexplicably, they had brought the old ways along for the journey nonetheless. It was as if . . . through some extraordinary mistake . . . they had been sewn into the linings of their coats!

No single paragraph—written by Wolfe or anyone else—better explains the paradox of modern California. It was built from scratch, overnight, at the farthest reaches of the world, land's end for Western civilization, on a foundation of virtues cultivated and nourished in Old Europe and the American heartland. But something in the character of the place and of the people who chose it drives them restlessly to seek (or invent) new virtues, new modes of living, to sweep aside all that has come before and start over, unencumbered.

Writer Virginia Postrel has commented on the extraordinary sensation of freedom that washed over her when she moved from Boston to Los Angeles. Arnold Schwarzenegger, arriving from Austria in 1968, was struck by how "everyone could come here and have opportunities." The old rules didn't apply in California. In his *Esquire* piece, Wolfe wrote that George Barris, the Giotto of the car customizers, "was making next to nothing at first but he never remembers feeling hard up, nor does any kid out there today I talked to. They have a magic economy or something." High expectations flow inexorably. And for a while, California had an uncanny knack for meeting those expectations. In hindsight, it's clear that the virtues sewn into the linings of those coats were at least as instrumental as any quality inherent in the land.

All that money, freedom, and sense of limitless possibility have the same effect on California writ large as they do on people who rocket overnight from steelworker's son to superstar. Out pours everyone's inner weird.

* * *

And enter Tom Wolfe. The car customizers were just the first revelers he noticed. He soon grew acquainted with their many orbiters, wannabes, hangers-on, and fellow travelers. These various "statuspheres" at first glance seemed distinct, but once investigated proved to be linked. The unifying element was, for lack of a better term, teen culture. In California, he found "a kind of Plato's Republic for teen-agers," he wrote.

There was, of course, the music. Record producer Phil Spector, born in the Bronx but raised in Los Angeles, earned millions before his 21st birthday by catering (or pandering) to the tastes of teenagers with money to spare. He wrote and produced the soundtrack not just to an era but to an entirely new way of life—born, developed, and consumed in California, and finally exported to all points on the map in the form of hits by the Ronettes, the Righteous Brothers, and Ike and Tina Turner, to name a few. Wolfe profiled Spector in a 1964 story called "The First Tycoon of Teen." Spector's own inner weird, by the way, was dark: later in life, he got into the habit of picking up women at West Hollywood nightclubs and limo-ing them back to his Alhambra mansion. Several allege that he held them at gunpoint to prevent their leaving. In 2003, one of them was shot dead in his home, and six years later, a Los Angeles County jury convicted him of second-degree murder. He is currently serving a 19-year sentence in Corcoran State Prison in the Central Valley.

I ask Wolfe, who spent a great deal of time with Spector at the height of his fame in the mid-1960s, if he had followed the trial. "I did, a little, though I had not spoken to him in years. When I knew him, I felt almost affectionate toward him. He had a lot of problems, all stemming from his high school days and being a shrimp. People gave him a hard time everywhere he went. . . . One time, we were having a drink in the Plaza Hotel"—this would have been in 1964—"and in those days his long hair still stood out. A woman kept staring at him and finally came up to him and demanded, 'What's your problem?' He looked at her and said, 'Premature ejaculation' without missing a beat."

Wolfe's next big idea for *The New Life Out There* was to examine another type of "tycoon of teen," the young men getting rich selling the surfing life-style. He started hanging around the big kahunas of Newport Beach, Balboa, and Dana Point. One of them suggested that an even better story lay farther south, in ritzy La Jolla, one of America's top surf spots. "That was the first time I ever heard of teenagers living communally, away from their parents, but in the same town," Wolfe says.

The result was the classic essay "The Pump House Gang." The surf tycoons made it into the piece, but Wolfe's focus was on the middle- and upper-middle-class kids, most of them younger than 20 and all under the "horror dividing line" of 25, whose lives revolved around Windansea Beach in La Jolla. The titular structure is a concrete sewage pump just above the beach. "Did you know there was a monument to me in La Jolla?" Wolfe asks me. "Somebody spray-painted TOM WOLFE IS A DORK on the side of the pump house. But it was cleaned up years ago."

One theme of "The Pump House Gang" is age segregation—voluntary and otherwise. In Southern California, Wolfe wrote,

> there are old people's housing developments, private developments, in which no one under 50 may buy a home. There are apartment developments for single persons 20 to 30 only. The Sunset Strip in Los Angeles has become the exclusive hangout of the 16 to 25 set. In 1966 they came close to street warfare to keep it that way, against the police who moved in to "clean up." . . . The Pump House Gang lived as though age segregation were a permanent state, as if it were inconceivable that any of them would ever grow old, i.e., 25. I foresaw the day when the California coastline would be littered with the bodies of aged and abandoned *Surferkinder*, like so many beached whales.

This refusal to grow up—which Wolfe saw 50 years ago, when the boomers were still children—is another of California's exports. Replace "*Surferkinder*" with "hippies," and you're describing a problem several orders of magnitude larger.

* * *

"I didn't know about the Pranksters when I went out to interview Kesey," Wolfe says about *Acid Test*, the book that made him a superstar, and its whimsical cast of characters centered on author Ken Kesey. "All I knew was that this very promising young novelist was in jail on serious drug charges after fleeing to Mexico. It sounded like a good piece for *The New Life Out There*."

The first thing Wolfe noticed when he got to the jail in San Mateo County was Kesey's "following of the faithful. They were hanging around the jail, all wearing white jumpsuits, like mechanics wear, with American flags sewn on them, and talking about Kesey with this . . . reverence." The sheriff gave Wolfe a paltry ten minutes with the author, so Wolfe stayed in California until Kesey was out on bail and then "went with him and his followers back to this garage in skid row"—Harriet Street, south of Market, in San Francisco—"that they called 'the Warehouse,' where they lived communally. He sat in the middle of this big open space and they all gathered 'round. He started speaking in parables that made no sense to me but which they treated as the most profound things they had ever heard. That's when I realized they were a band of believers, this was a religion."

What Wolfe witnessed was a kind of modern-day preaching of Jesus to the Apostles. The Pranksters were dissolute and frivolous, of course, but they had an enormous influence. The mainstreaming of "alternative lifestyles"—the drug culture, communalism, environmentalism, localism, Eastern spiritualism, the "Yoga-Industrial Complex," experimental art—flowed out from Kesey's compound to the rest of California, then to the country, and finally throughout the Western world.

At its best, the hippie Great Awakening gave birth to a heightened appreciation of nature, philosophy, and fine living that sanded some of the hard edges off mid-century California's rigid pragmatism and restored a sense of grace and ease to the land, or at least the coast. Most of those who lived it, though not all, settled down after waking from their post–Acid Test stupor. David Brooks, who has learned much from Wolfe, gently mocks the institutionalization of hippie culture as "boboism" even as he shows how it has done much good.

But there was a dark side. Wolfe mentions whole towns where "stranded hippies" who refuse or are unable to move on "make money by doing yard work." For every Alice Waters—the local-foods restaurateur who's managed to parlay the spirit of that age into a beneficent movement and successful business—hundreds more end up as burned-out wrecks. The Hensley family in *A Man in Full* are, in effect, Wolfe's second epilogue to *Acid Test*, like the captions at the end of movies that tell you what happened to the characters afterward. Conrad—the straitlaced, hardworking son of two Haight-Ashbury wastrels—is a reactionary in the precise sense, rebelling against the disorder of his parents' lives by becoming everything they are not.

In *The Right Stuff*, similarly, the test pilots of Muroc Field—later Edwards Air Force Base—in California's high desert are the Pranksters' mirror image.

The military culture that Wolfe describes suffused California before the end of the Cold War, when base closings and the decimation of the aerospace industry bled it white. Here, the old Protestant virtues thrived, sewn into the linings of the soldiers' uniforms.

* * *

Wolfe's next book after *Acid Test* was the tour de force *Radical Chic & Mau-Mauing the Flak Catchers* (1970). The titular radicals were the Black Panthers, founded in Oakland, California, four years earlier. That this anti-American group was welcomed into the bosom of the American establishment that it wanted to destroy was naturally treated by Wolfe as a farcical fad.

Wolfe's friend Harvey Mansfield once remarked that you haven't understood any paragraph in Machiavelli until you have found something funny in it. It's unnecessary to look for the comedy in Wolfe; it will find you, quickly, and never let up. However, you haven't understood any passage in Wolfe until you have found the seriousness beneath the surface. In the course of his research, Wolfe discovered that the Black Panther Party's vaunted "ten-point program" had been drawn up in the North Oakland Poverty Center—that is, in an office established, operated, and funded by the government. These offices, he wrote later, constituted "official invitations from the government to people in the slums to improve their lot by rising up and rebelling against the establishment, including the government itself." The comedic action of *Mau-Mauing*—tough-looking, angry-sounding ghetto warriors marching to downtown San Francisco to scare the bejesus out of a hapless white civil-service lifer so that he'd award their group a grant from the poverty program—would soon be institutionalized through the infamous Acorn and similar organizations. The rebels became a kind of parallel establishment and, eventually, the establishment itself.

I inform Wolfe that, as far as my research has discovered, *Mau-Mauing* contains the first publicly printed appearance of the now-ubiquitous term "community organizing." (It occurs twice, in fact.) "Really?" he says. "I didn't realize that." Alinsky's *Rules for Radicals*, the profession's manifesto, was published one year later. It's common, for someone charged with introducing Wolfe to a public gathering, to note how often he predicts coming headlines. Three months *after* the publication of *The Bonfire of the Vanities*, for example, the Tawana Brawley case exploded. Such feats of reportage are so routine for Wolfe that we have come to expect them. But it's hard to see how he can ever top having explained the rise of Barack Obama when the future president was only nine years old.

* * *

What Wolfe called the "New Journalism"—a style created by himself, Truman Capote, Hunter S. Thompson, and others—was characterized by four literary devices: extensive dialogue, scene-by-scene construction, a personal point of view instead of omniscient narration, and heavy inclusion of status details. But Wolfe's signature literary device is not, in the final analysis, any of these. It is rather to combine the big and the small, using the latter as a gateway into the former. "Great journalism is distinguished by the telling detail," Wolfe says, remembering the Samoans in *Mau-Mauing* who participate in the visit to intimidate the bureaucrat. They pound their carved tiki sticks on the floor to make a great ruckus, the better to strike fear into the heart of the Man, "although some of them press one end of the stick onto the sole of their sandal between their first two toes and raise their foot up and down with the stick to cushion the blow to the floor. They don't want to scuff up the Tiki cane." Forty-two years later, this "little thing" still makes Wolfe smile. That's what Machiavelli called such details—the *cose piccolo* through which the intentions of the gods can be discerned.

A writer can get such details only through on-scene reporting, "getting out of the house," Wolfe insists. His California is so richly realized because he has seen it and lived in it. It is no secret that he was stung by the critical reception of his 2004 book, the campus novel *I Am Charlotte Simmons*—and not by the intellectuals' sniggering at his supposed prudery and moralism, which he expected, but by the charge that the book was inaccurate. Wolfe says that he visited eight universities to do research (Stanford was the first). Bobo parents are desperate to believe that the campus bacchanalia that Wolfe describes can't be real—or that if they are, please God let them be confined to the lower orders. Wolfe makes us uncomfortable by showing that the boozing and especially the sex are not merely present at our elite institutions but happen even more there.

Should we be surprised? Nearly 30 years earlier, in the bravura essay "The Me Decade and the Third Great Awakening" (1976), which opens with a scene in the Los Angeles hotel ballroom where Robert Kennedy gave his last speech, Wolfe had explained the justifications offered for the "sexual revolution." That revolution had no Bastille or Winter Palace—it's impossible to say where it started—but it certainly had its Jacobins and Red Guards, of which California contributed more than its fair share:

> In Los Angeles it is not uncommon to see fifteen coin-operated newspaper racks in a row on the sidewalk. One will be for the *Los Angeles Times*, a second for the *Herald-Examiner*, and the other thirteen for the sex papers. . . . Sex had now become a religion, [with] a theology in which the orgasm had become a form of spiritual ecstasy. . . . At the Sandstone sex farm in the Santa Monica Mountains, people of all class levels gather for weekends in the nude, and copulate in the

living room, on the lawn, out by the pool, on the tennis courts, with the same open, free, liberated spirit as dogs in the park or baboons in a tree. In conversation, however, the atmosphere is quite different. The air becomes humid with solemnity. Close your eyes and you think you're at a nineteenth-century Wesleyan summer encampment and tent-meeting lecture series. It's the soul that gets a workout here, brethren.

The religious language was neither an accident nor intentionally ironic. The children of the adults who built California long ago spent down the stock of genuine virtue sewn into the linings of their ancestors' coats. But the words remained, ready to be twisted into rationales for whatever they wanted to do in the moment. Things have calmed down since. But that self-serving self-justification, like so much radioactive waste, will outlast us all, continuing to corrupt everything it touches, which is everything. So, for instance, the state—conservatively estimated to be at least $617 billion in debt—congratulates itself on spending $68 billion it doesn't have to build a train that no one will ride. That is but one of California's problems, but it's emblematic of a rot that Wolfe saw coming and that might have been avoided, had his analysis been heeded and understood.

Tom Wolfe's California is a literary continent scarcely explored by the scholars, historians, sociologists, theorists, cultural critics, and politicians who could most benefit from an extended sojourn. Much remains to be discovered. He has more to teach us. Or, more precisely, we have more to learn.

[2012]

VIII

KEEP HOPE ALIVE

28

The Silicon Lining

California's Innovative High-Tech Firms Keep Creating Wealth, but Will Bad State Politics Drive Them Out?

Guy Sorman

E RIC DEMERS CAN'T REMEMBER how many pseudo–Silicon Valleys he has seen around the world while traveling for Advanced Micro Devices. The globe's second-largest microchip designer and producer (after Intel), AMD was created 40 years ago in the authentic Silicon Valley in California. Demers, the firm's chief technology officer, has no intention of moving. Across the world, he points out, private and public attempts to create new Silicon Valleys have achieved only "pale copies" of the original.

That original has remained the undisputed cradle of high-tech and communications innovation. Historic leaders like Hewlett-Packard and Intel have stayed here; more recent giants Google, Facebook, and Twitter cluster around the pioneers. The valley's economy, concentrated in a 60-mile corridor running from San Francisco to San Jose, attracts one-third of all venture capital invested in new businesses in the United States—39 percent in 2009, though the $7 billion made it a slow year.[1] A new start-up launches every working day. From among these high-tech ventures will emerge the next Google or Intel.

Silicon Valley faces a serious threat, however: the fiscal and regulatory earthquakes rocking California. Measured by per-household state and local government spending, California ranks third-highest in the nation, behind Alaska and New York. The state government is trying desperately to squeeze money out of any profitable activity to meet the crippling costs. Further, California continues to impose onerous regulations on the private sector. High taxes and stifling regulations give companies a strong incentive to move

Illustration by Robert Pizzo.

elsewhere. In this increasingly business-hostile environment, will Silicon Valley's unique entrepreneurial spirit survive?

* * *

Forty years ago, when Silicon Valley began to expand and soon came to dominate the high-tech universe, most of its companies were manufacturing enterprises, producing microchips and computers right on the spot. No longer. Starting in the 1980s, valley firms began moving away from production to concentrate on inventing new products and services. AMD, for example, outsourced most of its manufacturing years ago to factories in countries like China, India, and Taiwan—places with lower wages and high production quality. The approximately 3,000 employees at the company's Sunnyvale offices are designers, marketers, accountants, and mechanical engineers; what tiny production lines remain are for building prototypes.

Was so much outsourcing necessary? Jason Clemens, research director for the Pacific Research Institute in San Francisco, one of California's few free-market think tanks, acknowledges that countries like Taiwan offer a powerful "pull" factor for shifting manufacturing to East Asia. But there has been a major "push" factor, too, Clemens argues: the Golden State's excessive income and property taxes and its web of regulations, which, he believes, have driven up outsourcing. As Berkeley-based journalist Francis Pisani puts it: "Outsourcing is the only answer to taxes and regulations."

California has piled every imaginable burden on businesses. Minimum-wage laws are among the highest in the country, and health and safety regulations are among the strictest; cities like San Francisco and San Jose require businesses to offer employees health insurance; labor laws are extremely union-friendly; environmental policies drive up energy costs—and on and on. Small firms have the toughest time in this business-toxic climate. A recent study by Sanjay Varshney, dean of the College of Business Administration at California State University in Sacramento, estimates that the cost of state regulations in 2007 reached an average of $134,122 per small business—the equivalent of one job lost per company. And it's not just the small guys: Google, which uses colossal amounts of electricity, is building its data centers in other states or abroad, where energy is much cheaper.

Hank Nothhaft is the CEO of Tessera, a firm in the field of semiconductor miniaturization. He shows me the vacant office parks and empty lots around his company's San Jose factory. Silicon Valley, he observes, lost more than a quarter of its computer, microchip, and communications-equipment manufacturing jobs from 2001 to 2008, and Tessera proved no exception. The company has kept some of its assembly lines and industrial operations going here, but it now produces two-thirds of its nanotechnology chips in less expensive

North Carolina and in various countries overseas, with China becoming the latest contender for a production facility. Just back from a trip there, Noth-haft says that he has been offered terms he "cannot decently refuse." Using the Internet and videoconferencing, he can manage Tessera factories around the globe without leaving his San Jose office. "The business environment is becoming awful in California," Nothhaft complains—just by moving his headquarters to Nevada, he'd save $5 million a year in taxes.

Why doesn't he, then? "Inertia," he answers. "We have a very good team here, which I wouldn't want to disband." He also holds out hope for change: "Things would turn around if the government became pro-growth."

* * *

Outsourcing has allowed local entrepreneurs and would-be entrepreneurs to remain as creative as ever—for now. The valley continues to attract inno-vators who share a "built-in start-up mentality," Pisani says, risk-takers who believe that "they can change the world through technical innovation and become billionaires while doing it." They've brought "permanent revolution" to the valley, he adds. After the microchip, the PC, and the Internet, Silicon Valley entrepreneurs might have rested on their laurels. But the innovation hasn't stopped. Smartphones inaugurated a new era of personal nomadic devices. Next came Apple's iPad.

These dazzling products have opened a new frontier for the software in-dustry: the seemingly infinite world of digital applications for mobile gadgets. Relatively cheap to launch and not requiring heavy investment or sophisti-cated equipment to create, apps could be invented anywhere, Pisani says. But it so happens that most of them are still created in Silicon Valley—or in other parts of the Bay Area that can offer cheaper rents. It is invaluable, Pisani ex-plains, to be "not farther than one hour's drive from Palo Alto and Sand Hill Road," where all the venture capitalists work.

The valley is a "vast, informal club," observes Jean-Louis Gassée, formerly with Apple and now a venture capitalist. Socializing and networking be-come vectors of creativity. Palo Alto's University Avenue cafés, school PTA meetings, and gyms become places where one can meet customers, vendors, collaborators, and investors. Skilled engineers and smart high-tech entrepre-neurs also cluster in the imitation Silicon Valleys of Bangalore, Saclay (near Paris), and Shanghai, Gassée acknowledges. But no hub can match the Val-ley's innovative start-up mentality.

Outsourcing has encouraged that creative spirit not just by keeping costs down but by bringing Silicon Valley firms into daily contact with other cul-tures. As a result, valley entrepreneurs recruit engineers in Africa, Asia, Eu-rope, and South America; a permanent two-way flow of people, products, and services unites the valley with hundreds of regions across the planet. Silicon Valley, observes Alan Eustace, a Google vice president at its Mountain View campus, has become a "high-tech melting pot within the U.S. melting pot." He adds that the array of ethnicities and backgrounds of Google employees is a tremendous benefit for the company. Google's search engine, based on what Eustace calls "the wisdom of the crowd," is a good example: it works well in any civilization, he maintains, because technicians from all civilizations have helped conceive it. Today, foreign-born entrepreneurs found half of the valley's start-ups.

Silicon Valley entrepreneurs, recognizing the benefits of this cross-fertilization, express frustration with current immigration law. The federal government's annual cap on H-1B visas—issued to professionals working in certain fields, many of them high-tech—is absurd, says Nothhaft. "Asian students are not allowed to stay in the U.S.; after they get a degree, they have to return to India or South Korea, where they become our competitors."

* * *

Where did Silicon Valley's entrepreneurial, creative spirit come from? There are as many answers to that question as there are political ideologies, says Kevin Kelly, founder of *Wired*, a magazine that in the 1990s was the paper expression of valley mystique. Kelly eventually sold *Wired* to Condé Nast (though he retains the title "Senior Maverick"). One could argue, he begins, that the government helped create Silicon Valley during World War II by installing military facilities there, which bought goods and services from surrounding private businesses and helped them flourish. Or maybe it was luck: working from his garage, David Packard initiated a technical revolution in radio transmission—and he just happened to live in Palo Alto.

Stanford University, Kelly continues, may be another explanation. Stanford not only trains some of America's best engineers; it also has a tradition of cooperating with the private sector. The university encourages students to start their own companies as soon as they've completed their studies, a practice that began with a professor of engineering in the 1930s, Frederick Terman, who would give his students small pots of money to help them test their ideas in the marketplace. Among his students were Packard and William Hewlett, who couldn't have started their firm without Terman's cash. When Terman returned to Stanford after the war to become dean of the School of Engineering, he expanded on this policy by leasing Stanford land to high-tech firms. Silicon Valley's venture capitalists consider Terman their "godfather," says Randy Komisar, a partner at one of the leading VC firms, Kleiner Perkins Caufield & Byers. Today, Silicon Valley is a "plug-and-play" environment where innovators can readily seek out funding—and also tap into the best accountants, engineers, public-relations professionals, and bankers, all available on the spot.

But it's the cultural explanation that Kelly likes best. He sees Silicon Valley as the ultimate Wild West: a geographic frontier and—at least in the beginning—an unregulated one. This helps explain how the valley won out over the Boston area as a high-tech center in the 1970s, Kelly believes. Home to MIT and leading high-speed computer manufacturers like Cray (which has since disappeared), Boston was the leader then. But Massachusetts was heavily taxed and regulated; at the time, California wasn't. The Silicon Valley pioneers thus had greater leeway than their Boston competitors to experiment, even to fail. They could explore fields like software, which wasn't considered valuable intellectual property yet but which would pay off hugely over time. The freewheeling Wild West triumphed over the more controlled New England. As Michael Bernstam, a scholar at Stanford's Hoover Institution, says: "Capitalism is most creative at the frontiers."

* * *

"We keep an edge over the rest of the world," says Komisar. "We know where the future is." Forty years ago, Silicon Valley capitalists knew that computers were the future; later, they knew that the Internet was the Next Big Thing, and later still, social networking. Knowing exactly which companies would flourish in these fields was, of course, more difficult. Only 10 percent of start-ups survive their first year, and half of those are still alive after two years, with just a few rising to the level of an Intel, a Google, or a Facebook.

"Alternative energy is the next big adventure," Komisar tells me. It's a plausible argument. True, alternative energy and energy-saving technologies won't replace the existing energy industry—they simply don't generate enough power. But Komisar contends that, in the long run, the cost of oil will only increase, while the cost of alternative energies, through innovation, can only drop. Even if cap-and-trade legislation goes nowhere and no global-warming treaty ever wins ratification, he says, companies will want to become more energy-efficient to improve their balance sheets. Amit Chatterjee, founder and CEO of Redwood-based Hara, a start-up financed by Komisar's fund, sells software that helps manage natural resources. "We do not sell green tech," he insists. "We sell cost reductions." Among Hara's first customers: Rupert Murdoch's News Corporation. "They count on us to become carbon-neutral in 2010," Chatterjee says.[2]

Not all of the valley's venture capitalists share Komisar's and Chatterjee's enthusiasm for green energy, it's important to add. Some competitors believe that the Obama administration's support is artificially boosting the momentum for alternative energy. The future may not be as green as some expect.

Komisar admits that public subsidies have played a major role in this latest valley mania, but he notes that the Internet enjoyed initial support from the government, too. "We think long-term," he says. "We are not playing with derivatives. We associate with entrepreneurial teams for many years and create real value."

Time will tell. Kleiner Perkins Caufield & Byers typically sells its participation in a project a full ten years after beginning to fund it. The pension funds, endowments, and wealthy individuals who trust their money with the roughly 20 elite venture-capital firms on Sand Hill Road aren't short-term speculators, either. Surrounding these top-tier firms are approximately 500 smaller, more adventurous, venture-capital companies that are willing to fund smaller, shorter-term investments, like social networks today. There aren't enough Facebooks and Twitters in Silicon Valley to make all the firms wealthy. Some will strike gold, however, and perhaps join the elite.

* * *

Given California's harsh business climate, it's remarkable that entrepreneurs still flock to Silicon Valley, Sonia Arrison wryly observes. She's a Pacific Research Institute scholar with a reputation for being a high-tech prophetess. "It's a trade-off," she says. "If you leave the valley, you lose a lot." The cost of doing business in the state is rising, but outside the valley, it remains more difficult to find venture capital and recruit brilliant students.

Will competitors displace Silicon Valley? "There is pervasive fear of Chinese competition," Arrison notes, but China lacks the valley's global appeal and "will not become a melting pot—at least not in the near future." Where does she see the next revolution taking place? "Smartphones are hot," she says, "and tablets are as hot as microprocessors were a generation ago. The next big thing could be cloud computing, and farther out, three-dimensional printers," which would be able to create objects in three dimensions, starting with basic plastic devices. Whatever the next innovation is, though, Arrison thinks that it will happen in the valley.

Carl Guardino concurs, up to a point: he calls the valley "the innovation leader of the world," but he won't rule out high-tech breakthroughs elsewhere. As president of the Silicon Valley Leadership Group, which represents the interests of the region's 300 most significant firms, Guardino looks closely at the competition. So far, he's less impressed by China and India than by Ireland and Singapore. "The error of many of our competitors is to copy Silicon Valley," he tells me. "They try to reproduce who we are and what we do: the Indian and Chinese governments built somewhat artificial high-tech parks without any real entrepreneurs working there." A more productive strategy, he thinks, is what Ireland and Singapore are doing: encouraging research and development by lowering taxes, loosening regulations, and improving education.

* * *

On January 27, 2010, two major events took place in the United States. In Washington, D.C., President Obama, in his first State of the Union address, announced steps to help small businesses create jobs. In San Francisco, Steve Jobs, Apple's visionary CEO, presented his last invention, the iPad. Which event will prove more significant to America's future and the world's?

Tessera's Hank Nothhaft suggests the answer when he tells me that his elder son has just created a start-up in the valley. "We can't help it," he says. "We're just a family of serial entrepreneurs." Innovation still tends to happen first in Silicon Valley. Even the sclerotic, near-failed state of California hasn't yet stifled the extraordinary energy of this unique place. A good thing, because California's economic recovery—and America's—will depend heavily on its continued vibrancy.

[2010]

Notes

1. In 2011, the latest year available, California attracted $14.5 billion in venture capital, according to a report by PricewaterhouseCoopers.

2. News Corporation CEO Rupert Murdoch announced that the company had reached its goal in a March 1, 2011 memo.

29

California, Here We Stay

Reasons Not to Flee an Imploding State

Victor Davis Hanson

CALIFORNIA'S MULTIDIMENSIONAL DECLINE—fiscal, commercial, social, and political—sometimes seems endless. The state's fiscal problems were especially evident in May 2012, when Governor Jerry Brown announced an "unexpected" $16 billion annual budget shortfall. Two months later, he signed a $92 billion budget that appears balanced only if voters approve an $8.5 billion tax increase in November. According to a study published by a public policy group at Stanford University, California's various retirement systems have amassed $500 billion in unfunded liabilities. To honor the pension and benefit contracts of current and retired public employees, state and local governments have already started to lay off workers and slash services.

Not just in its finances but almost wherever you look, the state's vital signs are dipping. The average unemployment rate hovers around 10 percent. In the reading and math tests administered by the National Assessment of Educational Progress, California students rank near the bottom of the country, though their teachers earn far more than the average American teacher does. California's penal system is the largest in the United States, with more than 165,000 inmates. Some studies estimate that the state prisons and county jails house more than 30,000 illegal aliens, at a cost of $1 billion or more each year. Speaking of which: California has the nation's largest population of illegal aliens, on whom it spends an estimated $10 billion annually in entitlements. The illegals also deprive the Golden State's economy of billions of dollars every year by sending remittances to Latin America.

Meanwhile, business surveys perennially rank California among the most hostile states to private enterprise, largely because of overregulation, stifling coastal zoning laws, inflated housing costs, and high tax rates. Environmental extremism has cost the state dearly: oil production has plunged 45 percent over the last 25 years, even though California's Monterey Shale formation has an estimated 15.4 billion barrels of recoverable oil, according to the U.S. Energy Information Administration. Geologists estimate that 3 trillion cubic feet of natural gas sit untapped as well. Those numbers could soar with revolutionary new methods of exploration (see chapter 12, "A Crude Awakening").

Between the mid-1980s and 2005, the state's aggregate population increased by 10 million Californians, including immigrants. But that isn't the good economic news that you might think. For one thing, 7 million of the new Californians were low-income Medicaid recipients. Further, as economist Arthur Laffer has noted, between 1992 and 2008, the number of taxpaying Californians entering California was smaller than the number leaving—3.5 million versus 4.4 million, for a net loss of 869,000 tax filers. Those who left were wealthier than those who arrived, with average adjusted gross incomes of $44,700, versus $38,600. Losing those 869,000 filers cost California $44 billion in tax revenue over two decades, Laffer calculated.

Worst of all is that neither the legislature nor the governor has offered a serious plan to address any of these problems. Soaring public-employee costs, unfunded pensions, foundering schools, millions of illegal aliens, regulations that prevent wealth creation, an onerous tax code: the story of all the ways in which today's Californians have squandered a rich natural and human inheritance is infuriating.

So why, you might ask, would anyone stay here?

* * *

For some of us, family heritage explains a lot. In the 1870s, my maternal great-great-grandmother homesteaded our farm and built the farmhouse in which I currently live, near what is now the town of Selma. I grew up working alongside her grandson—my grandfather, who was born in the same farmhouse in 1890 and died there in 1976. He worshiped California. Even in his eighties, he still marveled at the state's unique combination of rich soil, lengthy growing season, huge aquifer, and water flowing down from the Sierra Nevada mountains. He planted most of the fruit and nut trees growing in my yard today. On my father's side, my great-grandfather helped found the nearby Swedish colony of Kingsburg, where a plaque in a municipal park— thankfully not stolen during a recent wave of bronze thefts—marks Hanson Corner, the site of the ancestral family farmhouse.

My mother, a 1946 Stanford law graduate, was one of the state's first female appellate court justices and would lecture me about the brilliance of California's four-level court system. My father—a Pat Brown Democrat convinced that technical training was in short supply for the influx of Southeast Asian and Hispanic immigrants—helped found a vocational junior-college campus in the 1970s. Countless Californians are like me: determined to hold on to the heritage of our ancestors, as well as our memories of better times and the property on which we grew up. We feel that we played no part in our state's current problems, and we're reluctant to surrender to those who did.

Another draw to California is its culture. The California way, casual and even flaky, can sometimes become crass and self-indulgent; for evidence of that, just visit Venice Beach or Berkeley's Telegraph Avenue. But at its best, California still creates a 49er bustle of self-invention that makes little allowance for class, titles, or hierarchy. As someone who established a classics program with mostly minority students at California State University's Fresno campus, I can attest that real talent is often found unfettered by hierarchy. In a state with no majority culture, where it is almost impossible to determine a person's income by race, dress, accent, or bearing, performance tends to trump reputation or appearance. The proverbial "millionaires and billionaires" whom I see drinking coffee on University Avenue in Palo Alto on Monday are dressed no differently from the loggers I talk with in the Huntington Lake bar in the Sierra on Friday. Some of the wealthiest farmers in the world are indistinguishable from their tractor drivers. In California, one earns respect more from what one does than from what one has done.

Some of the reasons that people began migrating to California haven't changed, even in the twenty-first century: dysfunctional politics cannot so easily mar what nature has so abundantly bestowed. California will always be warm, dry, and beautiful, and it boasts an unparalleled diversity of climate and terrain. In the winter, I can leave my Sierra cabin (altitude 7,200 feet, with 20 feet of snow piled nearly to the roof) in the morning, drive down to 70-degree afternoons on my farm in the Central Valley, and arrive in the evening at the Stanford University campus, with its cool bay breezes. What's most striking about California isn't its rugged mountains, gorgeous beaches, and vast plains, but their proximity to one another. That nearness is an obvious incentive for Californians to stay put. In the winter, when midwestern sunbirds fly to Arizona and New Yorkers go to Florida, Californians are never farther than a few hours' drive from the coast.

This beauty is economically profitable as well. Thanks to its climate, California can grow three crops a year, while most states struggle with one or two. The long growing season—plus great soil, plenty of irrigation, vast agribusiness economies of scale, and technological support from nearby universities—means that California's farms can produce almost twice the usual tonnage of fruits and vegetables per acre. Not only are California's cotton, wine, fruit, and dairy industries more productive than any in the world; hundreds of millions of affluent Asian consumers translate into skyrocketing export-commodity prices for the state's farmers. In 2012, beleaguered

California farms—fighting water cutoffs, new regulations, and encroaching suburbanization—nonetheless exported over $17 billion worth of food overseas (see chapter 13, "The Water Wars"). In so mild a climate, moreover, outdoor construction is an all-year enterprise. It's hard to believe that the world's most productive farmers and most innovative builders would pack up and leave without a fight.

California also possesses enormous natural wealth in oil, gas, minerals, and timber. With commodity prices high and new technologies for energy exploration emerging all the time, the dollar wealth below California's surface is greater than ever. The existential stuff of any civilization remains food and fuel, and California has more of both than any other state. So we wait for sanity to return to our officials, as our natural untapped wealth grows ever more valuable.

And no explanation of California's appeal would be complete without mentioning how many top universities it hosts. In most rankings of the world's universities, Stanford, Caltech, UC Berkeley, and UCLA make the top 20. The industries that best explain why California is still the world's eighth- or ninth-largest economy—Silicon Valley, the Los Angeles aerospace industry, Napa Valley wineries, and central California agriculture—originated in the research and development programs of the state's vast public university system.

True, that system faces considerable budget pressure and has increasingly adopted a highly politicized and therapeutic curriculum. California State University, in particular, has lowered its standards, admitting students who don't meet traditional GPA and test-score thresholds, so that over half of entering freshmen must enroll in remediation courses. But the state's 50-year-old master plan for higher education—which instituted a tripartite arrangement of junior colleges, the California State University system, and the elite ten-campus University of California—remains viable. The schools still draw top scholars from around the world. And students come as well, especially engineering and computer students from China, India, South Korea, and Japan. Many end up settling here. Even in these bad times, it's difficult to destroy such an inspired system.

* * *

Another reason to feel hopeful about California is that it's reaching the theoretical limits of statism. To pay for current pensioners, the state simply can't continue to bestow comparable defined-benefit pension packages on new workers, no matter how stridently the public-sector unions claim otherwise. And as public insolvencies mount—with Stockton, Mammoth Lakes, and San Bernardino seeking bankruptcy protection a year after Vallejo emerged from it—public blame is finally shifting from supposedly heartless state taxpayers to the unions. The liberal unionism of an aging generation is proving untenable, as we saw in recent ballot referenda in which voters in San Diego and San Jose demanded that public-worker compensation plans be renegotiated.

Though the fiscal situation is dire, Californians can take comfort from the fact that their budget, unlike the federal government's, is smaller than at any time since 2006. The state constitution currently requires two-thirds of the legislature to approve any tax hike. Since Democrats have lacked the supermajority necessary to raise taxes, and since California cannot print its own money, the legislature has been forced to shrink budgets.

Californians are also fickle and can turn on a dime. For all its loud liberal credentials, the state is as likely to cut government as to raise taxes. Over the years, Golden State voters have passed ballot propositions limiting property taxes, outlawing free public services for illegal aliens, ending racial preferences, demanding "three-strikes" incarceration for repeat felons, and abolishing bilingual-education programs in public schools. Two statewide propositions at the ballot box in November would limit public unions' prerogatives and require balanced budgets. The state and federal courts and Sacramento bureaucracies overturn most resolutions of this kind or try to avoid enforcing them, but the referenda demonstrate how California can explode into conservative anger at any moment. No wonder the Democratic state legislature regularly tries to change the ballot process.

At some point, the state's southern border will finally be closed, and with it the unchecked yearly flow of illegal immigrants. The economic downturn in the United States, globalized new industry in Mexico, and increased border enforcement have already resulted in lower numbers of illegals. No national support exists for wholesale amnesty or for open borders. And with an enforced border, California will see not only decreased remittances to Mexico and Latin America and a reduced draw on state services but also, perhaps, a change in attitude within the state's largest ethnic group. After all, illegal immigration warps the politics of the Mexican-American community, which constitutes more than 40 percent of the state's population. The unlawful entry of Mexican nationals into California not only ensures statistically that Mexican-Americans as a group suffer from disproportionate poverty rates; it also means that affluent third- and fourth-generation Mexican-Americans become part of a minority receiving disproportionate state help. As one of my middle-class, third-generation Mexican-American college students once put it: "Without the illegal aliens in this school, I wouldn't get special treatment."

Without influxes of massive numbers of illegal immigrants, California Latinos could soon resemble California Armenians, Japanese, and Portuguese—whose integrated, assimilated, and intermarried ethnics usually earn more than the state's average per-capita income. With controlled borders,

Chicano studies departments should eventually go the way of Asian studies and Armenian studies—that is, they would become small, literary, and historical, rather than large, activist, and partisan. Indeed, the great fear of the liberal Hispanic hierarchy in government, media, and academia is that without illegal immigration, the conservative tendencies of the Hispanic middle class would cost the elites their positions as self-appointed spokespeople for the statistically underachieving.

* * *

To grasp a final reason for optimism about California's future, you need to understand that many of the state's political problems result from a bifurcation between the populous coastal strip from San Diego to San Francisco, where the affluent make state policy, and the vast, much poorer interior, from Sacramento to San Bernardino, where policy dreams about immigration, agriculture, public education, and resource use become nightmares in practice. But this weird juxtaposition of such different societies within one state is starting to change. Hispanic Redwood City, nestled next to tony Atherton and Palo Alto, now has as many illegal aliens per capita as do distant Madera and Tulare. Living in high-priced Bel Air, Brentwood, or old Pasadena no longer shields one from crime or from the decay of the California transportation system.

On the congested coastal strip, building regulations, zoning absurdities, and environmentalist prohibitions on new construction prohibit almost anyone under 40 without a sizable inheritance or an income in the upper six figures from acquiring a house. Elites in Santa Monica and Menlo Park are starting to notice that their once-premier public schools don't perform at the level that one might expect from the astronomical sales, income, and gas taxes. Shutting down thousands of acres of irrigated farmland in the state's interior, at a time when foreign buyers are lining up to buy California produce, translates into higher prices at the Santa Barbara food co-op. Soon, even the Stanford professor and the La Jolla administrator may learn that illegal immigration, cumbersome regulations, and terrible elementary schools affect them as well.

The four-part solution for California is clear: don't raise the state's crushing taxes any higher; reform public-employee compensation; make use of ample natural resources; and stop the flow of illegal aliens. Just focus on those four areas—as California did so well in the past—and in time, the state will return to its bounty of a few decades ago. Many of us intend to stay and see that it does.

[2012]

Index

List of Contributors

Brian C. Anderson is the editor of *City Journal* and the author of several books, including *Democratic Capitalism and Its Discontents* and *South Park Conservatives*.

Michael Anton is a fifth-generation Californian now writing from New York.

Ben Boychuk is an associate editor of *City Journal* and a regular columnist for the *Sacramento Bee*.

John Buntin covers law enforcement and urban affairs for *Governing*. A former resident of Santa Monica, he is the coauthor of *Governing States and Localities* and the author of *LA Noir: The Struggle for the Soul of America's Most Seductive City*.

Wendell Cox is principal of Demographia, a public policy firm specializing in urban issues, and served on the Los Angeles County Transportation Commission.

Tom Gray, a former editorial-page editor at the *Los Angeles Daily News*, writes on California's economy and politics.

Steven Greenhut is vice president at the Franklin Center for Government and Public Integrity and a Sacramento-based columnist.

Victor Davis Hanson is a contributing editor of *City Journal* and a senior fellow in classics and military history at the Hoover Institution at Stanford University.

Andrew Klavan is an award-winning and best-selling author of crime novels, as well as a screenwriter and an essayist.

Joel Kotkin is a distinguished Presidential Fellow in Urban Futures at Chapman University and a contributing editor to *City Journal*. He is also executive editor of the website newgeography.com and a member of the editorial board of the *Orange County Register*. His last book was *The Next Hundred Million: America in 2050*.

Arthur Laffer is chairman of Laffer Associates and author of *Eureka! How to Fix California*.

Heather Mac Donald is a contributing editor of *City Journal* and the John M. Olin Fellow at the Manhattan Institute.

Steven Malanga is the senior editor of *City Journal* and a senior fellow at the Manhattan Institute. His latest book is *Shakedown: The Continuing Conspiracy Against the American Taxpayer*.

Larry Sand, a retired public school teacher, is president of the California Teachers Empowerment Network.

Troy Senik, a former presidential speechwriter for George W. Bush, is the senior editor of *Ricochet* and a columnist and member of the editorial board for the *Orange County Register*.

William E. Simon, Jr. is cochairman of William E. Simon & Sons, LLC, which he cofounded in 1988 with his brother, Peter, and father, William E. Simon, Sr. He was the 2002 Republican gubernatorial nominee in California.

Guy Sorman, a *City Journal* contributing editor and French public intellectual, is the author of many books, including *Economics Does Not Lie: A Defense of the Free Market in a Time of Crisis*.

William Voegeli is a senior editor of the *Claremont Review of Books*, a visiting scholar at Claremont McKenna College's Henry Salvatori Center, and the author of *Never Enough: America's Limitless Welfare State*.